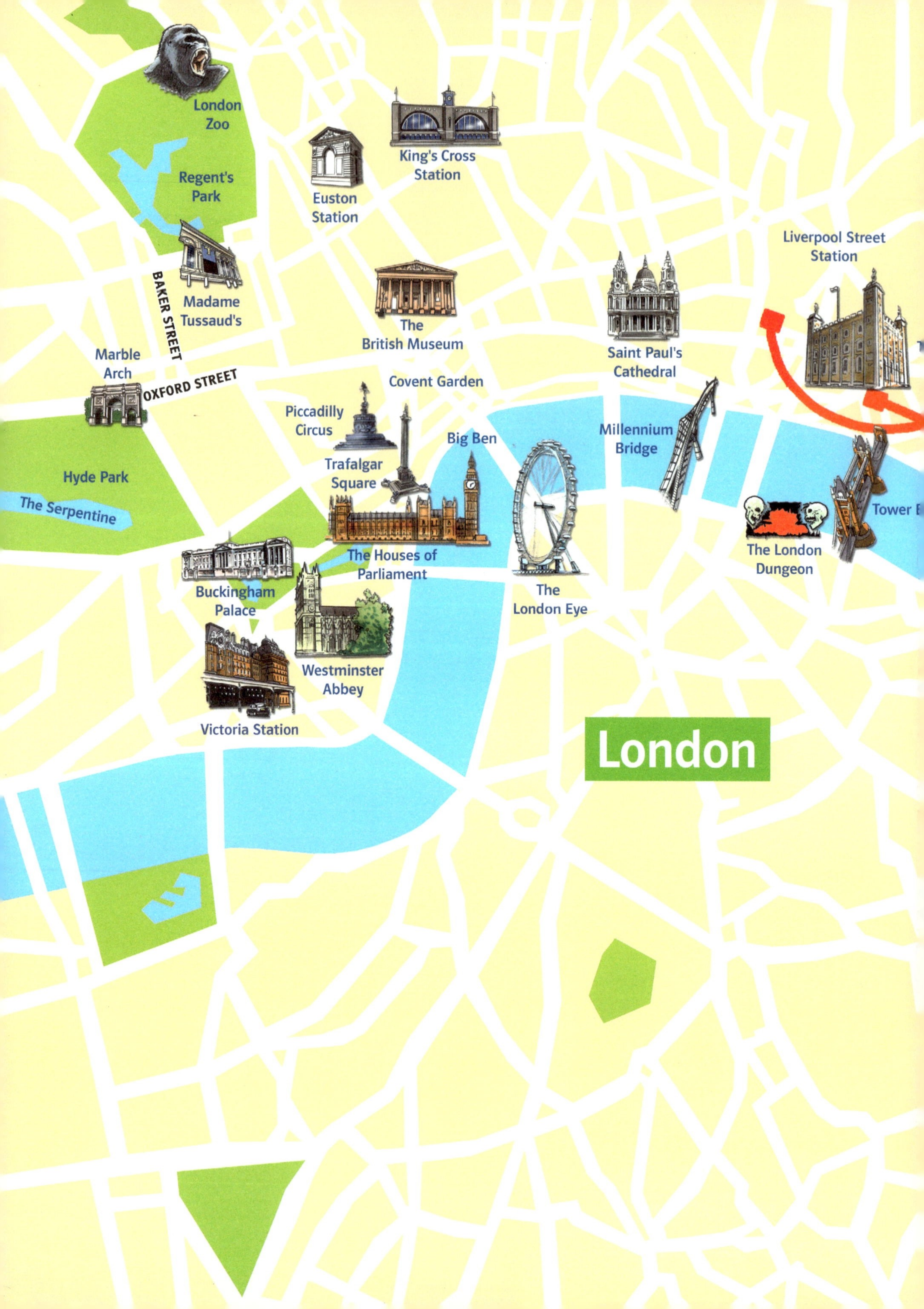
London Zoo
Regent's Park
Euston Station
King's Cross Station
BAKER STREET
Madame Tussaud's
The British Museum
Liverpool Street Station
Saint Paul's Cathedral
Marble Arch
OXFORD STREET
Covent Garden
Piccadilly Circus
Big Ben
Millennium Bridge
Trafalgar Square
Hyde Park
The Serpentine
The Houses of Parliament
The London Dungeon
Buckingham Palace
The London Eye
Westminster Abbey
Victoria Station
London

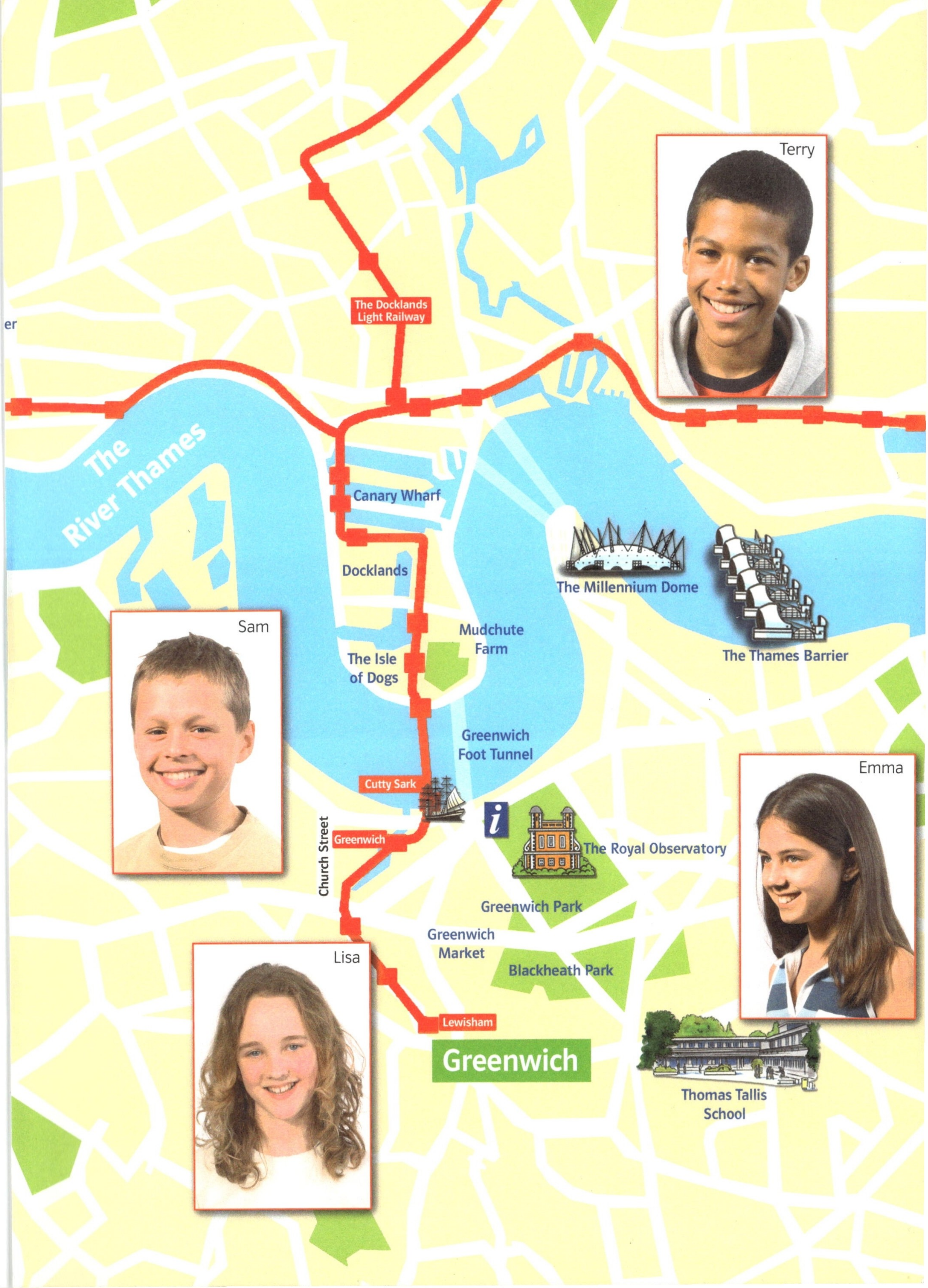

er
The Docklands Light Railway
Terry
The River Thames
Canary Wharf
Docklands
The Millennium Dome
Sam
Mudchute Farm
The Isle of Dogs
The Thames Barrier
Greenwich Foot Tunnel
Emma
Cutty Sark
Church Street
Greenwich
The Royal Observatory
Greenwich Park
Greenwich Market
Lisa
Blackheath Park
Lewisham
Greenwich
Thomas Tallis School

I'm Emma's sister Nasreen.
Hi! I'm Lisa's brother Ben, and this is our sister Jade.
Hi. My name is Emma.
Hello. My name is Sam.
Hi! I'm Lisa. Barker is my dog.
Hello. I'm Terry.

Hallo und herzlich willkommen bei Green Line!

Du kennst Englisch schon aus der Grundschule. Im Gymnasium wirst du vieles wieder erkennen und noch mehr Neues dazulernen. Das erste Kapitel, **Pick-up Unit 1**, und die **Pick-ups A, B** und **C** helfen dir, deine Englischkenntnisse aus der Grundschule anzuwenden.

Du beginnst mit **Zoom-in: Time for Greenwich**. Diese beiden Seiten zeigen dir den Handlungsort deines neuen Englischbuchs, nämlich Greenwich, einen Stadtteil Londons.
In sieben **Units** (Kapiteln) mit verschiedenen Themen lernst du die vier Lehrwerkskinder Lisa, Terry, Sam und Emma kennen.

IN JEDER UNIT FINDEST DU

Check-in: Hier geht's los! Auf zwei Seiten, die dich in die Unit einführen, lernst du neue Wörter und vieles über Land und Leute.
Language: Auf diesen 6 oder 8 Seiten erfährst du, wie du die englische Sprache anwendest. Außerdem erhältst du nützliche Hinweise, *wie* man etwas am besten behält.
Text: Im Textteil liest du Geschichten über die Lehrwerkskinder.
Wordwise: Alles über Wörter! Hier machst du Wortschatzarbeit und Wortspiele.
Check-out: Am Ende der Unit überprüfst du selbst, was du gelernt hast.

Nach den Units 3, 5 und 7 hast du in **Revision** (Wiederholung) die Möglichkeit, alles zu wiederholen.
Die **Trailers** (Anhänger) kannst du am Ende des Buchs „anhängen", wenn deine Lehrerin oder dein Lehrer es möchten. Verpflichtend sind die **Trailers** nur für Schülerinnen und Schüler in Hessen.
Manchmal ist es wichtig, zwischen Deutsch und Englisch zu vermitteln. Wie du das machst, lernst du in **Mediation** (Sprachmittlung).
In der **Free section** (Freier Teil) gibt es ein Tierprojekt, ein Theaterstück zum Aufführen und Informationen über Festtage in Großbritannien. Die spannende Fortsetzungsgeschichte *Stories for a ghost* (Geschichten für ein Gespenst) kannst du ab Unit 4 in jeder Unit finden.
Nun folgt der Grammatikanhang **Grammar** mit Beispielen, Übersichten, Regeln, Tipps.
Am Ende des Buches kannst du alle neuen Wörter der Units nachschlagen. Dieser Teil heißt **Vocabulary** (Vokabular) und enthält zahlreiche Tipps, wie du dir die Vokabeln am besten merkst.
Das **Dictionary** (Wörterbuch) listet die Vokabeln alphabetisch auf. Es ist zum Nachschlagen gedacht, wenn du einmal ein Wort vergessen hast.
Alles klar? Dann mach dich bereit für eine Reise nach Greenwich.
Viel Spaß und viel Erfolg beim Englischlernen!

- Diese Texte und Übungen sind nur auf den Lehrer-CDs zum Schülerbuch enthalten.
- Diese Texte und Übungen sind auf der Schüler-CD *und* auf den Lehrer-CDs.
- Diese Übungen/Übungsteile sind Partnerarbeit.
- Diese Übungen/Übungsteile sind Gruppenarbeit.
- Diese Übungen/Übungsteile sind Schreibübungen.
- Die Ergebnisse dieser Übungen/Übungsteile kannst du in deinen *English folder* heften.
- ⟨ ⟩ Diese Übungen/Übungsteile oder Kapitel sind wahlfrei (fakultativ).
- Diese Übungen/Übungsteile sind besonders knifflig oder anspruchsvoll.
- [ ] Diese Kapitel sind nur für bestimmte Bundesländer erforderlich; hier nur für Hessen.

Zoom-in Time for Greenwich

A

Millennium Dome

B

Greenwich Market

C

Thames Barrier

D

24-hour clock

E

Greenwich Park

1 Let's listen: Greenwich sounds

Listen and point.

F

Bus to Greenwich

2 ⟨A song: Let's get started!⟩

a) *Listen.*
b) *Sing the chorus:*
Let's get started!
We're on our way.
We're learning English!
Let's go! Hooray!

Musik: Thomas Brodbeck / Ulrich Hoffmann
Text: Sheila McBride

Pick-up Unit 1 Thomas Tallis School

1 Terry

My name is Terry Jackson.
1 twelve.
My new 2 is Thomas Tallis.
I'm 3 Greenwich. I'm in 4 7.

2 How to: Say hello

USEFUL PHRASES

Hello.
My name is / I'm …
I'm ten / eleven / …
I'm from …

3 What's your name?

A (You): What's your name?
B (Your partner): I'm ▢.
A: How old are you?
B: I'm ▢.
A: Where are you from?
B: I'm from ▢.

WB p. 3/1

4 Listening: Phone numbers

0 zero (phone number: 'oh')

1 one	**2** two	**3** three
4 four	**5** five	**6** six
7 seven	**8** eight	**9** nine
10 ten	**11** eleven	**12** twelve

a) *Listen and write the phone numbers.*

Lisa: ???
Terry: (home) ???
(mobile) ???

b) *Say your phone number or mobile number.*

My … is …

WB p. 3/2

5 Hands on: Your folder

a) *Start your English folder.*

My name is ▢.
I'm ▢.
I'm from ▢.
I'm in Year 5.
My phone number is ▢.
…

b) *Word bank: You know English from primary school. Say more about yourself.*

My name is Sven.
I'm ten.
I'm from Dortmund.
I'm in Year 5.
My phone number is 0231 …

My name is Julia.
I'm eleven.
I'm from Berlin.
I'm in Year 5.
My phone number is 030 …

My name is Marion.
I'm ten.
I'm from Stuttgart.
I'm in Year 5.
My phone number is 0711 …

A new friend

Hello. My name is Lisa. What's your name?
I'm Emma Brook. I'm from Bristol. I'm new in Greenwich.
I'm from Greenwich. But I'm new at Thomas Tallis.
It's a big school.
Here's Terry. He's my friend. He's from my old school.
Hi, Terry. This is Emma. She's new here.
Hi, Emma.
That's Mrs Carter. She's my tutor and my German teacher.
Hey – so you're in my tutor group, too.
What's your favourite sport, Emma?
Oh, you and your sport, Lisa!
My favourite sport is football. Here's a goal for England!
Oh! My shoe!
Here's your – er – your football.
Oh, thank you, Mr –
This is Mr Newman. He's the caretaker.
Mr Newman is OK!
A big new school is scary.

1 Thomas Tallis School

Example: Emma **is** new in Greenwich.

Emma Thomas Tallis Terry Mrs Carter Mr Newman Tom	+ is +	a tutor. a big school. new in Greenwich. a mouse. the caretaker. in Year 7.

2 This is Nina

1. A: This is Nina. **She's** eleven.
   She's from Stuttgart.
   B: Hello, Nina. My name is ___ .

2. B: This is Mehmet. **He's** ___ .
   He's from ___ .
   A: Hello, ___ . *Go on, please.*

WB p. 4/3

1

Nina, 11, Stuttgart

2

Mehmet, 12, Istanbul

3

Nadine, 10, Paris

4
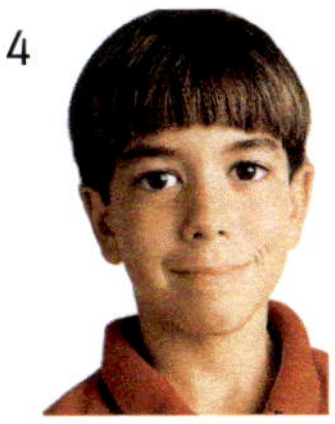
Francisco, 11, Madrid

5

Keiko, 12, Tokyo

6

Nelson, 9, Nairobi

3 A quiz game: What's my name?

Example:

A: What's my name? I'm eleven.
B: **You're** Lisa.
A: No. That's wrong. I'm from Madrid.
B: Oh, **you're** Francisco.
A: Yes, that's right!

WB p. 4/4

4 What is the right order?

Example: My • is • Lisa • name
→ My name is Lisa.

1. I'm • Thomas Tallis • at • new
2. Terry • my • is • friend
3. He's • old • school • my • from
4. Emma • Greenwich • in • is • new
5. She's • my • in • tutor group
6. My • sport • football • is • favourite
7. The • OK • caretaker • is

TIP
I'm
you're
he's
she's

(→ G 2)

WB p. 4/5

5 ⟨A song: Let's go⟩

Hi, hi, hi, hello!
Good morning, how are you?
Hi, hi, hi, hello!
I'm fine, and how are you?

Text und Musik: Karl-Heinz Böttcher

6 Your turn: This is my partner

This is … She's / He's …
… eleven.
…
… from Stuttgart.
… cool.
… my friend.

Sam

Lisa: Are we in the right classroom, Terry?
Terry: Yes, we are. But Mrs Carter isn't here.
Lisa: Are you sure this is the right room? Is Sam here?
Terry: Oh, no, he isn't.
Emma: Who's Sam? Is he a friend from your old school?
Lisa: Yes, he is. He's nice but he's always late!
Emma: You're lucky! I'm not from Greenwich. My friends aren't at Thomas Tallis.
Lisa: Oh, yes, they are. We're your new friends.
Terry: Here's Mrs Carter.
Mrs Carter: Good morning, girls and boys.
Lisa: And here's Sam. What's up? You're late!
Sam: I'm sorry, Mrs Carter.
Mrs Carter: That's OK. What's your name?
Sam: I'm Sam Spencer.
Mrs Carter: Where's your bag with your books?
Sam: It's in Cardiff.
Mrs Carter: Oh! Your home is Cardiff?
Sam: No, it isn't, it's in Greenwich. But my mum isn't – she's in Cardiff with my bag.
Mrs Carter: OK. But you're here.
Sam: Yes, Mrs Carter, I'm here.

7 Right or wrong?

Examples: Sam is in Cardiff.
→ That's wrong. ✗
Sam is always late.
→ That's right. ✓

1. Mrs Carter is the caretaker.
2. Terry, Emma and Lisa are in one tutor group.
3. This is the wrong classroom.
4. Emma is from Greenwich.
5. Sam and Lisa are friends.
6. Sam is here now.

WB p. 5/6

8 People at Thomas Tallis

Put in: I • you • he • she • it • we • you • they.

Example: I'm Lisa. I'm from Greenwich.
Go on, please.

1. That's Mrs Carter. ___'s my teacher.
2. Here's Terry. ___'s from my old school.
3. ___'s the right classroom. ___'m sure.
4. ___'re lucky. Terry and you are friends.
5. ___'re in my tutor group, Emma and Lisa.
6. Here are Sam and Terry. ___'re my friends.
7. Here's your new book. ___'re on page 5.

WB p. 5/7

9 Short and long forms

Write the long forms.

1. I'm ten. → I am ten.
2. She's eleven. → She is ...
3. We're new here. → ...
4. You're at Thomas Tallis, too. → ...
5. He's from Greenwich. → ...
6. I'm in your tutor group. → ...
7. They're friends. → ...
8. It's a big school. → ...

10 Emma and her diary

*Put in: **am, is** or **are**.*

Terry [1] so nice! He [2] in my tutor group at school. Sam and Lisa [3] my new friends, too. I [4] lucky, they [5] very nice. A new school [6] scary, but the teachers [7] OK! And the pupils at Thomas Tallis [8] OK, too.

GRAMMAR

short forms	long forms
I'm	I am
you're	you are
he's	he is
she's	she is
it's	it is
we're	we are
you're	you are
they're	they are

(→ G2)

11 That is not right

Look at the pictures and make sentences.

Example: **I'm not** a pupil. I'm a mouse.

1. The pupils ___ here. They ___ late.
2. I ___ from Greenwich. I ___ from Bristol.
3. It ___ a football. It ___ a shoe.
4. Mr Newman ___ a teacher. He ___ the caretaker.
5. Emma and I ___ twelve. We ___ eleven.
6. This ___ a book. It ___ a bag.

1

2

3

4

5

6

GRAMMAR

short forms	long forms
I'm not	I am not
you aren't	you are not
he isn't	he is not
she isn't	she is not
it isn't	it is not
we aren't	we are not
you aren't	you are not
they aren't	they are not

(→ G3)

WB p. 5/8

12 Make questions and answers

Example: Is Sam ten? No, he isn't.

Is

Tom, Terry, Lisa, Sam, Emma

from Greenwich? eleven? ten? a mouse? at a new school? a boy?

Yes, she is. Yes, he is. No, he isn't. No, she isn't.

TIP

Is Emma ... ?
– Yes, she is.
– No, she isn't.

(→ G4)

WB p. 6/9; 10

13 Your turn: At your school

Example: the girls and boys / OK → **Are** the girls and boys OK? → **Yes, they are.** → **No, they aren't.**

1. the teachers / always late?
2. the classrooms / big?
3. new schools / scary?
4. mobiles / OK in the classroom?
5. your friends / from your old school?
6. the caretakers / nice at your school?

WB p. 6/11

The schoolbag

In the bag	Lisa	Emma	Sam
a pencil-case	✓		
a pen	✓		
a pencil			
a rubber	✓		
a ruler			
a book			
an exercise book			
a sandwich			
an apple			
a mobile			

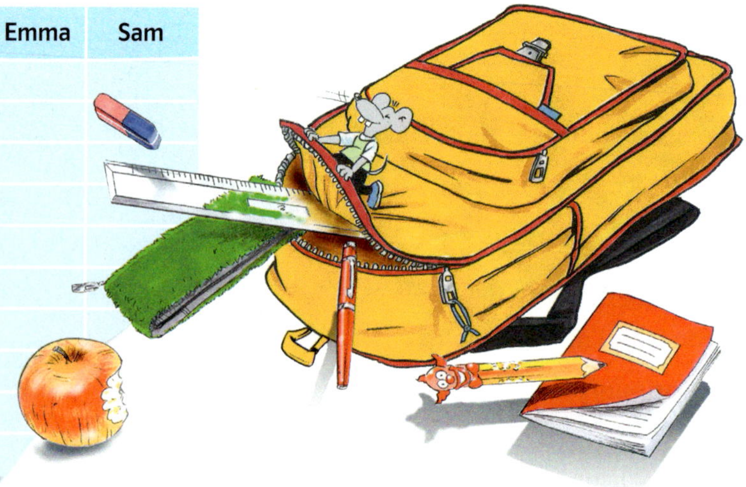

14 Listening: In the bag

a) *Copy the grid in your exercise book. Listen for the words and fill in your grid.*

b) *What is in the bag?*

A pencil, a ruler, … *Go on, please.*

c) *Look at your grid. What is the name on the bag in the picture – Emma, Sam, Lisa?*

WB p. 7/12

15 *A* or *an*?

1. Here's ___ exercise book.
2. And here's ___ pencil-case.
3. This is ___ English book.
4. Mmm, ___ apple.
5. Here's ___ shoe.
6. And that's ___ old ruler.

TIP

a ruler
an apple
an + a, e, i, o, (u)

(→ G 5)

16 Listening: Sounds [ðə] and [ði:]

Listen and write the words in two lists.

[ðə]	[ði:]
the pencil	the apple
…	…

17 Listening: Numbers

a) *Listen and say the numbers.*

b) A: What's 5 and 19 ?
B: It's 24. – What's … and … ?
A: … *Go on, please.*

c) *A game: Play 'buzz!' Say 'buzz!' for numbers with seven.*

One • Two • Three • Four •
Five • Six • **Buzz !** • Eight •
Nine • Ten • Eleven • Twelve •
Thirteen • **Buzz !** • Fifteen •
Sixteen • **Buzz !** • …

13 thirteen
14 fourteen
15 fifteen
16 sixteen
17 seventeen
18 eighteen
19 nineteen
20 twenty
21 twenty-one
22 twenty-two
23 twenty-three
24 twenty-four
25 twenty-five
26 twenty-six
30 thirty
40 forty
50 fifty
60 sixty
70 seventy
80 eighty
90 ninety
100 a/one hundred

WB p. 7/13

18 Plural

Here is one ruler.

Here **are** two rulers. *Go on, please.*

19 Your turn: What is in your bag?

Example: Two exercise books, one rubber, … *Go on, please.*

TIP

one pen	two pens
one sandwich	two sandwiches

(→ G7)

20 Listening: Sounds [z],[s] and [ɪz]

Listen and say.

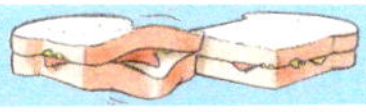

[z]	[s]	[ɪz]
1. *bag – bags:* The bags aren't new. *friend – friends:* My friends are OK.	2. *book – books:* My books are in my bag. *tutor group – tutor groups:* The tutor groups are big.	3. *sandwich – sandwiches:* Mmm – two big sandwiches! *pencil-case – pencil-cases:* Here are three pencil-cases.

WB p. 7/14

21 Alphabet rap

A (clap) B (clap) C D E
Here's a rap for Thomas T.
F (clap) G (clap) H I J
English lessons are OK.
K (clap) L (clap) M N O
Are you new here? Hi, hello.
P (clap) Q (clap) R S T
Say the numbers one, two, three.
U V W shout and clap
X Y Z (clap) do the rap.

a) *Say the alphabet rap.*

b) *Who is your favourite star?*

c) *Word bank: Spell more words that you know from primary school.*

⟨d)⟩ *Make word puzzles for your partner.*

A: Here are the letters: C–L–I–P–N–E
What's the word?
B: It's 'pencil'.

WB p. 7/15

The classroom

window
chair
board
poster
door
wall
table
cupboard
desk

22 What is in the classroom?

a) *Example:* **There's** a door. The door is A.
There are walls. The walls are B.

There's a ___.
There are ___.

b) *Word bank: Say more classroom words that you know from primary school. Work with a partner.*

23 What is where?

Example: on the wall –
There are posters **on the wall.**

1. on a chair
2. under the table
3. on a table
4. in front of the board
5. behind the door
6. in the cupboard
7. under a chair

24 Your turn: Your classroom

There is …
The classroom is (not) …
There are …
… on the wall.
… in the cupboard.
… under a desk.

My classroom

The classroom is not big.
There are 20 tables and a desk.
There are … on …
There is …

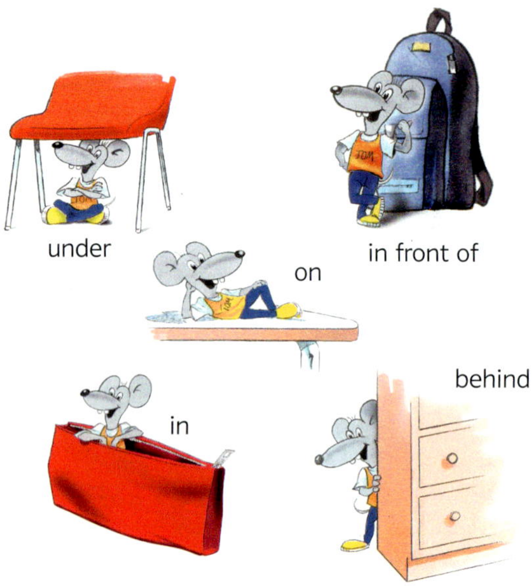

25 A game: Where is it?

Where's the pen?

Is it in the bag?

No, it isn't.

Is it on the chair?

No, it isn't.

Is it under the table?

Yes, it is.

WB p. 8/16

26 *Who* or *what*?

1. ___ is TTS? – It is Thomas Tallis School.
2. ___ is Mr Newman? – He is the caretaker.
3. ___ is from Bristol? – That is Emma.
4. ___ is 'mobile' in German? – The word is 'Handy'.
5. ___ is in the bag? – There are books and a pen.
6. ___ are Terry and Sam? – They are boys in Year 7.

27 Make questions for the answers

Example: **What's** under the chair? – There's a mouse under the chair.

1. What's under the chair?
2. Who's always late?
3. What's your name?
4. Who's Mr ___ ?
5. What's your ___ ?
6. Where ___ ?
7. ___ ?

My favourite sport is football. • There's a mouse under the chair. ✓ • It's in London. • Thomas Tallis School is in Greenwich. • He's the caretaker. • She's the girl from Bristol. • My name is Nina. • Sam is always late.

TIP

what? = was?
where? = wo?
who? = wer?

(→ G9)

28 How to: Use classroom phrases

USEFUL PHRASES

a) *You:*

What's 'Auf Wiedersehen' in English, please?
Good morning.
Sorry I'm late.
Where are we?
Thank you.
What's for homework, please?
Can I go to the toilet, please?

Your teacher:

That's OK. Sit down, please.
It's on the board.
You're welcome.
Yes, OK.
It's 'goodbye'. You can say 'bye', too.
Good morning, girls and boys.
We're on page 19 now.

b) *Word bank: Say more classroom phrases that you know from primary school.* WB p. 8/17

29 ⟨Role play: Act the dialogues⟩

Example: A (Teacher): Thank you.
B (Pupil): You're welcome.

1. Thank you.
2. Good morning.
3. Here's your exercise book.
4. Where's your book?
5. You're late.
6. Let's do a rap.

No problem!

A It is lunchtime.
Emma is in the cafeteria with Lisa.

Emma: Look – it's Terry. He's cool.
Lisa: Cool? He's –
Emma: Sssh!
Terry: Listen, you two. Here's a new joke. What's a word with twenty-six letters?
Emma: That's easy! The word is 'alphabet'. Right?
Terry: Uh, yes.
Lisa: That isn't a new joke, Terry. It's a boring old joke. Your jokes are always boring. You're terrible.
Emma: Lisa, that isn't very nice. You and Terry are friends.
Terry: No, we aren't. Goodbye, Lisa!

B Lisa and Emma are in the playground now. Lisa is good at sport. She is very good at football, but Emma is not. Football is not her favourite sport.

Watch out! Oh, no, now the ball is in a tree.

C Now Sam and Terry are in the playground, too.

Sam: Hi. What's the problem?
Emma: It's the ball. It's in the tree.
Sam: That's no problem.
Terry: Is it your ball, Emma?
Emma: No, it isn't.
Terry: Oh, is it your ball, Lisa?
Lisa: Yes, it is.
Terry: Hm. Your ball – your problem.
Sam: Terry! What's up? You and Lisa are friends.
Terry: Friends? No, we aren't. – My jokes are boring.
Lisa: I'm sorry, Terry. Your jokes are OK.
Emma: Please, Terry.
Terry: OK, OK. Here's the ball.
And here's a very new joke about …

1 What is the right order?

1. It is lunchtime.
2. Here is … *Go on, please.*

- Emma is not good at football.
- Here is Terry with an alphabet joke.
- It is lunchtime.
- Lisa and Emma are in the playground now.
- That is no problem for Terry and Sam.
- Lisa is sorry now.
- The ball is in the tree.
- Lisa is not nice.

2 ⟨Role play: Act a dialogue⟩

*Make groups. Act the dialogue in A **or** C.*

3 Write a dialogue

Write a dialogue for B. Complete the sentences with a partner. Put them in the right order.

Lisa: Let's play football, Emma.
Emma: OK. But I'm not …

Go on, please.

… good at …
Here's …
Where's …
Oh, no, it's …
Watch out!
That's OK!

4 Are the words polite?

a) *Example:* "You aren't my friend." – That isn't polite.

"Thank you." "It's your problem." "Hey, cool!" "No!" "She's nice." "I'm sorry." "Let's be friends." "You're terrible." "You're always wrong." "Yes, please." "You're boring."

🙂	☹️
I'm sorry.	No!
…	…

⟨b)⟩ *Hands on: Make a classroom poster – polite words and nasty words.*

1 Word webs

VOCABULARY SKILLS A B C D E F G H I

Neue Wörter behältst du am besten, wenn du sie im Zusammenhang lernst. Dabei kann dir ein **word web** helfen (Bild a). Übertrage dieses **word web** auf ein Blatt Papier und lege es in deinen **English folder.**

Vervollständige die beiden anderen **word webs** und lege auch diese in deinen **English folder.** Lass Platz für weitere Wörter, damit du die **word webs** im Laufe des Schuljahres ergänzen kannst.

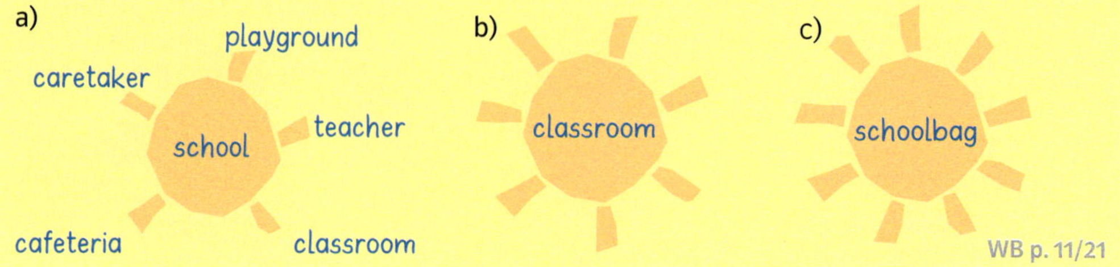

WB p. 11/21

2 The wrong word

Example: ruler – rubber – mouse – pencil
The wrong word is 'mouse'.

1. girl – tutor – boy – chair
2. sandwich – apple – crisps – book
3. who – what – hello – where
4. in – pen – on – under
5. goal – easy – scary – terrible
6. wall – window – joke – door

3 ⟨Mouth jogging⟩

a) *Listen and say.*

Rabba dabba dab,
Rabba dab,
Rabba dabba dab.
Ribba dibba dib,
Ribba dib,
Ribba dibba dib.
…

b) *Make new sounds.*
Example:

Razza dazza daz,
…
Rizza dizza diz,
…
Ruzza duzza duz,
…

4 ⟨Write two lists⟩

Who?	Where?
girl	classroom
…	…

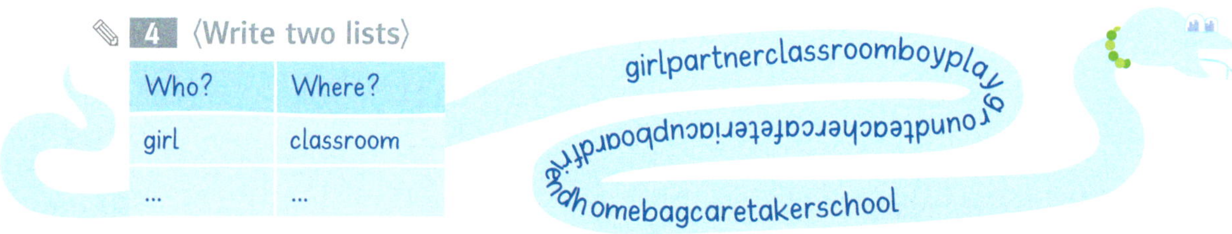

5 Find good adjectives

a) *Example*: Tom is a **nice** mouse. *Or:* Tom is a **cool** mouse.

1. My ___ sport is football.
2. A ___ school is always ___.
3. TTS is a ___ school. It's ___!
4. My English book is ___.
5. Emma is a ___ girl.
6. How ___ are you?
7. Here's Terry. He's ___.
8. Your jokes are ___, Terry.
9. Hey, that isn't ___!
10. This is a ___ party.

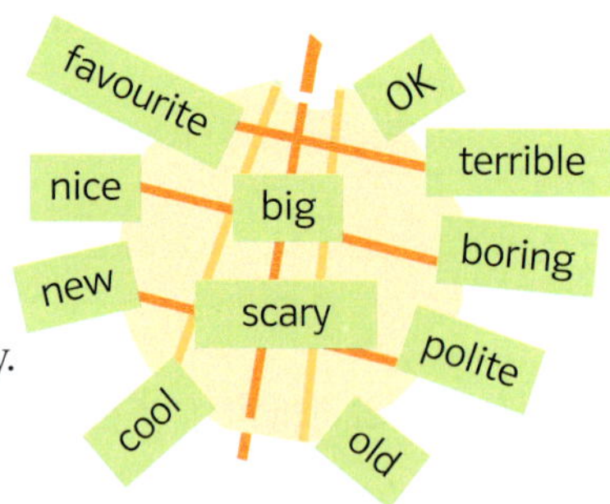

b) *Word bank: Make sentences with other adjectives that you know from primary school.*

6 ⟨Listening: Words⟩ *Write the letters. What are the words?*

DU KANNST JETZT

- ✓ Dich und andere vorstellen.
- ✓ Über die Schule reden.
- ✓ Das Verb *to be* verwenden.
- ✓ Sagen, wo sich etwas befindet.
- ✓ Fragen mit *who*, *what* und *where* stellen.
- ✓ Ein *word web* machen.

1 This is Lisa (→ G1, 2)

1. This is Lisa. She		in my tutor group, too.
2. Look, it's Terry and Sam. They	's	new here.
3. My name is Emma. I	+ 're +	from Bristol.
4. Here's Mr Newman. He	'm	eleven.
5. Hi, we		the caretaker.

WB p. 12/24

2 A friend from Bristol (→ G3, 4)

What is missing?

Emma: *(Ring! Ring!)* Oh, hi, Kim!
Kim: Hello, Emma. [1] your new school OK?
Emma: Yes, [2].
Kim: And your tutor and teachers? [3] they nice, too?
Emma: Yes, [4]. Mrs Carter is very nice.
Kim: [5] she your English teacher?
Emma: No, [6]. She's my tutor and my German teacher.
Kim: Hey, cool! You [7] lucky.
Emma: Yes, [8]. Bye, Kim!
Kim: Bye, Emma.

3 What is different? (→ G8)

Example:

In A there are two posters on the wall.
In B there is one poster on the wall.
Go on, please.

A B

4 Your turn: Your new school

Write five sentences about your new school.

5 *Who*, *what* or *where*? (→ G9)

Example: What is in the tree? / Who is in the tree?

1. [ ] is from Greenwich?
2. [ ] is Mr Newman?
3. [ ] is Thomas Tallis?
4. [ ] is Emma from?
5. [ ] is eleven?
6. [ ] is Greenwich?

WB p. 12/25; 26

Pick-up A Home sweet home

1 Listening: Rooms

a) *Listen and write the words on cards, one word per card.*

b) *Look at the picture and listen. Where is Tom? Hold up the correct card.*

c) *Word bank: Say other room words that you know from primary school.*

2 Colours

Pupil A: *Your book is open. Look at the picture. Ask questions.*

Pupil B: *Look at the picture, then close your book. Answer the questions.*

Example:

A: Is the kitchen yellow? – B: No, it isn't. It's pink.

1. Is the living room …?
2. Is the bathroom …?
3. Is the bedroom …?

Yes, it … .
No, it … . It's … .

3 Correct colours?

a) *Look at the words and say the correct colour.*

b) *Write the words in the correct colour.*

purple 1
grey 2
green 3
orange 4
yellow 5

4 Room rhyme

Hi, I'm Tom and here's my home
with table, chairs and bed.
Green and yellow, blue and purple
and my favourite colour, red.
Tiny pictures, tiny sofa,
in my funny, tiny house.
Tiny TV and computer –
this is home for Tom the mouse.

a) *Learn the rhyme by heart.*

b) *Your turn:*
Describe your room.

Start like this:

Hi, I'm … and here's my room with …

5 Funny furniture

Write and say the words.

1. c _ pbo _ rd
2. com _ _ t _ r
3. _ ha _ r
4. ta _ _ e
5. so _ a
6. pi _ tu _ e

WB p. 13/1

6 My dream house

a) *Talk to a partner.*

1. What are the rooms in your dream house?
2. What furniture is in the rooms?
3. What colours are in the rooms?

b) *Draw your dream house. Write the words for the rooms and the furniture in your picture. Put it in your folder.*

7 Listening: Tom Tiny and his family

Look at the pictures. Then listen and answer the questions.

Example:

1. Who is in picture A?
   That's his mother. She's 4.
2. Who is in picture B?
3. Who is in picture C?
4. Who is in picture D?
5. Who is in picture E?
6. Who is in picture F?

MOTHER (MUM) · BROTHER · SISTER · GRANDMOTHER (GRANDMA) · GRANDFATHER (GRANDAD) · FATHER (DAD)

8 Happy family!

a) *Write the family words.*

adragnd • itress • rohemt
tadogenrrmh • aertfh

b) *Word bank: Write more family words that you know from primary school.*

WB p. 13/2

9 Pick-up quiz

1. What are the rooms in the mouse house?
2. What colour are the rooms in the mouse house?
3. What furniture is in the rooms?
4. Who is in the Tiny family?

Unit 2 At home in Greenwich

A The Brook family

Our computer shop

Emma: This is my family – my parents, Rob and Farah Brook and my half-sister, Nasreen. Nasreen is fifteen, and my dad is her step-father. Our flat is in Holburne Road and it's over a computer shop. The shop is cool. My dad is its new manager, and I can play new computer games there with my friends. But the flat is very small, so Nasreen and I are in one room. And that's a big problem!

B The Jackson family

Terry: My parents are Grace and Ted Jackson. They're OK, but it can be boring at home. I'm an only child. There's our cat, Tiger, but she's only interested in mice. Our house is in Hither Farm Road, with a big garden. There's a shed in the garden. My drums are there and my chemistry set, too. It's *my* shed. Friends are OK there – but not parents or cats!

My shed in the garden

1 The Brooks and the Jacksons

Look at the pictures and texts.
Match the sentences with the names.

Example: I'm an only child. –
That's Terry Jackson.

Emma Brook   Terry Jackson

1. My sister and I are in one bedroom.
2. Our cat is only interested in mice.
3. My dad is the manager.
4. My drums are in my shed.
5. Grace and Ted are my parents.
6. Nasreen is my half-sister.

WB p. 14/1

3 Listening: A house in Hither Farm Road

Look at the photo and listen to Terry. Is this his house? Why or why not?

The door is …   … big windows upstairs.
… big windows downstairs.

WB p. 14/3

2 How to: Write a family text

Write a family text for Lisa.

USEFUL PHRASES

This is my family. My parents are …
My sister is … and Ben is my …
Our house is … Barker is our …

Our house and garden in Pond Road

WB p. 14/2

4 Your turn: My family

This is my family.
My parents are 1 and 2
I'm an only child. /
My brother / sister is 3 /
My brothers / sisters are 4
Our house / flat is in 5

Go on, please. Put the text in your folder.

Sam's family tree

The Spencer family

1 Make sentences about Sam's family

Example: Tim is **Sam's** uncle.

Sarah • James Tim • Rachel Elena • Phil	+	is	+	Sam's • Tracy's • Phil's • Susan's • David's	+	grandad • grandma • aunt • uncle • cousin • dad • mum • sister • brother

TIP
Sam's father
his **cousin's** sister

(→ G 10)

WB p. 15/4

2 ⟨A game: Who is where?⟩

There is a big family lunch at Sam's flat in Wendover Road.

Find the names for the letters at the table.

Five minutes!

1. The girls next to Sam are his cousins.
2. Tracy is on Sam's left.
3. Tracy is next to her Uncle David.
4. Susan is on her dad's left.
5. Phil is next to his dad.
6. David is on his mum's right.
7. Sam's aunt is on his grandma's left.

Sam
dad
3 cousins
uncle + aunt
grandma

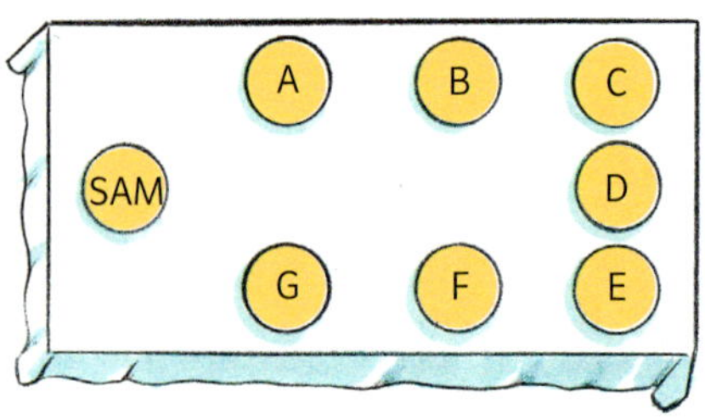

We're a very European family, Emma. My parents' name is Pilch. It's a Polish name because my father's family is from Poland. And the Spencers' family is from England. But Sam isn't only English and Polish because his mum is from a Greek family. Her parents' name is Stavros. And today our lunch is Italian! Here's your spaghetti, you two.

3 A European family

Write the sentences.

Example: My **(parents)** name is Stavros.
→ My **parents'** name is Stavros.

1. Emma is at the ___ (Spencer) flat today.
2. The ___ (Taylor) dog, Barker, is a nice dog.
3. The ___ (Brook) flat is over the computer shop.
4. The two ___ (sister) bedroom is a big problem.
5. The two ___ (girl) flat is very small.
6. There is a shed in the ___ (Jackson) garden.
7. His ___ (parents) name is Spencer.

WB p. 15/5

TIP
the **Spencers'** flat
his **parents'** home

(→ G 10)

4 Put in the right words

I – my | he – his | she – her ✓ | we – our | it – its | you – your | they – their

1. Emma: Is that your sister? – Lisa: Yes, it is. **Her** name is Jade. **She**'s five.
2. Terry: This is my shed. – Emma: ___'re lucky, Terry. ___ shed is cool!
3. Mrs Brook: Are the girls at home?
   Mr Brook: Yes, they are. ___'re in ___ room.
4. Grandma: Are you Sam's new friend?
   Emma: Yes, ___ am. ___ name is Emma.
5. Mr Taylor: Where's Ben?
   Lisa: ___'s at ___ friend's house.
6. Sam: Is Emma's flat over a shop?
   Terry: Yes, ___ is. ___'s a computer shop.
7. Lisa: Is this your sister's room, too?
   Emma: Yes, it is. ___ flat is small, so ___'re in one room.

WB p. 15/6

5 Your turn: Your family tree

a) *Where is your family from? Tell a partner.*

Examples:
A: Where are you from?
B: I'm from Germany. *Or:* I'm German.
B: Where is your family from?
A: My family is from England.
Or: My family is English. *Go on, please.*

TIP

Germany – German	Greece – Greek
England – English	Italy – Italian
Russia – Russian	Turkey – Turkish
Poland – Polish	Spain – Spanish

b) *Draw your family tree, with pictures or photos. Put it in your folder.*

c) *Word bank: Say more nationality words that you know from primary school.*

Emma, you're in big trouble!

Emma has got a big sister, Nasreen. Their bedroom is small, so they have only got one wardrobe. Nasreen hasn't got a lot of time. Her friends are outside, so she is in a hurry. But her new T-shirt is not in the wardrobe. Where is it?

Nasreen: Emma? Where's my new pink T-shirt? I'm late. Have you got it?
Emma: No, I haven't.
Nasreen: Has Mum ...?
Emma: No, she hasn't. Hmm. Look in the wardrobe where I've got my magazines.
Nasreen: It isn't here. Where is it? You've got two seconds!
Emma: OK, OK! Maybe it's on my chair with ...
Nasreen: On your chair! Aargh! Here it is, with your dirty old T-shirts! What a mess! Emma, you're in big trouble!

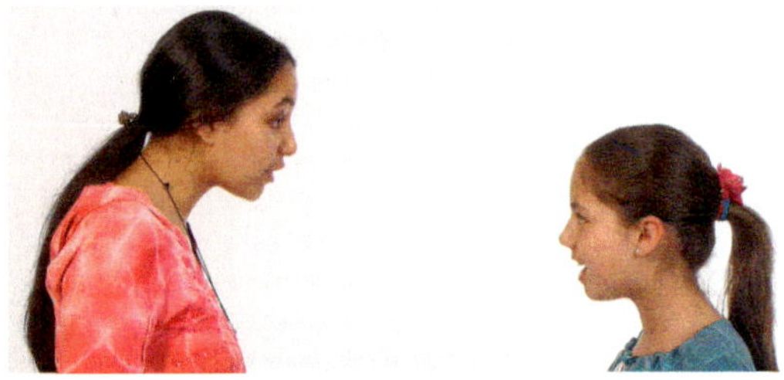

(Later)
Emma: Mum, Dad! Where's Nasreen? Has she got my Discman?
Mr Brook: Yes, she has.
Emma: Oh, no! Just because her silly T-shirt ...
Mr Brook: Well, that's your problem, Emma. Sort it out with your sister.

6 Emma and Nasreen

Emma Nasreen	+	has got hasn't got	+	a lot of time. her own room. a big sister. a new pink T-shirt. magazines in the wardrobe. a step-father.

GRAMMAR

+	–
I've got You've got	I haven't got You haven't got
He's got She's got It's got	He hasn't got She hasn't got It hasn't got
We've got They've got	We haven't got They haven't got

(→ G12)

7 Make sentences about the girls and their room

Examples:

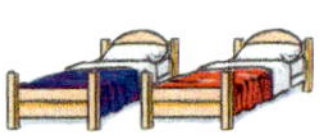

They**'ve got** beds in their room.

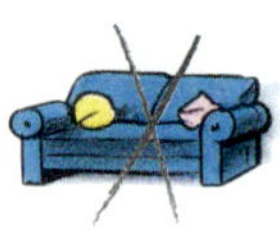

They **haven't got** a sofa in their room.

WB p. 16/7

8 Your turn: In your room

Examples: I**'ve got** a wardrobe in my room.
I **haven't got** a computer.

Go on, please.

WB p. 16/8; 9

9 ⟨A song: We're a funny family⟩

We're a funny family, my relatives and me
I think you can agree, we're a funny family.

10 Questions about Nasreen's father

Lisa is with Emma and Nasreen in their room.

Nasreen: My dad isn't in London. He's in Leicester.
Lisa: **Has he got** a new family?
Nasreen: **Yes, he has.**
Lisa: Has he got a flat?
Emma: **No, he hasn't.** *Go on, please.*

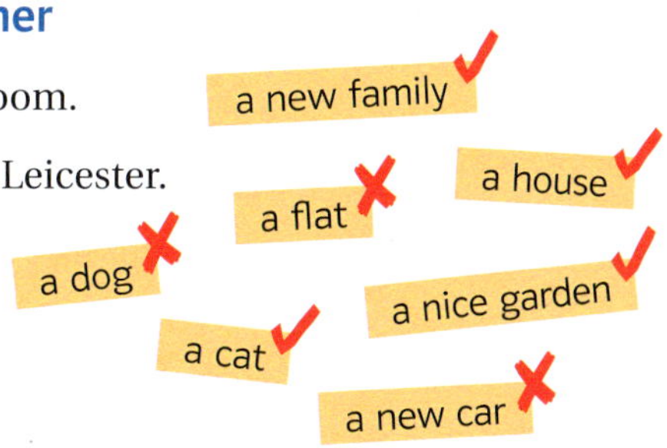

TIP
Has he got ...?
– Yes, he has.
– No, he hasn't.

(→ G 12)

11 A quiz: Their family

the Jacksons the Brooks the Taylors the Spencers	a computer shop three bedrooms a flat / house in ... Road a garden a cat / dog ...

A: My questions are about the Brooks.
Have they got a computer shop?
B: **Yes, they have.**
A: Have they got a cat?
B: **No, they haven't.**
A: Have they got ...?

Go on, please.

WB p. 17/10

12 ⟨Have you got a pen, please?⟩

You have not got your things at school.
Ask your partner.

A: I haven't got my pen.
Have you got a pen, please?
B: **Yes, I have.** Here you are.
Or: **No, I haven't.** Sorry. *Go on, please.*

13 Write the sentences with long forms

Example: **He's got** a nice grandma.
→ **He has got** a nice grandma.

1. They've got a small flat.
2. He hasn't got a big room.
3. You've got a nice T-shirt.
4. I haven't got your magazines.
5. She's got a problem.
6. We haven't got a computer.
7. He hasn't got a sister.
8. I've got new shoes.

WB p. 17/11

GRAMMAR

short form	long form
I've got	I have got
I haven't got	I have not got
He's got	He has got
He hasn't got	He has not got

(→ G 12, 13)

14 Your turn: Your school

Put in the right forms for the questions. What are your answers?

Example: **Has your school got** a cafeteria? – **Yes, it has. / No, it hasn't.**

1. ... your classroom ... computers? – ...
2. ... you ... a new table? – ...
3. ... your playground ... trees? – ...
4. ... the teachers ... their own room? – ...
5. ... you and your friends ... English books? – ...
6. ... your classroom ... a mouse? – ...

Rules for our room

Emma's friend Lisa is here. But where can they play? Nasreen has got a friend, too.

Now there is a different problem. Nasreen can't do her homework with Emma's music.

There are always problems, but now Nasreen has got an idea. They can make rules for their room. The rules can help.

Rules for our room:
1. Take turns with friends in the room.
2. Don't use your sister's school things.
3. Be quiet when your sister has got homework.
4. Don't play boring CDs.
5. Don't take your sister's T-shirts.
6. Don't make your own new rules.
7. Be nice to your sister!

15 What are the rules?

Find the girls' rules in the text for:

1. homework
2. new rules
3. school things
4. friends
5. T-shirts
6. music

WB p. 18/13

16 Don't!

TIP
Say the rap, Tom.
Don't play boring CDs.

Make rules with 'Don't ...'.
Are the rules Nasreen's idea or Emma's idea?

(→ G15)

Example: **Don't** use my things! → That's Nasreen's idea.

Don't	+	play use phone take	+	my T-shirt. my Discman. your friend Lisa on my mobile. your 'cool' CDs here. your dad in Leicester on my mobile.

WB p. 18/14

17 ⟨Your turn: Rules for your room⟩

Make a list for your brother or sister, or for your parents. (You can write funny rules, too.)

Don't use ...

Be nice to your brother.

Don't take my things.

18 Polite words

a) *Say the same thing with polite words.*

Example: Listen. → **Can you** listen, please?

1. Open the window.
2. Play a new CD.
3. Put your things in the wardrobe.
4. Help in the kitchen.
5. Make the sandwiches.
6. Be quiet.

WB p. 18/15

b) *Word bank: Say other polite words that you know from primary school. What can Tom say to the cat?*

19 Your turn: What can you do?

a) *Say what you can and can't do in your classroom.*

Example: We **can** use our English books.
We **can't** play football.

have a party • look at books • make a poster • phone our friends • do a rap • …

b) *Say what you can do at home.*

Example:

A: **Can you** play computer games in your room?
B: **Yes, I can. / No, I can't.**
A: Can you …? *Go on, please.*

WB p. 19/16

TIP
Can you …?
– Yes, I can.
– No, I can't.

(→ G16)

20 Listening: Emma at Terry's house

Listen and answer the questions.

Example: Has Terry got a small room? – No, he hasn't. He's got a big room.

1. Has Terry got football posters?
2. Has he got his own room?
3. Are the magazines great?
4. Are the magazines in the cupboard?
5. Is Emma good with cats?
6. Has Tiger got a rubber ball?

21 Listening: Sounds [u:] and [əʊ]

[u:]	[əʊ]	[u:] – [əʊ]
Who are you? Hey, cool shoes! It's a school rule.	Oh, no! That's an old joke. My poster is over my bed.	Please do your homework. Who's got a mobile? We've got two goals!

WB p. 19/18

22 Revision: What is missing?

I • you • it • they • he • we • she

Find the right words for Nasreen's e-mail to a friend in Bristol.

Hi, Nicola. Are 1 and your family OK? (Please say hello to your big brother – 2 's so cool!) 3 'm with my father and my new family in Leicester today. 4 've got a house here. 5 's a nice house because the rooms are nice and big! My two brothers are very funny. 6 're four and six years old. 7 's not easy in Greenwich because my sister and 8 are in one room. The flat is small, so 9 haven't got our own rooms. And there are always problems with Emma. 10 's terrible!
Bye, Nasreen.

Terry's shed

1 Before you read

What can you say about Emma and Terry, and about Terry's shed?

A One Saturday afternoon Terry is in his shed in the Jacksons' garden. Terry has got his dad's laptop. He is busy with a new music project. But he has got a problem. The laptop is not very good. It is slow. Terry is fed up. Can Emma help?

B Terry has got Emma's phone number. He is lucky, she is at home.

Terry: Hi, Emma. I'm in the shed. Can you help? I can't finish my music project. My laptop is so slow. Have you got a good laptop?
Emma: No problem, Terry. I can't help you here at home. Nasreen has got a friend in our room, and Nasreen is a pain. But I can come over with my dad's laptop now.
Terry: OK, great!

C Soon Emma is in Terry's shed.

Terry: Thanks, Emma!
Emma: No problem.

Terry is happy. Now he can do his music project. But it is boring for Emma. She is not very happy. What can she do? What is in the shed? There are Terry's drums! Emma can play his drums.

Terry: Emma, please, stop!
Emma: OK, sorry.

D What can she do now? Terry's old chemistry set is behind the door.
This is great – there are blue and yellow and red colours in the set. Emma is very happy. She can play with it. But then …

Emma: Oh, no! There's smoke everywhere!
Terry: Emma! What's that smell?
Emma: Yuk! Let's open the windows!
Terry: Oh, Emma. You're a pain.

E Now there is no smoke. But what is this?

Terry: Hey, look, Emma. Look at the beautiful crystal on the table. It's purple and green and orange. You aren't a pain, Emma. I'm sorry. Here – it's your crystal.

Emma: Oh, wow, Terry, your chemistry set is fun! Thanks for the crystal.

2 Find the right sentences

1. It is Saturday and …	… on the table.
2. Terry's laptop is not very good …	… with Terry's drums.
3. Emma can come over …	… is behind the door.
4. Emma can play …	… and he is fed up.
5. Terry's old chemistry set …	… with her dad's laptop.
6. There is a beautiful crystal …	… Terry is in his shed.

WB p. 21/21

3 Talk about the pictures

Who is happy? 🙂 *Who is not happy?* 🙁 *Say why.*

Example: In picture one Terry isn't happy. He's got a problem. His laptop is slow. WB p. 21/22

4 ⟨Role play: Act the story⟩

Make groups for ***B***, ***C***, ***D*** *and* ***E***.

5 How to: Talk about people and things in a text

a) *Sort the words.*

busy, not very good, new, slow, lucky, great, purple and green and orange, fed up, a pain, beautiful

Terry	Emma
busy	…
…	…

things
…
…

⟨b)⟩ *Use the words and write sentences.*

Example: Terry is busy in the shed.
Or: Terry is busy with a music project in his shed.

WB p. 21/23

1 Word groups

VOCABULARY SKILLS

A B C D E F G H I

It can help to learn words in a group.
Example: 'Ruler' is a new word. You can make a group with more words: ruler, pen, rubber … . The name for the word group is 'pencil-case'.

a) *Put the words in three groups.*

b) *Write the word groups in your exercise book.*

c) *One word in the group is the name for the word family. Underline the word.*

mother • red • kitchen • cousin • house • sister • white • family • bathroom • green • uncle • garden • bedroom • colour • yellow • grandad • blue

WB p. 22/24

2 What can you do?

Make lists.
1. You can play: a game, …
2. You can write: an e-mail, …
3. You can open: a bag, …
4. You can use: a pen, …

3 What can they say?

4 ⟨Picture words⟩

Make picture words. Examples:

5 ⟨Funny words⟩

a) *What is the right word?*

Example: bedroom

b) *Make your own funny words.*

~~bed~~ – board
lap – ~~room~~
play – top
ward – ground
cup – stairs
up – ball
foot – robe

NOW YOU CAN

- ✓ Talk about your family and home.
- ✓ Use *my, your, her, …* and s-genitive.
- ✓ Use *have got* and *has got*.
- ✓ Make rules.
- ✓ Use *please* and be polite.
- ✓ Use *can*.
- ✓ Learn words in a group.

1 Make one sentence (→ G10, 12)

a) *Example:* Lisa has got a dog. He is big.
→ Lisa's dog is big.

1. Ben has got two sisters. They are Lisa and Jade.
2. Their mum has got a bag. It is new.
3. Barker has got a ball. It is in the garden.

b) *Example:* The Taylors have got a house. It is in Pond Road.
→ The Taylors' house is in Pond Road.

1. The Taylors have got a garden. It is small.
2. The girls have got a brother. He is sixteen.
3. Their parents have got a car. It is old.

2 Your turn: Your family and your home

Write six sentences about your family. Use the Useful phrases on page 27.

3 Put in the right words (→ G11)

my | your | her | his | its | our | their | your

Lisa: Let's look at [1] pictures from Bristol, Emma. Who's the girl here?
Emma: She's a friend from [2] old school. [3] name is Fiona Green. The Greens have got a funny house. [4] house has got a living room upstairs – and [5] walls are pink and yellow! And Fiona's dad is funny, too. He's always got funny pictures on [6] T-shirts!
Lisa: Ha, ha! Is that a dog with Fiona – or a mouse?! We've got a dog, but [7] dog is big.
Emma: Yes, [8] dog is very big – but Fiona's dog is nice, too.

WB p. 23/27

4 What is missing: *have, 've, haven't, has, hasn't*? (→ G12, 13, 14)

1. Emma: My sister and I [1] got a small room. We [2] got a computer in our room. [3] you got a computer in your room, Terry?
   Terry: No, I [4] got a computer. But I [5] got Dad's old laptop.
2. Emma: The Jacksons [6] got a shed. [7] you got a shed, too, Lisa?
   Lisa: No, we [8]. But we [9] got a garden.
   Emma: [10] Sam got a garden?
   Lisa: No, he [11].

WB p. 23/28

5 At school (→ G15, 16)

WB p. 23/29

Pick-up B Tom in Hobbyland

1 Where can you do your hobby?

a) *Look at the grid and listen to what you can do in Hobbyland. Then answer the questions.*

Example: Where can you ride a bike?
You: You can ride a bike in **A1**. *Go on, please.*

b) *Ask your partner.*

Example: A: What can you do in **D1**?
B: You can draw a picture. *Go on, please.*

WB p. 24/1

2 Listening: What can Tom do?

What can Tom do in Hobbyland? What can't he do?

Start like this: Tom can play basketball in Hobbyland. But he can't …

WB p. 24/2

3 Your turn: Your hobbies

a) *Word bank: With your partner, collect hobby words that you know from primary school. Make a word web.*

b) *Now say what your hobby is.*

Example: I can play football and I …

4 Role play: Fun or boring?

Make dialogues about hobbies.
What is fun and what is boring?

A: Let's play computer games.
B: That's boring!
A: OK. Then let's watch videos.
B: No, that's boring, too.
But I've got an idea. Let's ride our bikes.
A: Yes, that's fun! Let's go!

Go on, please.

play computer games · watch videos · go swimming · draw pictures · play the guitar · play football · read books · ride our bikes · …

5 A game: What can you collect?

What can you collect? Start like this in your group:

"I can collect CDs." "I can collect CDs and books."
"I can collect CDs and books and …"

Go on, please.

6 A song: Seven days in a week

Musik: Karl-Heinz Böttcher
Text: Karl-Heinz Böttcher / Sheila McBride

7 Funny week

Write the days of the week. Example:

= Saturday

1. nduays 2. auetsyd 3. adonym 4. dnedawesy 5. yadrif 6. yhrdusta

WB p. 24/3

8 Pick-up quiz

1. What can you play in Hobbyland?
2. What can't you do in Hobbyland?
3. Spell the days of the week. Start like this: M-O-N- …

Unit 3 Hobbies and clubs

In British schools, clubs are very important. You can go there in your free time in the afternoons and meet your friends. There are a lot of clubs at Thomas Tallis:

Greenwich Orchestra

On Tuesdays from 3.00 pm to 4.00 pm

Cooking Club

On Mondays from 4.00 pm to 5.30 pm

Computer Club

On Thursdays from 3.30 pm to 4.30 pm

Emma: Hey, Sam, look at the clubs. How about the Greenwich Orchestra?
Sam: Hm, no. When is the Computer Club?
Emma: At half past three on Thursdays.
Sam: That's fine. Come on, Emma. See you there.
Emma: OK, and at the weekend we can go to the cinema. There's a new film with my favourite band '4U'. Can we meet at …?
Sam: Sorry, Emma, not a boy band! Ask Lisa! Terry and I can go to the Water Park. And then we can play basketball in Blackheath Park.

1 Free time in Greenwich

1. What clubs are there at Thomas Tallis?
2. When are the clubs?
3. Where can Emma and Lisa go at the weekend?
4. Where can Sam and Terry go?

WB p. 25/1

TIP
On Mondays
3.00 = three o'clock
3.30 = half past three

(→ G17)

2 What time is it, please?

Tell the time:

o'clock | half | quarter | past | to | minutes

1. 3.00: It's three **o'clock**.
   a) 4.00 b) 8.00 c) 11.00 d) 12.00
2. 3.15: It's **quarter past** three.
   a) 2.15 b) 4.15 c) 7.15 d) 11.15
3. 3.30: It's **half past** three.
   a) 5.30 b) 9.30 c) 1.30 d) 12.30
4. 3.45: It's **quarter to** four.
   a) 4.45 b) 8.45 c) 11.45 d) 12.45
5. 3.05: It's five **past** three.
   3.40: It's twenty **to** four.
   a) 4.05 b) 8.25 c) 11.50 d) 12.35
6. 3.06: It's six **minutes** past three.
   a) 1.11 b) 3.04 c) 6.46 d) 8.48

Or you can use only numbers:

7. 5.30: It's **five thirty**.
   a) 3.45 b) 9.15 c) 4.30 d) 8.45
8. 6.43: It's **six forty-three**.
   a) 10.41 b) 12.42 c) 7.43 d) 1.44
9. 1.09: It's one – **'oh'** – nine.
   a) 2.07 b) 3.02 c) 12.01 d) 6.08

WB p. 25/2; 3

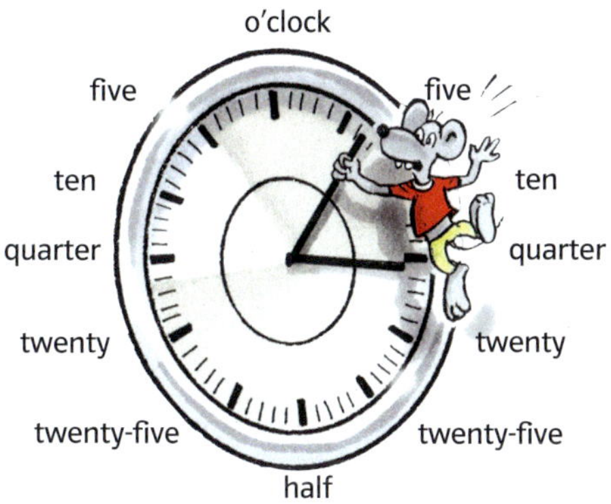

3 Listening: Let's go to the cinema

Right or wrong?

Example: Ben is Lisa's father. –
That's wrong! Ben is Lisa's brother.

1. There is a great film on Saturday.
2. The film is *From here to Cardiff*.
3. The film is at six o'clock.
4. It is at the Bristol Cinema.

4 How to: Meet a friend

What can you do at the weekend? Talk to a partner.

USEFUL PHRASES

Let's +	go to the park go swimming play …	+ this weekend. on Saturday. …	Great idea. Let's meet at my house See you at … + at six o'clock. at …
			Oh, no. That's boring. + Let's + go … play …

WB p. 25/4

5 Your turn: My hobbies and clubs

What clubs are there at your school or in your town? What can you do in your free time, and when?

Example: We can play basketball at the Sports Club. It is on Mondays from four fifteen to five fifteen. Basketball is great.

A phone call from Grandma

Mr Brook: Greenwich 84007433.

Grandma Brook: Hello, Rob, it's Mum here.

Mr Brook: Oh, hi, Mum. How are you?

Grandma Brook: I'm fine, thanks, Rob. How's Emma's new school? Is she there?

Mr Brook: She's here. Emma, it's your grandma.

Emma: Thanks, Dad. – Hi, Grandma.

Grandma Brook: Hello, Emma. How's your new school? Is it nice?

Emma: It's OK. I always get up early, at 7.15. Nasreen and I usually ride our bikes to school every morning. We start at 8.40.

Grandma Brook: What about lunch? Can you go home?

Emma: No, I can't. I eat lunch at school. The school day is from 8.40 to 3.20, but on Wednesdays we can go home at 2.30.

Grandma Brook: Oh, good! Then you've got a lot of time for homework on Wednesdays.

Emma: Yes, but it's never boring on Wednesday afternoons. After school I often go to my friend Lisa's house. We walk her dog in the park. Lisa is great fun. And at the weekend, Grandma, she and I sometimes go to the cinema.

Grandma Brook: I never go to the cinema now. I always watch films on TV in the evening, but I sometimes fall asleep on the sofa.

Emma: Oh, Grandma! – Can't you come and visit us? We can go to the cinema every day!

Grandma Brook: That's a great idea. – And what about your dancing lessons?

Emma: First I've got Computer Club on Thursdays. Then I usually go to dancing lessons after school. – Oh, here's Dad again. I've got homework now.

Grandma Brook: No problem, Emma. See you soon. Bye.

Emma: Bye, Grandma.

1 Look at the text

Say when. *Example:* I always get up early. – I always get up early, at 7.15.

1. Nasreen and I usually ride our bikes to school.
2. We can go home at 2.30.
3. It's never boring.
4. Lisa and I sometimes go to the cinema.
5. I usually go to dancing lessons.
6. I always watch films on TV.

WB p. 26/5

2 Your turn: Write about your day

I always get up at …
We start school at …
The school day is from …
After school I …

Put it in your folder.

3 Their free time

Say what they do in their free time.

Example: 1. **On Mondays** Sam and his father **play** cards.
2. On Tuesdays …

GRAMMAR

I	play basketball
You	
We	
They	

(→ G18)

Mondays | Tuesdays | Wednesdays | Thursdays | Fridays

1

Sam – his father

2

Emma – Sam

3

Lisa – Emma

4

Terry – his friends

5

Emma – Nasreen

WB p. 26/6

4 Find the rule

a) *Where can you put **never, always, usually, often**?*

I **usually** go to Cooking Club on Mondays.
I **always** do my homework.
We **often** go to the cinema.
It's **never** boring on Wednesday afternoons.

Write a tip box.

b) 1. We get up at 7.00. (usually)
2. My friends ride their bikes to school. (always)
3. We go swimming with my parents. (never)
4. I play football with my friends. (sometimes)
5. I go to my friend's house. (often)
6. It's fun at the Water Park. (always)
7. I read a book in the evening. (sometimes)
8. My friends and I play basketball at the Sports Club. (usually)

WB p. 26/7

5 How to: Make a phone call

USEFUL PHRASES

a)

Hi. / Hello. This is … / How are you?

Hi. / Hello, … / I'm fine, thanks.

Let's go to … / Can we … on Saturday?

Sorry, I always go to … on Saturdays. / OK, great idea! / Fine! / Cool! When can we meet?

How about … ?

Yes. That's fine. / See you at … / soon. Bye.

⟨b)⟩ *Role play: Phone a friend: Let's go to a sport club.*

WB p. 27/8

Sam and Tiger

It is four o'clock on Saturday afternoon. Terry and his family are in Bristol for the weekend. Sam goes to Terry's house. There is a note from Terry on the shed.

First Sam reads the note, then he goes into the shed. He cannot find the cat food, but then he sees the tin next to Terry's drums. "Mm – chicken flavour. This looks tasty! Tiger, where are you?" Tiger comes in and sees the tin. She says, "Purr-rrr." "Hi, Tiger. Here's your food," says Sam. First he makes a hole in the tin and then he opens the tin and feeds Tiger.

But Tiger sees a dog and runs away. "Tiger!" Sam shouts. First he walks round the garden. Then he looks in the neighbour's garden. No Tiger! After that he looks in the street. There she is. But Tiger is busy. "Tiger! Don't run away!" Sam chases the cat, and she runs away.

So finally Sam goes back to Terry's shed. It is seven pm. Sam waits and waits. Finally he falls asleep.
"Sam! There you are! Sam!" his father says.
"Oh, uh, ah, Dad. What time is it?"
"It's nine o'clock. It's time to go home."
"I can't go home! Where's Tiger?"

Tiger comes into the shed. She has got a mouse. "Tiger, no!" Sam shouts.

6 Put the sentences together

1. Terry is in Bristol
2. Sam cannot find the food
3. Sam feeds Tiger
4. First Sam looks in the garden
5. Finally Sam goes back to the shed
6. When Tiger comes back to the shed,

- and then in the neighbour's garden.
- but Tiger runs away.
- she has got a mouse.
- but then he sees the tin next to Terry's drums.
- so Sam helps with Tiger.
- and falls asleep.

7 A quiz: Say who it is

Example: She walks her dog in the park. –
It's Lisa. She walks her dog in Blackheath Park.

1. He plays the drums. – It's …
2. She sees a dog and runs away. – …
3. She falls asleep on her sofa. – …
4. He likes the Computer Club. – …
5. She gets up at 7.15. – …
6. He feeds Tiger on Saturday. – …

WB p. 28/10

TIP

He, she, it – *das s muss mit!*

she walks
he plays
she sees

(→ G 19)

8 In Blackheath Park

Put in the correct forms.

1. Lisa often goes to Blackheath Park with Barker. 2. She ▭ (love) Barker and he ▭ (love) Lisa. 3. Sometimes Lisa ▭ (meet) Terry or Emma in the park. 4. Barker usually ▭ (chase) a cat and Lisa ▭ (shout) at Barker. 5. At home Lisa often ▭ (watch) TV with Barker. He is a happy dog.

WB p. 29/12; 14

TIP

she goes
he chases
she watches

(→ G 19)

9 ⟨A game: I go – she goes⟩

10 *First, then, after that*

Start like this: **First** Terry **goes** to his shed. **Then** he plays … **After that** he …

	Terry's Saturdays	Emma's Saturdays	Lisa's Saturdays	Sam's Saturdays
first	go – shed	get up – 8.00	walk – her dog	get up – 9.30
then	play – the drums	go – swimming	play – football	phone – his mother
after that	play – basketball	do – homework	watch – TV	play – computer games

WB p. 29/13

11 Your turn: Your partner's weekends

First Then After that Finally	+	he she	+	get up … watch … play … phone … go to …

Talk to your partner about your Saturdays.
Then she / he says what you do.

A: First **I get up**. Then I …
B: First **she / he gets up**. …

WB p. 28/11

Sam's card trick

"I've got a good card trick, Terry," Sam says. "First take two cards! Uh, no, … sorry. Not those cards. Take these cards – this card on the top and that card on the bottom." "But then you know my cards," says Terry. "Yes, but this trick is cool. Just take these two cards," says Sam. "Now look at the two cards and then put the two cards back here." Terry looks at his cards and puts the cards back. Sam shuffles the cards. Then he holds the cards and bangs the cards on the table. He has only got two cards now. "Are these your cards here?" Terry can't believe his eyes. "Yes! That's great!"

How can you do this trick? Look at the bottom of this page!

12 Are these your cards?

A: Are **these** your cards?
B: No, they aren't.
Those are my cards there.
A: Is **this** … ?
B: Yes, it is.

Go on, please.

WB p. 30/15

cards ✗ apples ✓ CDs ✗ pen ✓ pencil ✗ exercise book ✗ magazines ✗ ruler ✓ rubber ✓ crisps ✗

TIP this these

TIP that those

(→ G 21)

13 Trouble in the classroom

Example: "Hey! This isn't your bag! That's your bag."

1

2

3
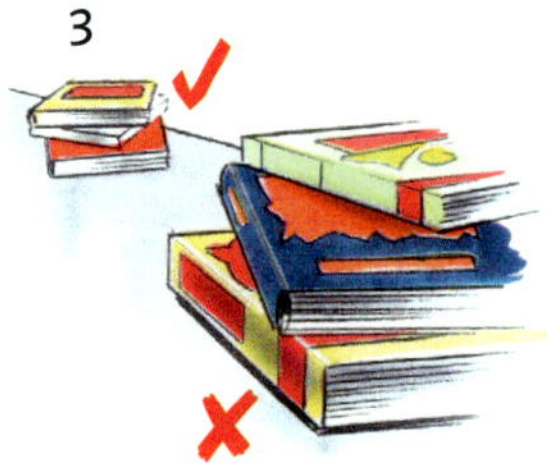

4
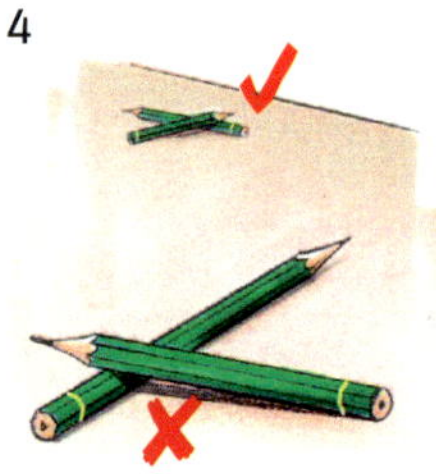

How this trick works:

First put the nine of diamonds on the top and the eight of hearts on the bottom. Then put the nine of hearts and the eight of diamonds on top of these two cards. When Terry looks at his cards, he knows the eight and nine are red. Then he puts the cards back. He forgets which is hearts and which is diamonds. Sam holds the nine of hearts and the eight of diamonds when he bangs the cards on the table. After that he shows Terry the cards, but the eight and nine are not the same.

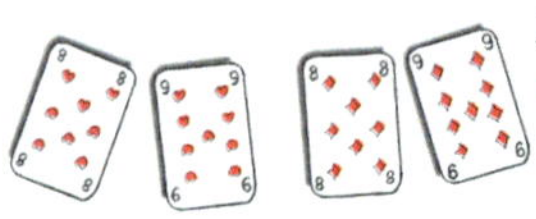

14 Listening: Saturday morning in the park

LISTENING SKILLS

When you listen to a text, always ask these questions first. They can help!

a) 1. **Who** is there? → 1. Lisa, …
2. **Where** are they? → 2. They are in …
3. **When** is it? → 3. It is … *Go on, please.*

Then always listen again. Ask these questions: What happens in the text?

b) 1. What happens first? → 1. First Pete kicks a ball and …
2. What happens then? → 2. Then Lisa … But the dog … Now there are …
3. What happens after that? → 3. After that Pete says … *Go on, please.*

WB p. 30/16

15 Listening: Sounds [ð] and [θ]

First listen. Then write these words in two lists:

Thursday • bathroom • brother • mother • this • then • thirty • thanks • three • those

[ð]	[θ]
brother	Thursday
…	…

WB p. 31/17

16 Listening: Linking sounds

First listen, then say: I've got‿a good card trick. Look‿at the two cards.
There‿is‿a note from Terry. Tiger sees‿a dog‿and runs‿away.
Tiger comes‿in‿and sees the tin. Sam waits‿and‿waits.

17 Revision: *Has got* or *have got?*

a) *Ask questions with* ***Has … got …?*** *or* ***Have … got …?***

1. Have the Jacksons ___ a house in Greenwich or Bristol?
2. Has Tiger ___ a mouse or a chicken?
3. ___ Lisa ___ a dog or a cat?
4. ___ Emma ___ a brother or a sister?
5. ___ Terry ___ drums or a guitar?
6. ___ Emma and Nasreen ___ a computer or a TV in their room?

b) *Now make answers for the questions in a). Start with she / he / it or they.*

Example: 1. They **haven't got** a house in Bristol. **They've got** a house in Greenwich.

18 Revision: In Greenwich

Write the sentences with the correct s-genitive.

Example: The Jacksons' house in Greenwich is at 39 Hither Farm Road.

1. Terry ___ shed is in the garden.
2. Mr Brook ___ computer shop is at 240 Holburne Road.
3. The Brook ___ flat is small.
4. The two girl ___ room is a problem.
5. Sam ___ flat is in Wendover Road.
6. His parent ___ name is Spencer; they are divorced.
7. Sam ___ family ___ flat is nice.

Barker's story

1 Before you read

1. Who is Barker? 2. What can you see in picture one?

1

Hello. I'm Barker. My people are the Taylors – Richard, Susan and Lisa, Ben and Jade. I help the Taylor family. I love the Taylors!

2

Lisa is my pet. Every morning at seven thirty I wake up Lisa and wash her face. Then she washes her face again and makes my breakfast. After that, she makes her own breakfast. Finally, her brother Ben and her sister Jade make their breakfast.

3

At twenty past eight Lisa and Ben ride their bikes to school. Then I wake up Susan and we go to the jazz café. It's her café, but I help when people come in. I'm very nice to the people.

4

It's nice outside in our garden. Sometimes Tiger, the Jacksons' cat, comes into our garden, but I always bark and then she runs away.

5

On Saturdays I take Lisa to the park. I teach Lisa tricks. I bring Lisa a ball and she throws the ball. Sometimes she gets lost in the park. Then she calls my name and I find Lisa.

6

On Sundays I usually take my people out in our car. There are always a lot of cars. Sometimes there are dogs in the cars, too. I bark at them and they bark at me. It's great fun!

7

My people like picnics. I like picnics, too, because there's no table. Sometimes Jade puts her drink next to me and it falls over. Silly girl!

8

In the evening my people often watch TV. Then we play a game. I watch TV, too, and they throw shoes at me. I take the shoes into Lisa's bedroom. I like shoes!

9

At nine o'clock I take Lisa to bed. She's nice to me, so she can always sleep in my bed. I've got a very nice bed. I usually fall asleep soon. After my busy day I'm dog-tired.

2 Answer the questions

Start like this: 1. Barker is in the story, and …

1. **Who** is in the story?
2. Say **when** Barker wakes up Lisa and when he goes to bed.
3. **What** can he and Lisa do in the park?
4. **Where** can Barker bark at the dogs?
5. **Why** are picnics fun for Barker?
6. **Why** can Lisa sleep in Barker's bed?

WB p. 32/20

3 Find names for the pictures

Example: Picture 1: Barker and his family

WB p. 32/21

4 Say why or why not

1. Is this a good story?
2. Is Barker a nice dog?
3. Are Barker's days fun?

Example: 1. The story is good because it's funny.
Or: … isn't nice because …

1 Collect words and phrases

1. Collect words and phrases for your day:

   Example: I get up, I wash my face, …

2. Collect words and phrases for the park:

   Example: I walk the dog, …

3. Collect words and phrases for free time:

   Example: I play football, …

Go on, please. You can use these words in exercise 4 on page 51.

2 Match the words

1. chase	a. a phone call
2. meet	b. the dog
3. open	c. a tin
4. make	d. a cat
5. walk	e. a friend
6. watch	f. your homework
7. ride	g. a bike
8. do	h. the guitar
9. play	i. a good film

WB p. 33/22

3 ⟨Make the rhymes⟩

a) *What is the rhyme word?*

Great school – very

Hey, look, you've got my

Come on, let's play every

?

b) *Can you find other rhymes with a partner?*

4 ⟨Five new words⟩

Draw five words from this unit.

Example:

5 Mixed bag

Put in the right words from this unit.

Barker is Lisa's [1]. Every morning at 7.30 he [2] up Lisa. She makes Barker's [3]. On Saturdays Lisa teaches Barker [4] in the park. Sometimes Barker gets [5] but Lisa [6] his name and finds Barker. Barker [7] at dogs and [8] cats. At 9 pm Lisa takes Barker to [9]. He usually falls [10] soon. After his busy day he is [11].

6 ⟨A poem: Break-dance is his thing⟩

There's a dog in our rap club,
And break-dance is his thing.
When he dances on the table,
All the children start to sing.

NOW YOU CAN

- ✓ Meet your friends and talk about your free time.
- ✓ Tell the time in English.
- ✓ Make a phone call.
- ✓ Talk about what you do every day in the simple present.
- ✓ Use the simple present in a story.
- ✓ Use *this, that, these* and *those*.
- ✓ Ask the right questions when you listen to a text.

1 At the weekend – Make the dialogue.

A

Hey – let's	at six at the Bristol Cinema?
There's a	let's see the film!
Oh, please –	great film about a girl and a boy.
How about Friday	go to the cinema.

B

A girl and a boy?! That's boring.
Good idea!
Oh – OK. When can we go?
Fine. See you on Friday. Bye.

2 What time is it? (→ G17)

a) *Say the time.*

b) *Write the time.*

3 A phone call

Put the dialogue in the right order. Start like this: Greenwich 84…

The Useful phrases on page 43 can help you. Then act the phone call.

Bye, Lisa. See you.
Oh – What's the problem?
Hi, Lisa. I'm fine. And you?
Yes, Lisa. No problem. I like Barker.
Greenwich 84007433.

Hi, Emma. It's Lisa. How are you?
Fine. Listen, Emma. I've got a problem.
Thanks a lot. See you. Bye.
I can't take Barker to the park this weekend. Can you help?

4 Your turn: Your free time

Write five sentences about your free time. Use the words from exercise 1 on page 50.

5 Saturdays with Jade (→ G17, 19)

Start like this: On Saturdays Jade gets up at …

1

get up 6.30
On Saturdays Jade …

2

make 6.45
Then …

3

wake up 7.15
After that …

4

play 10.30
At ten thirty …

5

feed 3.00
In the afternoon …

WB p. 34/25

⟨Revision A⟩ Unit 1–3

1 Emma's friend in Bristol (→ G11)

I	you	he	she	it	we	they
my	your	his	her	our	their	

Put in the right words for Emma's e-mail.

Hi, Fiona.
Thank you for your e-mail. Today 1 've got the room because Nasreen is with 1 friends. 2 're at the cinema. There isn't a lot of trouble at home now because Nasreen and 3 've got rules for 2 room. Nasreen is OK – sometimes, and 4 helps with my homework.
There's a nice boy in 3 tutor group. 4 name is Terry Jackson. 5 hasn't got a brother or a sister – only a cat. Terry is VERY nice! 6 're good friends. The Jacksons have got a shed in 5 garden. 7 isn't very big but 8 can meet there and play.
Can you come to Greenwich soon? 9 can meet 6 new friends. Please say hi to 7 family.
Bye, Emma.

2 Tiger's story (→ G1, 2)

Terry and his friends have got homework: 'Write your pet's story'. Terry shows his text to Sam. "Nice story, Terry," Sam says. "Maybe cats can talk, but they can't write!"

Read the text to your partner. Use short forms!

Hello, everyone. I am Tiger the cat, and Terry is my friend. He is nice, and I can play in his garden. It is a big garden, and there are not a lot of dogs. Dogs are not my friends – they are scary. But I like a nice mouse ...! Cats are very interested in tasty mice. Terry is not happy when I am in his shed. Then he says, "Don't sleep on my drums. They aren't your sofa!" I am not always on my 'sofa' in the shed. In the evening I go into the house with my people. When we are in the living room, I sleep on the sofa there. Terry says, "You're a lucky cat, Tiger. You've got two sofas."

Start like this: "Hello, everyone. **I'm** Tiger ..." *Go on, please.*

3 A game: Who is Jade? (→ G4, 9, 12)

Play the game with the Taylors. Put in the correct answers.

Jade: I know a new game. I'm not Jade. Who am I?
Ben: What's your name?
Jade: I can only say 'yes' and 'no'.
Ben: Oh, OK. Are you at Thomas Tallis?
Jade: **Yes, I am.**
Lisa: Are you a boy?
Jade: No, 1 .
Ben: So you're a girl. Have you got a brother?
Jade: No, 2 .
Lisa: Have you got a sister?
Jade: Yes, 3 .
Ben: Have you and your sister got a dog?
Jade: No, 4 .
Lisa: Is your sister eleven?
Jade: Yes, 5 .
Ben: Maybe your sister is Emma. Are you Nasreen?
Jade: Yes, 6 . Now you, Ben. Who are you?

4 Role play: Free time

Look at the information. Talk to your partner about Green Park Swimming Pool and Sportpark.

Let's go …
We can play … and …
How about …?
It's open …
…

Great idea!
When …?
Let's meet at …
…

Green Park Swimming Pool
Play in the water!
Open Mon. to Fri. from 9.00 am to 7.00 pm
Sat. and Sun. from 10.00 am to 5.00 pm
Cafeteria open every day 11.00 am to 5.00 pm

Come to
Sportpark
– Football – Basketball –
and a lot of sports and games
Open Mon. to Fri. 3.00 pm to 7.00 pm
Sat. and Sun. 11.00 am to 5.00 pm

5 Tom's Sundays (→ G17, 19)

Write what Tom does on Sundays.

Example: Tom gets up at 10.00 in the morning … First he … then … After that …

does homework
goes to bed
eats cheese
gets up
watches TV
makes breakfast

6 Polite or not so polite?

Are these words polite or not so polite? Make two lists.

Hey, you've got my CD! • That girl is a pain. • Yes, thank you! • You're welcome. • You and your silly T-shirts. • That's OK. • Can I help you? • That's your problem. • Sorry I'm late.

7 Make a phone call

Put the dialogue in the right order.

Phil:
- No, it isn't! Can you come over?
- Tim – I've got problems with my German homework.
- How about six o'clock?
- Hi, Tim. It's Phil. How are you?

Tim:
- Hello, Phil. I'm fine, thanks.
- Yes, fine. See you at six. Bye.
- OK, I can come over. No problem!
- German? But German is easy, Phil.

Start like this: Phil: Hi, Tim. …

Pick-up C In town

1 Listening: What is where?

a) *Listen to the words for places on the map. Say the words.*
b) *Now look at the map. Where are the places?*

in … Road
near
next to
opposite

Example: The museum is in Apple Tree Road.
The playground is opposite / next to / near … *Go on, please.*

WB p. 37/1

c) *Word bank: Say more town words that you know from primary school.*

2 A game: Where am I?

Your partner is at a place in Mousetown. Ask questions. Can you find the place?

Example: A: Is it near the river?
B: No, it isn't.

A: Is it opposite the playground?
B: Yes, it is.

A: Is it the castle?
B: Yes, it is.

Go on, please.

3 How can I get to … ?

Look at the map of Mousetown. You are at the school in Dog Street. How can you get to these places? Ask your partner.

Example:

A: Excuse me. How can I **get to** the park?
B: **Go down** Dog Street. **Turn right into** River Road. **Then turn left** into Brook Street. Turn right into Cat Street. **Go straight on.** Walk to the bridge. Cross the bridge, then turn left into Apple Tree Road. The park is **on your right**.
A: Thank you. Goodbye.

WB p. 37/2

Excuse me.
How can I get to
1. the police station?
2. the playground?
3. the café?
4. the church?

4 Listening: Tom in Mousetown

Tom is on his way to visit his aunt and uncle.

a) *Look at the map of Mousetown and listen to the text. Where is Tom?*

b) *Listen again. Where is the bus stop?*

5 A tour of Mousetown

Where can mice go in Mousetown?
How can they get there?
Make a tour of Mousetown.

Start at the information centre.
Go down Castle Road.
Turn left into Mouse Road.
The church is on your right.
Then go …

6 Pick-up quiz

What are these places in Mousetown?

1. It is near the castle. There are a lot of children there.
2. It is near the river. It is in Apple Tree Road. There are old books and pictures there.
3. It is near the church. It is in Mouse Road. There are a lot of sandwiches there.

Unit 4 Greenwich Project Week

This year there is a Greenwich Project Week at Thomas Tallis. The pupils work in teams. They collect information about interesting sights in Greenwich. Then they write about the sights. Emma, Lisa, Sam and Terry have got a tourist brochure for their project.

1

How to find the tourist information centre:
Take the Underground to Canary Wharf. Then take the Docklands Light Railway (DLR) train to the Cutty Sark station. The tourist information centre is opposite the Cutty Sark.

A. Greenwich Park is near the town centre. A lot of young people come here with their skateboards and bikes. There is a big playground, and you can play football here, too.

2

3

B. The Greenwich Foot Tunnel is under the Thames so you can walk under the river! It goes from Greenwich to the Isle of Dogs.

1 Match the texts and the six pictures

a) *Start like this:* Picture 1 goes with A / B / C … because … *Go on, please.*

b) *What is interesting for you in Greenwich? Say why.*

WB p. 38/1

2 How to: Show a visitor your town

What can visitors see or where can they go in your town? Look at the Useful phrases.

USEFUL PHRASES
In my town … we've got …
There is / are …
You can visit / see / go to …
… is famous / is interesting.

3 Your turn: Your town (Project part 1)

Collect pictures of sights in your town. Write 1–2 sentences for every picture. Put the pictures and the text in your folder.

4

5

C. World time "starts" on this line in the wall of the Royal Observatory in Greenwich Park. The time line is 'Greenwich Mean Time' or GMT. Visitors can put one foot in the west and one foot in the east. The 24 hour clock is there.

D. The Thames Barrier closes when there is too much water from the North Sea. People call the Barrier the Eighth Wonder of the World.

E. The Cutty Sark is a famous ship. It is 150 years old. It is now a museum near the River Thames. You can listen to stories about life at the sea there.

F. Church Street, near the River Thames, has got a lot of interesting shops. You can find things from all round the world there.

6

4 Listening: Sights of Greenwich

Which picture is right? Say why.

1

A 

B 

2

A 

B 

3

A 

B 

4

A 

B 

WB p. 38/2

Transport in Greenwich

Lisa, Emma, Terry and Sam are at Lisa's house in Pond Road. Where can they collect pictures and brochures for Project Week?

Lisa: Let's start at the tourist information centre.

Terry: OK. That's easy. We can take the 286 bus from Kidbrooke Park Road near our school. It takes us to Greenwich town centre.

Lisa: Look, this transport map shows the Underground, the Docklands Light Railway and all the buses.

Sam: Which bus takes us to the Millennium Dome?

Lisa: Hm … Just a second, there are lots of bus numbers here …

Emma: Ugh, the bus! Maybe we can go by Underground.

Sam: The Underground? Let's go by DLR! It's fun because there's no driver in the train.

Emma: No driver? Let's catch a bus – or walk! You can't take the DLR to the Dome.

Lisa: Oh, no! This isn't easy …

Terry: Don't listen to her … I know! I can phone my dad and ask him. He drives people all round London in his taxi. *(He phones his dad on his mobile.)* Hi, Dad, can I ask you a question? Can you tell me the way to the Dome from Greenwich town centre?

Dad: The Underground or the number 188 bus takes you to the Dome.

Terry: What? Lisa, Sam, quiet! What number, Dad?

Dad: Number 188. Catch it in the High Road. But we can …

Terry: What?

Dad: … we can go by taxi! I can pick you up at four o'clock – for a special tour of Greenwich!

1 Finish the sentences

Emma likes …	… the DLR.
Terry says: We can …	… the Underground.
Sam likes …	… about the number 188 bus.
Terry asks his dad …	… for a special tour of Greenwich.
Terry's dad can pick them up …	… take the 286 bus to Greenwich town centre.

2 Can you tell me the way?

Example: Can you tell **me** the way to the Dome?

1. Where's the information centre? I can't find ___ on the map.
2. We can't find the bus stop. Can you help ___?
3. Sorry, I can't help ___. I'm not from here.
4. The Greenwich brochures are there. Can you get ___ for me, please?
5. Is Mr Jackson there? Can I speak to ___, please?
6. Lisa knows the way. We can always ask ___.

WB p. 39/4

us, you, her, it, me ✓, him, them

3 Put in the pronouns

Here are Mrs Carter's tips for the class project:

1. **Amanda Peterson** at the tourist information centre is very nice. You can always phone **her**. 2. **Mr Jackson** drives people all round London. You can ask … about transport in Greenwich. 3. What about **people in shops**? You can ask … for information, too. 4. **I** know a lot about Greenwich. You can always come to … ! 5. Look at the **Thames Barrier** and draw … , or draw the Cutty Sark or the Royal Observatory. 6. Find nice **pictures and brochures** and collect … . 7. Please give … everything on Friday.

GRAMMAR
Pronouns

I	→	me
you	→	you
he	→	him
she	→	her
it	→	it
we	→	us
you	→	you
they	→	them

(→ G 22)

4 Jumbled sentences: Find the right order

a) 1. because • driver • a • it • I • hasn't got • like • it
2. takes • Dad • them • in his taxi • all round London
3. phone • him • I • can • and • the way • ask • him
4. pick • for • special • a • tour • Dad • can • us • up
5. the map • me • give • you • can • please?
6. wonder • of • the • eighth • people • it • call • the • world

⟨b)⟩ *Make three jumbled sentences with an object pronoun. Can your partner find the right order?*

5 Ask for information

COMMUNICATION SKILLS

You can use these phrases when you ask for information. Always be polite: Use **please** and **thank you**!

Excuse me! Can I ask you a question?
How can I get to …?/Can you tell me …?
Can you repeat that, please?/Excuse me?
Thank you. – You're welcome.

a) *You are in Greenwich. Use the new phrases.*

You: 1 me. Can I ask 2 ?
Girl: Yes, of course.
You: 3 the Millennium Dome, please?
Girl: Hm – go straight down Stockwell Street.
You: 4 ? Lockwell Street?
Girl: No, *Stockwell* Street! Turn right into Church Street and catch the number 188 bus there.
You: 5 ?
Girl: The number 188 bus. It takes you to the Dome.
You: 6
Girl: You're welcome. Bye!

b) *Role play: Look at the map on page 54 again. Ask your partner for information. Use the new phrases.*

WB p. 39/5

I don't know!

Terry's dad picks the kids up in his taxi. He drives them to the Cutty Sark first. They ask him a lot of questions for their project. Mr Jackson helps them.

6 Do they know it?

*Answer with **Yes, they do** or **No, they don't**.*

1. Do the kids know the name of the ship?
2. Do they know how long it is?
3. Do they know that it is a museum?
4. Do they know that time starts in Greenwich?
5. Do they see the Millennium Dome?
6. Do they know how many buses can park in the Millennium Dome?

7 Your turn: Friends and family

Make questions and then ask your partner.

Example: A: **Do** your friends go to town on Saturdays?
B: **Yes, they do.** / **No, they don't.**

TIP
Do you like me?
– Yes, I do. / No, I don't.

(→ G 24)

Do	+	your friends you and your parents you and your friends	+	go to	+	town the park the shops / the cinema	+	on Saturdays?

WB p. 40/6

8 ⟨Ask your partner⟩

Example: play • football • in • the school playground?
A: **Do** you play football in the school playground? – B: **Yes, I do.** / **No, I don't.**

1. like • museums? – Yes, ▭. / No, ▭. 2. often go to • the swimming pool? – ▭. 3. often go to • the sweet shop? – ▭. 4. meet • your friends • at the weekend? – ▭. 5. sometimes go • to • the park? – ▭.

(→ G 24)

9 Terry and his dad

a) Terry likes his dad. But …
Say how Terry and his dad are different. (→ G 23)

Example: like • same films – They **don't** like the same films.

1. know • same people
2. read • same magazines
3. play • same music
4. know • same things WB p. 40/7

⟨b)⟩ *Talk about you and your partner.*

Example:

We don't like the same teachers.

10 How to: Use public transport

Ask and answer questions. Start like this:

A: **Do** DLR trains go to the Thames Barrier?
B: **No, they don't.** Do Underground trains go to the Thames …?
A: … *Go on, please.*

USEFUL PHRASES

We can **go by** bus / DLR train / Underground / boat.
You can catch a bus.
We can take the bus / the Underground / the boat.
The bus takes us / you to …
We can walk.

	DLR trains	Underground trains	buses	boats
Thames Barrier	✗	✗	✓	✓
Greenwich Park	✗	✗	✓	✗
Millennium Dome	✗	✓	✓	✓
Cutty Sark	✓	✗	✓	✓

WB p. 41/8

11 Your turn: Your town (Project part 2)

*Make a grid about your partner's town. Write eight questions with **do**. Then ask your partner and write the answers in your grid.*

go to school by bus / Underground? • often ride your bike in your town? • think that your town is a nice place for young people? • … *Go on, please.*

Town: My partner's name:	✓	✗
1. Do you sometimes go to cafés in your town?	Yes, …	No, …
2. …		

The *does*-game

Greenwich Project Week ends with a test. The best team wins a prize. The friends are at Sam's flat.

Lisa: OK, let's see what we know for the test. Emma, does the river boat go to the Thames Barrier?
Emma: Yes, it does … that's easy-peasy.
Lisa: Correct!
Emma: It's my turn now. Sam, does the First Shop in the World sell chocolate?
Sam: … Yes, it does!
Emma: Oh, no, it doesn't! Not every shop sells chocolate, Sam!
Sam: Very funny! It's my turn now. Terry, does the Underground go to Canary Wharf? Come on, you know the answer to this question.
Terry: Me? Canary Wharf? No, it doesn't.
Sam: Wrong, silly. Of course it does.
Terry: It's my turn. Last question. Lisa, does Greenwich Market open on Sundays?
Lisa: Oh … er … I'm not sure. Yes, it does …er … No, it doesn't … er …!
Sam: Make up your mind, Lisa! You've only got five seconds.
Emma: Lisa! Come on!
Lisa: Can you repeat the question?
Sam: Does … Greenwich … Market … open … on … Sundays?

(Sam's grandma comes into the living room.)

Grandma: Yes, it does, dear. They've got very nice flowers there.
Lisa: Thanks, Mrs Spencer! Yes, it does!
Sam: Oh, Grandma …!
Lisa: I win! I win!
Sam: That's not fair!

12 Does Lisa answer the question?

Answer the questions with ***Yes, he / she / it does*** *or* ***No, he / she / it doesn't.***

Example: **Does** Terry start the game? – **No, he doesn't.**

1. Does the First Shop in the World sell chocolate?
2. Does Sam like chocolate?
3. Does Greenwich Market open on Sundays?
4. Does Sam repeat the question?
5. Does Mrs Spencer like flowers?
6. Does Lisa answer her question?
7. Does Sam win the game?

WB p. 42/10

TIP
Tom likes cheese.
Does Tom like cheese?

(→ G 25)

13 A quiz: Greenwich

Do you know Greenwich? Here are more questions for the test. What is the correct answer?

1. Does world time start at the Cutty Sark?
2. Does the Thames Barrier close when there is too much water?
3. Does the number 188 bus take you to the Dome?
4. Does GMT mean Greenwich Mean Time?
5. Does the Greenwich Foot Tunnel go from Greenwich Park to Thomas Tallis School?
6. Does the Cutty Sark open from 10–5?

14 Wrong names

Say who does what. Start like this:

1. That isn't Sam. He doesn't walk Barker. It's … *Go on, please.*

TIP
Tom likes cheese.
Tiger **doesn't** like cheese.

(→ G 25)

Sam?
1

walk Barker

Lisa?
2

play

Lisa's mum?
3

drive

Jade?
4

do

Tiger?
5

bark

WB p. 42/11

15 ⟨Answer the questions⟩

Start like this: 1. Does Emma help her dad in the computer shop? – Yes, …
(You can say "I don't know", too!)

2. Do the friends know a lot about Greenwich?
3. Does Lisa often go to Greenwich Park?
4. Does Tiger like Barker?
5. Does Terry like his dad?
6. Does Mrs Carter come from Greenwich?

16 A game: Twenty questions

One of you thinks of a thing and the others guess what it is.
They can ask only twenty questions. They can ask questions like these:

Is it in the classroom? – Yes, it is.
Is it small? – No, it isn't.
Can we all see it? – Yes, you can.
Do we use it every day? – Yes, …
Does our teacher use it? – Yes, …
Is it the board? – Yes, …

WB p. 42/12

GRAMMAR
Questions

Is it …? – Yes, it is. / No, it isn't.
Can you …? – Yes, I can. / No, I can't.
Do you …? – Yes, I do. / No, I don't.
Does she …? – Yes, she does. / No, she doesn't.

(→ G 4, 14, 24, 25)

The Greenwich test

Project Week ends with this test. The prize is a big book about the Cutty Sark. Here are the answers of teams A and B. Not every answer is correct.

TEAM A

Names: Elena Barker, Ben Carter, Rachel Wendover, Tom Nelson

1. Where can you see the 24 hour clock?
   At the Royal Observatory
2. What does GMT mean?
   Greenwich Minute Time
3. Where do you find things from all round the world?
   In Church Street
4. What does DLR mean?
   Docklands Long Railway
5. How do you walk under the Thames?
   In the Greenwich Foot Tunnel
6. How do you get to the Dome?
   You take the DLR.
7. Where do you get information about the sights in Greenwich?
   At the tourist information centre
8. When does the Cutty Sark museum open?
   At 10 am

TEAM B

Names: Lisa Taylor, Terry Jackson, Sam Spencer, Emma Brook

1. Where can you see the 24 hour clock?
   At the Royal Observatory
2. What does GMT mean?
   Greenwich Mean Time
3. Where do you find things from all round the world?
   In Church Street
4. What does DLR mean?
   Docklands Light Railway
5. How do you walk under the Thames?
   Fast!
6. How do you get to the Dome?
   You take the number 188 bus or go by Underground.
7. Where do you get information about the sights in Greenwich?
   At the tourist information centre
8. When does the Cutty Sark museum open?
   At 10 am

17 The prize

Correct the wrong answers of teams A and B. Who is the winner?

18 Find the rule

a) *Look at the test. How do you ask questions with question words?*

b) *Ask and answer questions.*

Where When How Why	+	do does doesn't	+	the friends see the sights in Greenwich? team A win? you get to the town centre? they say: The First Shop in the World? the Thames Barrier close? you listen to stories about the sea?

WB p. 44/15

TIP

who = wer
what = was
where = wo
when = wann
how = wie
why = warum

(→ G 26)

19 ⟨Your turn: Where do you live?⟩

What questions can you ask a friend? Make dialogues with your partner.
Example: A: **Where do** you live? – B: I live in …

Where?	When?	What?
live	eat breakfast	do after school
do your homework	go to bed	watch on TV
…	…	…

20 Listening: The Greenwich Foot Tunnel

This is what Sam says about the Greenwich Foot Tunnel. What is right?

1. Why does Sam like the Greenwich Foot Tunnel?
   a) because it is old.
   b) because it is under the Thames.
   c) because there are mice there.
2. Where does the Tunnel go?
   a) to the Cutty Sark.
   b) to the Isle of Dogs.
   c) to TTS.
3. Why does Sam's grandma not like the Tunnel?
   a) because it is long and scary.
   b) because it is under the Thames.
   c) because it is dirty.

21 Write a test (Project part 3)

Look at the test on page 64 again. Write a test with six questions about the town your school is in. Your partner does the test.

Example: 1. When does the swimming pool open?

22 Listening: Sounds [w] and [v]

Listen. What is the wrong sound?

1. very • of • evening • window
2. why • white • video • when
3. walk • TV • wash • weekend
4. water • word • very • with

23 Revision: Jade, Ben and Barker

Put in the correct words.

1. Jade is five years old. Sometimes **she** rides ___ bike to Greenwich Park with ___ brother Ben. 2. ___ helps ___ sister to cross the big roads. 3. Ben is 16 and ___ likes football, and ___ likes the playground in the park. 4. When Barker goes with ___, ___ play a lot. 5. ___ chases the dogs and the cats, and Jade and Ben chase ___.

24 Revision: Help for tests

eat | talk | watch | read | bring | read | look

This is Mrs Carter's help for tests. *(Watch out: Two sentences start with **don't**.)*

1. ___ a good breakfast. 2. ___ 2–3 pencils and a rubber with you to the test. 3. ___ to your partner! 4. ___ at your partner's test! 5. ___ your answers. Then ___ them again. 6. ___ out! Easy-peasy tests are often not easy-peasy!

Captain Terry and the pirates

1 Before you read

What can you usually find in a pirate story? Write down five things. The word list on page 193 can help you.

A Terry has got the book about the Cutty Sark at home. He is in his shed. It is a very interesting book. Terry reads and reads and reads. It is ten o'clock. And then …

*z*z*z*z*z*z*z*

B Everything is quiet. It is a beautiful day. "Emma! Where's my lunch?" Captain Terry asks. He is at the wheel of the Cutty Sark. He thinks that his first mate Samuel is in the crow's nest. But Captain Terry does not know that Samuel is in his bed. He is late again for his turn in the crow's nest.
The captain writes in his book:
'From Shanghai to London. We have got the tea and a TREASURE MAP of the Chocolate Islands with their tasty chocolate trees. The ship and sea are quiet. The first mate is in the crow's nest. No problems.'

C "Here's your lunch, Captain," Emma says. "Oh, sweet Emma. You've got my favourite food. Mmm, spaghetti. Very tasty."
But Captain Terry can't finish his lunch. There is a big bang.
"What's that?" shouts Captain Terry.
"I don't know," says Emma. "Phone Samuel in the crow's nest. Can't you find your mobile?"
Captain Terry looks everywhere.
"Hey! I haven't *got* a mobile!" the Captain says. And then he shouts, "Samuel! Samuel!"

D Captain Terry cannot believe his eyes. A big, black ship! Oh, no, and there she is – Lisa-Yoko, the terrible pirate of Tokyo! Now she is on the Cutty Sark with her scary pirates!
"You're lucky, Captain, I don't want your tea," says Lisa-Yoko. "You can sail to London with that. I only want your treasure map."
"No, no, no! We haven't got a treasure map, Lisa-Yoko. There's only tea on this ship," says Captain Terry. But he thinks, 'How does she know about the map?'
Here comes the first mate Samuel.
"Good morning, Captain. Isn't it a beautiful morning?"

"Samuel!" shouts Emma. "Why aren't you in the crow's nest?"

"Why? What time is it?" he asks. "Is it my turn? – Oh, no, pirates! What about the treasure map …?"

"Cool!" shouts Lisa-Yoko. "You're in big trouble now, Captain! Give me the treasure map or you can walk the plank!"

"Lisa-Yoko! You're a pain! And you, too, Samuel!" shouts Emma.

"Quiet!" Lisa-Yoko says to Emma. "Sort out your problem with the first mate. To the plank, Captain! And hurry up!"

Terry is fed up. "It's *my* ship and *my* map. Let's fight, Lisa-Yoko!"

"Oh, no, my Captain! Don't fight!" Emma shouts. "*Please* give Lisa-Yoko the map!"

"Never!" shouts Captain Terry.

E The pirate and the captain fight. Terry is big but Lisa-Yoko is fast. She is very good at football because she plays for the Tokyo Tigers. She runs all round Captain Terry. What can he do? He throws the spaghetti in Lisa-Yoko's face.

"Silly Captain!" she shouts and eats the spaghetti. Then she kicks Terry like a football, and wins the fight.

Captain Terry walks to the plank.

"Take the wheel, Samuel. Now it's your transport project. Bring the ship to London with the tea. Goodbye. Goodbye, sweet Emma."

And Captain Terry falls over into the water. The water from the sea is on his face. But it is funny. It is only on his face …

F Tiger is next to Terry's face.

"Oh – oh – it's you, Tiger. Don't lick me! Hey, you silly old cat …"

2 Talk about the pirate story

a) *Who is your favourite boy or girl in the story? Why?*

b) *Terry walks the plank: What does he think? Write down three sentences.*

WB p. 45/18; 19; 20

3 Role play: Act the story

In groups, act the story. One pupil reads the text.

4 ⟨A song: A jolly fine pirate⟩

I'm a jolly, jolly, jolly fine pirate
And my name is Grumpy Greg.
My left hand has three fingers
And I've got a wooden leg.
But I'm a jolly, jolly, jolly fine pirate
And my parrot's name is Peg.

Musik: Karl-F. Parnow-Kloth, Text: Sheila McBride

⟨Stories for a ghost[1]⟩ Chapter[2] 1

"Hey, Steven, look at this," Rebecca says to Steven.

Steven is Rebecca's friend. She likes him because they have got the same hobbies – they ride their bikes and they love history[3]. Steven likes football, too, and sometimes Rebecca takes photos[4] of his team.

Today they are in the Greenwich Public Library[5]. Rebecca and Steven are talking in quiet voices[6] at a big table near a window. Rebecca shows Steven a picture of the Queen's[7] House in a big, old book, *The Big History Book of Greenwich*. The pages of the book are yellow.

Rebecca and Steven are not very good at school, but they want to do a good school history project on "Greenwich and its history". They are doing their project about old buildings[8] in Greenwich.

Rebecca opens a new book about Greenwich and says: "Listen to this. It's very interesting. 'The Queen's House is from 1616, and it was[9] for Queen Anne of Denmark[10]. But she died[11] very soon. In 1805 the Queen's House was the home for 50 orphans[12].' "

Rebecca and Steven look at a picture of children with a ball in the garden.

"Football – yes! Let's play football now! Come on, Becca. We can come again on Monday," says Steven. But Rebecca reads the text about the Queen's House. "Wait! This is great for our project. The Queen's House has got ghosts!" Rebecca shouts. A girl in the library says 'Shhh!' In a quiet voice Rebecca reads to Steven about the ghosts in the building. "Listen, Steven: 'People do not use two rooms in the house because they believe that[13] ghosts live there. In 1966 a tourist took a photo[14] of ghosts in the house. It is a very famous picture.'"

"That's very interesting, Becca. But I don't believe in ghosts. What about you?" asks Steven.

"Well, no. But when there's a photo …," Rebecca says. "And look again in this old book, *The Big History Book of Greenwich*. Here's a rhyme about ghosts."

Rebecca reads:

Ghosts of white are ghosts that walk,
Listen, listen to them talk[15].
Beautiful queen and orphan children
They live[16] here – now come and find them.
Touch[17] the ghost and he touches you …

VOCABULARY SKILLS A B C

Mach' dir nichts daraus, wenn du nicht gleich alle Wörter in dieser Geschichte verstehst. Versuche zunächst, die Bedeutung eines neuen Worts aus dem Zusammenhang heraus zu erraten, ohne die Fußnote anzuschauen. Oft kommen die Wörter später noch einmal vor – dann verstehst du sie bestimmt auf Anhieb. Nach der ersten Lektüre eines Kapitels, lies es gleich noch einmal durch: Du verstehst dann viel mehr und kannst die Geschichte wirklich genießen!

[1] **ghost** [gəʊst] = Geist • [2] **chapter** ['tʃæptə] = Kapitel • [3] **history** ['hɪstri] = Geschichte • [4] **(to) take a photo** [teɪk‿ə 'fəʊtəʊ] = ein Foto machen • [5] **Greenwich Public Library** [ˌgrenɪdʒ ˌpʌblɪk 'laɪbrəri] = öffentliche Bibliothek von Greenwich • [6] **voice** [vɔɪs] = Stimme • [7] **queen** [kwi:n] = Königin • [8] **building** ['bɪldɪŋ] = Gebäude • [9] **was** [wəz] = war • [10] **Denmark** ['denmɑ:k] = Dänemark • [11] **died** [daɪd] = starb • [12] **orphan** ['ɔ:fn] = Waise • [13] **that** [ðət] = dass • [14] **took a photo** [tʊk‿ə 'fəʊtəʊ] = machte ein Foto • [15] **listen to them talk** [ˌlɪsn tə ðəm 'tɔ:k] = höre ihren Gesprächen zu • [16] **(to) live** [lɪv] = wohnen, leben • [17] **(to) touch** [tʌtʃ] = berühren

"Oh!" Rebecca says and cannot finish. Something[18] touches her foot. She gets up but she cannot move[19]. Then there is a boy's voice from under the table:

... then I put glue[20] in your shoe!

"Ha ha ha!" says a voice.

You can't walk and you can't run
Play with me, let's have some fun!

Suddenly[21] a young boy in funny clothes[22] is on the book on the table. He looks like someone[23] from an old film. It is scary for Steven and Rebecca, and they cannot believe their eyes.

"Thank you!" says the boy ghost. "I was in that big, old history book for 200 years and now I'm free[24]. Yippee!" The ghost dances on the book and laughs[25]. Then he suddenly does not look happy. "I'm free now but not for very long."

Rebecca looks at Steven.

"What do you say? Can you help me? Can you? Can you?" the ghost asks. He dances again. "Please say yes!" shouts the ghost.

"Shh!" Rebecca says. Steven looks at his friend Rebecca. "But how can we help you?" Steven asks.

The ghost laughs and says, "My name is George. I am eight years old – OK, I was eight years old in 1808. And here, read this. This is my ghost story:"

George's parents died in 1807. After that George lived with the other orphans in the Queen's House. But soon he died of a broken heart[26].

George's ghost stayed[27] in the Queen's House with Queen Anne of Denmark's ghost. Every day, George told[28] the Queen's ghost great stories (he knew[29] them from his parents), and the Queen's ghost was very happy. She liked good stories. But then George couldn't[30] find a good story for Queen Anne's ghost. So the Queen's ghost was angry[31]. "Stay in the history book until[32] you find a new story. Give me one great new story! Then you can live in my house again."

"And now you can help me. Please, please find a new story for the Queen. Please! Then I can live in the beautiful house again," George says. "I must[33] find a good story this year or live in this old book forever and ever[34]!"

"Oh no! It's five to six! The library closes at six," says Rebecca.

"We can help you but not today, George."

"How can we find you again?" asks Rebecca.

George says, "Come back here. It's easy-peasy! Open the book and read the rhyme. Come back soon – with a good story!" And WHOOOOSH! – George is back in the book. Rebecca and Steven go home.

"What can we do?" asks Steven.

"Let's meet in the morning at 11 at my house," Rebecca answers. "But don't say a word!"

[18]**something** ['sʌmθɪŋ] = etwas • [19]**(to) move** [mu:v] = sich bewegen • [20]**glue** [glu:] = Klebstoff • [21]**suddenly** ['sʌdnli] = plötzlich • [22]**clothes** [kləʊðz] = Kleidung • [23]**someone** ['sʌmwʌn] = jemand • [24]**free** [fri:] = frei • [25]**(to) laugh** [lɑ:f] = lachen • [26]**broken heart** ['brəʊkn hɑ:t] = gebrochenes Herz • [27]**stayed** [steɪd] = blieb • [28]**told** [təʊld] = erzählte • [29]**knew** [nju:] = kannte • [30]**couldn't** ['kʊdnt] = konnte nicht • [31]**angry** ['æŋgri] = verärgert, zornig • [32]**until** [ən'tɪl] = bis • [33]**must** [mʌst] = muss • [34]**forever and ever** [fə'revər‿ənd‿'evə] = für immer und ewig

1 The DLR

Put in the missing words.

under | to | from | at | of | next to | in

1. The DLR is a train **in** London.
2. It goes ___ the Thames.
3. You can go ___ Greenwich or Cutty Sark Gardens ___ the Isle of Dogs.
4. Trains are every 10 minutes ___ Monday ___ Friday.
5. The first train goes ___ 6.23 ___ the morning.
6. Sit ___ nice people – and the DLR is a lot ___ fun!

WB p. 46/22

2 The four friends

Find good words for Emma, Terry, Lisa and Sam. Make a list.

lucky • cool • boring • big • small • great • fair • interesting • quiet • slow • fast • nice • sweet • happy • funny • scary

3 Match the sentence parts

a)
1. Mr Jackson drives
2. You can ride
3. The DLR takes you
4. We can take
5. Tourists can go to the Millennium Dome

a. your bike to school.
b. by Underground.
c. his taxi to the town centre.
d. the number 286 bus from Kidbrooke Park Road.
e. to the Isle of Dogs.

b) *What can you drive? What can you take/go by?*

4 ⟨A word game⟩

Play this game in class. ***A*** *finds a word and writes it down.* ***B*** *starts with the last letter and makes a new word. Then* ***C*** *starts …*

5 Mixed bag: Ask for information

The Skills box on page 59 can help you.

German girl: Excuse [1]. Can I ask [2] a question? Do you know where the tourist [3] centre is?
Woman: Yes, I [4]. [5] the number 186 bus to the station.
Girl: Can you [6] that, please?
Woman: [7] the number 186 bus to the station.
Girl: And where can I find a bus [8] here?
Woman: It's there – next [9] the police [10]. Can you see [11]?
Girl: Oh, yes. Thank you! Bye.
Woman: You're [12]. Bye!

WB p. 46/23

NOW YOU CAN

- ✓ Talk about a town.
- ✓ Ask and tell the way.
- ✓ Talk about transport.
- ✓ Use object pronouns.
- ✓ Ask for information with *do* and *does* and *wh*-questions.
- ✓ Use *don't* and *doesn't*.

1 Your turn: From home to school

Write down how you get from your home to school.
Do you walk / take a bus / … to school?
The Useful phrases on page 61 can help you.

2 Find the pronouns (→ G 22)

you ✓ her him me them us it

Example: No problem, Emma. I can pick **you** up in ten minutes.

1. I'm not sure, but Mr Jackson knows the way. Ask ___.
2. Hey – we're lucky. My dad can pick ___ up for a special tour!
3. Mr Jackson drives the friends all round town. He takes ___ everywhere.
4. The Cutty Sark is great. I like ___ because it's so beautiful.
5. Emma always writes down everything about Greenwich. Ask ___.
6. I can't find the Dome. – It's easy-peasy! Please give ___ the map.

WB p. 47/24

3 Questions (→ G 24, 25)

Ask your partner questions.

Do Does	+ you your friends your teacher your friend	+ go to the park go to the town centre come to school	+ by bus? by train? by bike? by Underground?	Yes, No,	+ I / they do / don't. he / she does / doesn't.

WB p. 47/25

4 A quiz: Unit 4 (→ G 26)

Ask the correct questions and answer them.

Where When Why	+ does doesn't do	+ Mr Jackson know a lot about Greenwich? Mr Jackson pick the friends up for the tour? a lot of Greenwich kids go with their skateboards? Captain Terry win the fight?

WB p. 47/26

Unit 5 Birthday party

A

B

C

Sizes
S = small
M = medium
L = large
XL = extra large

D

E

1 Shops

music shop · newsagent · market · clothes shop · sports shop

a) *Look at the photos and find the right names for the places. What can you buy there?*

Photo **A** is a ___ because you can buy ___ there.

b) *Word bank: What other shops do you know? What can you buy there?*

WB p. 48/1

British money
There are 100 pence (p) in a pound (£).

1p	one p (= penny)
25p	twenty-five p (= pence)
£1	a/one pound
£1.50	one (pound) fifty
£2	two pounds
£3.70	three (pounds) seventy

2 How much is it?

Examples:

A: How much is the sweatshirt?
B: It's sixteen seventy-five.

A: How much is the T-shirt?
B: It's ten pounds.

A: How much are the crisps?
B: They're thirty-two p.

£1.20 · 60p · £11.99 · 45p · £16.75 · £179.50 · £44.95 · £3

3 How to: Go shopping

USEFUL PHRASES

a) *Read the dialogues. Then act them with a partner.*

A
Assistant: Can I help you?
Lisa: Yes, have you got the new 'Pets' magazine, please? I can't find it.
Assistant: It's there – next to the sports magazines.

B
Emma: Can you tell me how much this bag is, please?
Assistant: It's £15.95.
Emma: Hm. It's nice, but it's expensive.

C
Terry: Excuse me. Where can I try on this sweatshirt?
Assistant: There, on the left.
Terry: Thanks. I like the colour, but the size isn't right.
Assistant: No problem. We've got other sizes, too.

D
Assistant: Yes, please?
Sam: Can I buy just one apple, please?
Assistant: Yes, sure. That's 15p.
Sam: Here you are.
Assistant: Thank you. Here's your apple.

b) *Collect useful phrases from a). Write two lists – one for the customer and one for the assistant. Then make your own shopping dialogues. Take turns to be the customer and the assistant.*

Customer
Have you got ...?
...

Assistant
Can I help you?
...

WB p. 48/2

4 Listening: The sweatshirt

Listen, and put in the missing information.

Grandma Spencer goes to a 1 shop. She buys a 2. She likes the different 3 on it. The size of the sweatshirt is 4, and it is £ 5. It is not for Grandma – it is for 6.

WB p. 48/3

5 Your turn: Shopping in your town

In groups of four, talk about shopping in your town. What are your favourite shops? What do you buy there?

My favourite shops are ... • My friends and I sometimes meet at ... • I often buy ... • ...

Sam's invitation

Sam: Grandma, do you know what the third of March is?

Grandma: Hm, let's see … No school? Millennium Dome Day? Oh, I know! It's your birthday. What would you like to do on your big day? Would you like to have a party?

Sam: I'd like to invite my friends out to Angelo's, that new pizza place. It looks great!

Mr Spencer: It looks expensive! Sorry, Sam, I'd like to be rich, but I'm not.

Sam: It isn't fair! My friends can always do what they want on their birthday. They can go to pizza places or the cinema!

Grandma: No, they can't, Sam. And you know it! Why don't you invite your friends here?

Sam: What? For a little kids' party with silly games? No, thanks!

Mr Spencer: Don't be silly, Sam. You can do other things at your party.

Sam: But I don't want to have a party with you two here. I'm sorry, but – you know …

Mr Spencer: No problem. I'd like to be in the flat. But Grandma and I can be in our rooms.

Grandma: I'd like that. I can help with the food and drinks in the kitchen.

Sam: Oh thanks. That's great. But I'd like to make my own birthday cake.

Mr Spencer: Good idea, Sam. Do you want to write the invitations now?

Sam: No, Dad. That's for little kids. I can text my friends. I'd like to invite them to my party right now.

1 Make sentences about what they say

Example: Sam **would like** to invite his friends out to a pizza place.

Grandma Sam Mr Spencer	+	would like to	+	be rich. text his friends. make his own birthday cake. be in the flat for the party. help with the food and drinks.

GRAMMAR

long form	short form
I would like	I'd like

(→ G 27)

2 Write down what they want or do not want to do

Examples: 1. They **want to** ride their bikes.
2. The man does not want to …

1

2

3

4

5

WB p. 49/4

3 The months

a) *Listen to the song and say the months.*

September • May • August • December • June • January • March • July • October • February • April • November

b) *Make a **months** quiz for your partner.*

Examples:

A: It's got only three letters.
B: That's May.
A: It's the month after December / …
B: That's …

WB p. 49/5

4 Birthdays

Look at Sam's birthday list. When are the birthdays?

Example: His mum's birthday is on the twenty-first of May.

Mum – 21st May
Dad – 10th December
Grandma – 15th September
Terry – 23rd November
Lisa – 26th May
Emma – 17th September
My birthday! – 3rd March

TIP
You write: 21st May
You say: the twenty-first of May

(→ G 29)

5 Write a birthday invitation

a) *Look at Sam's text. What information is there in his invitation?*

b) *What information is not in these invitations?*

1. Can you come to my party? It's on 1st April at 36, London Road.
2. I'd like to invite you out to Angelo's. Please be there at 7 o'clock.

Please come to my birthday party at 36, Wendover Road on 3rd March at 5 o'clock! CU. Sam

c) *Write your birthday invitation. Put it in your folder.* WB p. 49/6

6 ⟨Role play: Please come!⟩

Act little dialogues.

Would you like to +	come to my party on …? go to the cinema …? go for a picnic on …? … with me at the weekend? …?	Oh yes, that's great! Sorry, I haven't got time then. Yes, I would. Thanks for the invitation. I'd like to, but I can't. …

7 Your turn: Your birthday

a) *Ask what your partner would like to do on her/his birthday.*

What **would you like to** do on your birthday? – **I'd like to** …

invite • watch • play • go to • …

b) *Word bank: Say other birthday words that you know from primary school.*

Shopping for Sam's birthday

Lisa and Emma are in a big department store today. They are looking for a birthday present for Sam.

GRAMMAR
Present progressive

I **am** look**ing**
You **are** watch**ing**
He **is** listen**ing**
They **are** talk**ing**

(→ G 30)

8 What is happening?

Finish these sentences with information from the pictures.

1. Two boys are watching …
2. Lisa and Emma are looking for …
3. A boy is chasing …
4. An assistant is selling …
5. A … is ringing.
6. A mother is taking her little boy to …
7. A … is waiting because … are talking.
8. Two girls are dancing on …

9 Just a minute

You are in a department store. Your friend is waiting. What do you say?

Example: Just a minute. I'**m looking** for a sweatshirt **right now**.

playing | watching | looking for | a sweatshirt | TV | bags | a computer game
buying | looking at | trying on | a magazine | a present for my | …

WB p. 50/7

10 Find the rule

a) *Look at the groups on the right. How do you spell the new forms?*

buy → buying	have → having	run → running
wait → waiting	make → making	put → putting
look → looking	dance → dancing	clap → clapping

b) *Write these sentences with the correct forms.*

1. Look who ___ (come) into the shop now!
2. Wow! You ___ (buy) a lot of things.
3. Great! They ___ (win) the game now.
4. I ___ (look) for a special present – but what?
5. She ___ (try) on jeans now.
6. The department store ___ (close) now.

11 Ask and answer questions

a) *What is happening in the department store today? Look at the pictures on page 76 again.*

Examples: Lisa and Emma • look for Sam now?
→ **Are** Lisa and Emma **looking** for Sam **now**?
– No, they **aren't**.
the big game • just start?
→ **Is** the big game **just starting**? – Yes, it **is**.

TIP
Are they **looking** for a present?
– Yes, they **are**. / No, they **aren't**.

(→ G 31)

1. the girls on TV • sing?
2. a customer • buy magazines now?
3. the boy in the yellow T-Shirt • read a magazine now?
4. boy's mobile • ring now?
5. Lisa and Emma • try on clothes?
6. the little boy • run to the toilet?
7. department store • just close?

b) *Make more questions about the pictures for your partner.*

12 ⟨In the department store⟩

Example: "Those assistants aren't very good."
– "No, they aren't helping the customers."

1. "Hey, that isn't nice!" – "No, it isn't their turn, they …"
2. "Why can't we find the jeans here?" – "Maybe we …"
3. "Your size isn't extra large." – "This T-shirt is for my dad, silly. I …"
4. "Look. That's how little kids get lost." – "Oh, yes, that mother …"
5. "These shoes are very small." – "Sure! You …"

- not wait behind us
- not look in the right place
- not try on the right size
- not watch her little girl
- not help the customers ✓
- not buy it for me

13 A game: What am I doing?

Take turns to act. Can the others guess what you are doing?

A: Look. What am I doing?
B: Are you playing basketball?
A: Playing basketball? No, I'm not.
C: Are you dancing?
A: Yes, I am – that's right!

- text a friend
- walk the dog
- play the drums / …
- …

The birthday cake

Today Sam is making his birthday cake. There is very little time now before his birthday. He is late again. Grandma has got lots of recipe books. "Here's a good recipe for a birthday cake," she tells Sam.
"Cool. How much sugar do I need? And how many eggs?" he wants to know.
Sam is having a lot of fun in the kitchen. But what a mess! The bag of sugar falls over. Then Sam sits down on a box of eggs, and a few eggs break. There is lots of flour everywhere in the kitchen, too.

"Oh, no! There aren't many cooks like you, Sam," Grandma laughs.
Sam needs a little help from Grandma. But there are no big problems, and finally Sam has got a cake.
On the morning of his birthday Sam finishes the cake with his name and twelve white candles. Sam is happy. "This," he says, "is the best cake in the world."

14 Answer the questions

a) 1. Does Sam know how to make the cake?
2. What has Sam got for the cake?
3. Why is there a mess?
4. What does he do on his birthday?

b) *Word bank: Say other words for food that you know.*

15 Put in *much* or *many*

TIP
How **many** eggs? – Not **many** eggs.
How **much** sugar? – Not **much** sugar.

(→ G 32)

1. Sam: You've got so ___ recipes for cakes!
2. Grandma: Let's see how ___ flour we need.
3. Sam: I don't need ___ help, Grandma.
4. Grandma: How ___ candles have you got there?
5. Sam: There aren't ___ letters in my name.
6. Sam: How ___ time have I got?

WB p. 52/11

16 Make sentences

1. It's time for lunch. I can make	+	a little	+	help.
2. I can't do this. I need		a few		friends.
3. Our teacher is nice. We've only got				sandwiches.
4. Do you like music? Let's listen to				pounds.
5. I can't buy this. I've only got				CDs.
6. I'd like a small party – with just				homework.

WB p. 52/12

TIP
a **few** eggs
a **little** sugar

(→ G 32)

17 Sugar, please?

You need help in the kitchen. What do you say?

Can you give me that	+	**bag of … ,** **tin of … ,** **box of … ,** **cup of … ,**	+	please?

1 

2 

3 

4 
5 

6 
7 

18 Listening: Chocolate crispies

Right or wrong? Say why.

1. Emma wants to make chocolate crispies.
2. Nasreen always takes the chocolate.
3. Mr Brook can help the girls.
4. Mr Brook is not the chocolate thief.

19 ⟨Hands on: Make chocolate crispies⟩

You need: 125 grams of plain chocolate • 4 tablespoons of rice crispies (or cornflakes) • a few raisins
What you do: Break the chocolate into small pieces. Melt it in a bowl over hot water. Put in the rice crispies (cornflakes) and the raisins, and mix until everything is covered with chocolate. Put spoonfuls into paper cases. When the chocolate is hard again, the chocolate crispies are ready!

20 Listening: Sounds in sentences

a) *In questions the sound often goes up. In sentences with information the sound usually goes down. Look and listen.*

Is he a good cook? ↗ – Yes, he's very good in the kitchen. ↘

Here's a present. ↘ – Oh, is it for me? ↗

b) *Listen and draw the correct sounds.*

21 People or things?!

Examples: The cake is beautiful. **(Sam)** → Sam**'s** cake is beautiful.
The colour is white. **(the candles)** → The colour **of** the candles is white.

1. The day is here! (the party)
2. The flat is upstairs. (the Spencers)
3. The living room is not very big. (the family)
4. The name is 'Party Music'. (the CD)
5. The game is fun. (the kids)
6. The size is OK. (the sweatshirt)

WB p. 53/14

TIP
people: 's or s'
Sam's birthday
the friends' presents
things: of
a photo of the cake
the colour of the candles

(→ G 34)

22 Revision: 's or s'?

Examples: Terry has got a big sandwich. → Terry**'s** sandwich is big.
The Brooks have got a small kitchen. → The Brooks**'** kitchen is small.

1. Sam has got a great cake.
2. The girls have got nice crisps.
3. The Spencers have got an old kitchen.
4. Grandma has got good recipe books.
5. The boys have got large pizzas.
6. Tiger has got tasty cat food.

1 Reading a story (part 1)

READING SKILLS

a) The title

The title of the story can give you ideas.
The title of the story is **Happy birthday, Sam!**
Talk about what can happen.

Maybe …
- the story is about Sam's …
- his friends give him …
- his party / his cake is …

Now read the story.

Happy birthday, Sam!

A There is a lot of food in the kitchen – sandwiches, crisps, chocolate crispies, and the birthday cake. Everything is ready for Sam's party. Now Sam is waiting for his friends.
Lisa and Emma get there first.
"Happy birthday, Sam!" they say. "Here's your present. Don't be late for school again!"
The present is in a box. Suddenly it rings. Sam laughs. "Oh, I can guess what it is. Yes! It's an alarm clock! Thank you! That's the right present for me."
In a few minutes all of Sam's friends are there. Terry's present is very special. He sings his own new birthday song for Sam, and then he gives Sam a CD of it. Sam is very excited. "Wow, Terry, my own song! Thanks. That's so cool!"
"Your sweatshirt isn't cool, Sam. All those colours – it's terrible!" says Lisa.
"I know," he answers. "But it's a present from my grandma. What can I do?!"

Stop here and look at **ex. 2b)** on page 81.

B Mr Spencer has got a surprise for Sam and his friends at the party. "A karaoke machine!" they shout. "Let's see what songs we can sing!"
Lisa wants to sing first. It is great fun. She is a pop star! She does not want to stop! But the others want their turn, too.
Only Emma does not want to sing in front of everyone.
"You can sing with me," Sam tells Emma.

"I need help. Let's sing Terry's new birthday song." Soon everyone is singing Terry's song – even Sam's dad.

C In the Spencers' flat everyone is having fun. But in the flat downstairs Ted Brown is not happy. He wants to write a new song on his computer, but there is a problem with it. *And* upstairs the Spencers are playing loud music! People are jumping and shouting, and they are laughing. Usually the Spencers are no problem for Ted, but today he does not like what is happening. He goes upstairs.

D Mr Spencer opens the door, and Ted sees a lot of kids behind him. They are dancing and singing a song.
"Oh, hi, Ted," shouts Mr Spencer. "We're very sorry that it's so loud. It's Sam's birthday today. He's having a party."
"It's his birthday, eh?! That's OK, then," Ted shouts. "But what's that song?"
"This is Terry's new birthday song for Sam," Lisa says.

"Who is Terry? Is he famous?" asks Ted. They all laugh and look at Terry. "Hey, Terry, are you famous?" Sam asks. Terry sees Ted Brown. "No, Sam," Terry says, "but do you know who that is? *He's* famous! That's London's great new radio DJ, Ted Cool Cat Brown. Don't you listen to the radio? He's in every magazine! What's he doing here?" "He lives downstairs," Sam shouts. "What?" Terry shouts.

E The music stops. "Hi, Sam. Happy birthday!" says Ted. "Hi, Mr Brown," says Sam. "Thank you. This is Terry. It's his music." "It's just a song for Sam's birthday," says Terry. "Cool song. Can you and Sam come to my radio station soon with a CD of it?" asks Ted. "I'd like to play it on the radio."

2 Reading a story (part 2)

READING SKILLS

b) Important ideas

1. Read part A of the story again. Look at the words in green. They are the important ideas in part A. You can use them to take notes.
2. Now go on with the story. Take notes of the important ideas in parts B – E. (Don't write too much!)

c) Headings

Find the correct headings for the parts of the story.
The heading for part A / B / … is …

The radio DJ | A surprise for Terry | Downstairs | Fun at the party | Sam's presents

d) Tell the story again

Look at your notes again. Can you remember the story? Can you tell it?

WB p. 55/17

3 ⟨A song: Terry's birthday song for Sam⟩

Let's sing a song
For … (you, Anne, Rolf …) –
For … (you, Anne, Rolf …). For you!
Happy birthday.
Happy birthday to you!

Party time!
It's … (your, Anne's, Rolf's …) day.
Fun and music –
That's OK.

Musik: Karl-Heinz Böttcher
Text: Karl-Heinz Böttcher / Sheila McBride

4 Your turn: A good birthday party

a) *Would you like to be at Sam's party? Say why or why not.*

b) *What is a good party for you?*

5 ⟨Hands on: A birthday card⟩

Make a card for a friend's birthday. Put it in your folder.

⟨Stories for a ghost⟩ Chapter 2

It is Monday afternoon. Rebecca and Steven run into the library. In her bag Rebecca has got a big picture book from her birthday with a story about a princess[1].

"This is a great story for a queen!" Rebecca says to Steven.

Steven finds the old book and Rebecca looks for the rhyme – but it is not there!

"Look!" says Steven. "A new rhyme!"

Put your hand[2] on the pictures.
Are ghosts coming or the witches[3]?
Witches black and ghosts of white,
See the flicker[4], watch the light[5].

Rebecca and Steven look, and the lights in the library flicker[6] – one, two, three. It is scary. Suddenly George is on the book, and he is laughing.

He says, "Hello! Have you got it? Have you got the story?"

"Yes, we've got a story for you," Rebecca says. "George, we can help you, but we want your help, too."

This is a surprise for George.

"We are doing a school project," Steven says. "If you like our story, we want to go into the book with you. We want to go back in history. Then we can see all the old buildings in Greenwich and Becca can take photos."

"Photos? What's that? Hm – OK," says George, but he does not laugh.

"Thanks, George. You're a nice ghost," says Rebecca. "Now look at the pictures. Here's the story:"

The paper bag[7] princess

1 Elizabeth is a beautiful princess. She lives in a castle and has got expensive clothes, and she wants to marry[8] Prince[9] Ronald.

2 But then a dragon[10] burns[11] her castle and her clothes with his breath[12] and takes Prince Ronald with him.

Elizabeth wants to chase the dragon and find Ronald. She looks everywhere for some[13] clothes but she can only find a paper bag. So she puts that on[14] and looks for the dragon. It is easy – the black trees and houses show her the way.

[1]**princess** [prɪn'ses] = Prinzessin • [2]**hand** [hænd] = Hand • [3]**witch** [wɪtʃ] = Hexe • [4]**flicker** ['flɪkə] = Flackern • [5]**light** [laɪt] = Licht • [6]**(to) flicker** ['flɪkə] = flackern • [7]**paper bag** [peɪpə 'bæg] = Papiertüte • [8]**(to) marry** ['mæri] = heiraten • [9]**prince** [prɪns] = Prinz • [10]**dragon** ['drægn] = Drache • [11]**(to) burn** [bɜːn] = verbrennen • [12]**breath** [breθ] = Atem, Atemzug • [13]**some** [sʌm] = ein paar • [14]**(to) put on** [pʊt 'ɒn] = anziehen

3 Finally Elizabeth comes to a cave[15] with a large door.

She bangs[16] on the door. The dragon opens the door and says, "Oh, a princess! I love tasty princesses, but I'm full[17] after that big castle today. I'm a very busy dragon. Come back another time[18]."

He closes the door. Elizabeth bangs on the door again.

The dragon opens the door and says, "Go away. I love tasty princesses, but I'm full now. Come back another time."

"Wait," shouts Elizabeth.

4 "… Is it correct that you are the nastiest[19] dragon in the world?"

"Yes, it is," says the dragon.

"Is it correct," asks Elizabeth, "that you can burn ten forests[20] with your breath?"

"Easy-peasy," answers the dragon, and he takes a big breath and makes so much fire[21] that he burns fifty forests.

"Great," says Elizabeth, "and can you fly[22] round the world in just ten seconds?"

"No problem," says the dragon. He runs and jumps and flies all the way round the world in just ten seconds. When he comes back, he is dog-tired, and he falls asleep.

Elizabeth says, "Hey, dragon!" But the dragon does not move.

5 So Elizabeth walks over the dragon, opens the cave door and sees Prince Ronald. He looks at her and says, "Elizabeth! You look terrible! Your hair[20] is a mess and you're wearing[24] a dirty old paper bag. Come back when you look like a princess."

"Ronny," says Elizabeth, "your clothes are very nice and your hair is beautiful. You look like a great prince, but you're a bum[25]."

Ronald and Elizabeth do not marry.

The …

"… end[26]!" Steven shouts. "And? Do you like it?" What can George say to the children? He likes the story, but he likes the fun with Rebecca and Steven, too. He does not want to go back to the Queen's House so soon.

"Yes, I like it," George starts, "but … Queen Anne knows everything about princes and castles and dragons. And she doesn't like … umm … uh … princesses like that! Princesses are polite and they don't fight dragons! Come back again!"

And George jumps into the book before Rebecca and Steven can say a word.

[15]**cave** [keɪv] = Höhle • [16]**(to) bang** [bæŋ] = hämmern, schlagen • [17]**full** [fʊl] = satt • [18]**another time** [əˈnʌðə taɪm] = ein anderes Mal • [19]**the nastiest** [ðə ˈnɑːstiəst] = der böseste • [20]**forest** [ˈfɒrɪst] = Wald • [21]**fire** [ˈfaɪə] = Feuer • [22]**(to) fly** [flaɪ] = fliegen • [23]**hair** [heə] = Haar(e) • [24]**(to) wear** [weə] = tragen *(Kleidung)* • [25]**bum** [bʌm] = Idiot • [26]**end** [end] = Ende

1 Finding words in a dictionary

VOCABULARY SKILLS

When you cannot guess a new word, you can use an English-German dictionary. (The Dictionary in your book is on page 208.) All the words are in alphabetical order.
Example: You do not know the word **flower**. First look for **F** in the dictionary, then **FL**, then **FLO**, etc. You can soon find the word. What is it in German?

a) *Revision: Say the alphabet in English.*

b) *Put these words in alphabetical order. Sometimes two or three words start with one letter, so look at the second or third letters of the word, too.*

- pence
- cake
- jeans
- dance
- egg
- pizza
- apple
- karaoke
- shoe
- try on
- expensive
- pop
- T-shirt
- sing
- CD
- buy
- recipe
- pound

WB p. 56/18

2 Word groups

a) *Put the words from exercise 1 into four groups.*

b) *Word bank: Do you know more words from these groups?*

music	money	food	clothes
...	...	...	...

3 ⟨Birthday ideas⟩

Look at these ideas. Then write your own birthday ideas.

Beautiful cake
Invitations for friends
Ready for my party
Thank you for the present
Happy, very happy
Day for fun
And music, too
Yes, birthdays are great!

4 ⟨Find the right words⟩

Thank you. | Happy birthday! | I can help you. | Come on! | Watch out! | Hey, great!

1. Your friend is twelve today.
2. Your friend helps you.
3. A car is coming, but your friend does not see it.
4. Your friend's team wins the game.
5. Your friend is looking at things in a shop. You don't want to wait.
6. Your friend has got a problem.

5 How to: Be polite!

These people are in shops or cafés. But they are not using very polite words. Can you help?

Example: "We want two pizzas."
→ "We'd like two pizzas, please."

1. "Give me those flowers."
2. "Where are the skateboards in this shop?"
3. "I need an alarm clock."
4. "That sandwich there."
5. "We want to try on these jeans."

TIP

"I'd like ..." → polite!
"I want ..." → not so polite!

(→ G 27)

USEFUL PHRASES

I'd / We'd like (to) ..., please.
Can you show / give me ...?
Can I ..., please?
Have you got ...?
Excuse me, do you sell ...?

NOW YOU CAN

- ✓ Go shopping and use British money.
- ✓ Say what you would like to do.
- ✓ Talk about parties and birthdays.
- ✓ Say what is happening.
- ✓ Use *much, many, a little, a few.*
- ✓ Look for important ideas in a story.
- ✓ Find words in a dictionary.

1 What are the customer's questions?

1. Customer: ___? – Assistant: It's £15.75.
2. Customer: ___? – Assistant: Let's see. – It's large.
3. Customer: ___? – Assistant: They're there, next to the pencil-cases.
4. Customer: ___? – Assistant: Yes, you can try them on.
5. Customer: ___? – Assistant: No, sorry. We don't sell them.

Write two more little shopping dialogues. Page 73, ex. 3 can help you.

2 Make questions or sentences with *would like (to)* (→ G 27)

1 

2 

3 

4 

3 At school (→ G 30, 31)

1. "Can I use your ruler, please?" – "Yes, OK. …" (I • not use it right now)
2. "Terry? He's in the school shop." – "Again?! …" (what • he • buy today?)
3. "Mrs Carter is late this morning." – "No, she isn't. Look, …" (she • come now)
4. "Aren't Lisa and Terry friends?" – "No. …" (they • not talk today)
5. "Hm. I'm not sure this is the right exercise." – "Oh no! …" (we • do the wrong homework?)

4 A great party (→ G 30)

Draw a picture of a party. What is happening? Write five sentences (present progressive!). WB p. 57/22

5 Put in the right words (→ G 32)

a little | a few | much | many

Mrs Taylor: What do we need from the shops, Lisa? How [1] flour have we still got?
Lisa: Let's see. There's only [2] flour here. And there isn't [3] sugar.
Mrs Taylor: And can you please look and see how [4] eggs we've got? I want to make a cake, so I need [5] eggs for that. Three or four.
Lisa: No, we don't need eggs. There are six in the box. But there's only [6] cheese. It's OK for a mouse, but not [7] for a big family!
Mrs Taylor: OK. So we need flour, sugar and cheese. Oh, and [8] tins of dog food, too. I know there aren't [9] tins in the cupboard. – Do you want to come to the shops with me, Lisa? I can use [10] help with the shopping. WB p. 57/23

⟨Revision B⟩ Unit 4–5

1 Questions at the jazz café (→ G 26)

It is Project Week at Thomas Tallis School. David Green and his team are collecting information about cafés in Greenwich. David is talking to Mrs Taylor in her jazz café. Here are her answers.

Write down David's questions. Look at the blue words.

When? | Where? | Why? | How? | Do / Does?

Example: I get to the café **by car**. – **How do you get** to the café? *Go on, please.*

1. The café opens **at 10 o'clock**. 2. We sell lots of sandwiches **because our customers like them**. 3. We make all the food **in the kitchen here**. 4. Yes, **the café opens on Sundays, too**. 5. My dog, Barker? He sleeps **in that room there in the café**. 6. Barker goes home with me **in the afternoon, after school**. 7. I like my day here **because I meet so many interesting people**.

2 Talk about a star (→ G 24, 25)

Lisa and Emma are talking about their favourite boy band 4U. Scott Free sings in the band.

You and your partner take Lisa's and Emma's roles. Answer your partner.

Example: Emma: Tell me about the boys in Scott's band.
Lisa: They come from Bristol but they **don't live** there now. What about … ?

Emma:
1. Tell me about the boys in Scott's band.
2. write his own songs (-)
3. Does he play music with his band?
4. sing on TV (+); make a lot of videos (-)
5. Is he interested in clothes?
6. go to cinema (+); do sport (-); play computer games (-)
7. Does he like music films?

Lisa:
1. come from Bristol (+); live there now (-)
2. What about Scott's songs?
3. play the drums (-); can play the guitar (+)
4. What about TV and videos?
5. wear jeans, T-shirts (+); like yellow things (-)
6. Can you tell me about his hobbies?
7. like music films (-); like funny films (+)

3 At the clothes shop

You want to buy new clothes.

Make a shopping dialogue with a partner.
One of you is the customer, the other is the assistant.

What would you like?
How much is … ?
I like …
…
I can't find …
You can try on …
We've got other …
The … isn't right.
Can I help you?
It's £ …
Excuse me. Have you got … ?

4 Put in the correct pronouns (→ G 22)

me you him it us them her

Nasreen is talking to her friend Sandra on the phone.

Nasreen: Hi, Sandra. It's **me**, Nasreen.
Sandra: Hi, Nasreen. How are [1] ?
Nasreen: OK. – Hey, I want to tell [2] about a new shop in Greenwich. They've got great clothes there, and a beautiful blue sweatshirt. But I can't buy [3] . It's SO expensive.
Sandra: Oh, no! – And have they got cool assistants?
Nasreen: Yes, and the people love [4] .
Sandra: Great! Let's go there on Saturday. Can you meet [5] at 10?
Nasreen: OK. Maybe Dad can take [6] to the shop in the car. I can ask [7] when he comes home. – It's Emma's birthday soon, and I'm looking for a present for [8] .
Sandra: How about a T-shirt?
Nasreen: A T-shirt … ? Good idea. She always takes my T-shirts. I can get [9] a nice pink T-shirt. She likes pink. And maybe a T-shirt for [10] – I need a T-shirt, too. See [11] on Saturday.
Sandra: See [12] at your flat at 10. Bye!

5 What are they doing? (→ G 30, 31)

Jade and her mother are looking at Jade's photos. They are not very good. So Jade tells her mother what the photos are about.

Start like this: 1. Mrs Taylor: **Is** Ben **looking** at pictures?
Jade: **No, he isn't**. He's … *Go on, please.*

look at pictures? – text friends

fight? – play football

have fun at swimming pool? – wash Barker

cook a chicken? – make spaghetti

play in park? – chase Tiger

listen to music? – sleep

Unit 6 Beach holiday

Greenwich is only 25 miles from the North Sea.
In Britain the sea is always near!

I'm Martin from Bamburgh. Our village is on the north-east coast of England. The lighthouse on the Farne Islands near Bamburgh is from 1776 and the castle is 900 years old! I play volleyball on the beach near our castle when it's not too windy.

My name is Scott and I live in Southend-on-Sea. It's a large town east of London and 176,000 people live here. It has got a pier a mile long and a lot of beaches. You can play arcade games at the 'Golden Mile'.

Hi, I'm Jonathan and I'm from Brighton. July is my favourite month because there's a great kite festival then. But you can fly your kites here even in the winter when it's cold!

Hi, my name is Elsie. I live in Cornwall in the town of Penzance. I like the beaches here because they're long and it's so warm here. I usually go surfing in the big waves at Sennen Beach.

Hi, I'm Debbie from Harlech. That's on the west coast of Wales. Our famous castle is 700 years old! People love our beaches in the summer. But we've got mountains, too; 500,000 people climb Mount Snowdon every year.

1 Match the people and the pictures

a) *Example:*
Picture number 1 goes with … because he / she is from …
The picture shows …

b) *Read the texts again. Where would you like to go? Why?*
These sentences can help you:

- I think … is nice because …
- … looks interesting because …
- I'd like to visit … because you can … there.
- I like …

WB p. 60/1

2 Listening: Where are they?

a) *Listen to the people on the CD.*
Where are these people and what can they do?
Take notes in a list like this.

	1	2	3
Where?	Penzance	Southend	…
What?	go surfing	…	…

b) *Look at the big map of Britain in your book. Where are these places?*

WB p. 60/2

1

2

3

4

5

3 A game: Find it on the map

In groups, look at the map in your book and find these things. Who can find them all first?

1. Find one ocean and one island.
2. Find two seas and two mountains.
3. Find three seaside towns.
4. Find five towns and say where they are: in the north, south, east or west.

4 Numbers and dates

a) 1. How many people live in Southend?
2. How many people climb Mount Snowdon every year?
3. How old is Harlech Castle?
4. How old is the Farne Islands lighthouse?

GRAMMAR

Large numbers

1,001 • a/one thousand and one
2,210 • two thousand two hundred and ten
44,440 • forty-four thousand four hundred and forty
666,789 • six hundred and sixty-six thousand seven hundred and eighty-nine

Dates

1600 • sixteen hundred
1838 • eighteen thirty-eight
2007 • two thousand and seven

(→ G 35)

b) *Read these dates:*

1. 1899
2. 1900
3. 1998
4. 2000
5. 2006
6. 2022

Lisa and Ben are surfing on the Internet. They want to find a new place for their family holiday. The home page of Penzance looks interesting.

Penzance

Penzance has got a lot of beautiful beaches and famous St Michael's Mount, a castle in the sea.
Penzance is great for everyone:

- Children always love the little beach in Mousehole Harbour.
- Mum and Dad can visit the old harbour in town.
- Do you like sport? You can always play a game of volleyball on the beach or you can go surfing at Sennen Beach.
- And Penzance has got shops for everyone.
- You can eat nice meals at the restaurants and cafés near the beach.

So plan your holiday trip to Penzance today!

Seasons
Autumn
Shopping
Holiday flats
Winter
St Michael's Mount
Spring
Music
Sport
Summer
Family fun
Children

"I don't want to go to Brighton again. We always go there in the summer. Penzance looks cool," says Ben.
Jade comes in and asks, "What's cool?"
"Penzance," says Lisa.
"Look at this! Penzance has got good beaches where you can play volleyball," says Ben. He clicks on 'Sennen Beach.'
"Surfing! This is the place for me!"
"Jade, you and I can build sand castles and go in the water every day," says Lisa. "We always get lots of ice-cream at the beach! And there's a castle in the sea."
"Then I must pack my wellies," says Jade.
"Wellies are for the rain, silly," says Lisa. "You take your swimsuit to the beach. And I need my sunglasses – oh, and my address book so I can write postcards, and my Discman, and …"
Mr Taylor comes into the room with sandwiches for the children.
"Oh, thanks, Dad! What do you think of Penzance?" asks Lisa.
"That's funny!" says Mr Taylor. "Your mother and I want to take you there in June. It's a great place for kids."
"We know!"

1 An interesting homepage

What words must Lisa and Ben click on to find more interesting pages?

2 What do they usually take?

What do the Taylors usually take with them when they go to the seaside?

Start like this: Ben **usually takes** his volleyball.
Go on, please. WB p. 61/3

3 Put in *bring* or *take*

1. Penzance: ___ the family here for a great holiday!
2. Can I ___ my wellies to the beach, Lisa?
   – No, we don't ___ wellies to the beach, Jade.
3. Please ___ me my address book.
4. The kids are upstairs. Can you ___ them some crisps?
5. Please ___ me that chair. I'd like to sit down. WB p. 61/4

TIP

Bring me that cheese.
Bring that cheese **here**.

Take him the cheese.
Take the cheese **over there**.

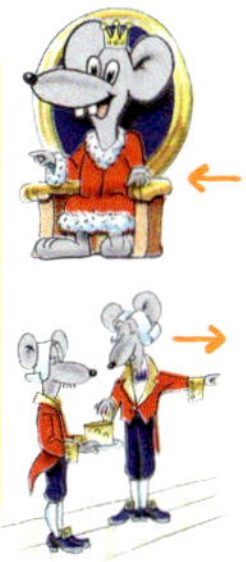

4 What are they doing now?

1

2

3

4

1. Ben and his sisters **are sitting** in Ben's room. They are … *Go on, please.* WB p. 61/5

5 ⟨A song: Leaving town⟩

Get up! We're leaving town.
Summer – the roof is down.
Oh, it's a beautiful day.
We're all OK.

We're getting near the coast.
Sun's hot enough to roast.
Let's find an ice-cream shop
Where we can stop.

Musik: Karl-F. Parnow-Kloth, Text: Sheila McBride

6 How to: Plan a trip

a) *Plan a trip for a weekend. Where do you want to go and what do you want to do?*

⟨b)⟩ *What do you pack? Make a list.*

USEFUL PHRASES

I sometimes / often go to … at the weekend.
It's fun to …
I want to go to / do … so I must take … with me.
I'm packing my … because …
Or we can take … / And we need …

WB p. 62/6

7 Your turn: Holidays in the four seasons

a) *What do you take or what don't you take with you when you …*

1. … go to the sea in the summer?

   Example: I **take** a swimsuit and my sunglasses but I **don't take** wellies.

2. … go to the mountains in the autumn?
3. … go to the mountains in the winter?
4. … ride your bike in the spring?

swimsuit • jeans • map • mobile • sunglasses • good shoes • sweatshirt • address book • bag • bike • wellies • alarm clock • T-shirts

b) *Word bank: What can you do in the four seasons?* WB p. 62/7

On the beach

The Taylors are in Penzance for a week.

8 What is happening here?

Lisa's mobile is ringing. It is Sam.

What are his questions?
Your partner answers them.

Example: 1. A: Where are you sitting?
B: We are sitting on the beach.

1. Where are you … ?
2. Who is sitting … ?
3. What are you … ?
4. Why isn't Ben … ?
5. What … Barker … ?

9 Now and never

Say what the Taylors are doing now and what they often / sometimes / never do at home.

Example: Lisa **is building** a sand castle **now**.
She **never builds** them at home.

1. Ben: play volleyball (now • sometimes)
2. Lisa: play with Jade (now • often)
3. Jade: eat an ice-cream (now • sometimes)
4. The T's: sit on the beach (now • never)
5. Lisa: go swimming (now • often)
6. Barker: eat Jade's ice-cream (now • never)

WB p. 63/9

10 Simple present and present progressive

GRAMMAR SKILLS G1 G2 G3 G4 G5 G6 G7 G8

Grammar can be easy if you know the right signal words.

Often and **never** are signal words.
They tell you: Use the **simple present**!
Example: Barker **often plays** with Lisa.

Now is a signal word.
It tells you: Use the **present progressive**!
Example: Barker **is playing** with Jade **now**.

How can you learn these words? – You can write them in your folder, or on a poster.

a) *Collect all the signal words for the simple present from pages 43 and 45. (often, …)*
b) *Collect all the signal words for the present progressive from pages 76 and 77. (now, …)*
c) *Write these signal words in your exercise book or make a poster for the classroom. Write three example sentences for the words.*

WB p. 63/10 (→ G 36)

11 At home and at the seaside

*Write down what Barker and Jade **usually do** at home and what they **are doing today**.*

1. Jade usually (get up) at 7.00. But today … (9.00).
2. Jade sometimes (have breakfast) with Mum in the kitchen. But this morning … (Dad • on the beach).
3. Barker usually (eat dog food). But today … (ice-cream).
4. Barker often (play) with Jade in the evening. But this evening he … (with new dog friends).
5. Jade usually (go to bed) at 8.00. But now … (7.00) because she is dog-tired!

WB p. 63/11

12 ⟨The present: simple or progressive?⟩

First find the signal words. Then put in the right forms.

1. The Taylors **often** ___ to the seaside for a weekend. 2. **Today** they ___ to Penzance. 3. Mr Taylor usually ___, but today he ___ at the map and Mrs Taylor ___. 4. Barker and Ben always ___ behind Lisa and Jade. 5. Jade ___ now and Barker ___ out of the window. 6. When he sees other dogs, he always ___ at them. 7. Now Lisa and Ben ___ about the music on the radio. This ___ very often! 8. But they usually ___ rules; now they ___ to Lisa's music.

go, bark, fight, drive, make, drive, sleep, sit, happen, look, look, go, listen

13 Your turn: Your idea of a good holiday

a) *Talk with your partner about your idea of a good holiday. These phrases can help you:*

I like … / I don't like …
I'd like to go / visit / play / eat …
You can … there.
I think … is interesting because …

My parents always go to … but I …
But I think … is very interesting because …
Yes, I'd like to …, too, because …
Yes, but … is fun, too.

b) *Now write down your ideas of a good holiday, with pictures. Put them in your folder.*

Some souvenirs of Penzance

It is the last day of the Taylors' week in Penzance. Lisa and Ben are in a shop at the harbour.

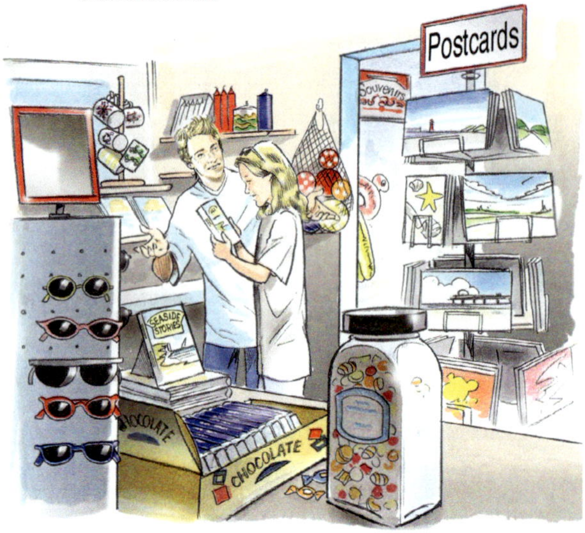

Lisa: I want a nice souvenir of Penzance.
Ben: Well, there are a lot of things in here. How about a mug?
Lisa: I can't see any mugs.
Ben: Take off your sunglasses! There are some mugs over there on the shelf.
Lisa: Oh, right. No, I don't like them.
Ben: Have you got any postcards of St Michael's Mount?
Lisa: No, no postcards. I want to *keep* the souvenir. Hey, I like these sunglasses!
Ben: But you've *got* three pairs of sunglasses.
Lisa: Maybe I want another pair. How much are these?
Ben: Come on, Lisa. You can't try on all the sunglasses in the shop! Dad is waiting for us. There's no time for that.
Lisa: Look, here are some candles. They're nice, but they're too expensive. It's not easy when you haven't got much money.
Ben: You're right. I don't see *any* cheap souvenirs here! Let's go!
Lisa: Maybe I can just buy some chocolate.
Ben: And where's your souvenir when you eat it? Come on now!
Lisa: No, wait! Here's a book of seaside stories. Hm. It looks interesting. Yes, that's fine. I can read it on the way home. That's my souvenir!

14 Look at the picture

a) *What is a good souvenir of Penzance?*

b) *Word bank: Say other souvenir words that you know.*

15 Right or wrong?

Correct the wrong sentences.

1. Lisa and Ben are on the beach.
2. Lisa wants to buy some mugs.
3. Lisa buys some postcards.
4. The sunglasses are too expensive.
5. Mr Taylor is waiting for Ben and Lisa.
6. Lisa hasn't got much money.
7. Ben is happy.
8. Lisa buys a book of seaside stories.

16 Find the rule

a) *Find the sentences with* ***some*** *and* ***any*** *in the dialogue. When do we use* ***some*** *and when do we use* ***any****?*

b) *Now complete these sentences.*

Lisa: Can you see [1] sunglasses?
Ben: What? Oh, sunglasses? There are [2] on the shelf over there. But I can't see [3] *nice* sunglasses.
Lisa: They look OK. I want [4] pink sunglasses. Ah, there they are.
Ben: Have you got [5] money?
Lisa: No, but maybe *you've* got [6] money!
Ben: That's funny! Do you know [7] more jokes?

WB p. 65/13

17 What is in the shop?

Look at the picture on page 94. Then write eight sentences with the right words.

Example: There are **a lot of** sweets in the shop.

There +	is • are isn't • aren't +	some • no a lot of • any +	sweets • postcards • CDs • candles • chocolate • books • mugs • volleyballs +	in the shop.

WB p. 65/14

18 ⟨Role play: In a souvenir shop⟩

A wants to buy a souvenir. B works in a souvenir shop. What does the shop sell? First make a list.

Start like this: A: Excuse me. Have you got **any** candles?
B: Yes, we have. There are **some** nice candles over there.
Or: B: No, we haven't got **any**. But we've got **some** …

19 Listening: Good souvenirs for little sisters

Listen to David's phone call. What does Scott say to David? Put the sentences in the right order.

1. Maybe you can buy her a T-shirt.
2. That's funny! Your sister can't even read!
3. What do you want to buy her?
4. No, they aren't. But what about a mug?
5. Hi, David, it's Scott. Where are you? WB p. 65/15

20 Listening: Sounds [ɜː]

a) *Listen, then say the words:*

girl • T-shirt • turn • her • learn • furniture • dirty • German • Germany • early • word • world

b) *Make three sentences with* [ɜː]. *Use one to three words with* [ɜː] *per sentence.*
Example: Look at the girl's dirty T-shirt.

21 Revision: Match the sentence pairs

1. Let's meet at the cinema.

2. It's a surprise for Sam.

3. They're expensive!

4. I don't like this sandwich!

Don't buy them!
Don't tell him!
Take another sandwich!
Don't be late!

22 Revision: Ask Nasreen's questions

Here are Ben's answers about Penzance. What does Nasreen ask him? Use ***do***.

Example: 1. When do you usually go to the beach?

1. We usually go to the beach in the morning.
2. I like it in Penzance because we always go surfing at Sennen Beach.
3. I always meet my friends on the beach.
4. I go to bed at 10.30.
5. I go to bed so early because I'm dog-tired.

Grace Darling's adventure

Lisa often reads stories to Jade. This evening she is reading the story about Grace Darling from her new book. Lisa asks Jade, "What do you know about storms, Jade?" "It rains a lot," answers Jade. "And what does the rain do, Jade?" "Pitter-patter." "And a strong wind?" "Woosh-shhh!" "And the waves on the rocks?" Lisa asks. "Crash!" "And when that happens all at once? Then we've got a storm! Pitter-patter, woosh-shhh, crash!"

A The evening of 7th September 1838 is very stormy. Young Grace Darling is asleep in her home on one of the Farne Islands near Bamburgh. She lives with her family in the old lighthouse.
The loud wind wakes Grace up. She goes to the window and sees the terrible storm outside. The big waves in the black sea are crashing against the rocks.

B Grace sees a ship near a rock.
"Father, wake up! A ship is sinking," she shouts. "And there are some people on Big Harcar Rock. They're in trouble. We must help them!"
Another great wave crashes against the lighthouse.
"Grace, we can't! It's too stormy. We must wait," says her father. "I can't row out to Big Harcar Rock in this storm!" "I can help you. I'm strong. Come on! There's no time!"says Grace.

C She wants to help the people, so she runs outside to their small boat. Her father is scared for her, but he knows Grace. She is not only strong but she has got a strong will, too. So he runs out to the boat and helps her. They start but it is a long, slow way to the rock. The waves are terrible but Grace and her father do not stop. They are near the nine scared people on the rock now. When they see the small boat, they shout, "Help! Help us, please!"
Grace calls, "We're coming," but they cannot hear her.

D Finally, the boat gets to the rock and Grace helps some of the people into the boat. But it is too small for all nine.
"Make two groups," says Grace's father. "We can row back to the lighthouse with the first group. Then we can come back for the others." They all want to go to the lighthouse.
Grace sees how scared the people are. So she says, "I can wait here with the second group."
"Grace, what are you saying?" asks her father.
"Don't worry, Father." Grace jumps from the boat.

E Five people get into the boat with Grace's father and start the long trip to the lighthouse. The storm is still terrible. Big waves crash on the rock. "Don't worry," Grace says to the four men. They wait and wait. Then Grace's father finally comes back. Grace and the four men jump into the boat. They row the boat back to the lighthouse. That day, forty-three people from the ship die, but nine lucky people survive.

Today people still talk about Grace Darling and her father. You can see their little boat in the Grace Darling Museum in Bamburgh.

"Zzzz." Jade is asleep.

1 Because

Finish the sentences with information from the text.

1. Grace wakes up because …
2. Grace runs outside to their small boat because …
3. The boat is slow because …
4. All of the people want to go back first because …
5. Some people must wait on the rock because …
6. Grace jumps from the boat because … WB p. 67/17

2 ⟨Look at the pictures⟩

a) *Find headings for the pictures.*

b) *Choose one picture. "Climb" into it. What can you see, what can you do?*

3 Which words or sentences in the text …

1. … tell you about Grace? *Start like this:* "She wants to help the people", …
2. … give you a picture of the sea?
3. … tell you about the storm?

4 How to: Retell a story

You are on a train. A boy next to you sees your English book and asks, "What story is that?"

1. Find the important information in the five parts of the story (A–E).
2. Take notes of the important words.
3. Make sentences with them.

Example: **A** It is 7th September 1838. A girl, Grace Darling, lives in the lighthouse on the Farne Islands with her parents. That night, there is a terrible storm, and the wind wakes Grace up.

Now tell parts **B – E** *of the story in your own words.* WB p. 67/19

5 Your turn: What do you think?

1. What do you think about the story? *Start like this:* It's interesting / boring / … because …
2. What do you think about Grace?
3. Do you know about other people like Grace? *Example:* I know about Robin Hood. He …

⟨Stories for a ghost⟩ Chapter 3

On Tuesday and Wednesday Rebecca and Steven do not go to the library. They cannot find any good stories. But when they meet at the school cafeteria on Thursday, Steven has got a good story from the Internet. "No castles," he tells Rebecca. "It's about the sea! A queen in Greenwich must love the sea."

That afternoon at the library, the children find a table and open the old book.

"Do you think there's another new rhyme?" Steven asks.

"Here it is!" Rebecca says and reads:

See the children, watch their eyes.
Listen to them, hear their sighs[1].

Rebecca and Steven look at the picture of the orphans in the garden. Rebecca reads:

Come to them, give them your hand.
They like playing in the sand.

Suddenly there is sand on the book. It is on Rebecca and Steven, too.

"George! That's not funny," Rebecca shouts. "Look at this mess!"

"Please don't shout, please don't be angry. Ghosts like fun, too!" George says.

"Funny fun, George," Steven laughs. "OK, OK, we're not angry. Listen to our story:"

Dylan and the Welsh[2] Wish[3] Fish

"Dylan! Where are you? Come home! Your little sister wants to play. I'm making lunch. Hurry up." "Dylan play with me! Now!"

Everyone always tells Dylan what he must do – his mother, his sister, his teacher, his father. Dylan is not happy. Every morning, he must fish[4] in the sea. Now he is alone in his little boat. It is time to go home for breakfast. Dylan's family lives in a small Welsh town, Harlech. His parents have got a small farm[5] and some animals[6].

"Fishing[7], fishing, fishing. Every morning. I wish[8], I wish … I want to do only what I want. That's what I wish!"

Dylan feels something on his fishing-line[9]. It is hard[10] but soon Dylan has got the fish out of the water. 'Wow!' he thinks, 'it's Rhys, the famous Wish Fish! Yippee!'

Rhys is long and beautiful and yellow. When you catch Rhys, your last wish comes true[11] and you get two new wishes. But you cannot keep Rhys. You must throw him back into the sea.

"I know your first wish, Dylan," says the fish. "Now you can do only what you want." Suddenly Dylan, his boat and the Wish Fish are on a faraway[12] island.

"The island is just for you," Rhys says.

"Cool! Wow! My island," Dylan shouts. Rhys is swimming away when Dylan shouts, "Wait! I've got two more wishes. I always want to have a lot of fish. I don't want to go fishing again."

"OK," says Rhys. "You've got your wish number two."

Dylan does not say thank you, and he runs away from Rhys. All round the beautiful island

[1]**sigh** [saɪ] = Seufzer • [2]**Welsh** [welʃ] = walisisch, aus Wales • [3]**wish** [wɪʃ] = Wunsch • [4]**(to) fish** [fɪʃ] = fischen • [5]**farm** [fɑːm] = Bauernhof • [6]**animal** ['ænɪml] = Tier • [7]**fishing** ['fɪʃɪŋ] = Fische fangen • [8]**(to) wish** [wɪʃ] = (sich) wünschen • [9]**fishing-line** ['fɪʃɪŋ laɪn] = Angelschnur • [10]**hard** [hɑːd] = schwierig, schwer • [11]**(to) come true** [kʌm 'truː] = wahr werden • [12]**faraway** [ˌfɑːrə'weɪ] = fern, weit entfernt

there is a beach with white sand. Dylan is having lots of fun.

Rhys watches the boy on the island. There are lots of fish in Dylan's boat on the beach. The fish are cooking[13] in the sun. Rhys swims away and says, "He's got only one more wish. Only one more."

On his first day on the island, Dylan swims in the sea and lies[14] in the sun a lot. There is no time for this at home. After a few hours on the beach, it is lunchtime. Dylan cooks two fish for lunch, and he is very happy. "Mmm," he says.

In the evening, he does not want to eat fish again, so he climbs a fruit[15] tree and eats a big, red fruit. 'Mmm, very sweet,' he thinks. 'I can eat this every evening.'

That evening Dylan does not want to sleep. He can go to bed when he wants.

"This is great," he says.

In the morning Dylan goes to his boat. But then he remembers – he has got a lot of fish in his boat. So Dylan swims in the sea again and lies on the beach. He finds a coconut[16] and kicks it. But it is not fun to play football alone. Then he throws stones into the water. But after ten stones it is boring.

He hasn't got any friends on the island. He is alone.

Dylan goes to his boat but now the fish stink[17]. He sees a big red fruit. 'Ugh!' he thinks. 'I don't want to eat that again. I can't eat the same thing every day.' He thinks about home and the good food that his mother makes.

After five days on the island, Dylan is sad[18].

There is nothing[19] to do. "It's so boring here. And I'm alone, alone, alone. This isn't fun. This is terrible! I wish, I wish … that everything was normal again!" Dylan shouts. Then Dylan sees a fish in the water. It is Rhys!

"Get in your boat," Rhys says to Dylan. Dylan kicks out the fish and jumps into his boat. Rhys pulls[20] him fast. Then Dylan sees Harlech.

"Thank you, Rhys," Dylan says. "Thank you, thank you, thank you."

"You're welcome," Rhys answers. "Bye."

Dylan hears his mother. She is calling him.

"Dylan! Come and help me!" His mother is making lunch and his little sister is playing with a ball. Everything is the same.

"Oh, Dylan. Please help me. I can't do this alone."

"Dylan, play with me!"

Dylan laughs at his little sister, kicks the ball to her and goes to help his mother.

"What's for lunch, Mum?"

"Do you like it?" Rebecca asks. George does not say a word. "I liked[21] it," she says.

"Yes, it's good, but …," George is thinking, "but … I know that story. Yes, that's right. In my story the boy's name is Ping … and the fish is a bird[22] and it's in China[23] … and there are 100 wishes. It's the same story. I can't use it. Tell me a new story, and then you can come with me. I promise[24]."

Rebecca and Steven are angry. They do not think that George is telling the truth[25]. When they look at the book again, George is not there. But what can they do? George is a funny ghost.

[13] **(to) cook** [kʊk] = kochen, braten • [14] **(to) lie** [laɪ] = liegen • [15] **fruit** [fru:t] = Frucht, Obst • [16] **coconut** ['kəʊkənʌt] = Kokosnuss • [17] **(to) stink** [stɪŋk] = stinken • [18] **sad** [sæd] = traurig • [19] **nothing** ['nʌθɪŋ] = nichts • [20] **(to) pull** [pʊl] = ziehen • [21] **liked** [laɪkt] = hat gefallen • [22] **bird** [bɜ:d] = Vogel • [23] **China** ['tʃaɪnə] = China • [24] **(to) promise** ['prɒmɪs] = versprechen • [25] **(to) tell the truth** [ˌtel ðə 'tru:θ] = die Wahrheit sagen

1 Guess new words

VOCABULARY SKILLS

A B C D E F G H I

a) *Read the information about the seaside. Talk about the words in blue. Can you guess what they mean?*
These questions can help you:

→ Is the word a noun? An adjective? Or what?
→ Can the other words in the sentence help?
→ Is it like a German word?
→ Does a picture help you with the word?

Example:
to spend (your holidays) is a verb.
I can guess what it means from the other words in the sentence. I think it's another word for **to go on holiday.** We say **in Urlaub *gehen*** or **den Urlaub *verbringen*** in German.

British families often spend their holidays at the seaside. The fresh sea air and the warm sun are nice. But the beaches are not always warm and sandy. Sometimes they are cold, windy and rocky. So people cannot spend the whole day – from morning to evening – in the water or on the beach. What can the holiday-makers do? They can enjoy the arcade games and ferris wheels.

b) *Look up the words in the Dictionary (p.208). Are your ideas about them correct?*

WB p. 68/20

2 Different plural forms

Look at Jade's picture book. Say the plurals.

You know some of these words:

GRAMMAR
Plural forms

foot – feet • tooth – teeth • child – children • man – men • woman – women • family – families • person – people • fish – fish • shelf – shelves • scarf – scarves

(→ G 38)

3 Mixed bag: Lisa's mobile

Read Lisa's text to Emma and write it in good English. What letters are missing?

```
hi ma¬ im in pnznce.
bn + jd r plyng in th
watr. mm + dd r on th
bch. dd s reding a
bk + mm is listng t
msic. c u sn¬ lisa
```

4 ⟨Seaside tongue twisters⟩

Listen to these tongue twisters. Can you say them?

1. Toy boat, toy boat, toy boat.
2. She sells sea shells by the seashore.
3. Fresh fried fish. Fish fresh fried.
   Fried fish fresh. Fish fried fresh.

NOW YOU CAN

- Talk about the seaside in Britain.
- Talk about the seasons.
- Plan a trip and use *bring* and *take*.
- Find signal words.
- Say what you are doing now (with the present progressive) and what you often / never do (with simple present).
- Use some plural forms.
- Use *some, any, a lot of* and *no*.
- Guess new words.

1 Your turn: A family trip

You would like to go on a trip with your family. Write six sentences about your plans. Start like this:

1. I would like to go to … because …
2. I would like to go swimming there and …
3. I want to take … with me because …

The Useful phrases on p. 91 can help you.

WB p. 69/22

2 Put in *bring* or *take*

The Taylors are packing the car before they drive home.

1. My Discman is still in the room. Jade, can you … me my Discman, please?
2. Can you … our bag to the car outside, Ben?
3. Lisa, can you please … me my wellies?
4. Please … the map to the car. Mum would like to look at it.
5. No, Barker, we can't … your new dog friend with us!

3 On holiday (→ G 36)

Here is Lisa's postcard to Terry. Put in the correct forms of the verbs.

Dear Terry,
We (be) in Penzance this year. I (sit) on the beach now. I can (see) St Michael's Mount from here.
Some people (surf) today. Mum and Dad always (go) in the water, but today it (be) too cold for me! Jade and I often (build) sand castles on the beach and (walk) Barker in town. Some kites (fly) over the beach now. Oops! One kite (fall) into the sea. CU soon.
Lisa

WB p. 69/23

4 Shopping with Lisa and Mr Taylor (→ G 37)

*Put in **some** or **any**.*

Mr Taylor: OK. Let's see what we've got. We've got 1 water. Now let's get 2 picnic food.
Lisa: Have they got 3 sandwiches here?
Mr Taylor: Yes, they have. And they've got 4 little cakes, too.
Lisa: Yes, nice. Have they got 5 apples?
Mr Taylor: OK, let's get 6 apples and 7 chocolate, too!
Lisa: And what about Barker? Is there 8 dog food here?
Mr Taylor: Yes, there is. They've got 9 tins of his favourite dog food over there.
Barker: Woof!

WB p. 69/24

Unit 7 Animals in the city

Cities are not only for people. There are lots of animals in cities, too. Many people have got pets, of course, but that is not all. In parks and gardens there are wild animals like foxes and birds, and in zoos you can see tigers, monkeys and other animals from all round the world. A big city like London has even got farms! *Look at this brochure.*

MUDCHUTE FARM

Mudchute Farm is in the centre of the city, so you can see green fields and the famous Canary Wharf at the same time! The farm is home to chickens, pigs, cows, and sheep. There are pets here, and you can learn to ride a horse or be a farmhand. Mudchute Farm is open to everyone, young and old. School groups can visit our farm, too. Our schools officer plans special activities for them.

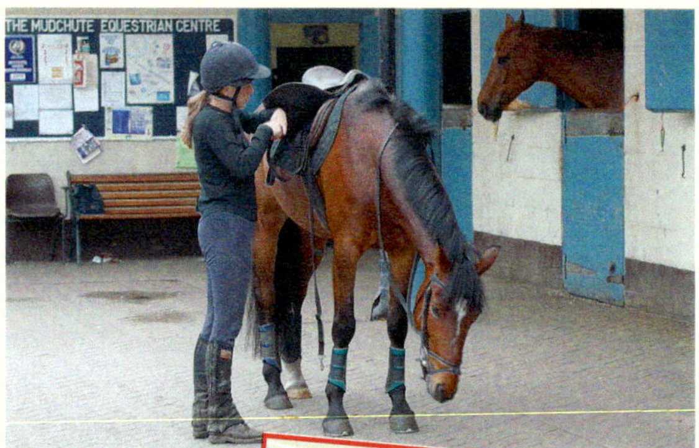

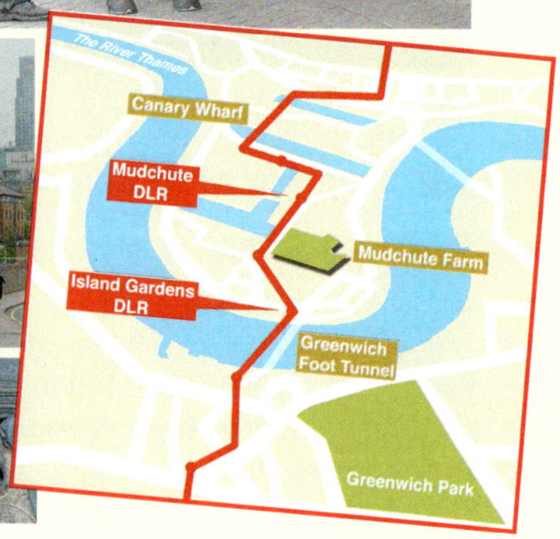

1 Mudchute Farm

Look at the brochure about Mudchute Farm on page 102. Say

- where Mudchute Farm is.
- how you can get there.
- what the farm has got.
- what you can see or do there.

2 ⟨A city farm⟩

Would you like to visit Mudchute Farm? Say why or why not.

3 Listening: A 'hands on' day

a) *Listen to the phone call and take notes. Listen for names, dates, times, and other important information.*

Mudchute Farm — schools officer — Mrs Carter — Year 7 class ...

WB p. 70/2

b) *Correct the wrong information.*

1. The schools officer at Mudchute is phoning Mrs Carter.
2. Mrs Carter can take her class to Mudchute on 5th July.
3. The pupils would like to learn about food.
4. The 'hands on' day is from half past ten to half past three.
5. School groups usually buy lunch in the café.

4 Role play: Tell us more!

a) *When Mrs Carter tells her class that they can go to Mudchute Farm, the pupils have got lots of questions for her. What can they ask? Write down six questions.*

Example: Can we ride the horses?
Where do we meet?

"Is there …?" "How do we …?" "…?"

b) *Make groups of three or four. Take turns to be Mrs Carter and answer the group's questions from a). When you do not know an answer, you can say "I'm not sure./I can't say./…"*

5 Hands on: An animal poster

a) *Word bank: How many animals do you already know? Make lists under these headings.*

Farm animals
Zoo animals
Wild animals in the city
Pets
…

⟨b)⟩ *Make a big poster for your classroom. Show the different groups of animals from a). Why do you like these animals? Write one or two sentences.*

On the farm

There is always a class trip before school closes for the summer. Today Mrs Carter's pupils are visiting Mudchute Farm. Lisa, Emma, Sam and Terry are with Denise, the schools officer. They have all got different ideas about what job they want to do.

Terry: Can we milk the cows? Please!

Lisa: No! I like horses! Can our group look after the horses, please?

Sam: I want to feed the sheep!

Lisa: You needn't feed the sheep, silly! They eat the grass in the field!

Denise: Ssh! I can't answer you all at the same time. And you mustn't shout like that when you're with animals. It makes them nervous. You must be calm with animals.

Emma: Have you got cats here? I mustn't go near cats. I'm allergic to them.

Denise: It's OK, Emma. There are no cats on Mudchute Farm. Now, come with me, please. I've got a nice job for your group. It's in this shed here.

Sam: Pooh! It stinks! It's the pig shed.

Emma: Oh, must we muck out the pig shed?

Lisa: That's fun. I like dirty jobs.

Terry: I don't like dirty jobs. But I like pigs. That's because I love bacon for breakfast.

Denise: Me, too. But let's not talk about bacon in front of our little friends here!

Emma: Oh, little pigs! Four of them! Aren't they sweet?

Denise: It's time for their milk now. Look, they can't wait. Who wants to give it to them?

Lisa: We all do!

Sam: There are four bottles here, so the pigs needn't fight over the milk.

Denise: And there are four of you, too. So you needn't fight over who feeds them!

1 Find the rule

Copy the list on the right. Find examples of the words in the text. What are the words in German? (There are two German words for ***can****.)*

English	German
1. can	dürfen,
2. can't	...
3. must	...
4. needn't	...
5. mustn't	...

2 Why?

1. Why needn't Sam feed the sheep?
2. Why must you be calm with animals?
3. Why mustn't Emma go near cats?
4. Why needn't the friends fight over who feeds the little pigs?

3 What must people on farms do?

Example: They must muck out the sheds.

collect | feed | muck out | milk | ...

4 Put in the right word: *must* – *needn't*

1. Lisa: I'd like to ride a horse.
   I ___ write my name on the list.
2. Denise: We don't only milk the cows in the morning.
   We ___ milk them in the evening, too.
3. Sam: It's OK, Emma. You ___ be nervous with the cows. They're nice animals.
4. Emma: Where are the toilets? I ___ wash my hands before I can eat my sandwiches.
5. Terry: We ___ go home by train.
   My dad can pick us up in his taxi.
6. Terry: A day at Mudchute is a good idea.
   We ___ go to school!

WB p. 71/3

TIP

Must we help with the pigs?
– Yes, you must. / No, you needn't.

(→ G 39, 40)

5 We mustn't do it!

a) *Emma is reading a list of rules for pupils on the farm. What does she tell the others?*

Emma: Look at these rules. We **mustn't** make the animals nervous.
We mustn't … *Go on, please.*

⟨b)⟩ *Your turn: Talk about the rules at your school. What must you do? What mustn't you do?*

WB p. 71/4

Please don't
- make the animals nervous.
- chase the chickens.
- write names or draw on the trees.
- go into the café with dirty shoes.
- feed the animals with your own food.
- eat the animals' food!

6 How to: Talk about jobs in the classroom

You want to help at school. Make polite dialogues.

Example: A: You needn't bring the map. I can do that.
B: Oh, thanks. That's a big help.

open the door • write the words on the board • put the tables / the … back • bring the books / the … • finish the poster / finish the … • take … to … • …

USEFUL PHRASES

You want to help:	**The answer is 'yes':**	**The answer is 'no':**
Can I … for you?	Thanks, that's nice of you.	Thanks, but I can do it.
I can help you to …	That's a big help.	I like the job.
You needn't … I can do that.	It isn't easy alone.	You needn't help.
Would you like some help with …?	Then I needn't do it.	That's OK.

WB p. 72/6

7 Your turn: Class trips

a) *Write about class trips at your school. What places do you visit? What must or mustn't you do on class trips?*

b) *Do you think class trips are a good idea? Why or why not?*

Cyberpets

Emma would like a pet, but the Brooks' flat hasn't got a garden for a dog and Emma is allergic to cats, and she is not good with them. So Sam shows her some interesting information on the Internet.

RSPCA

ADDRESS
HELP
PETS
CYBERPETS
MY RSPCA

Pets can be great fun. But before you ask your parents for a pet you should think!
Is your home a good place for a pet? Have you got time for a pet? Who can buy its food? What can you do with your pet when you are away from home in the school holidays?
A pet is not only for today. Many animals live for many years, so you must look after them for a long time. Are you sure that you want a pet? Or do you want to learn about it first? You can do this with your own cyberpet.
This is Bonza, just one of our cyberpets. She is waiting for an owner. But you needn't take your pet from our list.
You can make your own special pet. You can choose the colour, the eyes, the ears, and its name. When you have got your pet, you mustn't forget to look after it online. All the cyberpets want to go outside from time to time. They can all play with a ball and eat their food, so you must play games with them and feed them, too. When you are away or you cannot go online for a few days, you can put your pet in the cyberpets' holiday home. Cyberpets cannot die, even when their owners do not look after them. But we can see how you are looking after your pet, and we sometimes take pets away from bad owners. The best owners can see their names in our 'Cyberpet top 10'!

8 Make sentences with the correct information

You	+	can must mustn't	+	choose your cyberpet's name. feed your cyberpet. forget to look after your cyberpet. play games with your cyberpet. put your cyberpet in a holiday home. be a bad owner.

9 Your turn: A cyberpet

a) *What do you think? What is good about a cyberpet? What is not so good?*

Example: A cyberpet can't wake you up too early in the morning. That's good.
You can't love a pet on a computer. That isn't so good.

A cyberpet / You … can't run away with your shoes | needn't buy food | can't love you | can't hold your pet | must always be near a computer | can't die | …

b) *Talk about other pets (dogs, cats, …). What is or is not good about them?*

10 Put in: *needn't – mustn't*

1. Mr Jackson: Say hello to Tiger, Emma.
   Emma: No, I ___ go near cats.
2. Emma: Can you make your own cyberpet?
   Sam: Yes, you can. You ___ take a pet from the list.
3. Nasreen: You should play with your cyberpet.
   Emma: I know! You ___ tell me.
4. Jade: It's Barker's birthday on Saturday.
   Lisa: Yes, we ___ forget to buy a present.
5. Terry: Have we got food for Tiger?
   Mrs Jackson: Yes, we have. You ___ buy cat food today.
6. Lisa: Barker! Be quiet!
   Mrs Taylor: Yes, Barker! You ___ bark so much! Jade is sleeping.

WB p. 73/8; 9

11 ⟨Place and time⟩

a) *Sort the words and phrases on the right into two groups – **place** and **time**.*

b) *Word bank: Find other phrases of place and time that you already know.*

for many years • outside • away from home • for a few days • in the cyberpets' holiday home • in the school holidays • from time to time • online

TIP
Place before time!

12 Word order

Mice | look for | food | at school | in the evening

What are the right parts? Find the right order.

(→ G 41)

1. Lisa's face • in the morning • licks • Barker • in bed
2. the birds • watches • for many hours • in the trees • Tiger
3. Mrs Jackson • at the shop • cat food • every Saturday • buys
4. at the weekend • Barker • the Taylors • to the park • take
5. looks after • Emma • online • her cyberpet • after school
6. in the Underground • Sam • sees • from time to time • mice

WB p. 73/10

13 ⟨A game: What pet is it?⟩

Think of a pet. Tell your group about it. They must guess what it is.

can ride it | likes milk | sings | … | must take it to the park | swims

14 Your turn: My pet

Draw a picture of your own pet, or a funny pet. Then write a text about it. You can write down things like:

- *what its name is and what it looks like.*
- *what it can or cannot do.*
- *what you must or needn't do for it.*
- *why you like your pet.*

My pet
This is my pet Greeno.
He is green and he has got orange eyes. I take him to school every Friday.
I must feed him – he eats rubbers and pencils.

TTS school magazine

PHOTO CLUB

Thomas Tallis School

There are lots of good photos in July's 'Animal photo' competition, but the winner is Year 7 pupil Lisa Taylor with her photo of Crystal, a horse at Mudchute Farm. Her photo wins because it catches a great moment. When you look at the horse, it is talking to you! Lisa's prize is a new card for her camera, and she gets a big poster of her photo of Crystal, too. All the animal photos from the competition are in Room 20 where everyone can go and see them.

There are no more competitions before school closes for the holidays. The next competition is in September, so you have got a lot of time to take a good photo. The title of September's competition is 'A happy face'.

Happy holidays to you all!

15 Crystal

a) *Look at Lisa's photo of Crystal. What do you think Crystal is saying or asking? Think of funny ideas.*

Example: "I'm Crystal – and who are you?"
Or: "Have you got an apple for me?"

⟨b)⟩ *Find your own funny animal photos and bring them to school. What is your animal saying?*

16 Put in the right words

and | but | because | before | so | when

1. Hello, Crystal. I want to take a photo of you ___ you're so beautiful.
2. Hey, please don't run away ___ I can take your photo.
3. Look, I've got sugar for you, ___ here's an apple, too.
4. I'd like to win this competition, ___ I must take a good photo.
5. You can help me – just look at the camera ___ I call your name.
6. Thanks, Crystal. My photos usually aren't very good, ___ maybe I can win a prize with this!

17 ⟨A song: Oh please, Dad!⟩

Oh please, Dad, can we have a monkey?
The babies are really so sweet.
It can sleep in the shed
With a box as a bed
And a bag of bananas to eat.

Musik: Karl-F. Parnow-Kloth, Text: Sheila McBride

18 How to: Link sentences

a) *Look at these two texts. Say what is different.*

Lisa loves animals. She sometimes takes photos of them. She has got a big wall in her bedroom. She can put her photos there. Barker sees the pictures. He barks at them. He does not like the other animals in Lisa's room. He is her pet!	Lisa loves animals, *and* she sometimes takes photos of them. She has got a big wall in her bedroom where she can put her photos. When Barker sees the pictures he barks at them. He does not like the other animals in Lisa's room because he is her pet!

b) *It is good to link sentences in a text. What words can you use? Read the texts on page 106 and 108 again and make a list.*

but | because | …

c) *Link sentences in the text and write it again. Your list from b) can help.*

Start like this: Sam likes Mudchute Farm but his … *Go on, please.*

Sam likes Mudchute Farm. His favourite place for animals is London Zoo. He loves the monkeys. They are funny. They jump. They play games. They always get their food at 2 o'clock. Sam goes to the monkey house at that time. The monkeys talk to Sam. He answers them in their own language!

WB p. 75/12

TIP
Don't forget:
The English word order is always: S • V • O when you link two sentences.

(→ G 42)

19 Listening: Sounds [æ], [eɪ] and [ɑ:]

*The same letter can often have many different sounds. Listen and say these sounds for **a**.*

[æ] Look – two black cats! • Our family has got a flat. • This café sells sandwiches.
[eɪ] We've got the same name. • This is a famous place. • The bacon is on the table.
[ɑ:] It's half past two. • There's grass in the garden. • You can't park the car here!

20 Listening: Sentences

After the first part of a long sentence, the sound often goes up a little. When you finish the sentence, the sound goes down. Listen and say:

- There are lots of good photos, but the winner is Lisa Taylor.
- All the pictures are in Room 20 where everyone can see them.

21 Revision: Before the holidays

Put in the right verb forms: simple present or present progressive. Look for signal words.

1. It is the last week of the school year. The pupils **always** ___ (do) nice things then.
2. Right now Mrs Carter ___ (take) her class outside. They sometimes ___ (play) games on the grass.
3. Oh no! It always ___ (rain) when it shouldn't! Now everyone ___ (run) into the school again.
4. It is the last afternoon, and now the pupils ___ (put) all their things into their bags. School usually ___ (finish) early on the last day.
5. Now Mrs Carter ___ (say) goodbye to her class. Every year she – and the pupils – ___ (need) a nice long holiday!

WB p. 75/14

Sam's new friend

A "Oh! What's that?"
Sam and Lisa are playing football next to the flats in Wendover Road one evening. When the ball goes behind the garages, Sam runs after it. But he gets a shock. There is an old plank behind the garages, and in a dark hole under the plank Sam can see two eyes. They are looking at him.
"What's up, Sam?" Lisa looks under the plank. "Is it a cat? Or – no, it's a fox!"
"Wow! A fox? Are you sure?" Sam asks.
"Of course I'm sure. I know a fox when I see one! There are a lot of foxes in London," answers Lisa.
"What's it doing there? Does it live there?" Sam wants to know.
"I don't know. Oh, wait. That's why. Look at its leg. It can't walk!"

B The two friends go upstairs to Sam's flat and tell his grandma about the fox. She comes outside and looks into the hole where the fox is.
"Why do you think its leg is like that?" Lisa asks Sam's grandma.
"I'm not sure. A car, maybe. Cars are a big problem for foxes in cities."
"Should we take it to the vet?" Sam wants to know.
"No, you mustn't take a fox away from its territory. Another fox may come into the territory, and then you can't put the first fox back," Grandma explains.
But Sam is not happy. "I want to help it! It may die!"
"Yes, it may," says Grandma. "But maybe this is a lucky fox and its leg can mend. One thing is sure. It needs food. Like this it can't catch mice or birds."
"Oh, no! Must I catch mice and birds for it?"
Grandma smiles when she sees Sam's face.
"No, you needn't do that. We can't go to the shops now. But Lisa, I'm sure you've got food for the fox this evening. Just don't tell Barker!"

C Lisa rides her bike home to Pond Road and soon comes back to Sam's flat with a tin of dog food. But when Sam puts a bowl of food in front of the fox, it does not eat it. It does not even look at the food. It just watches Sam.
"It's tasty. Come on, you must eat," Sam tells the fox. But it still just watches and waits.
"Maybe it's because we're here," Lisa says. "We must be very scary for a little fox. Let's go, Sam."

D That night Sam does not sleep much. He is worried about the fox. But when he goes back the next morning, the bowl is empty. "Good. Maybe its leg can mend and it needn't die," he thinks.
After that he takes food and water to the fox every day. Grandma gives him money for dog food, so Lisa needn't bring Barker's food to Wendover Road.
Of course when Sam's other friends know about the fox, they all want to come and see it, too.
"You mustn't go too near and make it nervous," Sam tells them. "It's OK for me. It knows me now. We're friends!"
Sam is right. After a few days the fox is not so nervous of him. It even eats in front of him. Sam feels happy. He loves his new friend. He calls the fox Rusty.

E One morning Sam wants to visit Rusty before breakfast. Grandma sees him from the kitchen window upstairs. Sam is standing near the garages. He looks very sad.

1 What do you think?

Why does Sam look sad?

2 How can the story end?

Read F(1) and F(2).

F(1) Grandma runs downstairs to Sam. "The hole is empty. Rusty isn't there," says Sam, and he is very sad. "Oh, Sam. You should be happy, not sad. It means its leg is OK again – thanks to you!"

F(2) When Grandma goes outside, Sam is very sad. "He's dead, Grandma!"
"I'm sorry, Sam," Grandma says. "I'm very sad, too. But these things happen with wild animals. Life isn't easy for them."

Then explain why you like F(1) or F(2).
Start like this: I like **F(1)** / **F(2)** because …

I like happy / sad stories | the fox survives | I can believe F(1) / F(2) because … | …

3 Writing a picture story

WRITING SKILLS

a) Important ideas

If you want to write a picture story, collect ideas about the pictures first.
Take notes: What happens?
Who does what? Where? When?

1. Read the notes on the right. Match them with the first three pictures.
2. Finish these notes for pictures 4, 5 and 6.

A: put • the bowl • on the grass • near the shed • a fox • behind a tree • watch
B: Terry • in the kitchen • think • put • milk • into a bowl
C: take • the milk • into the garden • Tiger • asleep • on the shed

Picture 4: the fox • bring • … **Picture 5:** the little foxes • drink • … **Picture 6:** Tiger • …

b) Write the story

When you write the story, use your notes. Don't forget: simple present!
Start like this: One day Terry is in the kitchen. He thinks: '…', so … *Go on, please.*

c) Correct the text

Read your text to your partner. Can your partner help you to correct it? Is the information clear? Are the verb forms correct?

d) Title

Find a good title for your story.

WB p. 77/18

⟨Stories for a ghost⟩ Chapter 4

It is Saturday again. Rebecca and Steven are back in the library with their new story from the magazine *Teenie*. The story is about animals.

"Everyone likes animals," Rebecca says to Steven.

"But does the Queen's *ghost* like animals, Becca? We really need those photos soon."

"Steven," says Rebecca. "This is a great story."

"Page 372," Steven says and opens the old book on the library table.

"You read the rhyme today, Steven," Rebecca says.

"I can't. It's for you." Rebecca reads:

Dear[1] Rebecca, my dear friend,
All my jokes must have an end.
I won't bother[2], I won't bug you[3]
But pleeeeease, can I hug[4] you?!

Suddenly George hugs Rebecca.

"George," she laughs, "we like your jokes. But we need the photos for our project. When can we go with you?"

"First tell me the story."

Why the bear[5] has got a short tail[6]

Fox and Bear have got long, beautiful tails – one red tail and one big brown tail. Fox and Bear are friends – not real real friends because Bear is a terrible show-off[7]. And Fox does not like that. Do *you* like show-offs?

"A fox? Is the story about a fox?" asks George.

"George! Please!" says Steven.

"Sorry. But a fox is very good. Very good. Go on, please, Rebecca."

Bear always waves his tail around[8] and tells Fox how beautiful it is. Fox never tells Bear how beautiful his own tail is. Soon Fox is fed up with the show-off Bear, and then Fox gets a very clever idea.

"That's right! Foxes always get clever ideas."

"George! Shhh!"

It is winter so the lake[9] where Bear and Fox live is frozen[10]. Fox goes out onto the ice[11]

[1]**dear** [dɪə] = Liebe/r, lieb • [2]**I won't bother you** [aɪ wəʊnt ˈbɒðə juː] = ich werde dich nicht belästigen • [3]**I won't bug you** [bʌg] = ich werde dir nicht auf die Nerven gehen • [4]**(to) hug** [hʌg] = umarmen • [5]**bear** [beə] = Bär • [6]**tail** [teɪl] = Schwanz • [7]**show-off** [ˈʃəʊɒf] = Angeber • [8]**(to) wave around** [weɪv‿əˈraʊnd] = umherschwenken • [9]**lake** [leɪk] = See • [10]**frozen** [ˈfrəʊzn] = gefroren • [11]**ice** [aɪs] = Eis

and makes a hole in it. With his fast paws[12] he catches lots of fish and puts them around the hole. When he sees Bear, he puts his tail in a fish's mouth[13] and then puts his tail into the water with the fish on it.

Bear comes and asks, "Fox, what are you doing?"

"I'm catching fish," says Fox and shows Bear his tail with the fish.

Bear is excited – he loves fish – and wants to catch some fish, too. He sits down at Fox's hole.

"Stop!" shouts Fox. "There are no more fish[14] here. But I know a place where you can catch lots of fish. Come with me."

Fox takes Bear to a place on the lake where he knows there are no fish. Fox makes a hole in the ice for Bear.

Bear sits down and says: "But how do I know when there is a fish on my tail? I can't see behind me." He is nervous and wants to catch lots and lots of fish.

"I can help you," says Fox. "That's what friends are for[15]. First, be very quiet. I can stand behind you and watch. When a fish is on your tail, I can shout 'NOW!'. Then pull your tail out of the water."

"OK," Bear says.

Fox hides[16] behind a tree and watches. Soon Bear falls asleep and Fox goes home to his warm house.

The next morning Fox walks to the lake. Bear is still sitting on the ice, his tail is still in the hole and – Fox smiles – the hole is frozen round Bear's tail. "NOW!" shouts Fox.

Bear hears Fox and pulls very hard[17] on his tail. SNAP! His tail breaks off[18] and stays in the ice.

That is why bears have got short tails and that is why – even today – bears and foxes are not friends.

George is laughing. "The story is great, just great! OK, you can come with me now. Did you know: The Queen's favourite animal is the fox? She's got a pet fox."

"That's nice," says Steven.

"No – it isn't nice," answers George. "Because her fox is dangerous[19]. He can see and hear *everything*. So be careful[20]. And if the Queen catches you …"

George is very sad now.

"What happens then?" asks Rebecca.

"If she catches you, **POOF**! She can turn you into ghosts[21]. And remember: You've got only one hour in history," George says.

"An hour is OK," says Rebecca. "And we can be very careful, George. What do you think, Steven?"

"Let's go, Rebecca," Steven answers. "Now we can *see* history. This is great!"

The children are very excited. Rebecca takes her camera. They give George their hands.

"Ready?" asks George.

"Ready!" Rebecca and Steven shout.

"Then juuuuump!" shouts George and pulls them into the book with him.

[12]**paw** [pɔː] = Pfote, Tatze • [13]**mouth** [maʊθ] = *hier:* Maul • [14]**no more …** [nəʊ mɔː] = keine … mehr • [15]**that's what friends are for** ['ðæts wɒt frendz ə 'fɔː] = dafür hat man Freunde • [16]**(to) hide** [haɪd] = (sich) verstecken • [17]**hard** [hɑːd] = fest • [18]**(to) break off** [breɪk‿'ɒf] = abbrechen • [19]**dangerous** ['deɪndʒrəs] = gefährlich • [20]**careful** ['keəfl] = vorsichtig • [21]**(to) turn into** ['tɜːn‿'ɪntə] = verwandeln in

⟨Stories for a ghost⟩ Chapter 5

"Welcome[1]! Welcome to old Greenwich," George says.

Rebecca and Steven feel funny[2]. George is right – it is not easy to go into history. They feel strange[3] and their stomachs[4] feel funny. They look round and know the room from pictures in the history books. They are in the library of the Queen's House. And there is *The Big History Book of Greenwich* but it does not look old now. It is a new book in 1808. Rebecca takes a photo of the library and George with the book. Then she remembers the dangerous Queen and her dangerous fox.

"Uh, George. Let's go! The Queen is scary," she says and her stomach tickles[5].

George smiles: "OK."

They run down the stairs[6] and to the National Maritime Museum[7].

"Whew! Now I can breathe again!" laughs Rebecca. Steven feels good now, too.

"Look at all those people in funny clothes," he whispers to Rebecca. "This is like a film. Or TV. Wow! I love it! And look at all those horses. Here in the city!"

A rich man and a rich woman walk by[8]. Rebecca smiles at them and takes a photo of them.

"What strange children, and what a strange box that clicks[9]," says the woman.

"Maybe they're from the orphanage[10]," the man says to her.

George gives his cap[11] to Rebecca. "Here, so you don't look so strange," he says and smiles. "But I haven't got any clothes for you, Steven. Sorry."

"That's OK, George. Let's hurry. We haven't got much time. I want to see the market now," answers Steven.

The children walk down Turnpin Lane to the market. It is a small street and it stinks.

"Yuk," says Steven. "Why does it stink? Watch out, Becca. Don't walk there!"

George tells them that people throw everything from the kitchen into the street. When it rains, it all goes down the street. Rebecca and Steven just look at each other, and Rebecca takes a photo.

After the market they walk to the Thames.

"Where's the Cutty Sark?" Rebecca asks

"It's sailing to China just now. Why do you ask, Rebecca?" says George.

"Oh, nothing[12], nothing," says Rebecca.

"And look! Where is the Millennium Dome?" asks Steven.

Rebecca kicks him and then Steven remembers that it is 1808. But now they hurry back to the Queen's House. They have only got ten minutes. When they get back, Rebecca and Steven don't want to go in.

George smiles and says, "Any problems, my friends?"

"Um, ah, George, the Queen is scary," says Rebecca.

[1]**welcome** ['welkəm] = Willkommen • [2]**(to) feel funny** [fi:l 'fʌni] = sich komisch fühlen • [3]**strange** [streɪndʒ] = merkwürdig • [4]**stomach** ['stʌmək] = Magen • [5]**(to) tickle** ['tɪkl] = kitzeln • [6]**stairs** [steəz] = Treppe • [7]**National Maritime Museum** [ˌnæʃnl 'mærɪtaɪm mju:ˌzi:əm] = Nationales Schifffahrtsmuseum • [8]**(to) walk by** [wɔ:k 'baɪ] = vorbeigehen • [9]**(to) click** [klɪk] = klicken • [10]**orphanage** ['ɔ:fnɪdʒ] = Waisenhaus • [11]**cap** [kæp] = Mütze • [12]**nothing** ['nʌθɪŋ] = nichts

"Oh, yes," says Steven and now *his* stomach feels funny.

"Let's be very careful," George answers. "Quiet now – and up[13] the stairs to the library."

They tiptoe[14] up the old stairs. One step[15], two steps, three steps. They wait. Quiet.

Four steps, five steps, six steps.

They hear a noise[16]. What is it?

They feel a cold wind. Rebecca and Steven are shaking[17], and then George shouts: "The Queen's fox! And that means that Queen Anne is near. Fast! To the library! To the book!"

The fox runs to them and makes strange and wild noises. Suddenly the Queen's ghost jumps at them.

"Come here, my children, my sweet *real*[18] children, and you can live here forever!"

She tries[19] to hold Rebecca's T-shirt but then the Queen's ghost falls over her fox.

"Hurry, hurry!" George shouts. "Rebecca! Steven! Don't stand there like statues[20]."

Steven and Rebecca jump back and then run up the last steps. They are in the library and run to the table with the open book. They are shaking and shaking. Then they hear the Queen's ghost again.

"Come here my sweet children, come and be sweet ghosts and tell me stories forever!"

Rebecca looks back. Queen Anne's ghost and the fox are only two steps away. The Queen's ghost is holding Steven's T-shirt and he is shouting. Rebecca turns round[21] and takes one last photo. The Queen's ghost cannot see because of[22] the flash[23]. She and the fox stop and Rebecca and Steven jump into the book.

"Goodbye, George. And thank yoooooou!" Rebecca shouts.

"Whew!" says Steven. "We're safe."

"Whew!" says Rebecca. "These time trips[24] *aren't* boring."

Rebecca and Steven are sitting at the table in the Greenwich Public Library. The old book is open, and then Rebecca reads:

All good fun comes to an end
But you can always be my friend.
She loves the story, my Queen Anne.
Now one last time, give me your hand.

Rebecca and Steven smile and put their hands on the picture. Their stomachs feel good. Then they feel a warm wind and hear "Thank you."

***

"Thank you for your wonderful[25] project, Rebecca and Steven. That's a very good job. There's so much information about the buildings in Greenwich. And the photos! The photos are just wonderful. Wherever did you find them[26]?" asks Rebecca and Steven's teacher.

Rebecca and Steven smile at each other.

"Oh, that was the easy part," Rebecca says.

[13]**up** [ʌp] = hoch, nach oben • [14]**(to) tiptoe** ['tɪptəʊ] = auf Zehenspitzen gehen • [15]**step** [step] = Stufe, Schritt • [16]**noise** [nɔɪz] = Geräusch • [17]**(to) shake** [ʃeɪk] = zittern, beben • [18]**real** [rɪəl] = echt • [19]**(to) try** [traɪ] = versuchen, probieren • [20]**statue** ['stætʃu:] = Statue, Standbild • [21]**(to) turn round** [tɜ:n 'raʊnd] = sich umdrehen • [22]**because of** [bɪ'kɒz‿əv] = wegen • [23]**flash** [flæʃ] = Blitzlicht • [24]**time trip** ['taɪm trɪp] = Zeitreise • [25]**wonderful** ['wʌndəfl] = wunderbar • [26]**Wherever did you find them?** [weə'revə dɪd jə 'faɪnd ðəm] = Wo habt ihr sie nur gefunden?

1 Words with different meanings

VOCABULARY SKILLS A B C D E F G H I

When you find a new word in a dictionary, there are sometimes two or more meanings for it. The other words in the sentence can help you to choose the correct meaning for the new word.

a) *Look at the meanings for 'garage' on the right. What is the correct meaning in these sentences?*

1. There's a problem with my car. I must take it to the garage.
2. Our car is always in the street. We haven't got a garage.
3. Look, it says 'empty'. We must stop at the next garage.

gar·age ['gærɑːʒ, USA gə'rɑːʒ] ❶ *(zum Parken)* Garage ❷ *(zum Tanken)* Tankstelle ❸ *(für Reparaturen)* Werkstatt

b) *Put these phrases into German:*

1. **no**, thank you – **no** problem
2. **ride** a horse – **ride** a bike
3. the **right** answer – on the **right**
4. **catch** a bus – **catch** a mouse
5. **just** now – **just** a minute
6. **like** this – I **like** it

(Use the Dictionary on page 208.)

WB p. 78/19; 20

2 Where?

Look at the picture and make sentences with the words in the box

Example: The little pig is next to the big pig.

behind | in | on | under | next to | near | in front of

3 When?

Emma is telling her parents about the people on Mudchute Farm. Put in the missing words.

after | before | at | on | in

1. They're on the farm early ___ the morning.
2. They milk the cows ___ 6 o'clock every morning.
3. And they milk them again ___ the evening.
4. They do lots of jobs ___ lunch, and they are busy ___ the afternoons, too.
5. They must be tired ___ their long day.
6. They're often there ___ Sunday, too!

4 ⟨A poem: Hamsters⟩

Learn this poem by heart.

Hamsters are the nicest things
That anyone could own.
I like them even better than
Some dogs that I have known.

Their fur is soft, their faces nice.
They're small when they are grown.
And they sit inside your pocket
When you are all alone.

by Marci Ridlon

NOW YOU CAN

- Talk about animals and pets.
- Say what you *must*, *needn't* or *mustn't* do.
- Use phrases about place and time.
- Link sentences.
- Write a picture story.
- Find the correct meaning of a new word.

1 Your turn: Your favourite animal

*Write six sentences about your favourite animal. Give information about it and explain why you like it. Do not forget to link your sentences with **and**, **because** etc.*

2 Put in *must*, *needn't* or *mustn't*

(→ G 39, 40)

1. Are you busy? I can take the dog to the park today. You ___ do it.
2. Hey, you ___ throw water at the neighbours' cat. That isn't nice!
3. We've got chickens in our garden. So we ___ go to the shops for eggs.
4. My horse has got a problem with her leg. I ___ phone the vet.
5. We ___ forget to take a camera with us when we go to the zoo on Sunday.
6. The sheep eat the grass in the field, so we ___ feed them in the summer.

WB p. 79/21

3 Where and when?

(→ G 41)

Write the sentences again with more information. Explain where and when you do these things. You can use your own ideas for place and time, too.

Example: I often watch TV.
→ I often watch TV at my friend's house after school.

1. I do my homework.
2. I meet my friends.
3. I listen to music.
4. I have breakfast.

in the park | at … o'clock | at the weekend | in my room | at home

4 Link the sentences

(→ G 42)

Make one sentence from two. Use these words. and | but | so | because | …

Example: You can hear lots of birds in our street. We've got so many trees.
→ You can hear lots of birds in our street because we've got so many trees.

1. The trees are nice for the people here. They are nice for birds, too.
2. The birds start to sing early in the morning. They wake up my brother and me.
3. I like our 'alarm clock'. My brother doesn't like it.
4. I love birds. I think their songs are beautiful.
5. I always get up with the birds. I'm never late for school!

5 ⟨Tom's holiday rap⟩

The holidays are here, so goodbye
school!
School is OK, but holidays are cool.
It's time to say 'Bye!' to my Thomas
T house.
No more lessons – this is one
happy mouse!

So let's rap it, clap it, be excited
about it.
Let's tell the world that the
holidays are here.
Rap it, clap it, shout all about it!
Goodbye, everyone!
See you next year!

⟨Revision C⟩ Unit 6–7

1 What is Dave doing today? (→ G 36)

Dave works at Mudchute Farm.
On the right you can read a list of his **daily** jobs.
But **today** it is Dave's free day.

What does he do every day, and what is he doing now?

Example: 1. At six o'clock Dave usually **milks** the cows, but today he **is sleeping**.

1. 6.00 milk cows
2. 8.00 muck out pig shed
3. 9.30 feed chickens
4. 10.00 look for eggs
5. 10.30 ride a horse
6. 11.00 take a class on a tour

1

6.00 sleep

2

8.00 listen

3

9.30 have

4

10.00 surf

5

10.30 read

6

11.00 phone

2 Simple present or present progressive? (→ G 36)

Look for signal words. Put in the right verb forms.

Example: 1. It is a Sunday afternoon in June. **Today** Emma and Lisa **are sitting** in Lisa's room. It is a boring day.

2. They often (walk) to the park with Barker in the afternoon, but right now it (rain).
3. At the weekend the two girls sometimes (meet) Terry and Sam in Terry's shed, then they always (play) games or (have) a picnic there.
4. But today the Jacksons (visit) friends near Canary Wharf.
5. "Can you open the door, please, Lisa?" Mrs Taylor (bring) the girls a drink now.
6. Mrs Taylor has got an idea: "Let's make a nice big pizza for this evening!" – "Great!" says Emma. "We never (make) pizzas at home."
7. Now Emma and Lisa (stand) in the kitchen and they (have) fun.

3 Your turn: Your dream holiday

Tell your partner about your dream holiday or dream holiday island.
What has the place got and what can you do there? What is interesting / different there?
Use the Useful phrases on page 91.

4 Put in: can – must – mustn't – needn't (→ G 39, 40)

The Jacksons want to go to Wales for the weekend, and Sam can come, too.
Now Sam is packing his bag in his room. Terry is helping him.

1. Sam: **Can** we go to one of those cool castles on the coast?
   Terry: Dad says yes, we ___.
   But we ___ climb on the rocks when it's stormy.
2. Sam: Oh no! Look, my sunglasses are broken. I ___ buy new sunglasses in Wales.
3. Terry: We want to climb Snowdon, so you ___ pack good shoes.
4. Sam: I ___ forget my mobile. I want to text my friends, then I ___ write any postcards.

(Sam's grandma comes in.)

5. Grandma: I'd like a nice postcard, please, Sam. But you ___ buy me a present.
6. Sam: ___ I pack my alarm clock?
   Terry: No, you ___ take that. My dad always wakes me up.

5 Write a picture story (→ G 41, 42)

a) *Look at the pictures. Then take notes for the pictures. Start like this:*

1. Ben • play volleyball • with friends • Jade • ice-cream • say to Barker • …
2. Suddenly • ball • fly • Jade • cannot see it • Barker • want to help • jump at • …
3. Jade • …
4. Barker • …

b) *Now use your notes and write the story. Link your sentences with* ***and, because, when*** *etc. Use the simple present.*

Start like this: 1. Ben is playing volleyball with friends on the beach, and Jade **is** with Barker. She **has got** … *Go on, please.*

c) *Find a good title for your story.*

[Trailer 1] Summer with the Taylors

Sunday 30th July
Dear Lisa,
You asked for a postcard from Germany, so here it is. Berlin is great and Stefan is fun, too. Yesterday we were at the lake in the photo. Two girls there invited us to sail their boat with them. German girls are so cool! But some things are funny here. When I wanted to get into the car, I opened the wrong door. I think Stefan's dad was worried that I planned to drive! And it was a surprise to get cheese for breakfast. Must go now – things to do. See you soon.

Love, Ben

1 Finish the sentences

1. Lisa asked for …
2. Yesterday Ben and Stefan were at …
3. Two girls invited them to …
4. When Ben wanted to get into the car …
5. It was a surprise to get …

GRAMMAR
Past tense

am / is → **was**	ask + **ed**
are → **were**	invite + **d**
	plan + **n** + **ed**

(→ G 43, 44, 45)

2 Listening: Sounds [d], [t] and [ɪd]

a) *Listen and say these past forms.*

1. [d] opened – lived 2. [t] asked – watched 3. [ɪd] invited – needed

b) *Read the sentences and put the past forms in the right groups in a).*

1. Ben want**ed** to swim, so he jump**ed** from the boat into the lake.
2. Stefan laugh**ed** when Ben show**ed** him a funny photo of Barker.
3. Ben us**ed** the wrong word in German, so Stefan correct**ed** him.

3 Ben and Stefan in Berlin

Write down your ideas about the two boys' activities when Ben was in Berlin. Use the verbs in the box.

look at | play | talk about | visit | listen to | watch

Example: They **visited** museums. *or:* They **visited** Stefan's friends.

4 Lisa's diary

a) *Explain why Lisa is fed up.*

b) The past forms of these verbs are **irregular**. *Collect the forms from the text.*

have • say • go • run • get • find • come

c) *Word bank: What other irregular past forms do you already know? Start a list of irregular verbs and their past forms.*

Friday
I'm fed up! I had a bad day. First Emma phoned and said goodbye before her holiday. So now my best friend is away for two weeks. Then I went to the park with Barker. But he ran away and got lost. When I found him and came home, there was a postcard from Ben. It's OK for him. He's having fun in Germany, but it's BORING here.

5 Mr Taylor's idea

a) *Choose the right verbs and put in the irregular past forms. Use your list from exercise 4.*

be • come • say • get • go • find • have

When Lisa [1] up last Saturday she [2] still fed up. After breakfast she [3] into her room. But then her father [4] in. He [5] some interesting information for her. "Look, Lisa," he [6]. "I [7] this for you on the Internet. Summer activities for kids in Greenwich!"

b) Two days later, Lisa talked to Terry on the phone.

Regular or irregular? Put in the correct past forms.

"Hi, Terry. I [1] (start) a trampolining course yesterday. I [2] (love) it! We [3] (learn) to jump and dance in the air. It [4] (be) great. But one of the boys in my group [5] (have) a problem. He [6] (eat) too much chocolate before he [7] (jump), and suddenly his face [8] (look) very green. I'm not sure what [9] (happen) after that because he [10] (run) to the toilets and never [11] (come) back!"

6 How to: Write a postcard

You are in Greenwich. Write a postcard to your family in Germany. You can use some of the phrases on the right.

USEFUL PHRASES

Dear … ,
It's great here in … I'm having fun …
Yesterday we went to / visited …
It was cool / funny / … I saw / met / bought / …
I think British kids are …
I must go now because …
See you soon. Love, …

7 Your turn: Yesterday

Write six sentences about your day yesterday. Explain what you did or what happened.

I had a good / bad / funny / … day.
First … Then … After that … …

[Trailer 2] Old junk

Mr Jackson: I'm going to need some help this morning.
Terry: Why? What are you going to do?
Mr Jackson: I want to clear out the garage. There's so much old junk in it.
Terry: Oh, I can help you with that. Come on. Let's see what we can find!

In the garage:

Terry: Great! Here's an old skateboard! It hasn't got any wheels, but –
Mr Jackson: No, Terry! Throw it away. Put it outside with that old bath and all the other things.
Terry: OK, OK. Don't worry. I'm not going to keep it. – Hey, I think that girl wants to talk to us.

Girl: Are you going to throw these things away?
Terry: Yes, we are. We can't sell them. People aren't going to buy old junk.
Girl: Well, can I have that kite, please?
Mr Jackson: Yes, of course. Just take it.
Girl: Thanks a lot.
Terry: But what are you going to do with it? There's a hole in it, so you can't fly it.
Girl: That's OK. It's for my little brother. It's going to be a funny face. I can draw the eyes and the nose – and the hole can be the mouth!

1 Make sentences

1. Mr Jackson	+	is	+	going to	+	clear out the garage together.
2. He and Terry		is not				buy old junk.
3. Terry		are				be a funny face.
4. People		are not				need some help this morning.
5. The kite						fly the kite.
6. The girl						keep the old skateboard.

2 What are you going to do with it?

A: **What are you going to** do with that old bath?

B: I'm going to wash my dog in it.

old box
old drum
skateboard with no wheels
…
mend it
wake everyone up!
make a shelf with it
…

3 Summer fun?

Make the correct 'going to' forms with the verbs on the right.

not buy | fall | be | rain | get | not win

4 Terry's plans for next week

Take turns to ask and answer questions about Terry's plans for next week. You can ask questions with and without question words.

Examples:

A: **When is he going to** visit Mudchute?
B: He's going to do that on Friday.

A: **Is he going to** go swimming with Tiger?
B: **No, he isn't.** He's going to go with his father.

When is he going to … ?

Where is he going to … ?

What is he going to do on … ?

Monday:
get birthday present for Tiger
Tuesday:
play basketball
Wednesday:
clear out shed
Thursday:
go swimming with Dad
Friday:
visit Mudchute
Saturday:
look for new poster for shed
Sunday:
meet Lisa – 2 o'clock

5 Your turn: What are you going to do?

Talk about what you are going to do …

… after school today.
… next weekend.
… on your next birthday.
… in the holidays.
…

Example:

A: What are you going to do this evening?
B: Not much. I'm just going to listen to music.
C: I'm going to watch TV.
D: Me, too! What are you going to watch?

Mediation

Wenn man zum ersten Mal dolmetscht oder übersetzt, möchte man jedes einzelne Wort in die andere Sprache übertragen. Das geht selten gut, denn die englische und die deutsche Sprache drücken ein und dieselbe Sache manchmal ganz anders aus.
Damit du lernst, wie man richtig übersetzt oder dolmetscht, bekommst du in der Folge viele nützliche Tipps. Außerdem sind einige Problemstellen gelb angemalt, um dir bei den Übungen zu helfen.

UNIT 1 Im Pausenhof

Du triffst eine englische Gastschülerin im Pausenhof.
Wie könnte euer erstes Gespräch aussehen?

MEDIATION SKILLS

Wenn wir miteinander sprechen, benützen wir häufig feststehende Redewendungen. Du brauchst also oft nicht zu überlegen, wie die einzelnen Wörter im Englischen heißen. Du musst dich nur einfach an die gesamte Redewendung erinnern. Zum Beispiel: „Wie heißt du?" heißt *"What's your name?"*, „Wie geht's dir?" heißt *"How are you?"* und „Wo kommst du her?" heißt *"Where are you from?"*.

Example: You: *(Du sagst "Hallo", stellst dich vor und fragst die Schülerin, wie sie heißt.)*
Susanne: Hello, I'm Susanne. What's your name?

Fiona: Hello. My name is Fiona.
You: *(Du fragst, wo sie herkommt.)*
Fiona: I'm from Greenwich. That's in London.
You: *(Du sagst, wo du herkommst, und fragst sie, wie alt sie ist.)*
Fiona: I'm 11. And how old are you?
You: *(Du sagst, wie alt du bist.)*
Fiona: Who's your tutor?
You: *(Du sagst den Namen deiner Klassenlehrerin / deines Klassenlehrers.)*
Fiona: And is she / he nice?
You: *(Du bejahst die Frage.)*
Fiona: Is this your English book?
You: *(Du verneinst und sagst, dass das dein Sammelordner für Englisch ist. Du fragst Fiona, ob sie einen Lieblingssport hat.)*
Fiona: My favourite sport is football.
You: *(Du sagst, dass Fußball auch dein Lieblingssport ist.)*
Fiona: OK. Let's play football!

UNIT 2 Regeln für euer Zimmer

Dein Brieffreund in London teilt sich ein Zimmer mit seinem Bruder. Schreib ihm, welche Regeln du und dein Bruder / deine Schwester vereinbart habt, damit ihr euch nicht auf die Nerven geht.

MEDIATION SKILLS

Beachte beim Dolmetschen, dass die Wortstellung im Englischen nicht so frei ist wie im Deutschen. Beim s-Genitiv musst du besonders aufpassen. Zum Beispiel: „das Handy deines Bruders" heißt *your **brother's** mobile*. Das Hauptwort mit dem s-Genitiv *(your **brother's** mobile)* kommt vor dem Gegenstand, den man besitzt. Im Deutschen ist es anders herum (das Handy *deines Bruders*).

Here are our rules:

1. Wechselt euch ab, wenn ihr den Computer benutzt.
2. Benutze dein eigenes Handy, benutze nicht das Handy deines Bruders / deiner Schwester.
3. Spiele laute Musik nicht, wenn dein Bruder / deine Schwester Hausaufgaben macht.
4. Nimm nicht die Schulsachen deines Bruders / deiner Schwester.
5. Spiele deine CDs nicht auf dem Discman deines Bruders / deiner Schwester.
6. Sei nett zu den Freunden deines Bruders / deiner Schwester.
7. Nimm nicht die T-Shirts deines Bruders / deiner Schwester.
8. Kläre Probleme mit deinem Bruder / deiner Schwester.
9. Hilf deinem Bruder / deiner Schwester, wenn er / sie Probleme mit dem Computer hat.

UNIT 3 Was machen wir heute?

Susan, eine Austauschschülerin aus Cardiff, besucht deine Familie. Noch kann sie wenig Deutsch. Du möchtest mit Susan etwas in eurer Stadt unternehmen. Euer Nachbarsjunge Philipp möchte mitgehen, aber er kann noch kein Englisch. Also musst du dolmetschen.

MEDIATION SKILLS

Beim Übertragen eines deutschen Satzes ins Englische gibt es meist mehrere Möglichkeiten. Wenn dir ein Wort nicht einfällt, überlege zuerst, ob du ein anderes mit ähnlicher Bedeutung kennst. Oder kannst du den Satz umschreiben, um die Schwierigkeit zu umgehen? Zum Beispiel: „Wie wär's mit Basketball?" kannst du mit *"How about basketball?"* gut übersetzen; oder etwas freier: *"Can we play basketball?"*

Susan: What can we do today?
You: …
Philipp: Gehen wir schwimmen!
You: …
Susan: Oh no, that's boring.
You: …
Philipp: Gut, dann sag ihr, dass wir in den Park gehen können. Wie wär's mit einem Picknick?
You: …
Susan: Fine. What can we do in the park after the picnic?
You: …
Philipp: Wie wär's mit Basketball? Basketball ist mein Lieblingssport.
You: …
Susan: Basketball is OK but it's boring with just three people.
You: …
Philipp: Gut. Dann lass uns in der Stadt Fahrrad fahren.
You: …
Susan: OK. Is there a bike for me?
You: …
Philipp: Ja, du kannst das Fahrrad meines Bruders nehmen.
You: …
Susan: Great! What can we do in the evening?
You: …
Philipp: Ich habe Hausaufgaben auf. Aber ihr könnt danach zu mir kommen. Wie wär's mit acht Uhr?
You: …

UNIT 4 Ein Ausflug zur Cutty Sark

Stell dir vor, du bist in Greenwich und möchtest die *Cutty Sark* sehen. Du sprichst mit der Frau am Empfang deines Hotels.

MEDIATION SKILLS

Erinnerst du dich? Wenn du eine Frage ohne *to be, have/has + got* oder ohne *can* stellen möchtest, gebrauchst du die *to do*-Umschreibung. Das vergisst man leicht beim Dolmetschen oder Übersetzen. Doch ohne *to do* bei Fragen und Verneinungen geht es nicht. Zum Beispiel: „Wissen Sie, wo …?" heißt *"Do you know where …?"*

You: *(Du entschuldigst dich und fragst die Frau, ob sie dir helfen kann.)*
Woman: Sure, and how can I help you?
You: *(Du fragst, wo sich die Cutty Sark befindet.)*

Woman: It's in Greenwich near the River Thames.
You: *(Du fragst, was du dort machen kannst und wann die Cutty Sark geöffnet hat.)*
Woman: It's a museum now and it's open from 10 to 5. You can see the ship and listen to stories about the sea there.
You: *(Du fragst, ob der Bus zur Cutty Sark fährt.)*
Woman: No, the buses don't go to the Cutty Sark.
You: *(Du fragst, ob sie den Weg zur Cutty Sark kennt.)*
Woman: Yes, I do. You can walk! Here – I can show you on the map.
You: *(Du fragst, ob sie weiß, wo das Tourismusbüro ist.)*

Woman: The tourist information centre is opposite the Cutty Sark. You can get brochures there. Can I help you to find other sights in Greenwich?
You: *(Du fragst, wie du zur Isle of Dogs kommen kannst.)*
Woman: You can walk there from the Cutty Sark. The Greenwich Foot Tunnel goes under the Thames.
You: *(Du bedankst dich und verabschiedest dich.)*
Woman: You're welcome. Bye!

UNIT 5 Beim Einkaufen

Du machst Urlaub in London mit deiner Großmutter. Ihr wollt ein Geburtstagsgeschenk für deinen großen Bruder kaufen. Ihr geht ins Geschäft, aber du musst für deine Großmutter dolmetschen, weil sie kein Englisch kann.

MEDIATION SKILLS

Im Deutschen kann man mit dem Präsens Handlungen ausdrücken, die gewohnheitsmäßig oder gerade im Moment stattfinden. Im Englischen muss man je nach Situation *simple present* oder *present progressive* verwenden. Also aufgepasst! Zum Beispiel: *Emma often buys T-shirts.* (Das macht sie oft.) *She is buying a T-shirt now.* (Das tut sie gerade.)

Assistant: Hello. Can I help you?
You: …
Großmutter: Hallo. Wir suchen ein Geburtstagsgeschenk für seinen Bruder.
You: …
Assistant: That's nice, for your brother. How old is he?
You: He's 14 years old.
Großmutter: Wie wär's mit einem T-Shirt?
You: …
Assistant: We've got nice T-shirts and sweatshirts. What's his size – medium, large or extra large?
You: …
Großmutter: Seine Größe ist „large". Frag bitte nach dem Preis der T-Shirts und Sweatshirts.
You: …
Assistant: The sweatshirts are £ 18, and the T-shirts are £ 12.50.
You: …
Großmutter: Die Sweatshirts sind teuer. Aber ein T-Shirt ist in Ordnung.
You: …
Assistant: Look at these T-shirts. We've got them in lots of colours.
You: …
Großmutter: Sein Bruder mag schwarz. Er kauft keine anderen Farben.
You: …
Assistant: No problem. The black T-shirts are next to the jeans – where the boy with the red T-shirt is standing now. Please come with me. Here – here's a nice black T-shirt.
You: …
Großmutter: Ja – dieses T-Shirt sieht gut aus. Haben Sie es in Größe L?
You: …
Assistant: Yes, and here it is. That's £ 12.50.
You: *(Du sagst, das ist in Ordnung. Du bedankst dich.)*
Assistant: You're welcome.

UNIT 6 Urlaub in Cornwall

Du hast einen Brieffreund in Cornwall und schaust dir im Internet die Homepage von Penzance an. Dort kannst du dir einen Informationstext des Tourismusbüros anhören. Der Ort gefällt dir immer besser, je mehr du über Penzance erfährst. Du willst deinen Eltern davon berichten.
Sollten sich deine Eltern für Penzance als Urlaubsziel entscheiden, musst du ein Formular im Internet auf Englisch ausfüllen, um euch beim örtlichen Tourismusbüro anzumelden.

MEDIATION SKILLS

Wenn du einen Text für jemanden zusammenfassen willst, brauchst du nicht jedes einzelne Wort oder jeden Satz zu übersetzen. Das tust du nur sinngemäß. So ist es auch in diesem Fall: Wenn du deine Eltern überzeugen willst, wirst du nicht den gesamten Text über Penzance übersetzen. Das wäre ziemlich langweilig! Also musst du die wichtigsten Informationen herausziehen. Zuerst sagst du natürlich, dass du deinen nächsten Familienurlaub gerne in Penzance verbringen möchtest. Du erklärst deinen Eltern, wo das liegt. Dann erzählst du von den schönen Stränden …

a) *Hör dir den Text ein- bis zweimal an. Fasse ihn dann wie oben beschrieben zusammen.*

b) *Wie musst du das E-Mail-Formular für das zuständige Tourismusbüro ausfüllen, um euch anzumelden und um weiteres Informationsmaterial zu bekommen?*

Penzance Internet booking form[1]

Name:		Date of arrival[2]:	
Address:		Date of departure[3]:	
E-mail-address:		Number of nights[4]:	
Phone number:		Number of people:	
Fax number:		Sights interested in[5]:	
			Submit[6]

[1]**booking form** ['bʊkɪŋ fɔ:m] = Buchungsformular • [2]**date of arrival** [deɪt‿əv ə'raɪvl] = Ankunftsdatum • [3]**date of departure** [deɪt‿əv dɪ'pɑ:tʃə] = Abreisedatum • [4]**number of nights** ['nʌmbər‿əv naɪts] = Anzahl der Übernachtungen • [5]**sights interested in** [saɪts 'ɪntrəstɪd‿ɪn] = Sehenswürdigkeiten, für die man sich interessiert • [6]**(to) submit** [səb'mɪt] = *hier:* absenden

UNIT 7 Haustier im Cyberspace

Eine Freundin von dir möchte im Internet ein Cyberpet adoptieren und hat einen Text heruntergeladen, aber sie versteht nicht alles. Kannst du ihr helfen, damit sie ein Cyberpet bekommt und damit umgehen kann?

MEDIATION SKILLS

Fähigkeiten, Regeln und Verbote werden im Englischen mit *can, must* und *mustn't* ausgedrückt. Diese Modalverben sind manchmal nicht leicht zu übersetzen. Insbesondere der Unterschied von *mustn't* und *needn't* muss dir klar sein. Falls du unsicher bist, schau dir nochmals G 40 in der Grammatik an!

1. *Lies dir zuerst diesen Text ganz durch.*

Would you like your own little cyberpet? You needn't worry. We have got the right cyberpet for you! Take one from our list. Choose a name for your cyberpet, and then you are its owner. You can do things with your cyberpet in cyberspace[1]. Take it for a walk[2] outside. You can go to the park with your cyberpet, too. Play games with your cyberpet. Look after it online. Be nice to your cyberpet. Feed and wash it every day. You can go shopping for your cyberpet at the Internet pet shop. You sometimes need money because your pet must go to the vet. Every week we give you £ 20 cybermoney[3] for food etc. We can see how you look after your pet. When you cannot go online every day, you must put it in a holiday home. You mustn't forget your cyberpet. We can take cyberpets away from bad owners, and we give good owners a prize. All the best[4] for you and your cyberpet!

2. *Du möchtest die Informationen dieses Texts kurz für deine Freundin zusammenfassen.*
   Suche und schreibe dazu alle Sätze mit ***can*** *und* ***must / mustn't*** *heraus.*
3. *Übersetze nur diese Sätze schriftlich.*
4. *Sag deiner Freundin nun, was sie für das Cyberpet tun kann und was sie für das Cyberpet tun muss.*

[1]**cyberspace** ['saɪbəspeɪs] = Cyberspace; künstlicher Raum • [2]**take it for a walk** [teɪk ɪt fər‿ə 'wɔ:k] = geh mit ihm spazieren • [3]**cybermoney** ['saɪbəmʌni] = Cybergeld • [4]**all the best** [ɔ:l ðə 'best] = alles Gute

⟨A project⟩ Animals (after Unit 7)

Projects

Group projects are a good idea. You can get a lot of information about a topic[1] in your group. Then you can tell everyone in your class about your topic. And group projects are fun!

START HERE

Before you start a project in English, collect useful words and phrases for your topic. Make a word web with a partner:

animals
- how they live
- what they eat
- what they look like: brown, small …
- where they live
- …

GROUP SKILLS

1. Make groups of 4 or 5 pupils.
2. Look at the map and choose an animal for your group.
3. Look at the penguin[2] poster on the next page. Your job is: Make a poster like this for *your* animal.
4. Talk about this: Where can you find information for your project (your school books, magazines, your library[3], Internet, ask other teachers …)?
5. Find out everything about your animal. Everyone in your group has got a special little job!
6. Put your information on a poster. The poster can have pictures, short texts, lists, a vocabulary box. Don't forget: Make the vocabulary box BIG – everyone in your class wants to read the new words.
7. You can tell them a funny or sad story about your animal, too.

Then you **present**[4] your project to your class (next page).

[1]**topic** ['tɒpɪk] = Thema • [2]**penguin** ['peŋgwɪn] = Pinguin • [3]**library** ['laɪbrəri] = Bibliothek, Bücherei • [4]**(to) present** [prɪ'zent] = präsentieren, vorstellen

Group X – THE PENGUIN

- *Where does the penguin live?*
  It lives in the Antarctic[5] and loves the water. It is very cold near the South Pole[6].
- *What does it look like? How big/small is it?*
  The penguin is a bird, but it does not fly. It is small, under one metre[7], but the emperor[8] penguin is 1.2 m.
  It sits upright[9] – that can look very funny!
  It has got long wings[10] and a long beak[11].
- *What does it eat?*
  It eats fish, fish, fish and …
- *How many babies[12] has it got? How does it look after them?*
  The mother penguin lays[13] two eggs, and the parents look after the young penguins. The emperor penguins have even got a pouch[14] to protect[15] the eggs and the young penguins.
- *What is special about it?*
  (How fast is it, how long can it be without[16] food …)
  The penguin is slow on land[17] but fast in and under the water! A penguin can go without food for many weeks.

Vocabulary:
Antarctic, the South Pole, metre, emperor, upright, wing, beak, fish, baby, to lay, pouch, to protect, without, on land

YOUR PRESENTATION[18]

- Everybody in your group should present one part to your class.
- Don't just read your texts. Talk about what is on your poster.
- Use the Useful phrases for your presentation.
- Practise[19] your presentation before you present your project.
- Explain the new words in the vocabulary box.

USEFUL PHRASES

Here are some useful phrases for your presentation:

I'd/We'd like to tell you about … today.
Our presentation is about …
First we'd like to tell you about …
This is Susanne's job: … After that … Then …
Here is a picture of …/This picture shows you …
This list tells you …
These words in the vocabulary box can help you: … means …
Is everything clear?
Have you got any questions?

[5] **Antarctic** [æn'tɑ:ktɪk] = Antarktis • [6] **pole** [pəʊl] = Pol • [7] **metre** ['mi:tə] = Meter • [8] **emperor** ['emprə] = Kaiser • [9] **upright** ['ʌpraɪt] = aufrecht • [10] **wing** [wɪŋ] = Flügel • [11] **beak** [bi:k] = Schnabel • [12] **baby** ['beɪbi] = Junges • [13] **lay** [leɪ] = legen • [14] **pouch** [paʊtʃ] = Beutel • [15] **(to) protect** [prə'tekt] = schützen • [16] **without** [wɪ'ðaʊt] = ohne • [17] **on land** [ɒn 'lænd] = an Land • [18] **presentation** [ˌprezn'teɪʃn] = Präsentation, Vortrag • [19] **(to) practise** ['præktɪs] = üben

⟨A calendar⟩ Around the year[1]

People in Britain and people in Germany celebrate[2] the same religious holidays[3]. You know Christmas[4] and Easter[5]! But in Britain some of these holidays are different. And there are special days in Britain, too.

1 Valentine's Day[6] – February

On Valentine's Day in Britain you write a card to a girl or boy that you love. Sometimes it is a secret love[7]! Then you do not write your name on the card. The girl or boy must guess your name.

Make a Valentine's Day card.

2 Red Nose Day[9] – March

On this day a lot of people in Britain put on[10] a red nose and do funny things for charity[11]. Very many schools in Britain take part[12]. The pupils do funny things (they sing or wash all the teachers' cars) and collect money for charity. Famous pop stars and people on TV collect money, too. Red Nose Day is a big fund-raising[13] day. The money goes to poor[14] people in Britain and in other places. On Red Nose Day you have fun and help poor people, too. Red Nose Day is a British idea but many people in other countries celebrate it now, too.

Do you know any charities in your country?

3 A song: We wish[15] you a Merry Christmas[16]

We wish you a Merry Christmas, we wish you a Merry Christmas,
We wish you a Merry Christmas and a Happy New Year.
Chorus[17]: Good tidings[18] we bring to you and your kin[19],
We wish you a Merry Christmas and a Happy New Year.

[1]**around the year** [əˈraʊnd ðə ˈjɪə] = durch das Jahr • [2]**celebrate** [ˈseləbreɪt] = feiern • [3]**religious holiday** [rɪˈlɪdʒəs ˌhɒlədeɪ] = religiöser Feiertag • [4]**Christmas** [ˈkrɪsməs] = Weihnachten • [5]**Easter** [ˈiːstə] = Ostern • [6]**Valentine's Day** [ˈvæləntaɪnz deɪ] = Valentinstag • [7]**secret love** [ˈsiːkrət lʌv] = heimliche Liebe • [8]**(to) think of** [ˈθɪŋk‿əv] denken an • [9]**Red Nose Day** [red ˈnəʊz deɪ] = Tag der roten Nasen • [10]**(to) put on** [pʊt ˈɒn] = aufsetzen • [11]**charity** [ˈtʃærɪti] = guter Zweck • [12]**(to) take part** [teɪk ˈpɑːt] = sich beteiligen • [13]**fund-raising** [ˈfʌndˌreɪzɪŋ] = Wohltätigkeits- • [14]**poor** [pɔː] = arm • [15]**(to) wish** [wɪʃ] = wünschen • [16]**Merry Christmas** [ˌmeri ˈkrɪsməs] = Frohe Weihnachten • [17]**chorus** [ˈkɔːrəs] Refrain • [18]**tidings** [ˈtaɪdɪŋz] = Neuigkeiten • [19]**kin** [kɪn] = Familie

4 Christmas – 25th December

First, what do you know about Christmas?

Christmas Eve[20] (24th December): Parents tell their little children: In the night[21] Father Christmas[22] puts small presents in your stockings[23].

Christmas Day (25th December): In the morning the children open their stockings. Then they go downstairs and open the other presents under the Christmas tree.

Christmas dinner[24]:
Dinner is always on 25th December. It is great fun and always at lunchtime. Everyone in the family puts on paper hats[25] and pulls crackers[26]. For Christmas dinner there is usually a turkey[27] and plum pudding[28].

Other British Christmas traditions[29]: People in Britain always write a lot of Christmas cards. They usually hang them up[30] in the living room.

What is the same and what is different about Christmas in Britain and Germany?

5 Hands on

In groups, find information about one of the other special days or religious holidays in Britain. You can use the Internet or books from the library[31]. Collect the information for your English folder.

6 What do you do?

With a partner, talk about a special day or religious holiday where you live. What do you and your family do on that day?

USEFUL PHRASES

Let's talk about …	We always celebrate …
My favourite day is … because …	No, I don't like … / It's fun to …
What does your family do?	We never …

[20] **Christmas Eve** [ˌkrɪsməs ˈiːv] = Heiligabend • [21] **in the night** [ɪn ðə ˈnaɪt] während der Nacht • [22] **Father Christmas** [ˌfɑːðə ˈkrɪsməs] = Weihnachtsmann • [23] **stocking** [ˈstɒkɪŋ] = Strumpf • [24] **Christmas dinner** [ˌkrɪsməs ˈdɪnə] = Mittagessen am ersten Weihnachtsfeiertag • [25] **paper hat** [ˈpeɪpə ˌhæt] = Papierhut • [26] **(to) pull crackers** [pʊl ˈkrækəz] = Knallbonbons aufreißen • [27] **turkey** [ˈtɜːki] = Truthahn • [28] **plum pudding** [ˌplʌm ˈpʊdɪŋ] = *traditionelle Weihnachtsnachspeise* • [29] **tradition** [trəˈdɪʃn] = Tradition • [30] **(to) hang up** [hæŋ ˈʌp] = aufhängen • [31] **library** [ˈlaɪbrəri] = Bibliothek, Bücherei

⟨A play⟩ Turn[1] again, Whittington! (after Unit 6)

Place: London **Time:** The year 1380

Characters[2]:

Two storytellers[3]

1 Barny Forge *(a farmer[4])*
2 Sissy Forge *(his daughter[5], 13)*
3 Dick Whittington, 11
4 Lady Anne Fitzwarren
5 George Buckingham *(her brother)*
6 Stouty Burke *(her old cook)*
7 Alice Fitzwarren *(her daughter, 11)*
8 Two pickpockets[6], 12 and 13
9 The bells[7] of Bow Church in London
10 Blacky, the fast cat

Storyteller 1 Hello, my friends, please come and see our play[8]! The place is London, not today, but 1380, let us say. It tells of Dick and of his cat. He makes money out of that – and soon he wears[9] the Lord Mayor's[10] hat[11].

Scene[12] one

Storyteller 2 We are in a village, near London. There are a lot of animals[13] there. *(loud animal sounds)* A man on a horse[14] stops near a house.

Sissy Forge Good morning, good morning. What can I do for you?

Buckingham Can you tell me the way to London, please?

Sissy Yes, I can. But it isn't easy to find. Dick can show you the way. Dick! Dick!

Dick I'm coming! What's up, Sissy?

Sissy Can you show this man the road to London? He doesn't know the way.

Dick Sure! They say: There's gold[15] on the streets of London and all the houses are big – is that true?

Buckingham *(laughs)* Well, there are a lot of big houses in London but there isn't any gold on the streets. And the smell of London is terrible! Yuk! *(He makes funny sounds.)* But it's my town and I love the place. *(They walk together.)*

Dick Here we are now. Go over the river and the London Road is behind those trees.

Buckingham Thank you. *(throwing him a gold coin[16])* That's for your help.

Dick Wow! A gold coin! Thank you. Bye!

Barny Hey, Dick! What are you doing? Why aren't you working?

Dick Oh, hello, Mr Forge. I'm going home.

Barny Going home? What about the animals? You sleep in my kitchen, eat at my table and then you don't work. Pack your things and *go*!

Dick But…but where can I go, Mr Forge? I haven't got any family.

Barny That's your problem! *(shouts)* You can sort it out, you terrible boy!

[1] **(to) turn** [tɜ:n] = sich umdrehen • [2] **characters** ['kærəktəz] = Personen • [3] **storyteller** ['stɔ:ritelə] = Erzähler / -in • [4] **farmer** ['fɑ:mə] = Bauer, Bäuerin • [5] **daughter** ['dɔ:tə] = Tochter • [6] **pickpocket** ['pɪkˌpɒkɪt] = Taschendieb / -in • [7] **bell** [bel] = Glocke • [8] **play** [pleɪ] = Theaterstück • [9] **(to) wear** [weə] = tragen, anhaben • [10] **Lord Mayor** [lɔ:d 'meə] = Oberbürgermeister / -in • [11] **hat** [hæt] = Hut • [12] **scene** [si:n] = Szene • [13] **animal** ['ænɪml] = Tier • [14] **horse** [hɔ:s] = Pferd • [15] **gold** [gəʊld] = Gold • [16] **coin** [kɔɪn] = Münze

Scene two

Storyteller 1 Dick wants to go to London. He gets there after two days. Dick is very hungry[17]. He looks at his gold coin, but suddenly –

1st pickpocket Watch out, you!

2nd pickpocket Sorry! We're in a hurry.

Dick Wait! Where's my gold coin? I know – one of those boys has got it! Stop!

Pickpockets We haven't got your gold coin!

Stouty Burke What's up? Who's got a gold coin?

Dick They've got it. But it's *my* coin.

Stouty OK, boys! Give him his coin.

1st pickpocket What gold coin? We haven't got it.

Stouty Show me your hands[18].

1st pickpocket See! He's right!

Stouty And now your pockets[19]. Aha! A gold coin! That's funny. You haven't got it? So what's this, then? *(giving the coin to Dick)* Here you are, boy.

2nd pickpocket We're sorry, but we're hungry.

Stouty You've got a problem. – OK – here's an apple for you.

Pickpockets Mmm! Thank you. Bye!

Dick How can I thank you?

Stouty Hmm. You can come and help me in the kitchen. I work for a very important family and today I must cook[20] for the Lord Mayor.

Dick The Lord *who*?

Stouty The Lord Mayor of London. He's a very rich and very important man.

Dick Oh! Then I want to be Lord Mayor one day[21]!

Stouty What, *you*? *(laughs)* But you've got only one gold coin. The Lord Mayor is a very rich man.

Dick Well, I'm young and I can work.

Stouty *(laughs)* Come on!

Scene three

Storyteller 2 Dick helps the cook in the kitchen and then Dick wants to sleep. The cook shows him a bed in the kitchen. But there are mice there, and Dick can't sleep. In the morning Dick goes to a shop and takes four bags[22] back to the house. *(Dick puts the bags on the big table in the kitchen.)*

Cat Meow[23]! Meow!

Dick *(looks in one of the bags)* Oh, it's a little black cat! How sweet. What's your name? Hey! Where are you going? Are you hungry? Let's see … . Where are you? Oh! Behind the cupboard! What's that? Oh, it's a big mouse. Good cat. Come on! You can sleep here with me. But I can't call you 'Cat'. What about 'Blacky'? Do you like that name?

Cat Purr! Purr!!

Storyteller 2 Then Blacky catches a lot of mice and Dick can sleep.

Dick Zzzzzz.

[17] **hungry** ['hʌŋgri] = hungrig • [18] **hand** [hænd] = Hand • [19] **pocket** ['pɒkɪt] = Hosentasche • [20] **(to) cook** [kʊk] = kochen • [21] **one day** [ˌwʌn 'deɪ] = eines Tages • [22] **bag** [bæg] = Sack • [23] **meow!** [miːˈaʊ] = miau!

Scene four

Storyteller 1 One day Stouty Burke goes home to his family in Wales. A new cook comes. He doesn't like Dick and he doesn't like cats – Dick is not happy. He goes away. In the morning Dick and Blacky are sleeping outside near a big church. It's six o'clock and the bells are ringing. *(Dick wakes up.)*

Dick Listen, Blacky! The bells are talking. What are they saying?

Blacky Purr! Purr!!

Bells (Chorus)[24] Turn again, Whittington, Lord Mayor of London! Turn again, Whittington, Lord Mayor of London! Turn again, Whittington, Lord Mayor of London!

Dick Come on, Blacky! I want to be Lord Mayor one day and a Lord Mayor doesn't run away from problems! Let's go back and tell Lady Anne about the cook. Maybe she can find me a job in a friend's house.

Scene five

Storyteller 2 Dick goes back to the Fitzwarrens' house with Blacky. He goes into the living room. Lady Anne's brother is there, too. Suddenly Lady Anne screams[25].

Lady Anne *(standing on a chair)* Ah! Ah! There's a mouse! It wants the cake!

Buckingham *(laughs)* Oh, Anne! I've got thousands of mice on my ship.

Alice Please, Uncle George. Catch it!

Dick Oh, wait, we can help. Catch it, Blacky! Good cat! Bring it here! *(Blacky comes with the mouse, first to Lady Anne; she makes a funny face.)*

Lady Anne Oh! Uh, thank you, Dick. And thank *you*, Blacky.

Cat Purr! Purr!

Buckingham Dick? I know you. You showed me[26] the road to London.

Dick Yes, that's right.

Buckingham You've got a very fast cat here. Can I buy her for my ship? Here are three gold coins for her.

Blacky Meow! Meow! Meow! *(Blacky runs to Dick.)*

Dick I'm sorry, but Blacky is my friend and I love her. I can't sell her to you.

Buckingham Well, can I borrow[27] her? There are a lot of mice on my ship. They eat the silk[28]. You can have a gold coin for every ten mice that she catches[29]. She can come back to you soon.

Blacky Purr! Purr!!

Dick Well, thank you. Blacky likes the idea. It's time for a big, big trip, Blacky! – Uh, Lady Anne. Can I talk to you about the new cook, please … ?

Scene six

Storyteller 1 Stouty Burke soon comes back from Wales and Dick is very happy. Alice Fitzwarren likes Dick and sometimes she goes to the market with him and the cook. One day they see a big coach[30]. It's gold and black.

Dick Wow! A gold coach! I want to ride in a gold coach.

Stouty That isn't for people like you and me, Dick. That's the Lord Mayor's coach.

Dick Then I want to be Lord Mayor one day, too.

[24] **chorus** ['kɔːrəs] = Chor • [25] **(to) scream** [skriːm] = schreien, kreischen • [26] **you showed me** [ju 'ʃəʊd mi] = du hast mir gezeigt • [27] **(to) borrow** ['bɒrəʊ] = ausleihen • [28] **silk** [sɪlk] = Seide • [29] **… that she catches** [ðət ʃi 'kætʃɪz] = … die sie fängt • [30] **coach** [kəʊtʃ] = Kutsche

Alice I know, Dick. But you can't read and write.
Dick I can learn to read and write. A, B, C, D, E, uh, H … Hey, that coach is going very fast! Watch out, Alice! Alice!
Alice *(Dick pushes[31] her to the side[32] of the road)* Arrgh!
Stouty Are you OK?
Alice Yes, I'm OK now. Whew! These coaches are scary.
Stouty Can you get up?
Alice Yes, I can. Thank you, Dick. You saved my life[33]!

Scene seven

Storyteller 2 Stouty and Dick bring Alice to her mother. Lady Anne's brother is there again.
Lady Anne Come in! Ah, hello, children! Hello, Stouty.
Buckingham Alice! What –?
Alice Hello, Uncle George! Mum, a fast coach came[34] down the road. Dick pushed[35] me away and saved my life.
Lady Anne Oh, my dear! Dick, how can we thank you?
Alice I've got an idea, Mum. Dick wants to learn to read and write. Can we teach him?
Lady Anne Is that right, Dick?
Dick Yes, it is, Lady Anne.
Lady Anne Let me talk to Lord Fitzwarren about it. But first my brother wants to talk to you.
Buckingham Hello, young man. Here's your cat. *(giving him a bag)* And your gold coins are in this bag.
Dick Hello, Mr Buckingham. Blacky! *(shouting, is very happy)* Hooray! You're back!
Blacky Purr! Purr! Purr!!
Dick *(looks in the bag)* Wow – there are a lot of gold coins here.
Buckingham Because Blacky caught[36] a lot of mice. And I can sell my silk now for a lot of money.
Lady Anne You can put your money in a bank[37], Dick. And one day you can buy a house in London.
Dick No, Lady Anne. Please take my gold coins and borrow my cat again, Mr Buckingham. And please buy silk with the coins. Then you can sell the silk for me for a lot of money.
Buckingham *(laughs)* OK, Dick! What a boy[38]!

Storyteller 1 And this is where our story ends,
Of Dick and Blacky and their friends,
Of how a boy whose luck is down[39]
Is *thrice*[40] Lord Mayor of London Town!

Storyteller 2 Our Dick is soon a very rich man.
But this is not his only[41] plan[42].
A lot of people have no home,
And many kids are on their own[43].

They pick a pocket[44] just to eat,
Their only playground is the street.
So Dick gives money to the poor[45]
And helps them in this way[46] for sure[47].

[31]**(to) push** [pʊʃ] = schubsen, schieben • [32]**side** [saɪd] = Seite • [33]**you saved my life** [ju: 'seɪvd maɪ laɪf] = du hast mir das Leben gerettet • [34]**came** [keɪm] = kam • [35]**pushed** [pʊʃt] = hat geschubst / geschoben • [36]**caught** [kɔ:t] = hat gefangen • [37]**bank** [bæŋk] = Bank • [38]**what a boy** [wɒt‿ə 'bɔɪ] = was für ein Junge • [39]**whose luck is down** [hu:z lʌk‿ɪz 'daʊn] = der Pech hat • [40]**thrice** [θraɪs] = dreimal • [41]**only** ['əʊnli] = einziger • [42]**plan** [plæn] = Plan • [43]**on their own** [ɒn ðr‿'əʊn] = allein • [44]**(to) pick a pocket** [pɪk‿ə 'pɒkɪt] = Taschendiebstahl begehen • [45]**the poor** [ðə 'pɔ:] = die Armen • [46]**in this way** [ɪn 'ðɪs weɪ] = auf diese Weise • [47]**for sure** [fə 'ʃɔ:] = bestimmt, ganz sicher

Grammar

Liebe Schülerin, lieber Schüler,

in dem Bild herrscht völliges Durcheinander. Wenn man sich im Straßenverkehr nicht an die Regeln hält, kracht es. Wenn du dich in einer Sprache nicht an die Regeln hältst, dann könnte es sein, dass man dich falsch versteht.

Die Regeln, die den Verkehr ordnen, nennt man Straßenverkehrsordnung. Die Regeln der Sprache werden Grammatik (auf Englisch: *grammar)* genannt.
Im Grammatikteil deines Buches werden die Regeln zusammengefasst, die du aus dem Unterricht schon kennst.

Die Grammatik kann dir helfen,

- wenn du Hausaufgaben machst.
- wenn du dich auf einen Test oder eine Klassenarbeit vorbereitest.
- wenn du etwas nicht ganz verstanden hast.
- wenn du etwas wiederholen möchtest.
- wenn du etwas versäumt hast, weil du ein paar Stunden gefehlt hast.

Jeder Grammatikabschnitt hat eine Nummer, zum Beispiel G1, G2, mit einer deutlichen Überschrift (z. B. **Personalpronomen**), damit man weiß, worum es geht.

Jeder Abschnitt gehört zu bestimmten Seiten vorne in den Units. Diesen **Seitenverweis** (z. B. Seiten 10–14) findest du rechts oben vor jedem Grammatikabschnitt.
Meistens fängt ein Grammatikabschnitt mit einer kurzen **Einführung** an, die dir sagt, wie und wozu du die Formen verwenden kannst. Dann folgt eine **Übersicht** mit englischen Beispielen. Hinter den blauen Pfeilen ▶ stehen die **Regeln**. Diese Regeln müssen gelernt und natürlich befolgt werden.
An einigen Stellen findest du ein **!**. Hier stehen Dinge, auf die du ganz besonders achten musst.

Grammatical terms

English term	English example	Deutsche Bezeichnung / Übersetzung
adverb G20	We **often** play football at school.	Adverb / Umstandswort
auxiliary		Hilfsverb / Hilfszeitwort
can G16	**Can** you speak English?	können
must G39	We **must** make a poster.	müssen
mustn't G40	You **mustn't** make the animals nervous.	nicht dürfen
needn't G40	We **needn't** do any homework today.	nicht brauchen, nicht müssen
to be G1 bis G4	I **am**, she **is**, they **are**	sein
conjunctions G42	**and, but, because, so**	Konjunktionen / Bindewörter
definite article G6	**the** bag, **the** exercise	bestimmter Artikel / Begleiter
demonstrative pronoun G21	**This** is Terry. **Those** are your cards.	Demonstrativpronomen
do / don't G23 G24	**Do** you know him? – No, I **don't.**	*Do*-Umschreibung
does / doesn't G25 G26	**Does** he play the guitar? – No, he **doesn't**.	*Does*-Umschreibung
expressions of quantity G32 G33 G37	**much, many, a few, a little, some, any**	Mengenwörter
genitive		Genitiv / Wessen-Fall
s-genitive G10	Sam**'s** grandma, the girl**s'** mobiles	*s*-Genitiv
of-genitive G34	the name **of** the street	*of*-Genitiv
going to future G47	Terry is **going to** have fun.	*Going-to*-Futur / Zukunft
have got / has got G12 bis G14	We **have got** a new car. She**'s got** a dog.	haben / hat
imperative G15	**be** quiet, **don't use** your mobile	Imperativ / Befehlsform
indefinite article G5	**a** ball, **an** apple	unbestimmter Artikel / Begleiter
infinitive	**to play, to do**	Infinitiv / Grundform des Verbs
long forms	I **am**, it **is not**, he **has got**	Langformen des Verbs
negative (forms) G3 G13 G23 G25	She **isn't** here. I **can't** do it. He **doesn't** listen.	Verneinung
noun G7 G38	**book, mouse, classroom**	Nomen / Substantiv / Hauptwort
object G20	He plays **basketball.**	Objekt / Satzergänzung
object pronoun G22	**me, him, her** etc.	Objektform der Personalpronomen
ordinal numbers G28	the **first**, the **second**	Ordnungszahlen
personal pronoun G1	**I, you, he** etc.	Personalpronomen / persönliches Fürwort
plural G7 G38	book**s, men, children**	Plural / Mehrzahl
possessive determiner G11	**my, your, his, her, our, their**	Possessivbegleiter
present progressive G30 G31 G36	We **are winning**. **Are** you **listening**?	Verlaufsform der Gegenwart
question G4 G14 G24 bis G26 G31	**How old are** you? **Do you live** in London?	Frage
question word G9 G26	**What? When? Where?** etc.	Fragewort
short forms G2 G12	I**'m**, he **isn't**, we**'ve** got	Kurzformen des Verbs
simple past G43 bis G46	I **was**, she **asked**, he **went**	einfache Vergangenheit
simple present G18 G19 G36	She often **plays** football.	einfache Gegenwart
singular	**a** girl, **an** animal, **one** book	Singular / Einzahl
subject	**The children** are in the garden.	Subjekt / Satzgegenstand
verb	We **go** to school by bus.	Verb (Vollverb) / Zeitwort
word order G20 G41	**Lisa often plays football on Saturday.**	Satzstellung

Unit 1

IN DIESER UNIT LERNST DU

- ✓ wie man über Personen und Sachen sprechen kann. G1
- ✓ wie man die Formen von *to be* (sein) verwendet. G1 bis G4
- ✓ wie man *a/an* und *the* verwendet und ausspricht. G5 G6
- ✓ wie man im Englischen die Mehrzahl ausdrückt. G7 G8
- ✓ wie man mit *what, who, where* und *how* Fragen stellen kann. G9

G1 Die Personalpronomen und die Langformen von *to be*

The personal pronouns and the long forms of *to be*

Seiten 10–15

I, you, he, she, it, we, they sind die englischen Personalpronomen oder persönlichen Fürwörter (auf Deutsch: ich, du, er, sie, es, wir, ihr, sie).
To be (deutsch: sein) ist ein Verb. Bei den verschiedenen Personen hat es verschiedene Formen, genau wie im Deutschen. Die Form ***to be*** selbst ist der Infinitiv (die Grundform).

Singular	**I am**	twelve.	Ich bin	zwölf.
	You are	nice.	Du bist	nett.
	He is	my friend.	Er ist	mein Freund.
	She is	new here.	Sie ist	neu hier.
	It is	a big school.	Es ist	eine große Schule.
Plural	**We are**	at Thomas Tallis.	Wir sind	an der Thomas Tallis Schule.
	You are	OK, you two.	Ihr seid	in Ordnung, ihr zwei.
	They are	in the classroom.	Sie sind	im Klassenzimmer.

- ▶ Die Präsensformen (Formen der Gegenwart) von ***to be*** sind im Singular (in der Einzahl) ***am, are, is,*** im Plural (in der Mehrzahl) ***are.***
- ▶ ***I*** wird immer groß geschrieben.
- ▶ ***You*** kann **du, Sie** oder **ihr** heißen. ***You*** *are in my tutor group.* (**Du** bist …) ***You*** *are late, Mr Newman* (**Sie** sind …). ***You*** *are new, Lisa and Emma.* (**Ihr** seid …)
- ▶ Für eine männliche Person (z. B. *Terry, Mr Newman*) steht ***he***, für eine weibliche Person (z. B. *Lisa, Mrs Carter*) steht ***she***.
- ▶ Für Tiere, die man kennt und die einen Namen haben, verwendet man auch ***he*** oder ***she***. (*This is Tom.* ***He*** *is nice.*) Für Tiere, die man nicht kennt, sagt man ***it***.
- ▶ Für eine Sache steht immer ***it***. Im Deutschen ist dies anders: Da können **er, sie** oder **es** für Dinge stehen.

!

This is my football.	**It** is new.	**Er** ist neu.
The school is big. And	**it** is old.	… **sie** ist alt.
Here is the example.	**It** is right.	**Es** ist richtig.

G2 Die Kurzformen von *to be* The short forms of *to be*

Seiten 10–15

Die Formen von ***to be*** können als Langformen (siehe G1) oder als Kurzformen verwendet werden. Wenn man etwas schreibt, verwendet man meist die Langformen, wenn man spricht, meist die Kurzformen. Auch wenn man Gespräche aufschreibt oder an Freunde schreibt, verwendet man gewöhnlich die Kurzformen.

Wenn man Englisch spricht, wird oft eine Silbe verschluckt. So kann man schneller und flüssiger sprechen.

Langformen (long forms)			Kurzformen (short forms)				
I	**am**	at Thomas Tallis.	I▼**m** at Thomas Iallis. **a**	→	I	**'m**	at Thomas Tallis.
It	**is**	a nice school.	It▼**s** a nice school. **i**	→	It	**'s**	a nice school.
We	**are**	in the classroom.	We▼**re** in the classroom. **a**	→	We	**'re**	in the classroom.

▶ Ein Buchstabe wird „verschluckt". Wo der Buchstabe gewesen ist, schreibst du ein ' (einen Apostroph), um zu zeigen, dass etwas weggefallen ist.

	Die Kurzformen von *to be* (The short forms of *to be*)				
Singular	**I'm**	at Thomas Tallis.	Plural	**We're**	in the wrong room.
	You're	my friend.		**You're**	late, Sam and Terry.
	He's	from Greenwich.		**They're**	new here.
	She's	in my tutor group.			
	It's	a nice school.			

G3 Die Verneinung von *to be* The negation of *to be*

Seiten 14–15

Wenn du die Formen von ***to be*** verneinen möchtest, setzt du nach *am, is, are* einfach ***not*** ein: They are in the wrong room. + not → They are **not** in the right room.

	Langformen (long forms)			Kurzformen (short forms)		
Singular	I	**am not**	new here.	I	**'m not**	new here.
	You	**are not**	in my tutor group.	You	**aren't**	in my tutor group.
	He	**is not**	from Greenwich.	He	**isn't**	from Greenwich.
	She	**is not**	late.	She	**isn't**	late.
	It	**is not**	a scary school.	It	**isn't**	a scary school.
Plural	We	**are not**	on page five.	We	**aren't**	on page five.
	You	**are not**	from Bristol, Terry and Lisa.	You	**aren't**	from Bristol, Terry and Lisa.
	They	**are not**	my friends.	They	**aren't**	my friends.

- In der gesprochenen Sprache wird das ***not*** meist zu ***n't*** verkürzt und mit der Form von ***to be*** zusammengezogen *(**are not** → **aren't**, **is not** → **isn't**)*.
- Bei ***I*** (1. Person Singular) kann ***not*** jedoch nicht verkürzt werden *(I am not → **I'm** not)*.

G4 Fragen und Kurzantworten mit *to be*

Questions and short answers with *to be*

Seiten 14–15

Wenn du eine Frage mit den Formen von ***to be*** bilden möchtest, stellst du einfach Subjekt (Satzgegenstand) und Verb um. Das funktioniert genauso wie im Deutschen:

Terry **is** at Thomas Tallis.	**Terry** **ist** auf der Thomas Tallis Schule.
Is **Terry** at Thomas Tallis?	**Ist** **Terry** auf der Thomas Tallis Schule?

Frage	Kurzantwort	Kurzantwort
Am I late?	Yes, **you are**.	No, **you aren't**.
Are you eleven?	Yes, **I am**.	No, **I'm not**.
Is he at Thomas Tallis?	Yes, **he is**.	No, **he isn't**.
Is she from Cardiff?	Yes, **she is**.	No, **she isn't**.
Is it in your bag?	Yes, **it is**.	No, **it isn't**.
Are we on page 6?	Yes, **we are**.	No, **we aren't**.
Are you in my tutor group, Terry and Lisa?	Yes, **we are**.	No, **we aren't**.
Are they your friends?	Yes, **they are**.	No, **they aren't**.

- ***Yes*** und ***no*** allein klingen manchmal etwas unhöflich. Deshalb wird im Englischen häufig mit einem verkürzten Satz geantwortet (mit einer Kurzantwort oder ***short answer***).
- Bei den Ja-Antworten verwendet man immer die Langformen von ***to be*** *(am, is, are)*. Nur bei den Nein-Antworten stehen die Kurzformen.

!

Auf die Frage ***Is that …?*** antwortet man mit ***Yes, it is*** oder ***No, it isn't***, auch dann, wenn nach Personen gefragt wird, z. B.: Is **that** Mrs Carter? – Yes, **it** is.
Is **that** the caretaker? – No, **it** isn't.

G5 Der unbestimmte Artikel The indefinite article

Seite 16

Ein oder **eine** sind unbestimmte Artikel. Im Englischen heißen sie ***a*** oder ***an***.
Beispiel: Is that **a** ball? – Ist das ein Ball?

a [ə]			an [ən]		
Is that	**a**	ball?	No, it's	**an**	apple.
Here's	**a**	pencil.	And here's	**an**	exercise book.
That's	**a**	pencil-case.	Yes, it's	**an**	old pencil-case.

- Vor einem Konsonanten (einem Mitlaut) – *ball, pencil* – verwendet man ***a*** [ə].
- Vor einem Vokal (= *a, e, i, o*, manchmal *u*) – *apple, old* – verwendet man ***an*** [ən].

!

Es heißt ***a unit***, obwohl das Wort ***unit*** mit dem geschriebenen Vokal ‚u' beginnt. Die Aussprache ['ju:nɪt] entscheidet, nicht die Schreibung.

G6 Der bestimmte Artikel The definite article

Seite 16

Im Deutschen gibt es die drei bestimmten Artikel **der**, **die** und **das**. Im Englischen gibt es nur den einen bestimmten Artikel ***the***. ***The*** steht für männliche und weibliche Personen und für Sachen, im Singular und im Plural.

the [ðə]		the [ði]	
the	**b**ag	the	**e**xample
the	**n**ice apple	the	**e**xercise
the	**u**nit	the	**o**ld school

- Die Aussprache von ***the*** ist vor Vokalen [ði], ansonsten wird es [ðə] ausgesprochen
- Bei *unit* ['ju:nɪt] heißt es ***the*** [ðə] ***unit*** (vergleiche G5.)

G7 Die Pluralformen der Nomen The plural of nouns

Seite 17

Du kannst den Plural (Mehrzahl) der meisten englischen Nomen (Hauptwörter) bilden, indem du ein ***s*** direkt an die Singularform (Einzahlform) anhängst.

Singular (Einzahl)	Plural (Mehrzahl)
a book	two book**s**
one bag	three bag**s**
a page	five page**s**

[s]	[z]	[ɪz]
two boo**ks** [-ks]	two tr**ees** [-z]	two exerci**ses** [-zɪz]
three tutor grou**ps** [-ps]	five ba**gs** [-gz]	six sandwi**ches** [-dʒɪz]
four uni**ts** [-ts]	four frie**nds** [-dz]	ten pa**ges** [-dʒɪz]

- Nach den stimmlosen Lauten [p, t, k, f, θ] wird das Plural-*s* stimmlos (scharf) ausgesprochen [s].
- Nach Vokalen und stimmhaften Konsonanten [b, d, g, l, m, n, ð, v] wird das Plural-*s* stimmhaft (weich) ausgesprochen [z].
- Nach den Zischlauten [tʃ, dʒ, ʒ] wird die Pluralendung [ɪz] ausgesprochen und ***es*** geschrieben.

G8 There is ... / There are ...

Seite 18

Wenn du sagen möchtest, dass sich Personen oder Dinge irgendwo befinden, kannst du das mit ***there is*** oder ***there are*** tun. Es entspricht dem deutschen **es gibt** ... , **da sind** ... , **es liegen** ... oder **es stehen** ...

There is	a mouse in my classroom.	In meinem Klassenzimmer gibt es eine Maus.
There's	a nice boy in my group.	In meiner Gruppe ist ein netter Junge.
There are	five books on the table.	Da liegen fünf Bücher auf dem Tisch.
There are	four names on the board.	Es stehen vier Namen an der Tafel.

- ▶ ***There is*** (Kurzform: ***There's***) verwendest du, wenn es sich um **eine** Person oder Sache handelt.
- ▶ ***There are*** verwendest du, wenn es sich um **mehrere** Personen oder Dinge handelt.
- ▶ ***There is*** ... und ***There are*** ... stehen häufig am Anfang eines Satzes und leiten diesen ein.

G9 Die Fragewörter *where, who, what* und *how*

The question words *where, who, what* and *how*

Seite 19

Where	are you, Tom?	I'm under the chair.	Wo?
Where	's my book?	It's on the table.	
Where	are you **from**, Emma?	I'm from Bristol.	Woher?
Who	's that?	It's Mr Newman – the caretaker.	Wer?
Who	's always late?	That's Sam.	
What	's this, Tom?	It's my apple.	Was?
What	is this?	It is an apple.	
How	old are you, Terry?	I'm twelve.	Wie?

Du hast jetzt schon eine ganze Reihe von grammatischen Begriffen (Singular, Nomen usw.) gelernt. Weißt du noch, wo du diese Begriffe nachschlagen kannst?

!

Who fragt nach Personen. ***who?*** = wer?
Where fragt nach einem Ort. ***where?*** = wo?

In w***here*** steckt die Antwort ***here***.
Here steht für einen Ort.
Und in WH☺ ist ein Gesicht.
So kannst du dir das besser merken!

Unit 2

IN DIESER UNIT LERNST DU

- ✓ wie man sagt, dass Dinge zueinander gehören. G10
- ✓ wie man sagt, dass jemand etwas besitzt oder zu jemandem gehört. G11 G12 bis G14
- ✓ wie du auf Englisch sagen kannst, dass jemand etwas tun soll. G15
- ✓ und wie man sagt, dass jemand etwas kann. G16

G10 Der s-Genitiv
The s-genitive

Seite 28–29

Wenn du sagen möchtest, dass jemandem etwas gehört oder zugeordnet ist, kannst du das mit dem **s-Genitiv** tun. Er wird bei Personen und auch bei Tieren verwendet.

Singular	Sam	**'s**	grandma is nice.	Sams Oma …
	Mrs Carter	**'s**	computer is old.	Frau Carters …
	The cat	**'s**	name is funny.	Der Name **der** Katze …

▶ Im Singular hängst du zuerst einen Apostroph (') und dann ein **s** an das Nomen. Beachte die unterschiedliche Schreibung im Englischen und im Deutschen!
Sam's grandma – Sa**ms** Oma

Plural	The girl	**s'**	bikes are new.	Die Fahrräder **der** Mädchen …
	The sister	**s'**	bedroom is small.	Das Schlafzimmer **der** Schwestern …
	The Spencer	**s'**	flat is in Wendover Road.	Die Wohnung **der** Familie Spencer …

▶ Bei regelmäßigen Pluralformen mit der Endung ***s*** hängst du im Genitiv nur einen Apostroph (') an das ***s*** an. Die Aussprache des Nomens ändert sich dadurch nicht.

The **girl's** bike is new. ⟷

The **girls'** bikes are new.

G11 Die Possessivbegleiter
The possessive determiners

Seite 29

Mit den Possessivbegleitern kannst du ausdrücken, wem etwas gehört oder zu wem jemand gehört.

Personal pronouns		Possessive determiners	
I	'm from Greenwich.	**My**	name is Terry.
You	're in Year 7, Terry.	**Your**	tutor is Mrs Carter.
He	's twelve.	**His**	friend is eleven.
She	's in my tutor group.	**Her**	name is Lisa.
It	's the Brooks' flat.	**Its**	rooms are very small.
We	're in Year 7.	**Our**	classroom is nice.
You	're late, boys.	**Your**	bags aren't here.
They	're at Thomas Tallis School.	**Their**	school is in Greenwich.

▶ ***Your*** kann **dein, euer** oder **Ihr** heißen. Es kommt auf den Zusammenhang an:

I'm **your** new German teacher, Sam. – Ich bin **dein** …
I'm **your** tutor, boys and girls. – Ich bin **euer** …
Is this **your** pen, Mrs Carter? – Ist das **Ihr** …

you're	→ du bist → ihr seid	**You're** a nice cat, Tiger. **You're** funny, Tom and Tiger.
your	→ dein, euer	**Your** bag is under your chair, Sam.
he's [hi:z] **his** [hɪz]	→ er ist → sein	**He's** from Greenwich. **His** school is Thomas Tallis.
they're **their** **there**	→ sie sind → ihr → dort	**They're** our friends. **Their** caretaker is Mr Newman. **There's** an apple under the chair.
it's	→ er / sie / es ist	**It's** a nice computer shop.
its	→ sein, ihr	Mr Brook is **its** manager.

G12 Have got / has got

Seite 30–31

Wenn du sagen möchtest, dass jemand etwas **hat** oder **besitzt**, verwendest du das Verb ***have got*/*has got***. Z. B. ***I've got*** *an uncle in England.* – Ich habe einen Onkel in England. Auch von ***have got*** und ***has got*** gibt es Langformen und Kurzformen:

Langformen (long forms)			Kurzformen (short forms)		
I	**have got**	a small room.	I	**'ve got**	a small room.
You	**have got**	nice friends.	You	**'ve got**	nice friends.
He	**has got**	a new football.	He	**'s got**	a new football.
She	**has got**	a big sister.	She	**'s got**	a big sister.
It	**has got**	three bedrooms.	It	**'s got**	three bedrooms.
We	**have got**	a new English teacher.	We	**'ve got**	a new English teacher.
You	**have got**	two new folders.	You	**'ve got**	two new folders.
They	**have got**	five trees in their garden.	They	**'ve got**	five trees in their garden.

- Bei ***he, she, it*** (also in der 3. Person Singular) musst du ***has got*** verwenden.
- Ebenso wie bei den Formen von ***to be*** (vergleiche G1 und G2) benutzt man auch bei ***have got*/*has got*** die Langformen eher in der geschriebenen Sprache, die Kurzformen eher in der gesprochenen Sprache.

!

Verwechsle nicht die Kurzformen von ***has*** und ***is***:

She**'s** got a nice sister.	=	She **has** got a nice sister.
She**'s** nice.	=	She **is** nice.

G13 Die Verneinung von *have got / has got*

The negation of *have got / has got*

Seite 30–31

Have got und ***has got*** kannst du verneinen, indem du ***not*** zwischen ***have*** und ***got*** bzw. zwischen ***has*** und ***got*** einfügst.

Langformen (long forms)			Kurzformen (short forms)		
I	**have not got**	a computer.	I	**haven't got**	a small room.
You	**have not got**	a big room, Emma.	You	**haven't got**	a nice schoolbag.
He	**has not got**	a mobile.	He	**hasn't got**	a new football.
She	**has not got**	her English book.	She	**hasn't got**	a big sister.
It	**has not got**	a big garden.	It	**hasn't got**	three bedrooms.
We	**have not got**	a sofa in our classroom.	We	**haven't got**	a new English teacher.
You	**have not got**	your bags, Emma and Lisa.	You	**haven't got**	five trees in your garden.
They	**have not got**	a TV in their bedroom.	They	**haven't got**	new folders.

- In der gesprochenen Sprache wird ***not*** meist zu ***n't*** verkürzt und an ***have*** oder ***has*** angehängt. (Vergleiche die Verneinung der Formen von ***to be***, G3.)
- Ebenso wie bei den Formen von ***to be*** (Vergleiche G1 und G2) benutzt man auch bei ***have got/has got*** die Langformen eher in der geschriebenen Sprache, die Kurzformen eher in der gesprochenen Sprache.

G14 Fragen und Kurzantworten mit *have got / has got*

Questions and short answers with *have got / has got*

Seite 30–31

Wenn du Fragen mit ***have got*** und ***has got*** bilden möchtest, musst du einfach ***have*** oder ***has*** verschieben:

Terry **has got** a new mobile.

Has **Terry** **got** a new mobile?

Has und *Have* muss auf Wanderung gehen – *got* bleibt hinterm Subjekt stehen.

Have you **got**	a new mobile, Terry?	Yes, I **have**.
Has Emma **got**	a pink T-shirt?	Yes, she **has**.
Has Mr Brook **got**	a music shop?	No, he **hasn't**.
Has the Jacksons' house **got**	a big garden?	Yes, it **has**.
Have we **got**	a lot of time, Lisa?	No, we **haven't**.
Have the Taylors **got**	a flat in Holburne Road?	No, they **haven't**.

- Bei Fragen mit ***have got*** und ***has got*** stellt man ***have*** und ***has*** vor das Subjekt (Satzgegenstand). ***Got*** bleibt hinter dem Subjekt stehen.
- Bei den Kurzantworten wird ***got*** einfach weggelassen und nur ***have*** oder ***has*** wiederholt. Bei den bejahten Kurzantworten wird nur die Langform verwendet *(Yes, I have.)*. Bei den verneinten Kurzantworten gebraucht man meist die Kurzform *(No, she hasn't.)*. Das kennst du schon bei den Kurzantworten von ***to be***.
- Genau wie bei den Kurzantworten mit ***to be*** (vergleiche G4) klingen ***Yes, I have*** oder ***No, I haven't*** höflicher als nur ***Yes*** oder ***No***.

G15 Der Imperativ The imperative

Seite 32

Mit dem Imperativ (der Befehlsform) kannst du jemand auffordern, etwas zu tun oder nicht zu tun. Wie im Deutschen drückt der Imperativ eine Bitte, eine Warnung oder einen Befehl aus.

Open	your books, please.
Be	quiet, please.
Read	the sentence, please, Lisa.

- Den Imperativ (die Befehlsform) bildest du mit der Grundform des Verbs ohne *to*.

Don't	play football here, boys.
Don't	use your mobile in the classroom, Sam.
Don't	write in your English books, please.

- Der verneinte Imperativ wird mit ***don't*** gebildet (im geschriebenen Text: *do not*).

- Der Imperativ hat immer die gleiche Form, egal ob eine oder mehrere Personen angesprochen werden: ***Don't play** football in here.* – Spiel nicht … / Spielt nicht …

!

Der Imperativ ohne ***please*** klingt im Englischen oft unhöflich. Deshalb ist es besser, wenn du ***please*** zusammen mit der Befehlsform verwendest.

G16 Das modale Hilfsverb *can* The modal auxiliary *can*

Seite 32–33

Ein Hilfsverb ist ein Verb, das nicht allein ohne ein anderes Verb verwendet werden kann. Mit dem Hilfsverb ***can*** kannst du ausdrücken, dass jemand etwas tun **kann** oder **darf**.

I	**can**	say two words in Italian.
Terry	**can**	play in his shed.
We	**can**	do our homework in my room.
Tom	**cannot**	write his name on the board.
You	**can't**	play football in the classroom, Lisa.

Can you	help in the kitchen, please?	– Yes, I **can**.
Can I	help you with your homework?	– Oh yes, you **can**.
Can your friends	play the drums, Terry?	– No, they **can't**.

- Das modale Hilfsverb ***can*** bleibt in allen Personen gleich: *I can play/He can play.* Bei *he, she, it* bekommt es kein ***s***.
- ***Can*** steht immer mit der Grundform des Verbs ohne ***to***: *to play* → *we* ***can play***.
  Im Englischen steht das Verb immer direkt hinter ***can***, im Deutschen aber am Satzende:
  We ***can play*** *in the garden.* – Wir **können** im Garten **spielen**.
- Die verneinte Form von ***can*** [kæn] heißt ***can't*** [kɑːnt]. Beim Schreiben wird meistens die Langform ***cannot*** [ˈkænɒt] verwendet. *Cannot* wird immer zusammengeschrieben.
- Mit ***can*** kannst du auch jemanden fragen, ob du etwas tun darfst, oder jemanden bitten, etwas zu tun: *Can I help you? – Yes, you can. You can make the sandwiches.*

!

Während man im Deutschen **können** allein gebrauchen kann, muss im Englischen nach ***can*** immer ein Vollverb folgen:
Ich **kann** zwei Wörter auf Italienisch. – *I* ***can say*** *two words in Italian.*

Unit 3

IN DIESER UNIT LERNST DU

- ✓ die Uhrzeit auf Englisch. G17
- ✓ wie du auf Englisch sagen kannst, dass etwas in der Gegenwart regelmäßig, häufig oder nie geschieht. G18 G19
- ✓ wie du ausdrücken kannst, dass Ereignisse in der Gegenwart nacheinander ablaufen. G18 G19
- ✓ wie die Wortstellung in einem Satz ist und wo Angaben zur Zeit stehen. G20
- ✓ wie man *this, that* und *these, those* verwendet. G21

G17 Die Uhrzeit Telling the time

Seite 40–41

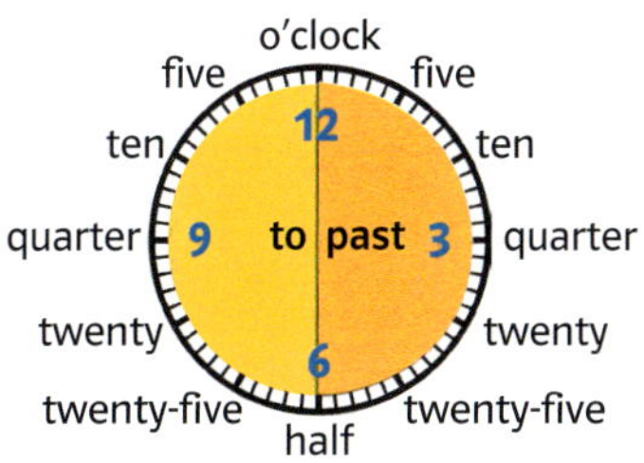

So kannst du auf Englisch Zeitangaben machen:

- Für die volle Stunde sagst du ***o'clock*** (10.00 : ***ten o'clock***).
- Für die ersten dreißig Minuten einer Stunde bezieht man sich auf die **vorhergehende** Stunde:
  10.05 : ***five past*** *ten* 10.15 : ***quarter past*** *ten* 10.30 : ***half past*** *ten*
- Bei den restlichen neunundzwanzig Minuten bezieht man sich auf die folgende Stunde:
  10.40 : ***twenty to*** *eleven* 10.45 : ***quarter to*** *eleven* 10.55: ***five to*** *eleven*

!

Vergleiche: 10.30 : englisch: ***half past ten***; deutsch: **halb elf**

- Bei Minutenangaben, die durch fünf teilbar sind (5, 10, 15 usw.), lässt man das Wort *minutes* meist weg. Bei allen anderen Zeitangaben muss *minutes* jedoch stehen: *It's 25 (minutes) past ten. – It's twenty-seven minutes past ten.*
- Du kannst die Uhrzeit aber auch ganz einfach ohne ***to*** und ***past*** angeben, ähnlich wie im Deutschen. In diesem Fall beziehen sich alle Zeitangaben auf die vorhergehende Stunde:

9.07	9.15	9.25	9.30	9.48
It's ***nine-oh-seven***	***nine fifteen***	***nine twenty-five***	***nine thirty***	***nine forty-eight***

- Im Englischen zählt man bei der Uhrzeit nur bis 12. Man fängt dann wieder mit eins für den Nachmittag an.
  Um Verwechslungen zu vermeiden, kann man die Zeitangaben von 0 bis 12 Uhr auch mit dem Zusatz ***am*** versehen. Die Zeitangaben von 12 bis 24 Uhr erhalten den Zusatz ***pm***:
  It's 7 ***am***. – Es ist 7 Uhr **morgens**.
  It's 7 ***pm***. – Es ist 7 Uhr **abends**.

G18 Die einfache Form der Gegenwart — The simple present

Seite 42–45

Bei ***I***, ***you***, ***we*** und ***they*** hat das ***simple present*** dieselbe Form wie der Infinitiv:

I sometimes	**play**	basketball.
You often	**play**	football.
We always	**play**	basketball at school.
But you	**play**	football.
Sam and his father	**play**	cards at the weekend.

Du verwendest das ***simple present***,

- wenn du sagen möchtest, dass etwas häufig oder regelmäßig geschieht, oder dass jemand etwas aus Gewohnheit tut. Deshalb steht das ***simple present*** oft zusammen mit Häufigkeitsadverbien wie ***always, sometimes, often, usually, never*** usw.
- um auszudrücken, dass etwas eine Tatsache ist: *Mice* ***like*** *cheese.*
- wenn du beschreiben möchtest, wie jemand mehrere Dinge nacheinander tut. Dies ist häufig so in einer Erzählung oder in einer Zusammenfassung: ***First*** *Sam* ***goes*** *to Terry's house.* ***Then*** *he* ***feeds*** *Tiger. But Tiger* ***sees*** *a dog and* ***runs*** *away …* ***After that*** *…* ***Finally*** *…*

G19 Das -s in der 3. Person Singular
The -s in the 3rd person singular

Seite 44–45

Bei ***he***, ***she*** und ***it*** (3. Person Singular) hängst du im ***simple present*** ein ***s*** an das Verb an.

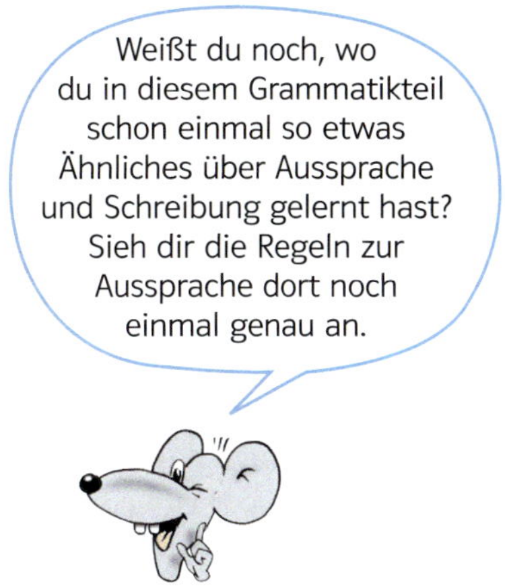

Besonderheiten beim Schreiben und Sprechen:

Emma She never	gets up walks	at 7.15. to school.	[s]
Terry Lisa sometimes	plays reads	the drums. a book after school.	[z]
Emma's school Grandma Brook	finishes watches	at 3.20. TV in the evening.	[ɪz]
Sam Terry sometimes	goes does	swimming on Tuesdays. his homework in his shed.	[gəʊz] [dʌz]

- Nach Zischlauten wie bei ***watch*** wird beim Schreiben ***es*** angehängt.
- ***Y*** am Ende des Verbs wird zu ***ies*** (***fly*** → ***flies***). Das ***y*** bleibt jedoch stehen, wenn davor ein Vokal kommt: ***say*** → ***says***.
- Auch an ***go*** und ***do*** wird beim Schreiben ***es*** angehängt. Sie werden aber unterschiedlich ausgesprochen.

!

Beachte die unregelmäßige Aussprache:

	to go **[gəʊ]**	–	he goes **[gəʊz]**
aber:	to do **[du:]**	–	she does **[dʌz]**
	to say **[seɪ]**	–	he says **[sez]**

G20 Die Satzstellung in Aussagesätzen
Word order in statements

Seiten 42–43

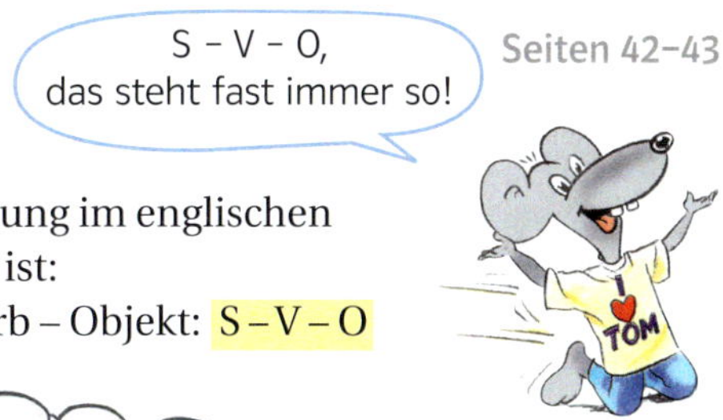

Subjekt	Verb	Objekt
Terry	**plays**	the drums.

- Die Satzstellung im englischen Aussagesatz ist: Subjekt – Verb – Objekt: S – V – O
- Zwischen Verb und Objekt darfst du kein anderes Satzteil stellen.

a) Aussagesätze mit einer Zeitangabe

Zeit	Subjekt	Verb	Objekt	Zeit
	Sam and his friends	play	football	**on Saturday.**
On Saturday	Sam and his friends	play	football.	

- Zeitangaben stehen in der Regel am Ende des Satzes. Wenn man die Zeitangabe stärker betonen möchte, stellt man sie an den Anfang des Satzes.

b) Aussagesätze mit Adverbien (Mittelwörtern) der Häufigkeit

Subjekt	Adverb	Verb		
Emma	**always**	rides	her bike to school.	Emma fährt immer …
Grandma Brook	**never**	goes	to the cinema.	Oma Brook geht nie …
Sam and Terry	**sometimes**	play	football after school.	Sam und Terry spielen manchmal …

- Im Englischen steht das Adverb der Häufigkeit meist zwischen Subjekt und Verb, im Deutschen meist nach dem Verb.

We **are**	**often**	in the park on Wednesdays.
We **can**	**always**	**go** there after school.
We **have**	**often**	**got** lessons in the afternoon.

- Wenn das Verb eine Form von ***to be*** ist, steht das Adverb der Häufigkeit dahinter.
- Wenn ein Hilfsverb (z. B. ***can***) verwendet wird, steht das Adverb zwischen diesem Hilfsverb und dem Infinitiv des Vollverbs (***go***). Dies gilt auch bei ***have got*** und ***has got***. Das Adverb steht immer zwischen ***have/has*** und ***got***.

G 21 Demonstrativpronomen *this / that, these / those*

Seite 46

Demonstrative pronouns *this / that, these / those*

- Wenn man Personen (auch Dinge) zeigen oder vorstellen möchte, benutzt man ***this*** oder ***that***. ***This*** benutzt du für Personen oder Dinge, die näher bei dir sind, ***that*** für solche, die weiter weg sind.
- Beim Vorstellen von zwei Personen sagt man zuerst ***this***, dann ***that***.
- ***These*** ist die Pluralform von ***this***, ***those*** ist die Pluralform von ***that***.

Unit 4

IN DIESER UNIT LERNST DU

- ✓ wie du die Objektformen der persönlichen Fürwörter verwendest (*me, him, her* usw.). G 22
- ✓ wie du Aussagen mit *don't* und *doesn't* verneinst. G 23 G 25
- ✓ wie du mit *do* und *does Yes / No*-Fragen stellst. G 24
- ✓ wie du *do / does*-Fragen mit den Fragewörtern *what, where, when* usw. bildest. G 26

G22 Die Objektformen der Personalpronomen

The object case of the personal pronouns

Seite 58–59

Du kennst schon die Subjektformen der Personalpronomen (*I, you, he* usw.). Diese Pronomen gibt es auch in der Objektform.

	Subjektform		Objektform		
Singular	I	Give	**me**	the brochure, please.	mir
		Can you see	**me**	in the photo?	mich
	you	Sorry, I can't help	**you**	with your homework.	dir
		This bus takes	**you**	to the Dome.	dich
	he	Is Sam at home? Can I speak to	**him,**	please?	ihm
		My dad? Yes, let's ask	**him.**		ihn
	she	Please give	**her**	these pictures.	ihr
		We can't find	**her.**		sie
	it	That's a basketball – you can't play football with	**it.**		ihm
		Sorry, but we can't use	**it.**		ihn
		Where's the ship? I can't see	**it.**		es
		Church Road? I can't find	**it**	on this map.	sie
Plural	we	Please help	**us**	with the poster, Terry.	uns
		Can you take	**us**	to school, Dad?	uns
	you	Sorry, boys. I can give	**you**	the money for the bus,	euch
		but I can't drive	**you**	to the Thames Barrier.	euch
	they	Lisa and Emma? We can talk to	**them**	about the project.	ihnen
		Yes, let's ask	**them.**		sie

▶ Im Englischen gibt es für jedes Personalpronomen nur **eine** Objektform, im Deutschen dagegen meist zwei.

G23 Verneinte Aussagen mit *don't* — Negative statements with *don't*

Seite 60–61

Du kennst schon verschiedene Formen der Verneinung:

I	**can't**	play basketball.
We	**haven't**	got our mobiles.
They	**aren't**	at school today.

▶ Enthält eine Aussage ein Hilfsverb wie ***can*** oder ***have/has (got)*** oder eine Form von ***to be,*** hängst du zur Verneinung einfach ***not (n't)*** an (vergleiche G3, G13, G15).

▶ Steht aber in einem Aussagesatz **keine** Form von ***to be*** und kein Hilfsverb, sondern nur das Vollverb, dann stellst du zur Verneinung das Hilfsverb ***don't*** vor das Vollverb.

Bejahte Aussage			Verneinte Aussage		
I	like	dogs.	I	**don't like**	mice.
You	know	Terry.	But you	**don't know**	his friends.
We often	go	swimming on Saturdays.	We	**don't go**	to museums.
Lisa and Emma	read	the same magazines.	But they	**don't like**	the same stories.

▶ ***Don't*** ist die Kurzform von ***do not***, ähnlich wie bei ***aren't (= are not)*** und ***haven't (= have not)***.

G 24 Entscheidungsfragen und Kurzantworten mit *do*

Yes / No questions and short answers with *do*

Seite 60–61

Entscheidungsfragen sind Fragen, die man mit Ja oder Nein beantworten muss.
Du kennst schon Entscheidungsfragen mit einer Form von ***to be***, mit ***can*** und mit ***have/has got***:

Aussage	Entscheidungsfrage		Kurzantwort
I **can** read this.	**Can**	you read this?	Yes, I **can**.
We **are** late.	**Are**	we late?	No, we **aren't**.
They **have got** new computers.	**Have**	they got new computers?	Yes, they **have**.

▶ So bildet man Fragen: Stellst du eine Frage mit einer Form von ***to be*** oder mit einem Hilfsverb wie ***can*** oder ***have/has (got)***, stellst du dieses einfach vor das Subjekt. Im Deutschen ist es ganz ähnlich.

▶ Bildest du aber einen Fragesatz ohne eine Form von ***to be*** und ohne ein Hilfsverb, so stellst du das Hilfsverb ***do*** an den Satzanfang.

▶ Die Antwort lautet dann: ***Yes, I do*** oder ***No, I don't***.

Aussage	Frage		Kurzantwort
I know the name of the ship.	**Do**	you know its name?	Yes, I **do**.
We often watch football on TV.	**Do**	you sometimes watch football?	No, we **don't**.
My friends play basketball.	**Do**	your friends play basketball, too?	Yes, they **do**.

G 25 Fragen und verneinte Aussagen mit *does* und *doesn't*

Questions and negative statements with *does* and *doesn't*

Seite 62–63

In Fragen mit ***he, she, it*** (3. Person Singular) gibt es eine besondere Regel. Erinnerst du dich noch an ***He, she, it*** – **das *s* muss mit?** Hier taucht das ***s*** wieder auf. Es wandert in der Frage vom Vollverb zu ***does*** und in der Verneinung zu ***doesn't***. Beim Vollverb fehlt das ***s*** dann natürlich.

Tom likes cheese.	**Does** he like chocolate, too?	Yes, he **does**. But he **doesn't** like cat food.

- Bei ***he, she*** und ***it*** (3. Person Singular) wird in der Frage ***does*** [dʌz] und in der Verneinung ***doesn't*** ['dʌznt] verwendet. ***Doesn't*** ist die Kurzform von ***does not***.
- Auf Entscheidungsfragen mit ***does*** antwortet man ***Yes, she does*** oder ***No, she doesn't***.

Hier sind alle Formen auf einen Blick:

Entscheidungsfrage	Kurzantwort	Verneinte Antwort
Do I **look** OK in this T-shirt?	**Yes**, you **do**.	But you **don't look** OK in those dirty shoes.
Do you **know** Mr Jackson?	No, I **don't**.	I **don't know** him.
Does Sam **like** chocolate?	**Yes**, he **does**.	But he **doesn't like** cheese.
Does Lisa **play** football?	**Yes**, she **does**.	But she **doesn't play** basketball.
Does GMT **mean** Greenwich Mean Time?	**Yes**, it **does**.	It **doesn't mean** 'girls mean trouble'.
Do we **start** here?	**No**, we **don't**.	We **don't start** here.
Do you **do** your homework at home?	**Yes**, we **do**.	We **don't do** it at school.
Do your friends **read** computer magazines?	**Yes**, they **do**.	But they **don't read** computer books.

G 26 Fragen mit Fragewörtern und *do / does*

Questions with question words and *do / does*

Seite 64–65

Du kannst Fragen mit Fragewörtern (***what, when, where*** usw.) mit einer Form von ***to be*** oder mit einem Hilfsverb stellen: ***What is*** *your name?* ***When can*** *we go to the Thames Barrier?*

Fragewort	Hilfsverb	Subjekt	Vollverb	restlicher Satz	Antwort
What	**does**	Lisa	watch	on TV?	She often watches sport.
When	**does**	the museum	open	in the morning?	It opens at 10.
Where	**do**	the Taylors	live	in Greenwich?	They live in Pond Road.
Why	**doesn't**	Mrs Spencer	like	the foot tunnel?	Because it's so long and scary.
How	**do**	I	get	to the Dome?	You can take the Underground.

- Stehen im Satz kein Hilfsverb und keine Form von ***to be***, setzt du das Hilfsverb ***do/does*** nach dem Fragewort ein.

Unit 5

IN DIESER UNIT LERNST DU

- ✓ wie du auf Englisch sagen kannst, dass du etwas möchtest oder willst. G 27
- ✓ wie du die Ordnungszahlen und das Datum schreibst und aussprichst. G 28 G 29
- ✓ wie du mit dem *present progressive* ausdrücken kannst, dass etwas gerade passiert. G 30 G 31
- ✓ wie du *much, many, a lot of* usw. verwendest. G 32
- ✓ wie du Mengenangaben mit *of* machst (*a box of* etc.). G 33
- ✓ wie du Besitz oder Zugehörigkeit mit *of* ausdrückst. G 34

G 27 *Want to* und *would like to* + Infinitiv

Want to and *would like to* + infinitive

Seite 74–75

Wenn du im Englischen einen Wunsch ausdrücken möchtest, kannst du ***would like to*** oder ***want to*** verwenden.

What do you	**want to**	do on your birthday, Sam?
	Would	you like to have a party?
Yes, I	**'d**	like to invite my friends.
But I don't	**want**	to have the party here.
My friends	**wouldn't**	like that.

- ***Want*** ist ein Vollverb. Es wird in Frage und Verneinung mit ***do/don't*** oder ***does/doesn't*** umschrieben.
- ***Would*** hingegen ist ein Hilfsverb. Es wird also in der Frage vor das Subjekt gestellt. Es wird mit ***not (n't)*** verneint.
- Die Kurzform von ***would*** ist ***'d: I'd*** *like to …*

!

I would like to (deutsch: Ich **möchte** / Ich **würde gern**) ist viel höflicher als ***I want to*** (deutsch: Ich **will**).

G 28 Die Ordnungszahlen The ordinal numbers

Seite 75

1st	the **first**	11th	the eleventh	21st	the twenty-**first**
2nd	the **second**	12th	the **twelfth**	22nd	the twenty-**second**
3rd	the **third**	13th	the thirteenth	30th	the thirt**ieth**
4th	the fourth	14th	the fourteenth	40th	the **fortieth**
5th	the **fifth**	15th	the fifteenth	50th	the fift**ieth**
6th	the sixth	16th	the sixteenth	60th	the sixt**ieth**
7th	the seventh	17th	the seventeenth	70th	the sevent**ieth**
8th	the **eighth**	18th	the eighteenth	80th	the eight**ieth**
9th	the **ninth**	19th	the nineteenth	90th	the ninet**ieth**
10th	the tenth	20th	the twent**ieth**	100th	the (one) hundredth

▶ Wenn du im Deutschen eine Ordnungszahl als Ziffer schreibst, setzt du einen Punkt nach der Zahl (z. B.: am 3. März). Im Englischen stehen statt dessen die beiden letzten Buchstaben der ausgeschriebenen Ordnungszahl: *first* = *1st*, *second* = *2nd*, *third* = *3rd*, *fourth* =*4th usw.*

G29 Das Datum The date

Seite 75

Im Englischen musst du zwischen der Schreibung des Datums und der Aussprache unterscheiden:

Man schreibt	Man spricht
22nd July **oder** July 22nd	"the twenty-second of July" **oder** "July the twenty-second"

▶ Du kannst das Datum aber auch ganz einfach mit Grundzahlen schreiben: ***22 July*** oder ***July 22***, aber auch dann musst du ***"the twenty-second of July"*** oder ***"July the twenty-second"*** sagen.

G30 Die Verlaufsform der Gegenwart
The present progressive

Seite 76–77

Du kennst schon die einfache Form der Gegenwart, das ***simple present***. Anders als im Deutschen gibt es im Englischen von allen Zeiten zwei verschiedene Formen, die man unterschiedlich verwendet. So gibt es in der Gegenwart neben dem ***simple present*** noch das ***present progressive*** (Verlaufsform der Gegenwart).

Singular	I	**am listening**	to the radio.
	You	**are doing**	your homework.
	He	**is looking at**	a magazine.
	She	**is watching**	a game on TV.
	It	**is starting**	right now.
Plural	We	**are making**	a poster.
	You	**are having**	a nice time.
	They	**are winning**	now.

▶ Du bildest die Verlaufsform so: Form von ***to be*** (*am, is, are*) + Vollverb (Infinitiv ohne *to*) + ***ing***-Endung: *She* ***is watch+ing*** *TV.*

▶ Mit der Verlaufsform der Gegenwart kannst du ausdrücken, dass jemand gerade dabei ist, etwas zu tun. Du kannst das ***present progressive*** auch verwenden, wenn du sagen möchtest, dass ein Vorgang gerade abläuft und noch nicht abgeschlossen ist.

- Diese Signalwörter helfen dir oft zu erkennen, dass du die **Verlaufsform** benützen musst: ***now, right now, just, today, still.***
- Im Deutschen gibt es die Verlaufsform nicht. Wenn du die Form im Deutschen wiedergeben möchtest, kannst du Ausdrücke wie **gerade**, **im Augenblick**, **im Moment** oder **jetzt** verwenden: *He **is looking** at a magazine.* = Er schaut sich **gerade** eine Zeitschrift an.

Besonderheiten beim Schreiben:

win	+ n	They are	win**n**ing	the game.
put	+ t	The boy is	put**t**ing	the CD in his bag.
danc**e**	~~e~~	Lisa and Emma are	danc**ing.**	
mak**e**	~~e~~	The boys are	mak**ing**	a poster.

- Steht ein kurzer Vokal (**a, e, i, o, u**) vor dem Konsonanten (**m, n, t** zum Beispiel) am Ende des Verbs, verdoppelt sich der Konsonant: *swim* → *swimming*
- Verben mit einem stummen **e** am Ende verlieren dieses **e** vor der *-**ing*** Endung: *writ*e → *writing.*

G31 Fragen und Kurzantworten in der Verlaufsform der Gegenwart Seite 76–77

Questions and short answers with the present progressive

Are	you	**listening to**	this new CD?	**Yes, I am.**	
Is	Emma	**looking for**	a birthday present?	**Yes, she is.**	
Is	Terry's mobile	**ringing?**		**No, it isn't.**	It's Sam's phone.
Are	you	**trying**	on clothes, girls?	**No, we aren't.**	We're buying a present.
Are	the boys	**watching**	a film on TV?	**Yes, they are.**	

- Bei Fragen in der Verlaufsform werden die Langformen von ***to be*** an den Satzanfang gestellt (vergleiche G4). Siehe jedoch auch G9: Wh- zuerst: ***What** are you doing?*
- Bei den Ja-Antworten verwendet man die Langformen von ***to be***, bei den verneinten Antworten meistens die Kurzformen von ***to be*** (vergleiche G4).
- Du kannst die Verneinung auch so bilden:
  Are you playing computer games again, Sam?
  *– No, I'm **not playing** computer games. I'm doing my homework.*
  Are you buying new clothes, girls?
  *– No, we **aren't buying** clothes. We're looking for a present.*

G32 Die Mengenwörter *much / many, a little / a few* Seite 78

Expressions of quantity with *much / many, a little / a few*

Mit ***much*** und ***many*** oder ***a little*** und ***a few*** kannst du angeben, wie viel oder wie wenig von einer bestimmten Menge vorhanden ist.

much	many
How **much sugar** have we got? – Not **much**. And we haven't got **much flour**.	There aren't **many eggs** here. How **many** do we need for the cake? – Not **many**. One or two.

!

In bejahten Sätzen verwendet man ***a lot of*** oder ***lots of*** und zwar bei zählbaren und nicht zählbaren Nomen:
*There are **a lot of/lots of** people in the shop today. They are having **a lot of/lots of** fun.*

- ***Much*** (= viel) wird zusammen mit Nomen verwendet, die im Singular stehen und nicht zählbar sind: ***not much flour***.
- ***Many*** (= viele) wird mit Nomen verwendet, die im Plural stehen und zählbar sind: ***not many candles***.
- ***Much*** und ***many*** werden fast nur in Fragen und verneinten Sätzen gebraucht.

a little	a few
I need **a little help**, Grandma.	Can we make **a few sandwiches**, too?

- ***A little*** (ein wenig, ein bisschen) wird zusammen mit Nomen verwendet, die im **Singular** stehen und **nicht zählbar** sind.
- ***A few*** (einige, ein paar) verwendet man mit Nomen, die im **Plural** stehen und **zählbar** sind.

G33 Mengenangaben mit *of* Expressions of quantity with *of*

Seite 78–79

a box	**of**	candles	eine Schachtel Kerzen
three tins	**of**	cat food	drei Dosen Katzenfutter
a pound	**of**	cheese	ein Pfund Käse
two bags	**of**	flour	zwei Tüten Mehl
a cup	**of**	tea	eine Tasse Tee

- Im Englischen werden diese Mengenangaben mit dem Wort ***of*** gebildet. Im Deutschen fehlt das ‚von': eine Dose Katzenfutter.

G34 Der *of*-Genitiv The of-genitive

Seite 78–79

Du kennst schon den *s*-Genitiv: *Sam's cake*. Es gibt noch eine zweite Form des Genitivs, den ***of***-Genitiv:

The door	**of** the house	is green.
On the	morning **of** his birthday	Sam puts the candles on the cake.
January is the first	month **of** the year.	
I don't know the	names **of** those streets.	

▶ Genau wie der *s*-Genitiv drückt auch der Genitiv mit ***of*** aus, dass etwas zueinander gehört oder einander zugeordnet ist. Der Genitiv mit ***of*** wird vorwiegend bei **Dingen** verwendet. Der *s*-Genitiv wird hauptsächlich verwendet, wenn **Menschen** oder **Tieren** etwas gehört oder zugeordnet ist.

!

Vergleiche:
This is Sam**'s** sweatshirt.
The colours **of** the sweatshirt are funny.

Unit 6

IN DIESER UNIT LERNST DU

- ✓ wie du Zahlen über 100 und Jahreszahlen schreibst und aussprichst. G 35
- ✓ wann du das *simple present* und wann du das *present progressive* benutzt. G 36
- ✓ wie du *some, any* und *no* verwendest. G 37
- ✓ einige Nomen kennen, die unregelmäßige Pluralformen haben. G 38

G 35 Zahlen über 100 und Jahreszahlen

Numbers over 100 and years

Seite 88–89

Du kennst schon die Grund- und Ordnungszahlen bis 100 (G 28) und kannst das Datum schreiben und aussprechen (G 29). So spricht und schreibt man Zahlen über 100 und die Jahreszahlen:

Numbers over 100

Man schreibt	Man spricht
145	a / one hundred and forty-five
1,000	a / one thousand
2,007	two thousand and seven
3,714	three thousand seven hundred and fourteen
55,555	fifty-five thousand five hundred and fifty-five
867,498	eight hundred and sixty-seven thousand four hundred and ninety-eight
1,000,000	a / one million

!

Tausender-Stellen werden im Englischen meist mit Komma angezeigt: 2,007.
Im Deutschen steht oft ein Punkt: 2.007

Years

Man schreibt	Man spricht
1492	fourteen ninety-two (*oder:* fourteen hundred and ninety-two)
1776	seventeen seventy-six (*oder:* seventeen hundred and seventy-six)
1900	nineteen hundred
2000	two thousand
2006	two thousand and six

G 36 Gegenüberstellung: Die Verlaufsform der Gegenwart und die einfache Form der Gegenwart

Seite 90–93

Present progressive and simple present

Look, Tom **is playing** football.

Tom **plays** football for Mousetown Football Club.

Wie du schon weißt, gibt es im Englischen zwei Formen der Gegenwart, das ***present progressive*** und das ***simple present***. Diese beiden Formen dürfen nicht verwechselt werden.

Ablaufende Handlungen:

Verlaufsform *(present progressive)*		
It's two o'clock **now**, and	**I'm having**	a picnic on the beach.
Lisa	**is building**	a sand castle **today**.
Look, they	**'re playing**	volleyball over there.

▶ Mit dem ***present progressive*** drückst du aus, dass etwas jetzt gerade geschieht und noch nicht zu Ende ist.

▶ Sehr oft steht das ***present progressive*** bei Signalwörtern wie ***now***, ***just***, ***right now*** und der Aufforderung ***look***. Häufig wird es auch mit ***this morning***, ***this afternoon***, ***this evening*** und ***today*** verwendet.

Gewohnheitsmäßige Handlungen:

Einfache Form *(simple present)*		
At home I **usually**	**have**	lunch at 12.
She **never**	**builds**	sand castles at home.
They **often**	**play**	volleyball on the beach.

▶ Mit dem ***simple present*** drückst du aus, dass etwas regelmäßig, oft, manchmal oder nie geschieht.

▶ Die Signalwörter ***usually***, ***never***, ***often***, ***always***, ***sometimes***, ***every day***, (auch: ***on Mondays***, ***on Tuesdays*** …) zeigen dir, dass du das ***simple present*** verwenden musst.

Aufeinander folgende Handlungen:

Einfache Form *(simple present)*

First Ben and Lisa **go** swimming. → **After that** they **play** volleyball on the beach. → Jade **wants** to build a sandcastle. → **Then** they **eat** ice-creams. → **Finally** they **go** home after a nice day on the beach.

- Man verwendet das ***simple present*** auch, wenn man berichtet, was nacheinander geschieht. Du kannst es für Zusammenfassungen und Inhaltsangaben gebrauchen.
- Häufig werden die Signalwörter ***First*** …, ***after that*** …, ***then*** … und ***finally*** verwendet.

Gewohnheitmäßige Handlungen Aufeinander folgende Handlungen →	**simple present**	Barker usually **eats** dog food.
Gerade ablaufende Handlungen →	**present progressive**	But just now he **is eating** ice-cream.

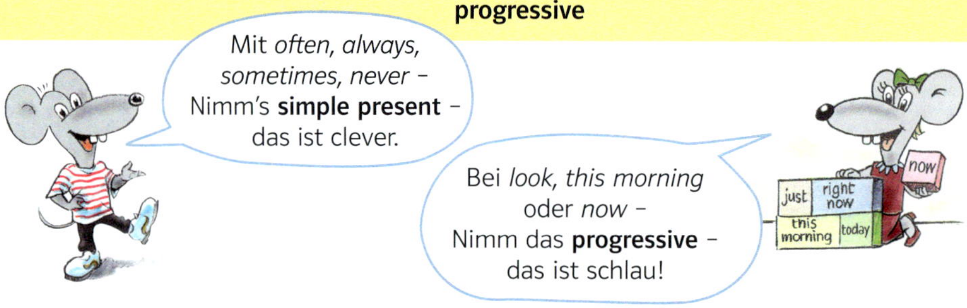

G 37 *Some* und *any, no*

Seite 94–95

Im Englischen drückt man eine unbestimmte Menge oder Anzahl (im Sinne von **etwas**, **einige** oder **ein paar**) mit ***some*** oder ***any*** aus.

Bejahte Aussagen mit *some* ✓	Fragen mit *any* ?	Verneinte Aussagen mit *not any* –
Let's buy **some** postcards. Kaufen wir (ein paar) Postkarten.	Have they got **any** postcards? Haben sie Postkarten?	No, there are**n't any** (postcards). Nein, es gibt keine (Postkarten).
We can get **some** chocolate. Wir können (etwas) Schokolade kaufen.	Do you see **any** chocolate? Siehst du Schokolade?	No, they have**n't** got **any** (chocolate). Nein, sie haben keine (Schokolade).

- In bejahten Sätzen verwendet man ***some***. In Fragen und verneinten Sätzen steht meist ***any***.
- ***Some*** und ***any*** entsprechen den deutschen Begriffen **etwas**, **einige** oder **ein paar**, sie bleiben aber oft unübersetzt: *Do you need **any** help?* Brauchst du Hilfe?
- Wenn das Nomen (***sunglasses***) schon genannt wurde, kann man es im Antwortsatz weglassen: *Have you got **any** sunglasses? – Yes, I can show you **some**.*

!

Anstelle von ***not any***, kann man auch ***no*** (kein / keine) verwenden: There are ***no*** postcards. (Es gibt keine Postkarten.)
No steht immer vor einem Nomen (***no*** postcards, ***no*** time).

G38 Der Plural der Nomen (unregelmäßige Formen)

Seite 100

The plural of nouns (irregular forms)

Wie du weißt, wird der Plural der meisten englischen Nomen gebildet, indem man ein *s* an die Singularform hängt: *one word – five words* (vergleiche G7). Bei einigen der Pluralformen, die auf *s* enden, gibt es bei Schreibung und Aussprache Besonderheiten:

Singular		Plural	
a shel**f**	[-f]	two shel**ves**	[-vz]
one scar**f**	[-f]	four scar**ves**	[-vz]
a thie**f**	[-f]	ten thie**ves**	[-vz]
one ba**by**		three ba**bies**	
a fami**ly**		two fami**lies**	
aber:			
a b**oy**		some b**oys**	

- Nomen, die auf *f* enden, haben meist die Pluralendung ***-ves***.
- Wenn ein Nomen auf einen Konsonanten + *y* (ba***by***) endet, so ist die Pluralendung bab***ies***. Steht vor dem *y* jedoch ein Vokal (b***oy***), so bleibt das *y* (b***oys***). Zur Aussprache vergleiche G7.

Es gibt eine kleine Zahl von unregelmäßigen Pluralformen, die du einzeln lernen musst. Du findest diese Pluralformen in der *Vocabulary*-Liste immer hinter der Singularform:

Singular		Plural	
one m**a**n	[mæn]	two m**e**n	[men]
a wom**a**n	['wʊmən]	four wom**e**n	['wɪmɪn]
one f**oo**t	[fʊt]	two f**ee**t	[fi:t]
a t**oo**th	[tu:θ]	32 t**ee**th	[ti:θ]
a child	[tʃaɪld]	three child**ren**	['tʃɪldrən]
one fish		hundreds of **fish**	
a person	['pɜ:sn]	lots of **people**	['pi:pl]

!

Wenn eine einzelne Person gemeint ist, benutzt man das Wort ***person***, eine Gruppe von Menschen sind ***people***.

Weißt du noch, wie man den *s*-Genitiv von Nomen im Singular und Plural bildet (vergleiche G10)?

!

Bei den unregelmäßigen Pluralformen, die nicht auf **s** enden, hängst du ein **'s** an.

The men	**'s**	bikes look great.
The women	**'s**	mobiles are new.
The children	**'s**	kites are red, blue and green.

Unit 7

IN DIESER UNIT LERNST DU

- ✓ wie man *must, mustn't* und *needn't* verwendet. G 39 G 40
- ✓ wo Orts- und Zeitangaben im Satz stehen. G 41
- ✓ wie du Sätze mit *because, when, but* … verbindest. G 42

G 39 Das modale Hilfsverb *must*

The modal auxiliary *must*

Seite 104–106

Du kennst schon das modale Hilfsverb ***can***. Es drückt aus, dass jemand etwas tun **kann** oder **darf** (vergleiche G 16). Das modale Hilfsverb ***must*** drückt aus, dass jemand etwas tun **muss**.

I	**must**	feed the pigs every morning.
You	**must**	be calm with the animals.
Emma	**must**	ask Mrs Carter about cats on the farm.
	Must	we muck out the pig shed?

- ▶ ***Must*** ist – genau wie ***can*** – in allen Personen gleich.
- ▶ Es wird zusammen mit dem Infinitiv eines Vollverbs ohne ***to*** verwendet (*to go: **I must go***).

!

Beachte die unterschiedliche Wortstellung im Englischen und im Deutschen:
Tom ***must*** do ***his homework***. → Tom **muss seine Hausaufgaben** machen.

G 40 *Mustn't* und *needn't*

Seite 104–107

Emma is allergic to cats.	She	**mustn't**	get near them.
People on farms **must** do a lot in the summer.	They	**needn't**	do so much in the winter.
Cows aren't bad.	You	**needn't**	be nervous, Emma.

- ▶ Mit ***mustn't*** ['mʌsnt] drückst du aus, dass jemand etwas **nicht** tun **darf**.
- ▶ Mit ***needn't*** drückst du aus, dass jemand etwas **nicht tun muss** oder **nicht zu tun braucht**.
- ▶ Die Formen ***mustn't*** und ***needn't*** sind für alle Personen gleich.

!

Mustn't und ***needn't*** darf man nicht verwechseln!

mustn't: nicht dürfen
*You **mustn't** make the animals nervous.*
Ihr dürft die Tiere nicht nervös machen.

needn't: nicht müssen / nicht brauchen
*You **needn't** take your wellies.*
Ihr braucht keine Gummistiefel zu tragen.

G41 Satzstellung Word order

Seite 107, 109

Die Satzstellung S – V – O in englischen Aussagesätzen kennst du schon. Du weißt auch, wo Zeitangaben in Aussagesätzen stehen (vergleiche G20). Wenn du aber in einem Satz gleichzeitig Ortsangaben (z. B. ***in** the park*) und Zeitangaben (z. B. ***after** school*) machen möchtest, gilt folgende Regel:

!

Ort vor Zeit – das ist gescheit.
Or in English:
Place before time – that is fine!

Zeit	Subjekt	Verb	Objekt	Ort	Zeit
	Lisa	plays	football	**in the park**	**after school.**
After school	Lisa	plays	football	**in the park.**	
	Mrs Jackson	buys	cat food	**at the shop**	**on Saturday.**
On Saturday	Mrs Jackson	buys	cat food	**at the shop.**	

- Ortsangaben und Zeitangaben stehen normalerweise am Ende des Satzes. Hierbei gilt die Regel: **Ort vor Zeit**.
- Wenn du die **Zeitangabe** stärker betonen möchtest, kannst du sie auch an den Anfang des Satzes stellen.

!

Auf keinen Fall darfst du Satzteile zwischen **Verb** und **Objekt** stellen.

Our English teacher **writes new words** on the board every day.
Unser Englischlehrer **schreibt** jeden Tag **neue Wörter** an die Tafel.

G42 Verknüpfung von Sätzen mit Konjunktionen
Linking sentences with conjunctions

Seite 108–109

Mit den Konjunktionen ***and***, ***but***, ***because***, ***so*** und ***when*** kannst du Sätze oder Satzteile miteinander verbinden. So werden Texte interessanter und lassen sich besser lesen.

Hauptsatz *(main clause)*		Hauptsatz *(main clause)*	
Lisa wins the first prize	**and**	Sam gets the second prize.	… und …
Terry doesn't like dirty jobs	**but**	he likes pigs.	… aber …

- ***And*** und ***but*** verbinden Hauptsätze.

Hauptsatz *(main clause)*		Nebensatz *(subordinate clause)*	
Lisa wins the prize	**because**	her photo is so nice.	… weil …
Barker always barks	**when**	he sees a dog on TV.	… wenn …
Sam often buys some food	**before**	he goes to the zoo.	… bevor …
Emma is allergic to cats	**so**	she mustn't go near them.	… weshalb …

- ***Because***, ***before***, ***when***, ***where*** und ***so*** verbinden einen Hauptsatz mit einem Nebensatz.

!

Die Wortstellung Subjekt – Verb – Objekt bleibt, anders als im Deutschen, auch im englischen Nebensatz erhalten.

Vergleiche:

		S	V	O
Barker likes places where		*he*	*meets*	*other dogs*.

	S	O	V
Barker mag Orte, wo	er	andere Hunde	trifft.

[Trailer 1]

G 43 Die einfache Vergangenheit: regelmäßige Formen

Seite 120–121

The simple past: regular forms

Das ***simple past*** verwendest du, wenn du über Handlungen sprechen möchtest, die in der Vergangenheit stattgefunden haben und **abgeschlossen** sind. Du kannst das ***simple past*** z. B. benutzen, um Geschichten zu erzählen oder um über Erlebnisse zu berichten.

Last week	Ben	**visited**	Stefan in Berlin.
Yesterday	they	**watched**	a German film on TV.

- Du bildest das ***simple past*** der regelmäßigen Verben, indem du die Endung ***-ed*** an den Infinitiv anhängst: ***help* + *ed* → *helped***.
- Die Form des ***simple past*** ist für alle Personen gleich.
- Mit dem ***simple past*** drückst du aus, dass etwas vorbei ist. Häufig stehen Zeitangaben der Vergangenheit in diesen Sätzen: ***yesterday, last year.***

G 44 Aussprache und Schreibung der einfachen Vergangenheit (regelmäßige Formen)

Seite 120–121

Pronunciation and spelling of the simple past (regular forms)

Beachte bei der Aussprache und der Schreibung folgende Regeln:

Beim Sprechen		Beim Schreiben	
open**ed** [-nd]	Nach Vokalen gefolgt von stimmhaften Konsonanten spricht man [d].	to lik**e** – lik**ed** to smil**e** – smil**ed**	Das stumme End-*e* fällt weg.
finis**hed** [-ʃt] hel**ped** [-pt] wal**ked** [-kt]	Nach stimmlosen Konsonanten spricht man [t]	to cop**y** – cop**ied** to worr**y** – worr**ied**	Verben, die auf Konsonant + *y* enden, erhalten die Endung *-ied*.
men**ded** [-dɪd] wan**ted** [-tɪd]	Nach [d] oder [t] spricht man [ɪd].	to sto**p** – sto**pped**	Ein Endkonsonant wird nach einem kurzen betonten Vokal verdoppelt.

G 45 Die einfache Vergangenheit von *to be* — The simple past of *to be*

Seite 120–121

Wie du weißt, kann man mit ***to be*** Aussagen, Fragen, Verneinungen und Kurzantworten bilden: *Emma* ***is*** *from Bristol. She* ***isn't*** *from Greenwich.* ***Is*** *she new at Thomas Tallis? – Yes, she* ***is***. Dies gilt auch für das ***simple past***.

Were	you in Wales in the holidays?	No, we **weren't**. We **were** in Germany.
Was	it good there?	Yes, it **was**. Berlin **was** cool.

▶ Im ***simple past*** gibt es zwei Formen von ***to be***: I / he / she / it **was** – you / we / they **were**

G 46 Die einfache Vergangenheit: unregelmäßige Formen

The simple past: irregular forms

Seite 121

Vorsicht bei den unregelmäßigen Verben im Englischen:

Infinitiv	simple past	
to have	**had**	Ben **had** a great time in Berlin.
to come	**came**	He **came** back last week.
to eat	**ate**	One morning he **ate** cheese for breakfast. Ugh!
to find	**found**	This morning I **found** a postcard from Ben.
to go	**went**	Stefan and Ben often **went** to a lake.
to say	**said**	Ben **said** 'Guten Tag' to the girls at the lake and they laughed.

▶ Die regelmäßigen Verben im ***simple past*** enden alle auf ***-ed***. Bei den unregelmäßigen Verben musst du die einzelnen Formen lernen.

▶ Auch bei den unregelmäßigen Verben sind die Formen des ***simple past*** für alle Personen gleich. (Die einzige Ausnahme ist ***to be*** – siehe oben.)

[Trailer 2]

G 47 Das *going-to*-Futur — The going to future

Seite 122–123

Du verwendest das ***going to future***, wenn du beschreiben willst, was du vorhast.

What **is** Terry	**going to do** this morning?		Was hat Terry heute morgen vor?
He	**is going to help**	his dad.	Er wird … helfen.
What	**are they going to do?**		Was planen sie?
They	**are going to clear out**	the garage.	Sie haben vor …
But they	**aren't going to fly**	the old kite.	… werden / wollen nicht …

▶ Das ***going to future*** wird gebildet aus ***am / is / are*** + ***going to*** + Infinitiv.

▶ Das ***going to future*** wird häufig für Vorhaben, Pläne und feste Absichten in der **nahen** Zukunft verwendet. (Z. B. *I'm going to help my dad* ***this morning***.)

▶ Du kannst das ***going to future*** auch verwenden, wenn klar ist, dass etwas demnächst passieren wird: *I must be there at 9 o'clock. It's already five to nine.* ***I'm going to be*** *late.* (Ich komme bestimmt zu spät.)

Vocabulary

Im ***Vocabulary*** findest du alle neuen englischen Wörter und Redewendungen. Sie stehen in der Reihenfolge, in der sie im Buch vorkommen. Das *Vocabulary* ist in drei Spalten aufgeteilt:

- Links stehen die englischen Wörter und Sätze. In Klammern ist das Wort in Lautschrift aufgeführt. Sie zeigt dir, wie du das Wort aussprichst. Die Erklärung der Lautschrift findest du am Ende dieser Seite.
- In der Mitte steht die deutsche Übersetzung.
- Rechts findest du Bilder, Beispielsätze, Erklärungen oder Hinweise auf Besonderheiten (siehe →).

Die **fett** gedruckten Wörter musst du lernen und anwenden können. Normal gedruckte Wörter sind nur zum Verständnis bestimmter Texte oder Übungen nötig.
In den Units und in der *Free section* findest du manchmal neue Wörter in Fußnoten unten auf der Seite. Auch diese helfen dir, die Texte zu verstehen. Du musst sie nicht lernen.
Auf das *Vocabulary* folgt ab Seite 208 das ***Dictionary (English-German)*** und ab Seite 226 das ***Dictionary (German-English)***. Falls du ein Wort vergessen hast, kannst du in diesen alphabetischen Wortlisten nachsehen. Englische Begriffe wie *e-mail*, *cool* oder *cornflakes*, die du auch im Deutschen verwendest, stehen nicht im *Vocabulary*. Du kannst ihre Aussprache und Übersetzung aber im *Dictionary* nachschlagen. Das gleiche gilt für Wörter, die auf Englisch und Deutsch fast gleich geschrieben und ausgesprochen werden, wie z. B. *park* oder *partner*.
Jede Unit im *Vocabulary* beginnt mit einer „Grundschul-Box". Dort stehen Wörter und Sätze, die du wahrscheinlich schon aus der Grundschule kennst. Diese Wörter findest du weiter unten im *Vocabulary* noch einmal als normalen Eintrag mit einem gelben Punkt (•).
Nach der „Grundschul-Box" kommen die *Vocabulary Skills* mit nützlichen Tipps zum Vokabellernen.
Und am Ende jeder Unit stehen die *Useful phrases*, die dir dabei helfen, auf Englisch über ein bestimmtes Thema zu sprechen.

Abkürzungen und Zeichen

pl	Mehrzahl (Plural)	!	Achtung!
sing	Einzahl (Singular)	↔	ist das Gegenteil von
5	In dieser Übung kommen die Wörter vor.	→	ist verwandt mit
		=	entspricht

Englische Laute

Mitlaute (Konsonanten)

[b]	**b**ed	[p]	**p**icture
[d]	**d**ay	[r]	**r**ed
[ð]	**th**e	[s]	**s**ix
[f]	**f**amily	[ʃ]	**sh**e
[g]	**g**o	[t]	**t**en
[ŋ]	morni**ng**	[tʃ]	**ch**air
[h]	**h**ouse	[v]	**v**ideo
[j]	**y**ou	[w]	**w**e, **o**ne
[k]	**c**an, mil**k**	[z]	ea**s**y
[l]	**l**etter	[ʒ]	revi**s**ion
[m]	**m**an	[dʒ]	pa**ge**
[n]	**n**o	[θ]	**th**ank you

Selbstlaute (Vokale)

[ɑː]	c**ar**
[æ]	**a**pple
[e]	p**e**n
[ə]	**a**gain
[ɜː]	g**ir**l
[ʌ]	b**u**t
[ɪ]	**i**t
[i]	happ**y**
[iː]	t**ea**cher
[ɒ]	d**o**g
[ɔː]	b**a**ll
[ʊ]	b**oo**k
[u]	Jan**u**ary
[uː]	t**oo**, t**wo**

Doppellaute

[aɪ]	**I**, m**y**
[aʊ]	n**ow**, m**ou**se
[eɪ]	n**a**me, th**ey**
[eə]	th**ere**, p**air**
[ɪə]	h**ere**, id**ea**
[əʊ]	hell**o**
[ɔɪ]	b**oy**
[ʊə]	s**ure**

[ː] der vorangehende Laut ist lang, z. B. *you* [juː]
[‿] der Bindebogen zeigt, dass zwei Wörter in der Aussprache verbunden werden
[ˈ] die folgende Silbe zeigt den Hauptakzent
[ˌ] die folgende Silbe zeigt den Nebenakzent
Alle anderen Zeichen werden genauso ausgesprochen, wie sie geschrieben werden, z. B. [b], [j], [l] usw.

Zoom-in Time for Greenwich

zoom-in [zuːmˈɪn]	Heranzoomen, Heranfahren
• **time** [taɪm]	Zeit
• **for** [fɔː; fə]	für
Greenwich [ˈɡrenɪdʒ]	
24-hour [twentiˌfɔː‿ˈaʊə]	24-Stunden
• **clock** [klɒk]	Uhr
• **bus** pl. **buses** [bʌs; bʌsɪz]	Bus
• **to** [tuː; tʊ; tə]	nach, zu, in
• **let's listen** [lets ˈlɪsn]	lass(t) uns zuhören
• **let's (= let us)** [lets; let‿ˈʌs]	Lass(t) uns
• to **listen** [ˈlɪsn]	zuhören
• **sound** [saʊnd]	Geräusch
• to **point** [pɔɪnt]	zeigen
let's get started [lets get ˈstɑːtɪd]	lass(t) uns beginnen, lass(t) uns anfangen
• to sing [sɪŋ]	singen
chorus [ˈkɔːrəs]	Refrain
we're on our way [wɪər‿ɒn‿aʊə ˈweɪ]	wir sind auf dem Weg
we're learning English [wɪə ˌlɜːnɪŋ‿ˈɪŋɡlɪʃ]	wir lernen Englisch
• Let's go! [lets ˈɡəʊ]	Lass(t) uns anfangen!/ Lass(t) uns gehen!
Hooray! [hʊˈreɪ]	Hurra!

Pick-up Unit 1 Thomas Tallis School

In dieser Box findest du Wörter und Sätze, die im *Vocabulary* der Unit 1 stehen und die du vielleicht schon aus der Grundschule kennst. Und los geht's mit dem Thema **Schule** und **Freunde kennen lernen**:

Hello.	Hallo.
Good morning.	Guten Morgen.
What's your name?	Wie heißt du?
My name is ...	Ich heiße ...
How old are you?	Wie alt bist du?
I'm ...	Ich bin ...
Where are you from?	Woher kommst du?
I'm from ...	Ich komme aus ...
boy	Junge
girl	Mädchen
friend	Freund, Freundin
pupil	Schüler, Schülerin
teacher	Lehrer, Lehrerin
school	Schule
classroom	Klassenzimmer
What's for homework?	Was haben wir auf?
please	bitte
Sit down, please.	Setz' dich/Setzt euch bitte hin.
Thank you.	Danke.
You're welcome.	Bitte; Nichts zu danken / Gern geschehen.
book	Buch
pen	Füller
pencil	Bleistift
pencil-case	Federmäppchen
schoolbag	Schultasche
picture	Bild
number	Nummer, Hausnummer; Zahl
game	Spiel
to play	spielen
Let's play a game!	Lass(t) uns ein Spiel spielen!
playground	Spielplatz
to listen	zuhören
to write	schreiben
Goodbye.	Auf Wiedersehen.
Bye.	Tschüss.

VOCABULARY SKILLS

Es gibt viele Tipps und Tricks, die dir das Vokabellernen erleichtern. Du findest sie hier im *Vocabulary* immer zu Beginn einer neuen Unit. Sie heißen *Vocabulary Skills*. Am besten lernst du Vokabeln in gewohnter und ruhiger Umgebung. Richte dir also einen festen Arbeitsplatz ein, an dem du alles greifbar hast, was zum Lernen nötig ist: Schreibzeug, Hefte, Bücher etc. Und schon kann's losgehen:

Schau dir die englischen Wörter, die deutsche Übersetzung und die Sätze und Bilder in der rechten Spalte genau an, am besten mehrmals hintereinander. Um sie dir noch intensiver einzuprägen, kannst du die Vokabeln auch abschreiben oder dir auf unterschiedliche Weise vorsagen, z. B. laut, leise, flüsternd oder auch singend!

pick-up ['pɪkʌp]	Pick-up, Kleintransporter	
to **pick up** [pɪk 'ʌp]	abholen, mitnehmen	
unit ['ju:nɪt]	Lektion, Kapitel, Einheit	
Thomas Tallis [ˌtɒməs 'tælɪs]		
°**school** [sku:l]	Schule →	Thomas Tallis is my new *school*.

Check-in

check-in ['tʃekɪn]	Einchecken	
°**Hello.** [hel'əʊ]	Hallo. →	
°**My name is ....** [maɪ 'neɪm‿ɪz]	Ich heiße .... →	! Englische Hauptwörter (Nomen) schreibst du immer klein, so wie hier *name*.
°**I'm (= I am)** [aɪm; aɪ‿'æm]	ich bin →	
eleven [ɪ'levn]	elf	
from [frɒm; frəm]	aus, von	
in [ɪn]	in	
London ['lʌndən]	→	London ist die Hauptstadt von Großbritannien.
a, an [ə; ən]	ein/-e →	! Vor Selbstlauten (Vokalen) wird *a* zu *an*.
°**pupil** ['pju:pl]	Schüler, Schülerin →	

TIP
Merk dir bei ***pupil***: Im Englischen gibt es oft nur ein Wort für weibliche und männliche Personen: Lisa is a *pupil* at Thomas Tallis.

at [æt; ət]	in, auf, bei, an	
twelve [twelv]	zwölf	
too [tu:]	auch →	! Satzstellung: I'm from Greenwich, *too*.
this [ðɪs]	diese/-r/-s	
new [nju:]	neu	
year [jɪə]	Jahr; Jahrgangsstufe, Klasse, Schuljahr →	! *Year* wird groß geschrieben, wenn es Jahrgangsstufe bedeutet: I'm in *Year* 7.
seven ['sevn]	sieben	
1 **tiny** ['taɪni]	klein, winzig	
mouse [maʊs]	Maus →	
one [wʌn]	eins	
and [ænd; ənd]	und	
home [həʊm]	Zuhause	
°**What's your name?** [wɒts jɔ: 'neɪm]	Wie heißt du? →	! *What's* ist die Kurzform von *what is*. *What's **your** name?* – **My** name is Lisa.
°**How old are you?** [haʊ‿'əʊld‿ɑ: 'ju:]	Wie alt bist du? →	*How old are you?* – I'm eleven.

	Where are you from? [ˌweər‿ə jə ˈfrɒm]	Woher kommst du? →
2	**How to …** [haʊ tə]	Wie man …
	to **say hello** [seɪ helˈəʊ]	jemanden begrüßen
	to **say** [seɪ]	sagen →
	useful [ˈjuːsfl]	nützlich, hilfreich
	phrase [freɪz]	Satz, Redewendung
	ten [ten]	zehn
4	**Listening** [ˈlɪsnɪŋ]	*hier:* Hörverstehensübung
	phone number [ˈfəʊn ˌnʌmbə]	Telefonnummer
	number [ˈnʌmbə]	Nummer, Hausnummer; Zahl

TIP

Wenn vor einem Zeitwort (Verb) das Wörtchen *to* steht, weißt du, dass es die Grundform (der Infinitiv) ist, wie hier bei *to say*.

Numbers 1–12

1	**one** [wʌn]	5	**five** [faɪv]	9	**nine** [naɪn]
2	**two** [tuː]	6	**six** [sɪks]	10	**ten** [ten]
3	**three** [θriː]	7	**seven** [ˈsevn]	11	**eleven** [ɪˈlevn]
4	**four** [fɔː]	8	**eight** [eɪt]	12	**twelve** [twelv]

	mobile [ˈməʊbaɪl]	Handy, Mobiltelefon →
	ring! [rɪŋ]	klingeling!
	or [ɔː]	oder
	to **write** [raɪt]	schreiben
	the [ðə; ði]	der, die (*auch pl.*), das →
5	**Hands on** [hændz‿ˈɒn]	Pack's an! →
	folder [ˈfəʊldə]	Ordner, Mappe
	to **start** [stɑːt]	anfangen, beginnen
	English [ˈɪŋglɪʃ]	Englisch
	word bank [ˈwɜːd ˌbæŋk]	Wortsammlung →
	word [wɜːd]	Wort
	to **know** [nəʊ]	kennen; wissen
	primary school [ˈpraɪmri ˌskuːl]	Grundschule →
	more [mɔː]	mehr; weitere
	about [əˈbaʊt]	über
	yourself [jɔːˈself]	dich selbst

! *The* wird vor Selbstlauten (Vokalen) [ði] gesprochen.

Bei diesen Übungen bastelst du etwas.

Hier sammelst du Wörter, die du aus der Grundschule kennst.

Language 1: A new friend

language [ˈlæŋgwɪdʒ]	Sprache
meeting people [ˈmiːtɪŋ ˌpiːpl]	Leute kennen lernen, Leute treffen
friend [frend]	Freund, Freundin →

TIP

Merk dir bei *friend:* Du weißt, im Englischen gibt es oft nur ein Wort für weibliche und männliche Personen: Lisa is my *friend*, and Terry is my *friend*, too.

	but [bʌt]	aber	
	it's (= it is) [ɪts; ɪt‿ˈɪz]	es ist	**BIG**
	big [bɪg]	groß →	
	here's (= here is) [hɪəz; hɪə‿ˈɪz]	hier ist →	! *Here's* ist die Kurzform von *here is*: *Here's* Terry.
	he's (= he is) [hi:z; hi:‿ˈɪz]	er ist →	! *He's* ist die Kurzform von *he is*: *He's* from Greenwich.
	she's (= she is) [ʃi:z; ʃi:‿ˈɪz]	sie ist →	! *She's* ist die Kurzform von *she is*: This is Lisa. *She's* eleven.
	that's (= that is) [ðæts; ðæt‿ˈɪz]	das ist →	! *That's* ist die Kurzform von *that is*: *That's* Emma.
	Mrs [ˈmɪsɪz]	Frau *(Anrede)*	
	tutor [ˈtju:tə]	Klassenlehrer, Klassenlehrerin	
	•**German teacher** [ˈdʒɜ:mən ˌti:tʃə]	Deutschlehrer, Deutschlehrerin →	I'm your *German teacher.*
	so [səʊ]	also, folglich, deshalb	
	you're (= you are) [jɔ:; jɔ:‿ˈɑ:]	du bist; ihr seid; Sie sind →	! *You're* ist die Kurzform von *you are*: So *you're* in my tutor group, too.
	tutor group [ˈtju:tə gru:p]	Klasse *(in einer englischen Schule)*	
	favourite [ˈfeɪvrɪt]	Lieblings- →	Mrs Carter is my *favourite* teacher.
	sport [spɔ:t]	Sport, Sportart →	! Achtung Aussprache
	football [ˈfʊtbɔ:l]	Fußball →	a *football*
	goal [gəʊl]	Tor	
	•**England** [ˈɪŋglənd]	England	
	shoe [ʃu:]	Schuh →	! Achtung Schreibung
	•**thank you** [ˈθæŋk ju]	danke	
	Mr [ˈmɪstə]	Herr *(Anrede)*	
	caretaker [ˈkeəteɪkə]	Hausmeister, Hausmeisterin →	I'm the *caretaker* at TTS. Mr Newman
	scary [ˈskeəri]	beängstigend, unheimlich	
1	**example** [ɪgˈzɑ:mpl]	Beispiel	
2	**Go on, please.** [gəʊ‿ˈɒn pli:z]	Mach'/Macht bitte weiter.	
	•**please** [pli:z]	bitte →	**TIP** Wenn du um etwas bittest oder nach etwas fragst, denk daran, dass im Englischen *please* meist am Satzende steht: What's your phone number, *please?*
3	•**game** [geɪm]	Spiel	
	wrong [rɒŋ]	falsch	
	right [raɪt]	richtig →	*right* ↔ wrong
4	**order** [ˈɔ:də]	Reihenfolge	
	tip [tɪp]	Tipp, Ratschlag →	! Achtung Schreibung
5	Good morning. [gʊd ˈmɔ:nɪŋ]	Guten Morgen.	
	How are you? [ˌhaʊ‿ɑ: ˈjə]	Wie geht es dir/Ihnen?	
	I'm fine. [ˌaɪm ˈfaɪn]	Mir geht es gut.	
6	**Your turn.** [ˈjɔ: tɜ:n]	Du bist dran.	

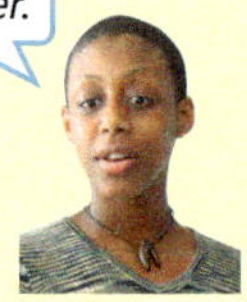

Language 2: Sam

long [lɒŋ]	lang	
short [ʃɔ:t]	kurz →	*short* ↔ long
form [fɔ:m]	Form	

Die Grundform (Infinitiv) von *I am/ you are …* ist *to be*. Viel Wissenswertes dazu findest du im Grammatikanhang unter G1-G4.

are [ɑː] – bist, sind, seid →
we [wiː; wi] – wir
•**classroom** [ˈklɑːsrʊm] – Klassenzimmer
Yes, we are. [jes wi‿ˈɑː] – Ja (das sind wir).
isn't (= is not) [ɪznt; ɪz‿ˈnɒt] – ist nicht →

! *Isn't* ist die Kurzform von *is not*: Mrs Carter *isn't* here.

sure [ʃɔː; ʃʊə] – sicher
room [ruːm] – Zimmer, Raum
No, he isn't. [ˌnəʊ hi‿ˈɪznt] – Nein, ist er nicht. →

no ↔ yes

who's (= who is) [huːz; huː‿ˈɪz] – wer ist →

! *Who* heißt **wer**, wo heißt *where*.

nice [naɪs] – nett, sympathisch →

always [ˈɔːlweɪz] – immer
He's late. [hiːz ˈleɪt] – Er kommt zu spät. / Er ist spät dran.
You're lucky. [jʊə ˈlʌki] – Du hast Glück/Ihr habt Glück.
not [nɒt] – nicht
aren't (= are not) [ɑːnt; ɑː‿ˈnɒt] – bist, sind, seid nicht
they [ðeɪ] – sie
•**Good morning.** [gʊd ˈmɔːnɪŋ] – Guten Morgen.
•**girl** [gɜːl] – Mädchen
•**boy** [bɔɪ] – Junge →

a *girl* and a *boy*

What's up? [wɒts‿ˈʌp] – Was ist los?
I'm sorry. [aɪm ˈsɒri] – Es tut mir Leid. →

Sam, you're late. – *I'm sorry*, Mrs Carter.

bag [bæg] – Tasche →

a *bag* 

with [wɪð] – mit
•**book** [bʊk] – Buch
mum [mʌm] – Mama
7 **now** [naʊ] – jetzt, nun, gerade
8 **people** *(pl.)* [ˈpiːpl] – Leute *(pl.)*, Menschen *(pl.)* →

! *People* ist eine Ausnahme. Das Hauptwort (Nomen) steht immer in der Mehrzahl (Plural), hat aber kein Mehrzahl-s: The *people* here **are** nice.

to **put in** [pʊt ˈɪn] – einsetzen
on [ɒn] – auf, an
page [peɪdʒ] – Seite →

10 **her** [hɜː] – ihr/-e
diary [ˈdaɪəri] – Tagebuch
so [səʊ] – so
very [ˈveri] – sehr
grammar [ˈgræmə] – Grammatik
11 to **look at** [ˈlʊk æt] – anschauen, ansehen
•**picture** [ˈpɪktʃə] – Bild →

Look at the *picture*.

to **make** [meɪk] – machen, bilden
sentence [ˈsentəns] – Satz
12 **question** [ˈkwestʃən] – Frage →
answer [ˈɑːnsə] – Antwort →

Question: How old are you?
Answer: I'm ten.

Language 3: The schoolbag

school things *(pl.)* [ˈskuːl ˌθɪŋz] – Schulsachen *(pl.)*

	schoolbag ['sku:lbæg]	Schultasche →
	pencil-case ['pensl keɪs]	Federmäppchen
	pen [pen]	Füller
	pencil ['pensl]	Bleistift
	rubber ['rʌbə]	Radiergummi
	ruler ['ru:lə]	Lineal
	exercise book ['eksəsaɪz ˌbʊk]	Heft →
	apple ['æpl]	Apfel
14	to **copy** ['kɒpi]	abschreiben, abmalen
	grid [grɪd]	Raster, Tabelle
	to **listen for** ['lɪsn fə]	heraushören →
	to **fill in** [fɪl‿'ɪn]	ausfüllen
16	**sound** [saʊnd]	Laut →
	list [lɪst]	Liste
17	to **play** [pleɪ]	spielen

! Achtung Schreibung: *exercise*

! Achtung Aussprache: Das ‚t' ist stumm.

! Achtung Aussprache: Das ‚s' muss zischen wie eine

Numbers 13–100 (Zahlen 13–100)

13	**thirteen** [θɜ:'ti:n]	20	**twenty** ['twenti]	40	**forty** ['fɔ:ti]
14	**fourteen** [fɔ:'ti:n]	21	**twenty-one** ['twenti'wʌn]	50	**fifty** ['fɪfti]
15	**fifteen** [fɪf'ti:n]	22	**twenty-two** ['twenti'tu:]	60	**sixty** ['sɪksti]
16	**sixteen** [sɪks'ti:n]	23	**twenty-three** ['twenti'θri:]	70	**seventy** ['sevnti]
17	**seventeen** [sevn'ti:n]	24	**twenty-four** ['twenti'fɔ:]	80	**eighty** ['eɪti]
18	**eighteen** [eɪ'ti:n]	...		90	**ninety** ['naɪnti]
19	**nineteen** [nain'ti:n]	30	**thirty** ['θɜ:ti]	100	**one hundred** [wʌn'hʌndrəd]

18	**plural** ['plʊərl]	Plural, Mehrzahl
21	**alphabet** ['ælfəbet]	Alphabet →
	to **clap** [klæp]	klatschen
	lesson ['lesn]	Unterrichtsstunde
	to **shout** [ʃaʊt]	rufen, schreien
	to **do** [du:; də; du]	machen, tun →
	to **spell** [spel]	buchstabieren →
	words that you know from Primary School [ˌwɜ:dz ðæt ju: ˌnəʊ frɒm 'praɪmri sku:l]	Wörter, die du aus der Grundschule kennst
	word puzzle ['wɜ:d ˌpʌzl]	Worträtsel
	letter ['letə]	Buchstabe

the *alphabet*

Do exercise 7 and write it in your exercise book, please.

Spell "Thomas Tallis":
T-H-O-M-A-S T-A-L-L-I-S

The alphabet (Das Alphabet)

a [eɪ]	**e** [i:]	**i** [aɪ]	**m** [em]	**q** [kju:]	**u** [ju:]	**y** [waɪ]
b [bi:]	**f** [ef]	**j** [dʒeɪ]	**n** [en]	**r** [ɑ:]	**v** [vi:]	**z** [zed]
c [si:]	**g** [dʒi:]	**k** [keɪ]	**o** [əʊ]	**s** [es]	**w** ['dʌblju:]	
d [di:]	**h** [eɪtʃ]	**l** [el]	**p** [pi:]	**t** [ti:]	**x** [eks]	

Language 4: The classroom

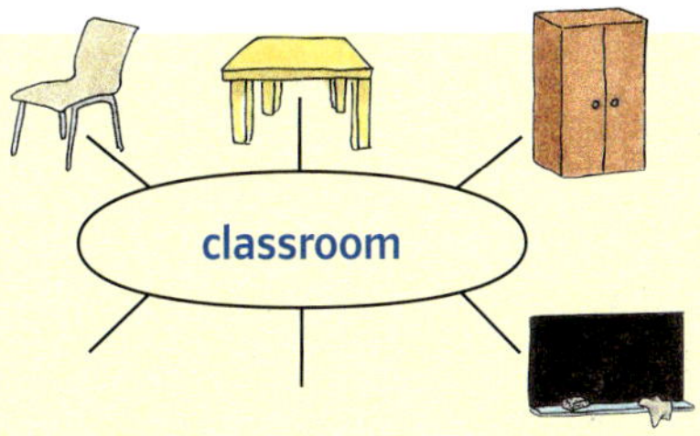

window ['wɪndəʊ]	Fenster	
chair [tʃeə]	Stuhl →	
board [bɔ:d]	Tafel, Brett	
poster ['pəʊstə]	Poster	
door [dɔ:]	Tür	
wall [wɔ:l]	Wand, Mauer	
table ['teɪbl]	Tisch	
cupboard ['kʌbəd]	Schrank	
desk [desk]	Schreibtisch	
there's (= there is) [ðeəz; ðeə‿'ɪz]	da ist, es gibt →	! *There's* ist die Kurzform von *there is*: *There's* a schoolbag on the chair.
there are [ðər'ɑ:]	da sind, es gibt →	*There are* two apples on the table.
crisp [krɪsp]	Kartoffelchip	
under ['ʌndə]	unter →	*under* ↔ on
behind [bɪ'haɪnd]	hinter	
chocolate ['tʃɒklət]	Schokolade	
in [ɪn]	im →	The pupils are *in* the classroom.
to **phone** [fəʊn]	anrufen	
23 **in front of** [ɪn 'frʌnt‿əv]	vor →	*in front of* ↔ behind
28 to **use** [ju:z]	benutzen, nutzen	
classroom phrases *(pl.)* ['klɑ:srʊm ˌfreɪzɪz]	Sätze für den Unterricht	
in English [ɪn‿'ɪŋglɪʃ]	auf Englisch	
Sorry I'm late. [ˌsɒri‿aɪm 'leɪt]	Tut mir Leid, dass ich zu spät komme.	
°**What's for homework, please?** [wɒts fə 'həʊmwɜ:k ˌpli:z]	Was haben wir als Hausaufgabe auf, bitte? →	
Can I go to the toilet, please? [kən‿aɪ ˌgəʊ tə ðə 'tɔɪlət pli:z]	Kann ich bitte zur Toilette gehen?	
°**Sit down, please.** [sɪt 'daʊn pli:z]	Setz' dich/Setzt euch bitte.	
°**You're welcome.** [jɔ: 'welkəm]	Nichts zu danken./Gern geschehen. →	
°**goodbye** [gʊd'baɪ]	auf Wiedersehen	
°**bye** [baɪ]	tschüss →	! Achtung Schreibung
29 role play ['rəʊl ˌpleɪ]	Rollenspiel	
to act [ækt]	spielen	
dialogue ['daɪəlɒg]	Dialog →	Let's act a *dialogue*!

Eine Übersicht der Fragewörter steht im Grammatikanhang unter G9.

Text: No problem!

text [tekst]	Text	
no [nəʊ]	kein/-e	
problem ['prɒbləm]	Problem →	Oh, I'm sorry. – *No problem.*
eatery ['i:tri]	Restaurant, Kantine	
lunchtime ['lʌnʃtaɪm]	Mittagszeit, Mittagspause →	It's *lunchtime*. The pupils are at the eatery.
cafeteria [kæfə'tɪəriə]	Cafeteria →	! Achtung Aussprache

	Look! [lʊk]	Schau mal! / Sieh mal! →	
	joke [dʒəʊk]	Witz	
	letter ['letə]	Buchstabe	
	easy ['i:zi]	leicht, einfach	
	boring ['bɔ:rɪŋ]	langweilig	
	terrible ['terəbl]	schrecklich, schlimm, furchtbar	
	• **playground** ['pleɪgraʊnd]	Schulhof; Spielplatz	
	she is good at … [ʃi‿ɪz 'gʊd‿ət]	sie ist gut in/bei … →	Lisa *is good at* football.
	to **watch out** [wɒtʃ 'aʊt]	aufpassen	
	ball [bɔ:l]	Ball →	! Achtung Aussprache
	tree [tri:]	Baum →	
2	group [gru:p]	Gruppe	
3	**dialogue** ['daɪəlɒg]	Dialog	
	to **complete** [kəm'pli:t]	vervollständigen →	*Complete* the sentences with a partner.
	to **put** [pʊt]	stellen, setzen, legen	
	them [ðem; ðəm]	sie	
4	**polite** [pə'laɪt]	höflich	
	you're wrong [jɔ: 'rɒŋ]	du hast Unrecht, du irrst dich	
	nasty ['nɑ:sti]	böse, gemein →	

Wordwise

	wordwise ['wɜ:dwaɪz]	„wortschlau", „wortgewandt"	
1	**word web** ['wɜ:d web]	Wortnetz	
	vocabulary [və'kæbjəlri]	Vokabular, Wortschatz	
	skill [skɪl]	Fertigkeit	
3	mouth jogging ['maʊθ ˌdʒɒgɪŋ]	„Sprachjoggen"	
5	to **find** [faɪnd]	finden	
	good [gʊd]	gut	
	adjective ['ædʒɪktɪv]	Adjektiv, Eigenschaftswort →	! Ein *adjective* ist ein Eigenschaftswort (Adjektiv), z. B. *good, polite, old, new*.
	other ['ʌðə]	andere/-r/-s, weitere/-r/-s	

Check-out

	check-out ['tʃekaʊt]	Auschecken	
2	**What is missing?** [ˌwɒt‿ɪz 'mɪsɪŋ]	Was fehlt?	
3	**different** ['dɪfrnt]	anders, unterschiedlich →	two *different* balls 

USEFUL PHRASES

Hier findest du die wichtigsten *classroom phrases* aus Unit 1.
Welche Antworten würde dir dein Lehrer/deine Lehrerin darauf geben?
Überlege dir drei weitere *classroom phrases*, die du bereits kennst.

Good morning.
Sorry I'm late.
Where are we?
What's … in English, please?

Thank you.
What's for homework, please?
Can I go to the toilet, please?

Pick-up A Home sweet home

VOCABULARY SKILLS

So kannst du dir Vokabeln einfach einprägen: Schau dich in deinem Zimmer um und überlege dir, welche Gegenstände du schon auf Englisch kennst. Schreibe dann das englische Wort auf einen selbstklebenden Zettel und hefte ihn auf den entsprechenden Gegenstand (z. B. auf dein Bett, den Tisch …). Nun übst du jedes Mal, wenn du den Gegenstand benutzt oder darauf schaust, ganz nebenbei das englische Wort!

	home sweet home ['həʊm ˌswi:t 'həʊm]	trautes Heim *(Sprichwort)*	
	sweet [swi:t]	süß →	Chocolate is *sweet*.
	purple ['pɜ:pl]	violett, lila	
	grey [greɪ]	grau	
	green [gri:n]	grün	
	black [blæk]	schwarz	
	white [waɪt]	weiß	
	pink [pɪŋk]	rosa, pink	
	red [red]	rot →	Tom is grey and the pencil-case is *red*. 
	blue [blu:]	blau	
	orange ['ɒrɪndʒ]	orange	
	brown [braʊn]	braun	
	yellow ['jeləʊ]	gelb	
1	**card** [kɑ:d]	Karte, Spielkarte →	 *cards* 
	per [pɜ:; pə]	pro	
	to **hold up** [həʊld 'ʌp]	hochhalten →	
	correct [kə'rekt]	richtig →	Lisa is from Greenwich. – That's *correct*.
2	**colour** ['kʌlə]	Farbe →	Orange is my favourite *colour*.
	open ['əʊpn]	geöffnet, offen, aufgeschlagen →	The book is *open*. 
	to **ask** [ɑ:sk]	fragen →	Can I *ask* you a question?
	then [ðen]	dann, danach →	Look at exercise 5 on page 26. *Then* complete it with your partner.
	to **close** [kləʊz]	schließen, zumachen	
	to **answer** ['ɑ:nsə]	(be)antworten →	to ask ⟷ *to answer*
	kitchen ['kɪtʃɪn]	Küche	
	living room ['lɪvɪŋ ru:m]	Wohnzimmer	
	bathroom ['bɑ:θru:m]	Bad(ezimmer)	
	bedroom ['bedru:m]	Schlafzimmer →	**TIP** Merk dir: Du schreibst *bedroom* und *bathroom*, aber *living room*.
4	**rhyme** [raɪm]	Reim	
	bed [bed]	Bett	
	sofa ['səʊfə]	Sofa, Couch →	 ! Achtung Aussprache
	funny ['fʌni]	lustig, witzig	
	house [haʊs]	Haus →	 a *house*
	TV [ˌti:'vi:]	Fernseher	
	to **learn by heart** [ˌlɜ:n baɪ 'hɑ:t]	auswendig lernen →	*Learn* the song *by heart*, please.

	• to **describe** [dɪ'skraɪb]	beschreiben →
	• **like this** [laɪk 'ðɪs]	so, auf diese Weise
5	• **furniture** ['fɜ:nɪtʃə]	Möbel →
6	• **dream** [dri:m]	Traum →
	• to **talk (to)** [tɔ:k]	sprechen (mit), reden (mit)
	• to **draw** [drɔ:]	zeichnen →
7	• **his** [hɪz]	sein/-e
	• **family** ['fæmli]	Familie →
	• **mother** ['mʌðə]	Mutter
	• **grandfather** ['græn,fɑ:ðə]	Großvater →
	• **grandad** ['grændæd]	Opa
	• **brother** ['brʌðə]	Bruder
	• **sister** ['sɪstə]	Schwester
	• **father** ['fɑ:ðə]	Vater
	• **dad** [dæd]	Papa, Vati
	• **grandmother** ['græn,mʌðə]	Großmutter
	• **grandma** ['grænmɑ:]	Oma
8	• **happy** ['hæpi]	glücklich, fröhlich →
9	• **What colour are … ?** [wɒt 'kʌlə_ɑ:]	Welche Farbe haben … ?

Look at the house in the picture. Then *describe* it, please.

! *Furniture* hat <u>keine</u> Mehrzahl (Pluralform): What *furniture* **is** in the room?

Let's *draw* a picture!

the Tiny *family* = die Familie Tiny

grandmother —— *grandfather*

mother —— *father*

brother —— sister

Tom is *happy*.

Unit 2 At home in Greenwich

Hier findest du noch weitere Wörter, um deine **Familie** vorzustellen. Sie sind dir vielleicht schon aus der Grundschule bekannt.

parents (pl.)	Eltern	**English**	englisch, aus England
child pl. children	Kind, Kinder	**Germany**	Deutschland
aunt	Tante	**German**	deutsch, aus Deutschland
uncle	Onkel	**Where are you from?**	Woher kommst du?
cousin	Cousin, Cousine	**I'm from Germany.**	Ich komme aus Deutschland.
England	England	**I'm German.**	Ich bin Deutsche / Deutscher

VOCABULARY SKILLS

Vokabeln kannst du gut mit Hilfe einer Vokabelkartei lernen. Dazu brauchst du Karteikarten und einen Karton mit fünf Fächern. Schreibe jeweils das englische Wort auf die Vorderseite der Karteikarte und die deutsche Übersetzung auf die Rückseite. Als Merkhilfe kannst du zusätzlich zum englischen Wort auch ein Bild malen oder einen Beispielsatz aus dem Buch aufschreiben. Stelle alle Karten in das erste Fach.
Trainiere jeden Tag 5–10 Minuten, und zwar so: Nimm eine Karte nach der anderen heraus und prüfe, ob du die Übersetzung weißt (deutsch-englisch und englisch-deutsch!). Wenn ja, wandert die Karte in das zweite Fach. Wenn nein, bleibt sie im ersten Fach.
Mache so lange weiter, bis das erste Fach leer ist. Das zweite Fach bearbeitest du dann genauso, allerdings nicht jeden Tag, sondern einmal in der Woche, das dritte Fach alle zwei Wochen und so weiter …

	at home [æt 'həʊm]	zu Hause →	Emma is *at home*. Her mother and father are *at home*, too.

Check-in

	• **parents** *(pl.)* ['peərənts]	Eltern →	mother and father = *parents*
	half-sister ['hɑ:fˌsɪstə]	Halbschwester	
	step-father ['stepˌfɑ:ðə]	Stiefvater	
	our [aʊə; ɑ:]	unser/-e	
	flat [flæt]	Wohnung →	a *flat* 
	road [rəʊd]	Straße	
	over ['əʊvə]	über →	The flat is *over* the shop.
	computer shop [kəm'pju:tə ˌʃɒp]	Computerladen	
	shop [ʃɒp]	Geschäft, Laden	
	its [ɪts]	sein →	! This is our computer shop. **It's** a cool shop. My father is ***its*** manager.
	small [smɔ:l]	klein →	*small* ↔ big
	Nasreen and I are … [nʌs'ri:n‿ənd‿aɪ‿ɑ:]	Nasreen und ich sind …	
	only child [ˌəʊnli 'tʃaɪld]	Einzelkind →	The Jackson family: Mr Jackson, Mrs Jackson and Terry → Terry is an *only child*.
	• **child** pl. **children** ['tʃaɪld; 'tʃɪldrn]	Kind →	! Achtung Aussprache: one *child* – two *children*
	cat [kæt]	Katze	
	tiger ['taɪgə]	Tiger →	! Achtung Aussprache
	only ['əʊnli]	nur	
	interested in ['ɪntrəstɪd]	interessiert an	
	mice *(pl.)* [maɪs]	Mäuse *(pl.)* →	! one mouse, two *mice*
	garden ['gɑ:dn]	Garten	
	shed [ʃed]	Schuppen, Gartenhäuschen	
	drums *(pl.)* [drʌmz]	Schlagzeug →	Can you play the *drums*?
	chemistry set ['kemɪstri set]	Chemiekasten	
1	to **match** [mætʃ]	zuordnen	
2	**dog** [dɒg]	Hund →	 a *dog*
3	• **photo** ['fəʊtəʊ]	Foto →	! Achtung Schreibung und Aussprache
	to **listen to** ['lɪsn tə]	jemandem zuhören	
	why [waɪ]	warum	
	upstairs [ʌp'steəz]	oben, im Obergeschoss	 *upstairs*
	downstairs [daʊn'steəz]	unten, im Untergeschoss →	*downstairs*

Language 1: Sam's family tree

	nationality [ˌnæʃn'æləti]	Nationalität →	What's your *nationality*? – I'm German.
	family tree ['fæmli ˌtri:]	Familienstammbaum	
	married to ['mærid tə]	verheiratet mit →	Ted is *married to* Grace.
	• **aunt** [ɑ:nt]	Tante	
	• **uncle** ['ʌŋkl]	Onkel →	! Du schreibst alle Familienbezeichnungen in Verbindung mit einem Namen groß: *Aunt* Maria, *Uncle* Tim etc.
	divorced from [dɪ'vɔ:st frəm]	geschieden von →	David is *divorced from* Elena.
	• **cousin** ['kʌzn]	Cousin, Cousine	
2	lunch [lʌnʃ]	Mittagessen	
	minute ['mɪnɪt]	Minute	
	next to ['nekst tə]	neben	

	on the left [ɒn ðə 'left]	auf der linken Seite, links
	on the right [ɒn ðə 'raɪt]	auf der rechten Seite, rechts
3	**European** [ˌjʊərə'piːən]	europäisch, aus Europa
	Polish ['pəʊlɪʃ]	polnisch, aus Polen; Polnisch
	because [bɪ'kɒz]	weil, da →
	Poland ['pəʊlənd]	Polen
	English ['ɪŋglɪʃ]	englisch, aus England →
	Greek [griːk]	griechisch, aus Griechenland; Griechisch
	today [tə'deɪ]	heute
	lunch [lʌnʃ]	Mittagessen
	Italian [ɪ'tæliən]	italienisch, aus Italien; Italienisch
	your [jɔː]	euer, eure; Ihr(e)
4	**their** [ðeə]	ihr, ihre *(Plural)*
5	to **tell** [tel]	erzählen, sagen →
	Germany ['dʒɜːməni]	Deutschland →
	Russia ['rʌʃə]	Russland
	Russian ['rʌʃn]	russisch, aus Russland; Russisch
	Greece [griːs]	Griechenland
	Italy ['ɪtli]	Italien
	Turkey ['tɜːki]	Türkei →
	Turkish ['tɜːkɪʃ]	türkisch, aus der Türkei; Türkisch
	Spain [speɪn]	Spanien
	Spanish ['spænɪʃ]	spanisch, aus Spanien; Spanisch

The pupils are happy *because* it is lunchtime.

TIP

Merk dir: Nationalitäten schreibst du im Englischen immer groß: Terry is *English*.

Where's your family from? *Tell* your partner!
I'm from *Germany*. = I'm German.

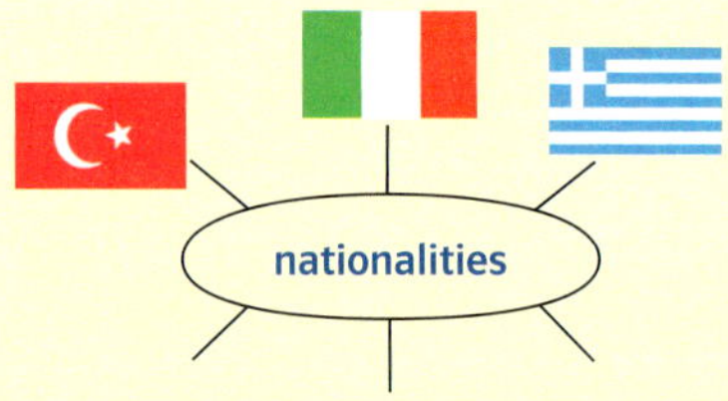

My, your, his, her, our, their

my	mein/meine	**My** brother and **my** parents are in the garden.
your	dein/deine	**Your** friends are nice.
	euer/eure	**Your** teacher is OK.
	Ihr/Ihre	Mr Brook, is **your** computer new?
his	sein/seine	**His** drums are in **his** shed.
her	ihr/ihre	**Her** sisters are at **her** grandma's house.
our	unser/unsere	**Our** flat is over **our** shop.
their	ihr/ihre	**Their** uncle and **their** cousins are from Greece.

Language 2: Emma, you're in big trouble!

saying what you've got ['seɪɪŋ ˌwɒt jʊv 'gɒt]	sagen, was jemand hat
You're in big trouble. [jɔːr ɪn 'bɪg ˌtrʌbl]	Du steckst in großen Schwierigkeiten.
she has got ... [ʃi həz 'gɒt]	sie hat ... →
only ['əʊnli]	nur, bloß
wardrobe ['wɔːdrəʊb]	Kleiderschrank
a lot of [ə 'lɒt əv]	viel/-e, eine Menge →
outside [ˌaʊt'saɪd]	außen, draußen, im Freien; außerhalb

I've got *a lot of* friends.

	She is in a hurry. [ˌʃi‿ɪz ɪn ə ˈhʌri]	Sie hat es eilig. →	She hasn't got a lot of time. *She is in a hurry.*
	to **look** [lʊk]	nachschauen, suchen →	Where is my ruler? – *Look* in your pencil-case.
	magazine [ˌmægəˈziːn]	Zeitschrift	
	second [ˈseknd]	Sekunde	
	maybe [ˈmeɪbi]	vielleicht	
	Here it is. [ˈhɪər‿ɪt‿ɪz]	Hier ist es. →	Where is my German book? – *Here it is*!
	dirty [ˈdɜːti]	dreckig, schmutzig	
	What a mess! [wɒt‿ə ˈmes]	Was für eine Unordnung!	
	later [ˈleɪtə]	später	
	just [dʒʌst]	nur	
	silly [ˈsɪli]	albern, dumm	
	well [wel]	tja, nun	
	to **sort out** [sɔːt ˈaʊt]	klären, regeln →	I've got a problem with Nasreen – Then *sort it out* with her!
6	**her own room** [hər‿ˌəʊn ˈruːm]	ihr eigenes Zimmer →	**TIP** Merk dir: *own* verwendest du immer mit *my, your, his, her* etc.: Emma hasn't got **her** *own* room.
9	relative [ˈrelətɪv]	Verwandter, Verwandte	
	to agree [əˈgriː]	zustimmen	
10	**car** [kɑː]	Auto	
12	Here you are. [ˌhɪə ju‿ˈɑː]	Bitte schön.	

Language 3: Rules for our room

	rule [ruːl]	Regel	
	can't (= cannot) [kɑːnt; ˈkænɒt]	nicht können →	! Achtung Aussprache: can ↔ *can't*
	CD [ˌsiːˈdiː]	CD →	! Achtung Aussprache
	How can I do my homework? [ˈhaʊ kən‿aɪ ˌduː maɪ ˈhəʊmwɜːk]	Wie soll ich meine Hausaufgaben machen?	
	music [ˈmjuːzɪk]	Musik	
	idea [aɪˈdɪə]	Idee	
	to **help** [help]	helfen	
	to **take turns** [teɪk ˈtɜːnz]	sich abwechseln	
	Don't use ... [dəʊnt ˈjuːs]	Benutze nicht ... →	
	quiet [kwaɪət]	leise, ruhig, still	
	when [wen]	wenn, als	
	to **play** [pleɪ]	(ab)spielen *(CD, Radio etc.)* →	*to play* a CD = eine CD (ab)spielen *to play* a game = ein Spiel spielen
	to **take** [teɪk]	(weg)nehmen	
18	**the same** [ðə ˈseɪm]	der-/die-/dasselbe, der/die/das Gleiche →	The two schoolbags are *the same*.
	to **open** [ˈəʊpn]	öffnen, aufmachen →	*to open* ↔ to close
19	to **have a party** [hæv ə ˈpɑːti]	eine Party feiern →	
20	**great** [greɪt]	toll, großartig	
	Emma is good with ... [ˌemə ɪz ˈgʊd wɪð]	Emma kann mit ... gut umgehen	
	rubber ball [ˌrʌbə ˈbɔːl]	Gummiball	
22	**revision** [rɪˈvɪʒn]	Wiederholung	
	to [tuː; tʊ]	an	

to **say hello to** [seɪ hel'əʊ tə]	grüßen, Grüße ausrichten →	**TIP** Wenn du auf Englisch Grüße an jemanden ausrichten möchtest, sagst du z. B.: *Say hello to* your sister. Oder: *Say hello to* Richard.
I'm **with ...** [aɪm 'wɪð]	Ich bin bei ...	

Text: Terry's shed

before [bɪ'fɔː]	bevor	
one Saturday afternoon [wʌn 'sætədeɪ ˌɑːftə'nuːn]	an einem Samstag Nachmittag	
busy (with) ['bɪzi ˌwɪð]	beschäftigt (mit) →	I'm *busy with* my homework.
project ['prɒdʒekt]	Projekt →	! Achtung Schreibung und Aussprache
slow [sləʊ]	langsam →	My computer is old. It's very *slow*.
he is fed up [hiː ɪz fed 'ʌp]	er ist sauer / er hat die Nase voll	
to **finish** ['fɪnɪʃ]	(be)enden, fertig stellen	
Nasreen is a pain. [nʌs'riːn‿ɪz ə 'peɪn]	Nasreen geht mir auf die Nerven.	
to **come over** [kʌm 'əʊvə]	herüberkommen, vorbeischauen →	Can you *come over* this afternoon?
soon [suːn]	bald	
thanks [θæŋks]	danke →	! *Thanks* ist die Kurzform von *thank you*.
to **stop** [stɒp]	aufhören, beenden →	*to stop* ↔ to start
smoke [sməʊk]	Rauch	
everywhere ['evriweə]	überall	
smell [smel]	Geruch, Duft, Gestank	
yuk [jʌk]	i, igitt	
beautiful ['bjuːtɪfl]	schön, wunderbar →	*beautiful* ↔ terrible
crystal ['krɪstl]	Kristall	
... is fun [ɪz 'fʌn]	... macht Spaß	
3 to **talk about** [tɔːk ə'baʊt]	sprechen über	
4 story ['stɔːri]	Geschichte, Erzählung →	Do you know the *story*? Let's talk about it!
5 to **sort** [sɔːt]	sortieren	

Wordwise

1 **group** [gruːp]	Gruppe	
to **underline** [ˌʌndə'laɪn]	unterstreichen	

USEFUL PHRASES

Wenn du auf Englisch über deine Familie sprechen möchtest, helfen dir die folgenden *phrases*:

This is my family. My parents are ...
I've got ... sister(s) and ... brother(s).
My sister's/my brother's name is ...
Our house/our flat is in ...
We've got a big/small garden ...
I've got a pet, it's a ... and his/her name is ...

Pick-up B Tom in Hobbyland

VOCABULARY SKILLS

Vielleicht fällt dir das Vokabellernen leichter, wenn du nicht im Sitzen lernst, sondern ab und zu aufstehst und z. B. Zeitwörter (Verben) mit einer bestimmten Bewegung oder Eigenschaftswörter (Adjektive) mit einem passenden Gesichtsausdruck verbindest (bei *to clap* könntest du beispielsweise in die Hände klatschen). Um dir ein Wort besser zu merken, kannst du dir auch eine witzige Situation überlegen, die dazu passt.

	Hobbyland ['hɒbilænd]	Hobbyland
	hobby pl. **hobbies** ['hɒbi; 'hɒbiz]	Hobby
	land [lænd]	Land
	to **ride** [raɪd]	reiten, fahren
	bike [baɪk]	Fahrrad
	to **watch** [wɒtʃ]	ansehen; beobachten
	guitar [gɪ'tɑ:]	Gitarre →
	to **go swimming** [gəʊ 'swɪmɪŋ]	schwimmen gehen
	to **swim** [swɪm]	schwimmen
	to **read** [ri:d]	lesen →
	to **collect** [kə'lekt]	sammeln, einsammeln
4	**role play** ['rəʊl pleɪ]	Rollenspiel
	Let's go! [lets 'gəʊ]	Lass(t) uns anfangen!/ Lass(t) uns gehen!

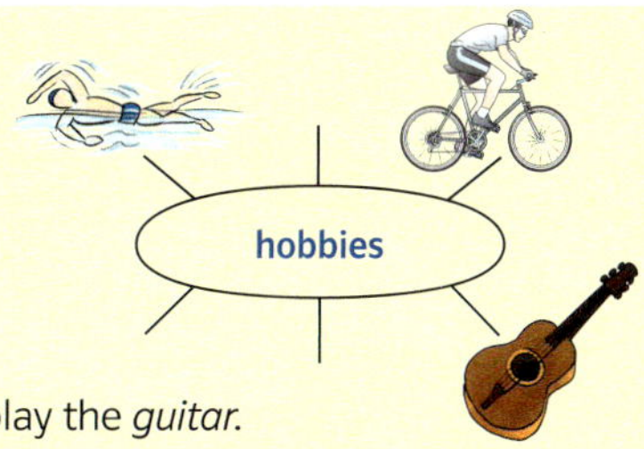

I play the *guitar.*

to read

Let's ...! (Lass(t) uns ...!)

Let's start!	Lass(t) uns beginnen!/ Lass(t) uns anfangen!
Let's listen!	Lass(t) uns zuhören!
Let's sing a song!	Lass(t) uns ein Lied singen!
Let's play a game!	Lass(t) uns ein Spiel spielen!
Let's look at the picture!	Lass(t) uns das Bild anschauen!
Let's read a book!	Lass(t) uns ein Buch lesen!
Let's talk about our school!	Lass(t) uns über unsere Schule reden!
Let's ride our bikes!	Lass(t) uns Fahrrad fahren!
Let's watch a video!	Lass(t) uns ein Video anschauen!
Let's go!	Lass(t) uns gehen!

6	**days of the week** *(pl.)* [ˌdeɪz_ɒv ðə 'wi:k]	Wochentage *(pl.)*
	day [deɪ]	Tag
	week [wi:k]	Woche →

There are seven days in a *week.*

Days of the week (Wochentage)

Monday ['mʌndeɪ]	Montag
Tuesday ['tju:zdeɪ]	Dienstag
Wednesday ['wenzdeɪ]	Mittwoch
Thursday ['θɜ:zdeɪ]	Donnerstag
Friday ['fraɪdeɪ]	Freitag
Saturday ['sætədeɪ]	Samstag
Sunday ['sʌndeɪ]	Sonntag

Unit 3 Hobbies and clubs

Erinnerst du dich noch an andere Grundschul-Wörter zum Thema **Freizeit** und **Hobbies**? Bestimmt erkennst du einige aus dieser Box wieder.

club	Klub, Verein	**to dance**	tanzen
Come on!	Komm schon! / Komm jetzt!	**to sing**	singen
film	Film	**Can we sing a song, please?**	Können wir bitte ein Lied singen?
Let's watch a film!	Lass(t) uns einen Film anschauen!	**What time is it, please?**	Wie spät ist es, bitte?
to like	mögen	**It's five o'clock.**	Es ist fünf Uhr.
I like English.	Ich mag Englisch.	**to get up**	aufstehen
to meet	treffen, sich treffen	**to walk**	gehen (*zu Fuß*)
Let's meet at the playground.	Komm, wir treffen uns auf dem Schulhof/Spielplatz.	**to run**	laufen, rennen

VOCABULARY SKILLS

Mehrere kleine, leichte Pakete kannst du nacheinander besser heben als ein großes, schweres! Genauso merkst du dir neue Wörter schneller und leichter, wenn du sie in kleinen Päckchen von 10-15 Vokabeln lernst. Außerdem behältst du neue Wörter besser, wenn du sie erst einmal fünf Minuten lang lernst, sie dann nach einer halben Stunde wiederholst und schließlich am Ende deiner Hausaufgaben oder am Abend vor dem Einschlafen noch einmal überprüfst.

•**club** [klʌb]	Klub, Verein

Check-in

British ['brɪtɪʃ]	britisch
important [ɪm'pɔ:tnt]	wichtig
there [ðeə]	dorthin, dahin
free time ['fri: ˌtaɪm]	Freizeit →
•to **meet** [mi:t]	treffen, sich treffen →
orchestra ['ɔ:kɪstrə]	Orchester →
on Tuesdays [ɒn 'tju:zdeɪz]	dienstags →
from ... to ['frəm tə]	von ... bis
pm [ˌpi:'em]	nachmittags *(Uhrzeit)*
cooking club ['kʊkɪŋ ˌklʌb]	Kochklub
am [ˌeɪ'em]	vormittags *(Uhrzeit)* →
How about ... [haʊ ə'baʊt]	Wie wäre es mit ...
when [wen]	wann →
at half past (three) [ət ˌhɑ:f pɑ:st 'θri:]	um halb (vier)

! Achtung Aussprache

! on Mondays, *on Tuesdays* ... = jeden Montag, jeden Dienstag ... (regelmäßig etwas tun!)

TIP

Merk dir: Im Englischen sagst du zu 8 Uhr, 9 Uhr ... 8 *am*, 9 *am*, und zu 13 Uhr, 14 Uhr, 15 Uhr ... 1 *pm*, 2 *pm*, 3 *pm* ...
Du kannst es dir am Besten so merken: Im Alphabet kommt ‚a' vor ‚p'.

When is the cooking club? – It's at 4 pm on Mondays.

	fine [faɪn]	in Ordnung, gut	
	• **Come on!** [kʌm‿'ɒn]	Komm schon!/Komm jetzt! →	*Come on*! Let's go!
	See you there. [siː jə 'ðeə]	Wir sehen uns dort. →	
	at the weekend [æt ðə ˌwiːk'end]	am Wochenende →	Saturday and Sunday = the *weekend*
	cinema ['sɪnəmə]	Kino	
	• **film** [fɪlm]	Film →	There's a new *film* at the cinema. Let's go and see it!
	boy band ['bɔɪ ˌbænd]	Boygroup	
	water ['wɔːtə]	Wasser	
1	• **o'clock** [ə'klɒk]	Uhr (*Zeitangabe bei vollen Stunden*) →	It's six *o'clock*!
2	• **What time is it, please?** [wɒt 'taɪm‿ɪz‿ɪt pliːz]	Wie spät ist es, bitte?	
	to **tell the time** [ˌtel ðə 'taɪm]	die Uhr lesen	
	half [hɑːf]	halb	
	quarter ['kwɔːtə]	Viertel	
	past [pɑːst]	nach (*bei Uhrzeitangaben*) →	3.15 pm = quarter *past* three
	to [tə]	vor (*bei Uhrzeitangaben*) →	2.45 pm = quarter *to* three
	minute ['mɪnɪt]	Minute →	1 *minute* = 60 seconds 
4	**at my house** [ət 'maɪ haʊs]	bei mir zu Hause	
5	**town** [taʊn]	Stadt	

Language 1: A phone call from Grandma

daily ['deɪli]	täglich →	! Achtung Schreibung: day → *daily*
routine [ruː'tiːn]	Routine	
phone call ['fəʊn ˌkɔːl]	(Telefon)Anruf	
It's Mum here. [ɪts 'mʌm ˌhɪə]	Hier spricht Mama. →	
How are you? [ˌhaʊ‿ɑː 'jə]	Wie geht es dir/Ihnen?	
I'm fine, thanks. [aɪm 'faɪn ˌθæŋks]	Mir geht es gut, danke.	
nice [naɪs]	schön, gut →	How is the new film at the cinema? – It's very *nice*.
• to **get up** [get 'ʌp]	aufstehen	
early ['ɜːli]	früh →	*early* ↔ late
usually ['juːʒli]	gewöhnlich, normalerweise	
every ['evri]	jede/-r/-s	
What about … ? [wɒt‿ə'baʊt]	Was ist mit … ?	
to **go home** [gəʊ 'həʊm]	nach Hause gehen	
to **eat** [iːt]	essen	
school day ['skuːl deɪ]	Schultag	
never ['nevə]	nie, niemals →	*never* ↔ always
after ['ɑːftə]	nach; nachdem →	*after* ↔ before
often ['ɒfn]	oft, häufig	
to **walk the dog** [wɔːk ðə 'dɒg]	den Hund ausführen →	Lisa *walks* Barker. 
to **walk** [wɔːk]	gehen (*zu Fuß*)	

	Lisa is great fun. ['li:sə ɪz 'greɪt ˌfʌn]	Lisa ist echt witzig. →
	sometimes ['sʌmtaɪmz]	manchmal
	on TV [ɒn ˌti:'vi:]	im Fernsehen
	in the evening [ɪn ði‿'i:vnɪŋ]	abends
	to **fall asleep** [fɔ:l‿ə'sli:p]	einschlafen →
	to **visit** ['vɪzɪt]	besuchen
	us [ʌs; əs]	uns →
	dancing lessons *(pl.)* ['dɑ:nsɪŋ ˌlesnz]	Tanzunterricht, Tanzstunden
	first [fɜ:st]	zuerst, als Erstes
	again [ə'gen]	wieder, noch einmal, nochmal →
4	**box** [bɒks]	Box, Kasten, Kästchen, Schachtel
5	**this is ...** [ðɪs‿ɪz]	hier ist ... *(am Telefon)*

TIP

Um auszudrücken, dass eine Person witzig ist oder dass dir eine Sache Spaß macht, benutzt du ... *is fun*: Lisa *is* great *fun*. My school project *is fun*.

In the evening, I usually *fall asleep* at 9 o'clock.

Please visit *us* at the weekend = Please come to our house at the weekend.

vor/nach (zeitlich)

It's twenty **to** five. — Es ist zwanzig **vor** fünf.

Please do your homework **before** you go to dancing lessons. — Bitte mache deine Hausaufgaben, **bevor** du in den Tanzunterricht gehst.

It's quarter **past** ten. — Es ist viertel **nach** zehn.

Let's go to the park **after** school. — Lass(t) uns **nach** der Schule in den Park gehen.

vor/hinter (räumlich)

The mouse is **in front of** the bag. — Die Maus ist **vor** der Tasche.

The mouse is **behind** the cupboard. — Die Maus ist **hinter** dem Schrank.

Language 2: Sam and Tiger

third person singular [θɜ:d 'pɜ:sn 'sɪŋgjələ]	dritte Person Singular (Einzahl) →
note [nəʊt]	Notiz, Nachricht
help [help]	Hilfe →
tin [tɪn]	Dose, Büchse
cat food ['kæt ˌfu:d]	Katzenfutter
food [fu:d]	Essen, Nahrung, Nahrungsmittel
into ['ɪntə]	in (hinein)
next to ['nekst tə]	neben →
chicken flavour ['tʃɪkɪn ˌfleɪvə]	Geschmacksrichtung „Hühnchen"
to **look** [lʊk]	aussehen
tasty ['teɪsti]	lecker →
to **come in** [kʌm 'ɪn]	hereinkommen

help → to help

Emma is *next to* Lisa and Sam is *next to* Terry.

hole [həʊl]	Loch	 
to **feed** [fi:d]	füttern →	
to **run away** [rʌn‿ə'weɪ]	weglaufen	
to **run** [rʌn]	laufen, rennen →	
round the garden [raʊnd ðə 'gɑ:dn]	durch den ganzen Garten	
neighbour ['neɪbə]	Nachbar, Nachbarin →	Your *neighbour's* house is the house next to your house.
after that ['ɑ:ftə ðət]	danach	
street [stri:t]	Straße →	! *street* – road: Mit ***street*** meinst du eine Straße mit Häusern **in einem Ort** (Don't play in the *street*.). Mit **road** meinst du eine Verkehrsstraße **außerhalb eines Orts** (Where is the road to Greenwich?).
There she is. ['ðeə ʃi‿ɪz]	Da ist sie ja.	
to **chase** [tʃeɪs]	verfolgen	
finally ['faɪnli]	schließlich, endlich, zum Schluss →	first → then → after that → *finally*
to **go back** [gəʊ 'bæk]	zurückgehen	
to **wait** [weɪt]	warten	
It's time to go home. [ɪts ˌtaɪm tə gəʊ 'həʊm]	Es ist Zeit, nach Hause zu gehen. →	*It's time to go home.* = It's time to go back to the house.
6 **together** [tə'geðə]	zusammen; gemeinsam	
7 to **like** [laɪk]	mögen	
8 to **love** [lʌv]	lieben →	

Language 3: Sam's card trick

card trick ['kɑ:d ˌtrɪk]	Kartenkunststück	
those [ðəʊz]	diese (dort), jene	
these [ði:z]	diese (hier) →	*These* are my books. Those are your books.
on the top [ɒn ðə 'tɒp]	oben	
on the bottom [ɒn ðə 'bɒtəm]	unten →	*on the bottom* ↔ on the top
just [dʒʌst]	einfach →	! The exercise is **easy**. ***Just*** read it again.
to **shuffle** ['ʃʌfl]	mischen	
to **hold** [həʊld]	halten, festhalten	
to **bang** [bæŋ]	knallen, schlagen	
He can't believe his eyes. [hi kɑ:nt bɪˌli:v hɪz 'aɪz]	Er traut seinen Augen nicht.	
to **work** [wɜ:k]	funktionieren	
nine of diamonds [naɪn‿əv 'daɪəməndz]	Karoneun *(beim Kartenspiel)*	
eight of hearts [ˌeɪt‿əv 'hɑ:ts]	Herzacht *(beim Kartenspiel)* →	
on top of [ɒn 'tɒp‿əv]	auf … hinauf, oben (auf)	
to **remember** [rɪ'membə]	sich erinnern (an)	
to **forget** [fə'get]	vergessen →	*to forget* ↔ to remember
which [wɪtʃ]	welche/-r/-s	
to **show** [ʃəʊ]	zeigen	
14 to **happen** ['hæpn]	passieren, geschehen	
to **kick** [kɪk]	schießen; treten →	When you play football, you *kick* the ball.
16 **linking sounds** [ˌlɪŋkɪŋ 'saʊndz]	das Verbinden von Lauten	
to **link** [lɪŋk]	verbinden	

Text: Barker's story

story ['stɔ:rɪ]	Geschichte, Erzählung
pet [pet]	Haustier →
to **wake up** [weɪk‿'ʌp]	aufwecken; aufwachen →
to **wash** [wɒʃ]	waschen
face [feɪs]	Gesicht
breakfast ['brekfəst]	Frühstück →
to **bark** [bɑ:k]	bellen →
to **take** [teɪk]	(mit)nehmen, bringen
to **teach** [ti:tʃ]	unterrichten, lehren, beibringen →
to **bring** [brɪŋ]	(mit)bringen
to **throw** [θrəʊ]	werfen
me [mi:]	mich; mir
to **get lost** [get 'lɒst]	sich verirren →
to **call** [kɔ:l]	rufen, schreien
to **take out** [teɪk‿'aʊt]	ausführen
to **bark at** ['bɑ:k‿ət]	anbellen
them [ðem; ðəm]	sie *(Plural)*
drink [drɪŋk]	Getränk →
to **fall over** [fɔ:l 'əʊvə]	umfallen, hinfallen
to **sleep** [sli:p]	schlafen
dog-tired [dɒg'taɪəd]	hundemüde →
2 to **go to bed** [ˌgəʊ tə 'bed]	zu Bett gehen

Barker and Tiger are *pets*. Tom isn't a *pet*.

to wake up ↔ to fall asleep

to teach → teacher

In a big town, it is easy to *get lost*.

Tom is *dog-tired*.

Wordwise

5 **mixed bag** [ˌmɪkst 'bæg]	bunte Mischung
mixed [mɪkst]	gemischt
6 poem ['pəʊɪm]	Gedicht
… is his thing [ɪz hɪz 'θɪŋ]	… macht er gerne/ … kann er gut
to dance [dɑ:ns]	tanzen
all [ɔ:l]	alle
to sing [sɪŋ]	singen

Check-out

simple present [ˌsɪmpl 'preznt]	Gegenwart, Präsens

USEFUL PHRASES

In einer Fremdsprache zu telefonieren ist manchmal schwieriger, als sich mit jemandem direkt zu unterhalten. Aber mit diesen *phrases* wird es dir ganz leicht fallen.

Hi./Hello. This is … How are you?	Hi./Hello, … I'm fine, thanks. And you?
Can we … on Saturday?	OK, great idea! Fine! / Cool! When can we meet?
Let's go to … !	No, sorry, I can't, I've always got … on Saturdays.
How about … ?	Yes. That's fine. / See you at …/soon. Bye.

Pick-up C In town

VOCABULARY SKILLS

Lerne ein neues Wort möglichst in einem ganzen Satz, z. B. *museum*: *Let's go to the museum.* So kannst du dir das Wort besser einprägen. Auch merkst du dir dann, wie man es in einem Satz benutzt.

map [mæp]	Stadtplan, Landkarte	
of [ɒv; əv]	von	
museum [mju:'zi:əm]	Museum	
river ['rɪvə]	Fluss →	
bridge [brɪdʒ]	Brücke →	Let's meet on the *bridge*.
information centre [ˌɪnfə'meɪʃn 'sentə]	Touristeninformation	
information *(no pl.)* [ˌɪnfə'meɪʃn]	Information, Informationen →	**!** *Information* hat keine Mehrzahl (Pluralform): I've got a lot of *information* about Greenwich.
police station [pə'li:s 'steɪʃn]	Polizeirevier, Polizeiwache	
police [pə'li:s]	Polizei →	**!** The *police* **are** on the bridge.
bus stop ['bʌs ˌstɒp]	Bushaltestelle →	
castle ['kɑ:sl]	Burg, Schloss →	**!** Achtung Aussprache: Das ‚t' ist stumm.
sweet shop ['swi:t ˌʃɒp]	Süßwarenladen	
church [tʃɜ:tʃ]	Kirche →	
1 **place** [pleɪs]	Ort	
near [nɪə]	nahe, in der Nähe von →	The church is *near* the information centre.
opposite [ɒpəzɪt]	gegenüber	
3 to **get to** ['get tə]	kommen zu, kommen nach, erreichen	
Excuse me. [ɪk'skju:s mi]	Entschuldigung./ Entschuldigen Sie. →	*Excuse me.* Where's the police station, please? – It's opposite the museum.
to **go down** [gəʊ 'daʊn]	hinuntergehen; entlanggehen	
down [daʊn]	herunter, hinunter, nach unten, hinab	
to **turn right** [ˌtɜ:n 'raɪt]	(nach) rechts abbiegen	
to **turn** [tɜ:n]	einbiegen, abbiegen	
right [raɪt]	rechte/-r/-s; rechts	
left [left]	linke/-r/-s; links →	*left* ↔ right
straight on [streɪt‿'ɒn]	geradeaus →	
straight [streɪt]	gerade(aus); direkt	
to **cross** [krɒs]	überqueren, über … gehen	
on your right/left [ɒn jə 'raɪt/'left]	rechts/links, auf der rechten/linken Seite →	Go down Mouse Road. Then turn left into Castle Road. The castle is *on your right*.
4 **on his way** [ˌɒn hɪz 'weɪ]	auf dem Weg, unterwegs →	**!** He is on his way. I am on my way.

Unit 4 Greenwich Project Week

Wie du nach dem Weg fragst oder deine Stadt beschreibst, weißt du ja schon aus Pick-up C. Vielleicht kennst du auch einige der folgenden Wörter und Sätze zum Thema **Verkehrsmittel** aus der Grundschule.

train	Zug
Underground	U-Bahn
Let's go by Underground.	Lass(t) uns mit der U-Bahn fahren.
ship	Schiff
boat	Boot
We can take the boat.	Wir können das Boot nehmen.

VOCABULARY SKILLS

Je öfter du eine Vokabel hörst, umso leichter kannst du sie dir merken. Nimm hierfür neue Wörter auf Kassette auf. Sprich zuerst das englische Wort, mache dann eine kleine Pause und sage schließlich die deutsche Bedeutung. In einem zweiten Durchlauf kannst du die gleichen Vokabeln in umgekehrter Reihenfolge (deutsch/englisch) aufnehmen. Hör dir die Kassette immer mal wieder an – z. B. im Bus – und übe den neuen Wortschatz, indem du dir während der Sprechpause die deutsche bzw. englische Bedeutung überlegst oder laut vorsagst.

Check-in

to **work** [wɜːk]	arbeiten	
interesting [ˈɪntrəstɪŋ]	interessant	
sights *(pl.)* [saɪts]	Sehenswürdigkeiten →	You can find information about interesting *sights* in Greenwich at the information centre.
tourist [ˈtʊərɪst]	Tourist, Touristin →	! Achtung Aussprache
brochure [ˈbrəʊʃə]	Broschüre	
Underground [ˈʌndəgraʊnd]	U-Bahn	
train [treɪn]	Zug	
station [ˈsteɪʃn]	Station, Bahnhof	
young [jʌŋ]	jung →	*young* ↔ old
here [hɪə]	hierher, hierhin →	Come *here*! ↔ Go there!
tunnel [ˈtʌnl]	Tunnel →	! Achtung Aussprache
to **go** [gəʊ]	führen →	The Greenwich Foot Tunnel *goes* from Greenwich to the Isle of Dogs.
world [wɜːld]	Welt →	the *world*
line [laɪn]	Linie; Zeile	
Greenwich Mean Time (= GMT) [ˌgrenɪdʒ ˈmiːn ˌtaɪm]	westeuropäische Zeit	
visitor [ˈvɪzɪtə]	Besucher, Besucherin →	*visitor* → to visit
foot pl. **feet** [fʊt; fiːt]	Fuß →	! one *foot* – two *feet*
west [west]	Westen	
east [iːst]	Osten	
hour [aʊə]	Stunde	
too much [tuː ˈmʌtʃ]	zu viel →	
North Sea [ˌnɔːθ ˈsiː]	Nordsee	

	north [nɔ:θ]	Norden →	
	sea [si:]	Meer, die See →	! *the sea* = **die** See = das Meer
	to **call** [kɔ:l]	nennen	
	wonder ['wʌndə]	Wunder	
	famous ['feɪməs]	berühmt →	A lot of people know David Beckham. He is very *famous*.
	•**ship** [ʃɪp]	Schiff	
	life pl. **lives** [laɪf; laɪvz]	Leben →	! Achtung Schreibung in der Mehrzahl (im Plural): *life* – *lives*
	from all round the world [frəm‿'ɔ:l ˌraʊnd ðə 'wɜ:ld]	aus aller Welt	
1	to **go with** [gəʊ 'wɪð]	passen zu, gehören zu	
3	**part** [pɑ:t]	Teil →	In this picture you can only see one *part* of the room.

Language 1: Transport in Greenwich

	finding the way [ˌfaɪndɪŋ ðə 'weɪ]	den Weg finden	
	transport *(no pl.)* ['trænspɔ:t]	Verkehrsmittel, Beförderung →	! Achtung Aussprache: Im Englischen liegt die Betonung bei *transport* vorne (auf der ersten Silbe).
	all [ɔ:l]	alle/-s; ganz →	In England, *all* children from 5 to 16 go to school.
	•**by (Underground)** [baɪ]	mit (der U-Bahn), per →	Let's go *by Underground*!
	driver ['draɪvə]	Fahrer, Fahrerin	
	to **catch** [kætʃ]	nehmen *(Bus, Zug)*; (ein)fangen	
	to **drive** [draɪv]	fahren →	*to drive* → driver
	taxi ['tæksi]	Taxi →	! Achtung Aussprache
	special ['speʃl]	besondere/-r/-s	
2	to **get** [get]	holen, bringen; bekommen	
	to **speak** (to) [spi:k tə]	sprechen (mit)	
3	**pronoun** ['prəʊnaʊn]	Pronomen, Fürwort →	
	class [klɑ:s]	(Schul-)Klasse	
	to **give** [gɪv]	geben; schenken	
	everything ['evriθɪŋ]	alles	
4	**jumbled** ['dʒʌmbld]	durcheinander geraten, vermischt	
	object pronoun ['ɒbdʒɪkt ˌprəʊnaʊn]	Objektpronomen	
5	to **ask for ...** ['ɑ:sk fə]	nach ... fragen →	When you have got a problem, you can *ask for* help.
	communication skills [kəˌmju:nɪ'keɪʃn ˌskɪlz]	Sprechfertigkeiten, Kommunikationsfertigkeiten	
	to **repeat** [rɪ'pi:t]	wiederholen →	Can you *repeat* that, please? = Can you say that again, please?
	of course [əv 'kɔ:s]	natürlich, selbstverständlich	

Language 2: I don't know!

	I don't know! [ˌaɪ dəʊnt 'nəʊ]	Ich weiß (es) nicht! →	What's 'famous' in German? – Sorry, *I don't know*!
	kid [kɪd]	Kind, Jugendlicher, Jugendliche →	*kid* = child: Hey, *kids*, let's go swimming!

	English	German	Example
	to **park** [pɑːk]	parken	
	to **write down** [raɪt ˈdaʊn]	aufschreiben →	What's for homework? – It's on the board. *Write* it *down*, please. 
	to **give tours** [gɪv ˈtʊəz]	Stadtrundfahrten leiten	
	first [fɜːst]	erste/-r/-s →	Today is my *first* day at the new school.
	How many ... ? [haʊ ˈmeni]	Wie viele ... ? →	*How many* people are in the picture?
	You've got me there! [jʊv ˈgɒt mi ˈðeə]	Da habt ihr mich kalt erwischt!	
8	swimming pool [ˈswɪmɪŋ ˌpuːl]	Schwimmbad, Schwimmbecken	
10	**public** [ˈpʌblɪk]	öffentlich	
	boat [bəʊt]	Boot, Schiff →	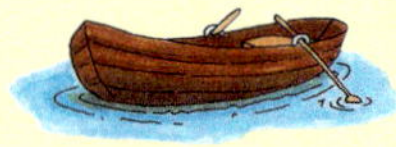 a *boat*
11	to **think** [θɪŋk]	finden, glauben, (nach)denken →	Do you like your town? Do you *think* it's a nice place?

Language 3: The does-game

	English	German	Example
	to **end** [end]	enden →	How does the film *end*?
	test [test]	Test, Prüfung	
	best [best]	beste/-r/-s →	Tom, you are my *best* friend!
	to **win** [wɪn]	gewinnen	
	prize [praɪz]	Preis, Gewinn →	You can win a *prize* for the best school project. 
	easy-peasy [ˌiːziˈpiːzi]	babyleicht	
	to **sell** [sel]	verkaufen →	At this shop they *sell* books. 
	Me? [miː; mi]	Ich?	
	silly [ˈsɪli]	Dummkopf	
	last [lɑːst]	letzte/-r/-s →	*last* ↔ first
	market [ˈmɑːkɪt]	Markt	
	Make up your mind! [ˌmeɪk‿ˈʌp jə ˈmaɪnd]	Entscheide dich!	
	dear [dɪə]	Schatz →	**TIP** Wenn du in Großbritannien in ein Geschäft kommst, kann es sein, dass du mit *Hello, dear!* begrüßt wirst. *Dear* ist in solch einem Fall kein Kosename, sondern eine freundliche Anrede, mit der oft auch Fremde begrüßt werden. 
	flower [flaʊə]	Blume	
12	**cheese** [tʃiːz]	Käse →	! *Cheese* hat im Englischen keine Mehrzahl (Pluralform).
16	to **guess** [ges]	(er)raten; vermuten	

Kein, keine

I **don't** like cheese.	Ich mag **keinen** Käse.
He **doesn't** eat apples.	Er isst **keine** Äpfel.
Sarah **can't** speak German.	Sarah kann **kein** Deutsch (sprechen).
James **hasn't got** a bike.	James hat **kein** Fahrrad.
It's a flat, **not** a house.	Es ist eine Wohnung, **kein** Haus.
No idea.	**Keine** Ahnung.

Language 4: The Greenwich test

	question word ['kwestʃən ˌwɜːd]	Fragewort →
	to **mean** [miːn]	bedeuten; meinen →
	fast [fɑːst]	schnell →
17	to **correct** [kə'rekt]	korrigieren, berichtigen
	winner ['wɪnə]	Gewinner
19	to live [lɪv]	leben, wohnen
21	**swimming pool** ['swɪmɪŋ ˌpuːl]	Schwimmbad, Schwimmbecken

When, what, where, why, who und *how* sind Fragewörter. Mehr Information dazu findest du im Grammatikanhang unter G9 und G26.

What does 'easy-peasy' *mean*?
– It *means* 'very easy'!
fast ↔ slow

Text: Captain Terry and the pirates

	captain ['kæptɪn]	Kapitän →
	pirate ['paɪrət]	Pirat, Seeräuber
	wheel [wiːl]	Steuerrad, Steuer, Rad
	that [ðæt; ðət]	dass
	mate [meɪt]	(Schiffs)Offizier; Freund, Freundin
	crow's nest ['krəʊz ˌnest]	Ausguck, Krähennest
	tea [tiː]	Tee
	treasure map ['treʒə ˌmæp]	Schatzkarte
	island ['aɪlənd]	Insel
	bang [bæŋ]	Knall, Schlag
	to **want** [wɒnt]	wollen, mögen
	to **sail** [seɪl]	segeln
	to **walk the plank** [ˌwɔːk ðə 'plæŋk]	über eine Schiffsplanke ins Wasser getrieben werden *(alte Strafe für Seeleute)*
	to **hurry up** [ˌhʌri 'ʌp]	sich beeilen →
	to **fight** [faɪt]	kämpfen; sich streiten
	She runs all round him. [ʃi ˌrʌnz ɔːl 'raʊnd hɪm]	Sie rennt um ihn herum.
	to **lick** [lɪk]	(ab)lecken
3	to **act** [ækt]	spielen
4	jolly ['dʒɒli]	lustig, vergnügt
	finger ['fɪŋgə]	Finger
	wooden ['wʊdən]	hölzern, aus Holz
	leg [leg]	Bein
	parrot ['pærət]	Papagei

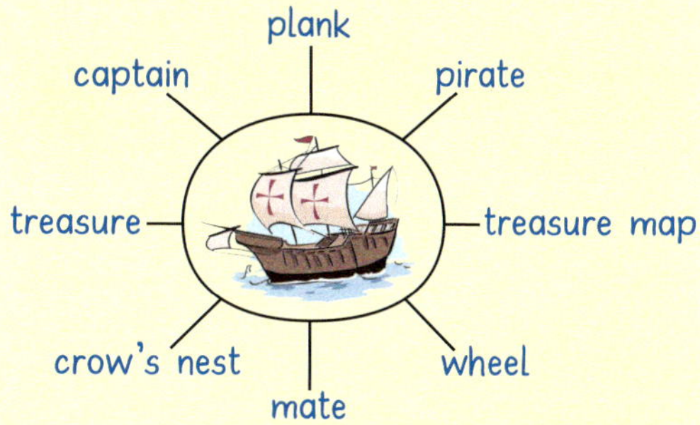

Hurry up, we're late!

Wordwise

1	**every ten minutes** [ˌevri ten 'mɪnɪts]	alle zehn Minuten →

There is a bus to the centre of Greenwich *every ten minutes*.

Check-out

2	**He takes us everywhere.** [hi ˌteɪks‿əs‿'evriweə]	Er bringt uns überallhin. →

My father *takes us everywhere* in his taxi.

USEFUL PHRASES

Mit den folgenden *phrases* fragst du auf Englisch nach dem Weg oder gibst eine Wegbeschreibung.

Excuse me, how can I get to … ?	You can go by bus/by Underground/by … / You can take bus number … / You can walk.
Can you tell me the way to …, please?	Go down … / Then turn left/right (into) / Go straight on. / … is on your left/right.
Can you repeat that, please?	…
Thank you.	You're welcome!

Unit 5 Birthday party

Hier gibt's was zu feiern! Einige Wörter zum Thema **Geburtstag** und **Party** und zum **Einkaufen** kennst du bestimmt noch aus der Grundschule:

birthday	Geburtstag
When's your birthday?	Wann hast du Geburtstag?
My birthday is in March.	Ich habe im März Geburtstag.
Happy Birthday!	Alles Gute zum Geburtstag!
birthday party	Geburtstagsfeier
to invite	einladen
I would like to invite you to my birthday party.	Ich möchte dich gerne zu meiner Geburtstagsfeier einladen.
present	Geschenk
cake	Kuchen, Torte
candle	Kerze
to buy	kaufen
How much is … ?	Wie viel kostet … ?
It's …	Es kostet …

VOCABULARY SKILLS

Gewöhne dir an, neue und unbekannte Wörter in einem Wörterbuch nachzuschlagen. Wie du ein Wörterbuch benutzt, kannst du so üben:
Nimm ein Päckchen Karteikarten aus deinem Karteikasten und ordne die Wörter in alphabetischer Reihenfolge. Wie beim Nachschlagen in einem Wörterbuch musst du hierzu nicht nur auf den ersten, sondern auch auf die nachfolgenden Buchstaben achten. Hier ein Beispiel: Unter ‚S' steht das Wort *shop* vor *sport*, weil das ‚h' im Alphabet vor dem ‚p' kommt.

• **birthday party** ['bɜːθdeɪ ˌpɑːti]	Geburtstagsfeier
• **birthday** ['bɜːθdeɪ]	Geburtstag →

Check-in

• **present** ['preznt]	Geschenk →
size [saɪz]	Größe →

a *present*

Have you got this T-shirt in a different *size*, please?

	medium (M) ['miːdiəm]	mittel(groß)	
	large (L) [lɑːdʒ]	groß	
	extra large (XL) ['ekstrə ˌlɑːdʒ]	besonders groß →	S (small) – M (medium) – L (large) – *XL (extra large)*
	• **How much is ... ?** ['haʊ mʌtʃ‿ɪz]	Wie viel kostet ... ?	
	• **It's two pounds.** [ɪts ˌtuː 'paʊndz]	Es kostet zwei Pfund. →	Das Symbol für britische Pfund ist £. Es steht immer vor der Zahl, wird beim Sprechen aber nach der Zahl genannt.
1	• to **buy** [baɪ]	kaufen →	*to buy* ↔ to sell
	newsagent ['njuːzˌeɪdʒnt]	Zeitschriftengeschäft →	You can buy magazines at a *newsagent*.
	clothes *(pl.)* [kləʊðz]	Kleidung, Kleider →	**!** Das Wort *clothes* steht immer in der Mehrzahl (im Plural): David's *clothes* **are** nice.
	sports shop ['spɔːts ˌʃɒp]	Sportgeschäft	
2	**money** ['mʌni]	Geld →	
	penny pl. **pence** [peni; pens]	Penny, Pence (*brit. Währungseinheit*) →	In Großbritannien spricht man *penny* oder *pence* immer als Kurzform *p* (wie den Buchstaben *p* [piː]): *one penny = 1 p, five pence = 5 p.*

3	to **go shopping** [gəʊ 'ʃɒpɪŋ]	einkaufen gehen →	Can we *go shopping* this afternoon?
	assistant [ə'sɪstnt]	Verkäufer, Verkäuferin	
	expensive [ɪk'spensɪv]	teuer	
	to **try on** [traɪ‿'ɒn]	anprobieren →	
	• **Here you are.** [ˌhɪə ju‿'ɑːt]	Bitte schön. →	*Here you are.* – Thank you.
	customer ['kʌstəmə]	Kunde, Kundin →	*customer* ↔ assistant

Language 1: Sam's invitation

	date [deɪt]	Datum	
	invitation [ˌɪnvɪ'teɪʃn]	Einladung	
	the third of March [ðə ˌθɜːd‿əv 'mɑːtʃ]	der dritte März →	Du sagst: "Today is *the third of March*", aber du schreibst: 3rd March.
	• **I'd like to. (= I would like to)** [aɪd 'laɪk tə]	ich möchte ... / ich würde gerne ...	**TIP** Merk dir, dass du nach *want to* und *would like to* immer ein Zeitwort (Verb) in der Grundform (Infinitiv) verwendest: He *would like* ***to* listen** to a CD.
	I want to ... [aɪ 'wɒnt tə]	ich möchte ... / ich will ... →	
	to **invite ... out** [ɪnˌvaɪt 'aʊt]	... (zu etwas) einladen	
	• to **invite** [ɪnˌvaɪt]	einladen →	*to invite* → invitation
	pizza place ['piːtsə ˌpleɪs]	Pizzeria	
	rich [rɪtʃ]	reich	
	Why don't you invite ... ? [waɪ dəʊnt jə ɪn'vaɪt]	Warum lädst du nicht ... ein?	
	little ['lɪtl]	klein →	I'm twelve. My *little* sister is five.
	• **cake** [keɪk]	Kuchen, Torte	
	to **text** [tekst]	eine SMS schicken	
	right now [raɪt 'naʊ]	jetzt, sofort, gerade	
2	**man** pl. **men** [mæn; men]	Mann →	**!** Achtung unregelmäßige Mehrzahl (Pluralform): *man – men*
3	**month** [mʌnθ]	Monat →	day → week → *month* → year

Months (Monate)

January ['dʒænjuri]	Januar	**July** [dʒʊ'laɪ]	Juli
February ['februri]	Februar	**August** ['ɔ:gəst]	August
March [mɑ:tʃ]	März	**September** [sep'tembə]	September
April ['eɪprl]	April	**October** [ɒk'təʊbə]	Oktober
May [meɪ]	Mai	**November** [nə'vembə]	November
June [dʒu:n]	Juni	**December** [dɪ'sembə]	Dezember

Ordinal numbers (Ordnungszahlen)

first [fɜ:st]	erste (-r/-s)	**fifteenth** [fɪf'ti:nθ]	fünfzehnte (-r/-s)
second ['seknd]	zweite (-r/-s)	**sixteenth** [sɪks'ti:nθ]	sechzehnte (-r/-s)
third [θɜ:d]	dritte (-r/-s)	**seventeenth** [sevn'ti:nθ]	siebzehnte (-r/-s)
fourth [fɔ:θ]	vierte (-r/-s)	**eighteenth** [eɪ'ti:nθ]	achtzehnte (-r/-s)
fifth [fɪfθ]	fünfte (-r/-s)	**nineteenth** [naɪn'ti:nθ]	neunzehnte (-r/-s)
sixth [sɪksθ]	sechste (-r/-s)	**twentieth** ['twentiɪθ]	zwanzigste (-r/-s)
seventh ['sevnθ]	siebte (-r/-s)	**twenty-first** [ˌtwenti'fɜ:st]	einundzwanzigste (-r/-s)
eighth [eɪtθ]	achte (-r/-s)	**twenty-second** [ˌtwenti'seknd]	zweiundzwanzigste (-r/-s)
ninth [naɪnθ]	neunte (-r/-s)	**twenty-third** [ˌtwenti'θɜ:d]	dreiundzwanzigste (-r/-s)
tenth [tenθ]	zehnte (-r/-s)	...	...
eleventh [ɪ'levnθ]	elfte (-r/-s)	**thirtieth** ['θɜ:tiəθ]	dreißigste (-r/-s)
twelfth [twelfθ]	zwölfte (-r/-s)	...	...
thirteenth [θɜ:'ti:nθ]	dreizehnte (-r/-s)	**hundredth** ['hʌndrədθ]	hundertste (-r/-s)
fourteenth [fɔ:'ti:nθ]	vierzehnte (-r/-s)		

5 **CU (= See you)** ['si: ju] — bis bald *(Abkürzung in SMS oder E-Mail)*

6 to go for a picnic [gəʊ fər‿ə 'pɪknɪk] — ein Picknick machen

Language 2: Shopping for Sam's birthday

Wenn du wiederholen möchtest, wie und wann du das *present progressive* verwendest, schau im Grammatikanhang unter G30/G31 nach.

using the present progressive ['ju:zɪŋ ðə ˌpreznt prə'gresɪv] — das *present progressive* benutzen →

department store [dɪ'pɑ:tmənt ˌstɔ:] — Kaufhaus → — You can buy a lot of things in a *department store*: clothes, CDs, food ... .

just [dʒʌst] — gerade (eben), soeben

to **dance** [dɑ:ns] — tanzen → — The music is great – let's *dance*!

to **look for** ['lʊk fə] — suchen (nach) → — Where's my new T-shirt? – *Look for* it in your bag.

still [stɪl] — noch, immer noch → — Hurry up, it's late. – No problem, we've *still* got time.

thief pl. **thieves** [θi:f; θi:vz] — Dieb → — ! Achtung Schreibung in der Mehrzahl (im Plural): *thief – thieves*

11 to **sing** [sɪŋ] — singen

12 to watch [wɒtʃ] — aufpassen auf, achten auf

13 **the others** [ði‿'ʌðəz] — die anderen

Language 3: The birthday cake

little ['lɪtl] — wenig

Wann benutzt man *much* und wann *many*? Mehr Information dazu findest du im Grammatikanhang unter G32.

before [bɪ'fɔː]	bis (zu), vor	
lots of ['lɒts‿əv]	viel/-e, jede Menge	
recipe ['resɪpi]	Rezept	
How much ...? [haʊ 'mʌtʃ]	Wie viel ... ? →	
sugar ['ʃʊgə]	Zucker	
to **need** [niːd]	brauchen →	Tom *needs* a cake and lots of chocolate for his birthday party.
egg [eg]	Ei	
to **want to know** [ˌwɒnt tə 'nəʊ]	wissen wollen	
to **have fun** [həv 'fʌn]	Spaß haben, sich amüsieren →	The children *are having fun* at the party.
a bag of ... [ə 'bæg‿əv]	eine Tüte ...	
a box of ... [ə 'bɒks‿əv]	eine Schachtel ..., ein Karton ...	
a few [ə 'fjuː]	ein paar, einige; wenige	
to **break** [breɪk]	(zer)brechen, kaputtgehen	
flour [flaʊə]	Mehl	
many ['meni]	viele	
cook [kʊk]	Koch, Köchin	
to **laugh** [lɑːf]	lachen →	! Achtung Aussprache
a little [ə 'lɪtl]	ein wenig, etwas →	I've only got a few eggs and *a little* sugar.
candle ['kændl]	Kerze	
in the world [ɪn ðə 'wɜːld]	auf der Welt	
16 to **count** [kaʊnt]	zählen	
17 **a cup of** [ə 'kʌp‿əv]	eine Tasse ...	

Mengenangaben

How much sugar/flour/money ...?	Wie viel Zucker/Mehl/Geld ... ?	**a little** help	ein wenig Hilfe
How many eggs/apples ... ?	Wie viele Eier/Äpfel ... ?	**a bag of** apples	eine Tüte Äpfel
a lot of/lots of money/books	viel Geld/viele Bücher	**a box of** eggs	eine Schachtel Eier
a few eggs	ein paar/einige Eier	**a cup of** tea	eine Tasse Tee

18 **chocolate crispies** *(pl.)* ['tʃɒklət ˌkrɪspɪz]	Schokoplätzchen	
19 gram [græm]	Gramm	
plain chocolate [ˌpleɪn 'tʃɒklət]	(Halb)Bitterschokolade	
tablespoon ['teɪblspuːn]	Esslöffel	
rice crispies *(pl.)* ['raɪs ˌkrɪspɪz]	Reis-Knusperflocken	
raisin ['reɪzn]	Rosine	
piece [piːs]	Stück	
to melt [melt]	schmelzen	
bowl [bəʊl]	Schüssel →	*a bowl*
hot [hɒt]	heiß	
to mix [mɪks]	verrühren	
until [ʌn'tɪl]	bis	
covered ['kʌvəd]	bedeckt	
spoonful ['spuːnfʊl]	Löffel *(Mengenangabe)*	
paper case ['peɪpə ˌkeɪs]	Papierbackförmchen	
hard [hɑːd]	hart	
ready ['redi]	fertig	

20	to **go up** [gəʊ 'ʌp]	nach oben gehen	
	to **go down** [gəʊ 'daʊn]	nach unten gehen →	*to go down* ↔ to go up

Text: Happy birthday, Sam!

1	**reading a story** ['ri:dɪŋ ə 'stɔ:ri]	eine Geschichte lesen	
	title ['taɪtl]	Titel →	! Achtung Schreibung
	•**Happy birthday!** [ˌhæpi 'bɜ:θdeɪ]	Alles Gute zum Geburtstag! →	
	ready ['redi]	fertig, bereit →	Are you *ready*? – Yes, let's go!
	to **be late for school** [bi ˌleɪt fə 'sku:l]	zu spät zur Schule kommen →	Sam *is* often *late for school*.
	suddenly ['sʌdnli]	plötzlich, auf einmal	
	alarm clock [ə'lɑ:m ˌklɒk]	Wecker →	an *alarm clock* 
	excited [ɪk'saɪtɪd]	aufgeregt, begeistert →	Today is my birthday. I'm having a party with my friends. I'm very *excited*!
	surprise [sə'praɪz]	Überraschung	
	karaoke machine [ˌkæri'əʊki mə'ʃi:n]	Karaokegerät	
	everyone ['evriwʌn]	jeder →	*Everyone* is at the party: Lisa, Emma, Terry … .
	even ['i:vn]	sogar, selbst	
	loud [laʊd]	laut →	*loud* ↔ quiet
	to **jump** [dʒʌmp]	springen →	
	What's that song? [wɒts ðæt 'sɒŋ]	Was ist das für ein Lied?	
	radio ['reɪdiəʊ]	Radio →	! Achtung Aussprache
	Don't you listen to the radio? [dəʊnt jə ˌlɪsn tə ðə 'reɪdiəʊ]	Hörst du kein Radio?	
	to **live** [lɪv]	wohnen, leben →	! Achtung Schreibung und Aussprache: *to live* ↔ life
	radio station ['reɪdiəʊ ˌsteɪʃn]	Radiosender	
2	to **take notes** [teɪk 'nəʊts]	sich Notizen machen	
	heading ['hedɪŋ]	Überschrift, Titel →	*heading* = title

Wordwise

1	**finding words** [ˌfaɪndɪŋ 'wɜ:dz]	Wörter finden	
	dictionary ['dɪkʃnri]	Wörterbuch →	a *dictionary* 
	alphabetical [ˌælfə'betɪkl]	alphabetisch →	alphabet → *alphabetical*
	etc. (= **et cetera**) [ɪt'setrə]	usw. (= und so weiter)	

USEFUL PHRASES

Hier findest du die wichtigsten *shopping phrases* aus Unit 5.

I'd like / We'd like to … , please.
Have you got … ?
Excuse me, do you sell … ?
Can you help me, please?

Can you show me / give me …, please?
What size is it?
Can I try it on, please?
How much is … ?

Unit 6 Beach holiday

Über die **Jahreszeiten** und das **Wetter** hast du schon in der Grundschule gesprochen. Bestimmt auch über **Urlaub**. Kennst du die folgenden Wörter und Sätze noch?

spring	Frühling	**cold**	kalt
summer	Sommer	**holidays**	Ferien, Urlaub
autumn	Herbst	**What are you doing in the holidays?**	Was macht ihr in den Ferien?
winter	Winter	**We are going to England.**	Wir fahren nach England.
I often fly my kite in autumn.	Im Herbst lasse ich oft meinen Drachen steigen.	**beach**	Strand
warm	warm	**mountain**	Berg

VOCABULARY SKILLS

Du kannst deine Englischkenntnisse auch in vielen Alltagssituationen üben, z. B. wenn du deine Mutter oder deinen Vater das nächste Mal zum Einkaufen begleitest. Versuch doch einfach, den Einkaufszettel auf Englisch zu schreiben! Oder mache dir einen Wochenplan und trage alles, was du geplant hast, auf Englisch ein.

Check-in

• **beach holiday** ['bi:tʃ ˌhɒlədeɪ]	Strandurlaub →	
holiday(s) ['hɒlədeɪ]	Ferien, Urlaub	
mile [maɪl]	Meile →	Eine Meile entspricht 1,609 Kilometern.
from [frɒm; frəm]	von … entfernt →	Bristol is 108 miles *from* London.
Britain ['brɪtn]	Großbritannien →	*Britain* → British
east of ['i:st‿əv]	östlich von →	Poland is *east of* Germany.
a pier a mile long [ə 'pɪə ə ˌmaɪl 'lɒŋ]	ein Pier, der eine Meile lang ist	
arcade games *(pl.)* [ɑ:'keɪd ˌgeɪmz]	Spielautomaten	
in the town of Penzance [ɪn ðə 'taʊn‿əv pen'zæns]	in der Stadt Penzance →	*Penzance* ist eine Hafenstadt im Südwesten Englands, in Cornwall.
• **warm** [wɔ:m]	warm →	Today is a very *warm* day.
to **go surfing** [gəʊ 'sɜ:fɪŋ]	surfen gehen	
wave [weɪv]	Welle, Woge	
kite festival ['kaɪt ˌfestɪvl]	Drachenfest →	
• to **fly a kite** [flaɪ ə 'kaɪt]	einen Drachen steigen lassen →	I like to *fly my kite* at the beach.
to **fly** [flaɪ]	fliegen	
• **winter** ['wɪntə]	Winter	
cold [kəʊld]	kalt →	*cold* ↔ warm
coast [kəʊst]	Küste →	The *coast* is where the land ends and the sea starts.
• **summer** ['sʌmə]	Sommer	
• **mountain** ['maʊntɪn]	Berg →	the *mountains*
to **climb** [klaɪm]	(hinauf)steigen, hinaufklettern, erklimmen	

	village ['vɪlɪdʒ]	Dorf →
	lighthouse ['laɪthaʊs]	Leuchtturm →
	windy ['wɪndi]	windig
	south [saʊθ]	Süden
3	**ocean** ['əʊʃn]	Ozean →
	seaside town [ˌsi:saɪd 'taʊn]	Küstenstadt

village ↔ town

a *lighthouse*

There are three *oceans*: The Atlantic Ocean [ət'læntɪk ˌəʊʃn], the Pacific Ocean [pə'sɪfɪk ˌəʊʃn] and the Indian Ocean ['ɪndiən ˌəʊʃn].

Language 1: Penzance

	planning your holidays [ˌplænɪŋ jə 'hɒlədeɪz]	den Urlaub planen
	to **surf on the Internet** [ˌsɜ:f‿ɒn ði‿'ɪntənet]	im Internet surfen
	harbour ['hɑ:bə]	Hafen
	meal [mi:l]	Mahlzeit, Essen →
	restaurant ['restrɑ:ŋ]	Restaurant, Gaststätte
	season ['si:zn]	Jahreszeit; Saison
	autumn ['ɔ:təm]	Herbst
	spring [sprɪŋ]	Frühling →
	family fun ['fæmli ˌfʌn]	Spaß für die ganze Familie
	to **click on** ['klɪk‿ɒn]	anklicken
	to **build** [bɪld]	bauen
	sand castle ['sænd ˌkɑ:sl]	Sandburg
	sand [sænd]	Sand
	ice-cream [ˌaɪs'kri:m]	Eiscreme, Eis
	must [mʌst]	müssen
	to **pack** [pæk]	(ein)packen
	welly pl. **wellies** ['weli; weliz]	Gummistiefel →
	rain [reɪn]	Regen
	swimsuit ['swɪmsu:t]	Badeanzug
	sunglasses *(pl.)* ['sʌnˌglɑ:sɪz]	Sonnenbrille
	address book [ə'dres ˌbʊk]	Adressbuch
	postcard ['pəʊskɑ:d]	Postkarte →
	to **think of** ['θɪŋk‿əv]	halten von, denken über
3	**over there** [ˌəʊvə 'ðeə]	(nach) dort drüben
5	the roof is down [ðə 'ru:f‿ɪz ˌdaʊn]	*hier:* das Faltdach (am Auto) ist heruntergeklappt
	to get near [get 'nɪə]	sich nähern
	sun [sʌn]	Sonne
	hot [hɒt]	heiß
	enough [ɪ'nʌf]	genug
	to roast [rəʊst]	braten, rösten

I usually eat a big *meal* at lunchtime. Now I'm only eating a big apple.

The four seasons: *spring*, summer, autumn and winter.

Gummistiefel heißen auf Englisch *wellies* oder *wellingtons*, weil sie in England vom ersten **Herzog von Wellington** getragen wurden.

to bring/to take

Can you **bring** me the ball, please?	Kannst du mir bitte den Ball **bringen.** (=herbringen)
Can you **take** the ball **to** Jade, please?	Kannst du Jade bitte den Ball **bringen.** (= hinbringen)
I can **take** you home.	Ich kann dich nach Hause **bringen.** (= hinbringen)

Language 2: On the beach

present progressive [ˌpreznt prəˈgresɪv]	Verlaufsform des Präsens/der Gegenwart	
on the beach [ɒn ðə ˈbiːtʃ]	am Strand →	You can do a lot of nice things *on the beach*: build sandcastles, play volleyball, fly a kite …
to **ruin** [ˈruːɪn]	zerstören, ruinieren	
safe [seɪf]	sicher, ungefährlich	
alone [əˈləʊn]	allein →	*alone* ↔ together
thanks a lot [ˌθæŋks‿ə ˈlɒt]	vielen Dank	
Hooray! [hʊˈreɪ]	Hurra!	
tooth pl. **teeth** [tuːθ; tiːθ]	Zahn →	! Achtung unregelmäßige Mehrzahl (Pluralform): ***tooth*** – ***teeth***
doghouse [ˈdɒghaʊs]	Hundehütte	
10 **signal word** [ˈsɪgnl ˌwɜːd]	Signalwort →	TIP Ein Signalwort für das *present progressive* ist beispielsweise *now*.

11 to **have breakfast** [ˌhæv ˈbrekfəst]	frühstücken →	Tom is *having breakfast* now.
this morning [ðɪs ˈmɔːnɪŋ]	heute morgen	

Language 3: Some souvenirs of Penzance

some [sʌm]	einige, ein paar; etwas →	*some* = not all
any [ˈenɪ]	irgendein-e/-er; irgendwelche →	I can't see *any* birds. = I can see no birds.
souvenir [ˌsuːvnˈɪə]	Andenken, Souvenir	
in here [ɪn ˈhiːə]	hier drin →	

mug [mʌg]	Becher	
to **take off** [teɪk‿ˈɒf]	abnehmen, ausziehen, herunternehmen →	You *take off* your clothes before you go to bed.
shelf pl. **shelves** [ʃelf; ʃelvz]	Regal, Regalbrett →	! Achtung Schreibung in der Mehrzahl (im Plural): *shelf* – *shelves*
I don't like them. [aɪ dəʊnt ˈlaɪk ˌðəm]	Sie gefallen mir nicht. →	Do you want these trousers? – No, sorry, *I don't like them*.
to **keep** [kiːp]	behalten, aufbewahren	
pair [peə]	Paar	
another [əˈnʌðə]	noch ein/-e; ein/-e andere/-r/-s →	the same ↔ *another*
to **wait for** [ˈweɪt fə]	warten auf	
cheap [tʃiːp]	billig, preiswert →	*cheap* ↔ expensive
on the way home [ˌɒn ðe weɪ ˈhəʊm]	auf dem Weg nach Hause	
17 **sweets** *(pl.)* [swiːts]	Süßigkeiten →	*sweets*
19 **not even** [nɒt ˈiːvn]	(noch) nicht einmal	

Text: Grace Darling's adventure

adventure [ədˈventʃə]	Abenteuer	
to **read to** [riːd ˈtə]	jemandem vorlesen	
storm [stɔːm]	Sturm, Unwetter, Gewitter	
to **rain** [reɪn]	regnen →	It's *raining*.

	to **pitter-patter** ['pɪtəˌpætə]	prasseln, klopfen, trappeln	
	strong [strɒŋ]	stark, kräftig	
	wind [wɪnd]	Wind →	*wind* → windy
	rock [rɒk]	Fels, Riff, Stein	
	to **crash** [kræʃ]	aufprallen, zusammenstoßen	
	at once [ət 'wʌns]	auf einmal; sofort	
	stormy ['stɔːmi]	stürmisch →	It's *stormy* today.
	against [ə'genst]	gegen	
	to **sink** [sɪŋk]	untergehen, sinken →	*to sink* ↔ to swim
	great [greɪt]	groß, riesig →	*great* ↔ tiny
	to **row** [rəʊ]	rudern	
	out [aʊt]	heraus, hinaus, nach draußen	
	to **be scared for** [bi 'skeəd fə]	Angst haben um	
	scared [skeəd]	verängstigt →	This film is scary. I'm *scared*.
	will [wɪl]	Wille	
	to **hear** [hɪə]	hören →	**!** My parents are coming home. I can ***hear*** their car. ↔ I'm **listening to** my new CD.
	Don't worry. [dəʊnt 'wʌri]	Mach' dir keine Sorgen. →	
	to **get into** [get‿'ɪntə]	(ein)steigen	
	that day [ðæt 'deɪ]	an jenem Tag	
	to **die** [daɪ]	sterben →	*to die* ↔ to live
	to **survive** [sə'vaɪv]	überleben	
4	to **retell** [riː'tel]	nacherzählen; nochmals erzählen	
	on a train [ɒn‿ə 'treɪn]	im Zug	
5	to **think about** [θɪŋk‿ə'baʊt]	halten von, denken über →	

Wordwise

1	**noun** [naʊn]	Nomen, Hauptwort	
	verb [vɜːb]	Verb, Zeitwort	
	to **look up** [lʊk‿'ʌp]	nachschlagen, nachschauen →	You can *look up* words in a dictionary.
2	**woman** pl. **women** ['wʊmən; 'wɪmɪn]	Frau →	**!** Achtung unregelmäßige Mehrzahl (Pluralform): *woman – women*
	person pl. **people** ['pɜːsn; piːpl]	Person, Mensch →	**!** one *person* → many people
	fish pl. **fish** [fɪʃ]	Fisch →	
	scarf pl. **scarves** [skɑːf; skɑːvz]	Schal, Tuch	
4	tongue twister ['tʌŋ ˌtwɪstə]	Zungenbrecher →	A *tongue twister*: Jonathan's birthday is on the third Thursday of this month.
	toy [tɔɪ]	Spielzeug	
	shell [ʃel]	Muschel	
	seashore ['siːʃɔː]	Strand, Meeresküste	
	fried [fraɪd]	gebraten	

Check-out

3 **Oops!** [uːps] Hoppla!

USEFUL PHRASES

Mit diesen *phrases* drückst du aus, dass du etwas regelmäßig und gerne tust oder dass du etwas interessant findest.

I sometimes / often go to …
I think … is interesting because …
… looks interesting because …
It's fun to …
I want to go to … / I want to do …
I like …

Unit 7 Animals in the city

Auf einem **Bauernhof** gibt es viel zu tun und zu sehen, vor allem Tiere. Diese Wörter kennst du bestimmt noch aus der Grundschule:

animal	Tier	**bird**	Vogel
horse	Pferd	**fox**	Fuchs
cow	Kuh	**I can help you to feed the pigs.**	Ich kann dir helfen, die Schweine zu füttern.
pig	Schwein	**Thanks, that's nice of you.**	Danke, das ist nett von dir.
sheep	Schaf		

VOCABULARY SKILLS

Wie du schon weißt, merkt man sich Vokabeln am besten in Zusammenhang mit einem Satz oder in Verbindung mit anderen Wörtern zum gleichen Thema (z. B. als *word web*). Du kannst neue Wörter aber auch lernen oder wiederholen, indem du Zeitwörter (Verben) mit Hauptwörtern (Nomen) verbindest. Für das Zeitwort *to write* kannst du z. B. folgende Wortkette bilden: *I'm writing a postcard /a letter / a story …* Oder du machst es umgekehrt und überlegst dir, was man mit dem Hauptwort *story* alles verbinden kann: I'm *reading / writing / listening to … a story.*

Check-in

• **animal** ['ænɪml]	Tier
city ['sɪti]	Großstadt →
wild [waɪld]	wild →
• **fox** [fɒks]	Fuchs
• **bird** [bɜːd]	Vogel
zoo [zuː]	Zoo →
monkey ['mʌŋki]	Affe
farm [fɑːm]	Bauernhof
field [fiːld]	Wiese, Weide, Acker
at the same time [ət ðə ˌseɪm 'taɪm]	zur selben Zeit, gleichzeitig
chicken ['tʃɪkɪn]	Huhn; Hähnchen, Hühnchen
• **pig** [pɪg]	Schwein
• **cow** [kaʊ]	Kuh →

village → town → city
wild animals ↔ pets

! Achtung Aussprache

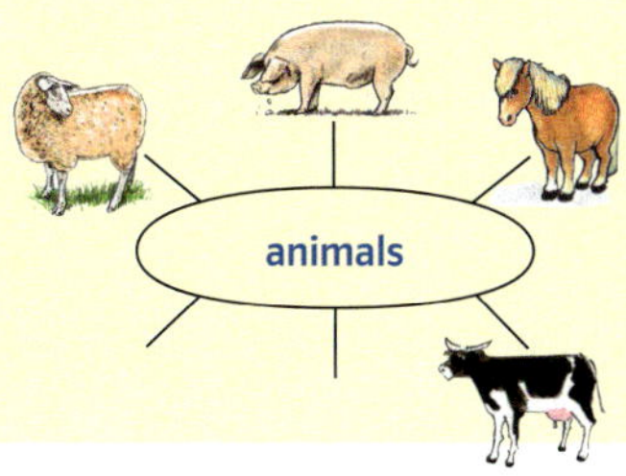

• **sheep** pl. **sheep** [ʃi:p]	Schaf	
• **horse** [hɔ:s]	Pferd	
farmhand ['fɑ:mhænd]	Landarbeiter, Landarbeiterin →	
schools officer ['sku:lz ˌɒfɪsə]	*(hier:) Beauftragter/ Beauftragte für Schulklassen*	
activity [æk'tɪvəti]	Aktivität	
5 **already** [ɔ:l'redi]	schon, bereits →	Have you got this CD? – Yes, I've *already* got it.

Language 1: On the farm

duty ['dju:ti]	Pflicht	
class trip [ˌklɑ:s 'trɪp]	Klassenfahrt, Klassenausflug	
to **milk** [mɪlk]	melken →	On Mudchute farm, they *milk* the cows in the morning and in the evening.
to **look after** [lʊk‿'ɑ:ftə]	sich kümmern um; aufpassen auf	

to look

Look! There's a tiny monkey. It **looks** very sweet.	**Guck' mal**, da ist ein kleiner Affe. Er **sieht** sehr süß **aus**.
They are **looking at** the photos of their class trip.	Sie **schauen** sich die Photos von ihrem Klassenausflug **an**.
Where are my wellies? – **Look for** them in the shed.	Wo sind meine Gummistiefel? – **Schau** im Schuppen **nach** / **such** sie im Schuppen.
My parents are at the cinema. I'm **looking after** my little sister.	Meine Eltern sind im Kino. Ich **passe** auf meine kleine Schwester **auf**.

grass [grɑ:s]	Gras	
mustn't ['mʌsnt] (= must not)	nicht dürfen →	! you must = du musst you *mustn't* = du darfst nicht
nervous ['nɜ:vəs]	nervös, aufgeregt	
calm [kɑ:m]	ruhig, friedlich →	*calm* ↔ nervous
allergic to [ə'lɜ:dʒɪk tə]	allergisch auf	
shed [ʃed]	Stall →	Du erinnerst dich sicher noch daran, dass *shed* auch Schuppen oder Gartenhäuschen heißt: The cows are in the *shed*. ↔ Terry spends a lot of time in his shed.
Pooh! [pu:]	Igitt! →	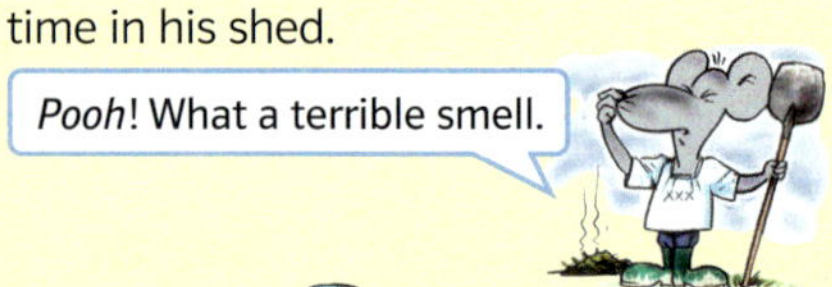
to **stink** [stɪŋk]	stinken	
to **muck out** [mʌk‿'aʊt]	ausmisten	
bacon ['beɪkn]	(Schinken)Speck	
four of them [fɔ:r‿əv ðəm]	vier davon (Personen, Tiere, …)	
milk [mɪlk]	Milch →	*milk* → to milk
bottle ['bɒtl]	Flasche →	a *bottle* of milk
to **fight over** [faɪt‿'əʊvə]	sich streiten um →	Emma and Nasreen often *fight over* their CDs.
4 **hand** [hænd]	Hand →	! Achtung Aussprache

Language 2: Cyberpets

	looking after a pet [ˌlʊkɪŋ ˌɑ:ftər‿ə 'pet]	sich um ein Tier kümmern	
	cyberpet ['saɪbəpet]	virtuelles Haustier	
	should [ʃʊd]	sollte/-est/-en/-et	
	owner ['əʊnə]	Besitzer, Besitzerin →	This is my parents' house. They are the *owners* of the house.
	to **choose** [tʃu:z]	(aus)wählen	
	ear [ɪə]	Ohr	
	from time to time [frəm ˌtaɪm tə 'taɪm]	von Zeit zu Zeit →	Barker wants to play in the park every day, not only *from time to time*. 
	holiday home ['hɒlədeɪ ˌhəʊm]	*(hier:)* Tierpension	
	bad [bæd]	schlecht; böse →	good ↔ *bad*
12	**word order** ['wɜ:d‿ɔ:də]	Wortstellung, Satzstellung	
	subject ['sʌbdʒɪkt]	Subjekt, Satzgegenstand	
	object ['ɒbdʒɪkt]	Objekt, Satzergänzung	
	for many hours/years ... [fə ˌmeni 'aʊəz; jɪəz]	stundenlang/jahrelang ... →	Barker sleeps *for many hours* every day.
13	to **think of** [θɪŋk‿'əv]	(sich) ausdenken, sich etwas einfallen lassen	
14	**what it looks like** [ˌwɒt‿ɪt 'lʊks laɪk]	wie es aussieht	

to think

I **think** TTS is a great school.	Ich **finde**, TTS ist eine tolle Schule.
What do you **think about/of** our new German teacher?	Was **hältst** du **von** unserem neuen Deutschlehrer?
This game is boring. Why don't we **think of** a new game?	Dieses Spiel ist langweilig. Warum **denken** wir uns nicht ein neues Spiel **aus**?

Language 3: TTS school magazine

	competition [ˌkɒmpə'tɪʃn]	Wettbewerb →	He wants to win the *competition*.
	moment ['məʊmənt]	Moment, Augenblick	
	card [kɑ:d]	Chip, Speicherkarte *(für Digitalkamera)*	
	camera ['kæmrə]	Fotoapparat, Kamera →	! Achtung Schreibung und Aussprache
	to **take a photo** [ˌteɪk‿ə 'fəʊtəʊ]	ein Foto machen →	! *to **take** a photo*: Can you *take a photo* of us, please?
15	to **think of** [θɪŋk‿'əv]	(sich) ausdenken, sich etwas einfallen lassen →	This game is silly. Let's *think of* a new game.
17	baby ['beɪbi]	Baby, Säugling	
	really ['rɪəli]	wirklich	
	as [æz; əz]	als	
	banana [bə'nɑ:nə]	Banane	

Text: Sam's new friend

	one evening [wʌn‿'i:vnɪŋ]	eines Abends	
	garage ['gærɑ:ʒ]	Garage; Werkstatt; Tankstelle →	The car is in the *garage* next to our house. Our car doesn't work. I must take it to the *garage*.

	to **run after** [rʌn‿'ɑːftə]	hinterherrennen	
	shock [ʃɒk]	Schock, Schreck	
	dark [dɑːk]	dunkel	
	I know a fox when I see one! [aɪ ˌnəʊ ə 'fɒks wen‿aɪ ˌsiː wʌn]	Ich erkenne einen Fuchs sofort!	
	leg [leg]	Bein →	
	vet [vet]	Tierarzt, Tierärztin	
	territory ['terɪtri]	Gebiet, Revier, Territorium	
	may [meɪ]	(vielleicht) können; dürfen →	**TIP** Wenn du auf Englisch nach etwas fragst oder um etwas bittest, beginne deine Frage mit *may*. Das ist höflicher: *May* I take another piece of cake, please?
	to **explain** [ɪk'spleɪn]	erklären	
	to **mend** [mend]	heilen; reparieren	
	to **smile** [smaɪl]	lächeln	
	bowl [bəʊl]	Schüssel	
	night [naɪt]	Nacht →	*night* ↔ day
	worried ['wʌrɪd]	beunruhigt, besorgt	
	to **be right** [bɪ 'raɪt]	Recht haben →	*to be right* ↔ to be wrong
	to **stand** [stænd]	stehen	
	sad [sæd]	traurig →	*sad* ↔ happy
2	**empty** ['emti]	leer	
	thanks to ['θæŋks tə]	dank (dir/Ihnen), wegen →	Thank you for your help. *Thanks to* you we can go home earlier.
	dead [ded]	tot	
3	**if** [ɪf]	wenn, falls; ob	
	to **drink** [drɪŋk]	trinken	
	clear [klɪə]	klar, verständlich	

Wordwise

1	**meaning** ['miːnɪŋ]	Bedeutung →	*meaning* → to mean: What's the *meaning* of 'to describe'? – It means: to say what a thing or a person looks like.
	in the street [ɪn ðə 'striːt]	auf der Straße →	! The kids are playing *in the street* ↔ The cars are on the road.
	next [nekst]	nächste/-r/-s	
	just now [ˌdʒʌst 'naʊ]	gerade, im Augenblick	
4	hamster ['hæmstə]	Hamster	
	the nicest [ðə 'naɪsɪst]	die schönsten, die nettesten	
	anyone ['eniwʌn]	irgendjemand; jeder (beliebige)	
	could [kʊd]	könnte/-n	
	to own [əʊn]	besitzen	
	better ['betə]	besser, mehr	
	than [ðæn; ðən]	als *(bei Vergleichen)*	
	I have known [aɪ həv 'nəʊn]	ich habe gekannt, ich kannte	
	fur [fɜː]	Fell	
	soft [sɒft]	weich	
	grown [grəʊn]	ausgewachsen; erwachsen	
	inside [ˌɪn'saɪd]	in	
	pocket ['pɒkɪt]	Hosentasche	
	all alone [ˌɔːl‿ə'ləʊn]	ganz allein	

USEFUL PHRASES

Möchtest du jemandem auf Englisch deine Hilfe anbieten, kannst du die untenstehenden *phrases* verwenden. Überlege dir, welche Antworten (positiv und negativ) zu den einzelnen Sätzen passen.

Can I help you?	Let me help you with …
Can I … for you?	You needn't … . I can do that.
I'm good at/with …	Would you like some help with … ?
I can help you to …	Do you want me to … ?

[Trailer 1 Summer with the Taylors]

trailer [treɪlə]	Anhänger
past [pɑ:st]	Vergangenheit
dear [dɪə]	Lieber … , Liebe … *(Anrede in Briefen)*
yesterday ['jestədeɪ]	gestern
lake [leɪk]	See
love [lʌv]	Liebe Grüße, Herzliche Grüße *(am Briefende)*
irregular [ɪ'regjələ]	unregelmäßig
regular ['regjələ]	regelmäßig
trampolining ['træmpəli:nɪŋ]	Trampolin hüpfen

Past form: irregular verbs

to be	**was**	He **was** very tired yesterday evening.	Er **war** gestern Abend sehr müde.
	were	Last week we **were** in the mountains.	Letzte Woche **waren** wir in den Bergen.
to have	**had**	Yesterday, I **had** a funny dream.	Gestern **hatte** ich einen lustigen Traum.
to say	**said**	She **said** she would like to go swimming.	Sie **hat gesagt**, sie würde gerne schwimmen gehen.
to go	**went**	Last Saturday we **went** to London.	Letzten Samstag **sind** wir nach London **gegangen**.
to run	**ran**	I was late, so I **ran** to the bus stop.	Ich war zu spät, deshalb **bin** ich zur Bushaltestelle **gerannt**.
to get	**got**	He **got** a beautiful bike for his birthday.	Er **hat** ein schönes Fahrrad zu seinem Geburtstag **bekommen**.
to find	**found**	Yesterday, I **found** a bag in the park.	Gestern **habe** ich eine Tasche im Park **gefunden**.
to come	**came**	They all **came** to the party.	Sie **sind** alle zur Party **gekommen**.
to eat	**ate**	Yesterday, Tom **ate** all the chocolate.	Gestern **hat** Tom die ganze Schokolade **gegessen**.
to see	**saw**	I **saw** many interesting sights in London.	Ich habe in London viele interessante Sehenswürdigkeiten **gesehen**.
to meet	**met**	I **met** nice people in Wales this summer.	Ich habe diesen Sommer nette Leute in Wales **getroffen**.
to buy	**bought**	Emma **bought** a funny souvenir for Lisa.	Emma hat ein lustiges Souvenir für Lisa **gekauft**.

[Trailer 2 Old junk]

plan [plæn]	Plan
junk [dʒʌŋk]	Gerümpel, Abfall; Ramsch
to clear out [klɪə 'aʊt]	ausräumen; entrümpeln
bath [bɑ:θ]	Badewanne
nose [nəʊz]	Nase
mouth [maʊθ]	Mund

Dictionary (English–German)

In dieser alphabetischen Wortliste findest du das gesamte Vokabular von *Green Line* 1.
Namen stehen in einer extra Liste am Ende des ***Dictionary***.
Einträge, die aus mehreren Wörtern bestehen, kannst du meist unter verschiedenen Stichwörtern nachschlagen. So ist z. B. *at home* unter *at* und unter *home* eingetragen.
Die Fundstellen stehen immer hinter dem jeweiligen Wort und zeigen dir an, wo es zum ersten Mal vorkommt, z. B.
always ['ɔ:lweɪz] immer **I U1,** 14 kommt zum ersten Mal vor in Band I, Unit 1, Seite 14
colour ['kʌlə] Farbe **I PUA,** 24 kommt zum ersten Mal vor in Band I, Pick-up A, Seite 24
U = Unit, PU = Pick-up
Bei Wörtern, die nicht zum Lernwortschatz zählen, steht die Fundstelle in Spitzklammern, z. B.
banana [bə'nɑ:nə] Banane ⟨**I U7,** 108⟩

A

a(n) [ə; ən] ein/-e **I U1,** 10
a lot of [ə 'lɒt‿əv] viel/-e, eine Menge **I U2,** 30
aargh! [ɑ:g] Grrrr! **I U2,** 30
about [ə'baʊt] über **I U1,** 11
to **act** [ækt] spielen **I U4,** 67; ⟨**I U1,** 19⟩
activity [æk'tɪvəti] Aktivität **I U7,** 102
address [ə'dres] Adresse **I U6,** 90
address book [ə'dres ˌbʊk] Adressbuch **I U6,** 90
adjective ['ædʒɪktɪv] Adjektiv, Eigenschaftswort **I U1,** 22
adventure [əd'ventʃə] Abenteuer **I U6,** 96
after ['ɑ:ftə] nach; nachdem **I U3,** 42
after that ['ɑ:ftə ðæt] danach **I U3,** 44
afternoon [ˌɑ:ftə'nu:n] Nachmittag **I U2,** 34
again [ə'gen] wieder, noch einmal, nochmal **I U3,** 42
against [ə'genst] gegen **I U6,** 96
to **agree** [ə'gri:] zustimmen ⟨**I U2,** 30⟩
air [eə] Luft **I U6,** 100
alarm clock [ə'lɑ:m ˌklɒk] Wecker **I U5,** 80
all [ɔ:l] alle/-s; ganz **I U4,** 58; alle/-s ⟨**I U3,** 50⟩
all alone [ˌɔ:l‿ə'ləʊn] ganz allein ⟨**I U7,** 116⟩
allergic to [ə'lɜ:dʒɪk tə] allergisch auf **I U7,** 104
alone [ə'ləʊn] allein **I U6,** 92
all alone [ˌɔ:l‿ə'ləʊn] ganz allein ⟨**I U7,** 116⟩
alphabet ['ælfəbet] Alphabet **I U1,** 17
alphabetical [ˌælfə'betɪkl] alphabetisch **I U5,** 84
already [ɔ:l'redi] schon, bereits **I U7,** 103
always ['ɔ:lweɪz] immer **I U1,** 14
am [ˌeɪ'em] vormittags *(Uhrzeit)* **I U3,** 40
and [ænd; ənd] und **I U1,** 10
animal ['ænɪml] Tier **I U7,** 102
another [ə'nʌðə] noch ein/-e; ein/-e andere/-r/-s **I U6,** 94
answer ['ɑ:nsə] Antwort **I U1,** 15
to **answer** ['ɑ:nsə] (be)antworten **I PUA,** 24
any ['enɪ] irgendein-e/-er; irgendwelche **I U6,** 94
anyone ['eniwʌn] irgendjemand; jeder (beliebige) ⟨**I U7,** 116⟩
apple ['æpl] Apfel **I U1,** 16
April ['eɪprl] April **I U5,** 75
arcade games *(pl.)* [ɑ:'keɪd ˌgeɪmz] Spielautomaten **I U6,** 88
are [ɑ:] bist, sind **I U1,** 10
Nasreen and I are ... [nʌs'ri:n‿ənd‿aɪ‿ɑ:] Nasreen und ich sind ... **I U2,** 26
as [æz; əz] als ⟨**I U7,** 108⟩
to **ask** [ɑ:sk] fragen **I PUA,** 24
to ask for ... ['ɑ:sk fə] nach ... fragen **I U4,** 59
asleep [ə'sli:p] schlafend **I U3,** 42
to fall asleep [fɔ:l‿ə'sli:p] einschlafen **I U3,** 42
assistant [ə'sɪstnt] Verkäufer, Verkäuferin **I U5,** 73
at [æt; ət] in, auf, bei, an **I U1,** 10
at half past (three) [ət ˌhɑ:f pɑ:st 'θri:] um halb (vier) **I U3,** 40
at home [æt 'həʊm] zu Hause **I U2,** 26
at my house [ət 'maɪ haʊs] bei mir zu Hause **I U3,** 41
at once [ət 'wʌns] auf einmal; sofort **I U6,** 96
at the weekend [æt ðə ˌwi:k'end] am Wochenende **I U3,** 40
August ['ɔ:gəst] August **I U5,** 75
aunt [ɑ:nt] Tante **I U2,** 28
autumn ['ɔ:təm] Herbst **I U6,** 90
away [ə'weɪ] weg **I U3,** 44

B

baby ['beɪbi] Baby, Säugling ⟨**I U7,** 108⟩
back [bæk] zurück **I U3,** 44
bacon ['beɪkn] (Schinken)Speck **I U7,** 104
bad [bæd] schlecht; böse **I U7,** 106
bag [bæg] Tasche **I U1,** 14
a bag of ... [ə 'bæg‿əv] eine Tüte ... **I U5,** 78
ball [bɔ:l] Ball **I U1,** 20
rubber ball [ˌrʌbə 'bɔ:l] Gummiball **I U2,** 33
banana [bə'nɑ:nə] Banane ⟨**I U7,** 108⟩
band [bænd] Band, Musikgruppe **I U3,** 40
boy band ['bɔɪ ˌbænd] Boygroup **I U3,** 40
bang [bæŋ] Knall, Schlag **I U4,** 66
to **bang** [bæŋ] knallen, schlagen **I U3,** 46
to **bark** [bɑ:k] bellen **I U3,** 48
to bark at ['bɑ:k‿ət] anbellen **I U3,** 49
basketball ['bɑ:skɪtbɔ:l] Basketball **I PUB,** 38
bathroom ['bɑ:θru:m] Bad(ezimmer) **I PUA,** 24
to **be** [bi:; bi] sein **I U1,** 15
Emma is good with ... [ˌemə ɪz 'gʊd wɪð] **Emma kann mit ... gut umgehen** **I U2,** 33
he is fed up (with) [hi: ɪz fed 'ʌp wɪð] er ist sauer, er hat die Nase voll (von) **I U2,** 34
He's late. [hi:z 'leɪt] Er kommt zu spät./Er ist spät dran. **I U1,** 14
How are you? [ˌhaʊ‿ɑ: 'jə] Wie geht es dir/Ihnen? **I U3,** 42; ⟨**I U1,** 13⟩
I'm (= I am) [aɪm; ˌaɪ'æm] ich bin **I U1,** 10

I'm fine. [ˌaɪm 'faɪn] Mir geht es gut. **I U3,** 42; ⟨**I U1,** 13⟩
I'm sorry. [aɪm 'sɒrɪ] Es tut mir Leid. **I U1,** 14
I'm with ... [aɪm 'wɪð] Ich bin bei ... **I U2,** 33
... is fun [ɪz 'fʌn] ... macht Spaß, ... ist witzig **I U2,** 35
Nasreen is a pain. [nʌsˌriːn‿ɪz ə 'peɪn] Nasreen geht mir auf die Nerven. **I U2,** 34
No, he isn't. [ˌnəʊ hi‿'ɪznt] Nein, ist er nicht. **I U1,** 14
she is good at [ʃi‿ɪz 'gʊd‿ət] sie ist gut in/bei ... **I U1,** 20
She is in a hurry. [ˌʃi‿ɪz ɪn ə 'hʌri] Sie hat es eilig. **I U2,** 30
this is ... ['ðɪs‿ɪz] hier ist ... *(am Telefon)* **I U3,** 43
to be right [bɪ 'raɪt] Recht haben **I U7,** 110
to be scared for [bi 'skeəd fə] Angst haben um **I U6,** 96
What is missing? [ˌwɒt‿ɪz 'mɪsɪŋ] Was fehlt? **I U1,** 23
You're lucky. [jʊə 'lʌki] Du hast Glück./Ihr habt Glück. **I U1,** 14
you're wrong [jɔː 'rɒŋ] du hast Unrecht, du irrst dich **I U1,** 21
beach [biːtʃ] Strand **I U6,** 88
beach holiday ['biːtʃ ˌhɒlədeɪ] Strandurlaub **I U6,** 88
on the beach [ɒn ðə 'biːtʃ] am Strand **I U6,** 92
beautiful ['bjuːtɪfl] schön, wunderbar **I U2,** 35
because [bɪ'kɒz] weil, da **I U2,** 29
bed [bed] Bett **I PUA,** 25
to go to bed [gəʊ tə 'bed] ins Bett gehen **I U3,** 49
bedroom ['bedruːm] Schlafzimmer **I PUA,** 24
before [bɪ'fɔː] bevor **I U2,** 34; bis (zu), vor **I U5,** 78
behind [bɪ'haɪnd] hinter **I U1,** 18
to **believe** [bɪ'liːv] glauben **I U3,** 46
He can't believe his eyes. [hi kɑːnt bɪˌliːv hɪz 'aɪz] Er traut seinen Augen nicht. **I U3,** 46
best [best] beste/-r/-s **I U4,** 62
better ['betə] besser, mehr ⟨**I U7,** 116⟩
big [bɪg] groß **I U1,** 12
bike [baɪk] Fahrrad **I PUB,** 38
bird [bɜːd] Vogel **I U7,** 102
birthday ['bɜːθdeɪ] Geburtstag **I U5,** 72
birthday party ['bɜːθdeɪ ˌpɑːti] Geburtstagsfeier **I U5,** 72
Happy birthday! [ˌhæpi 'bɜːθdeɪ] Alles Gute zum Geburtstag! **I U5,** 80
black [blæk] schwarz **I PUA,** 24
blue [bluː] blau **I PUA,** 24
board [bɔːd] Tafel; Brett **I U1,** 18
boat [bəʊt] Boot, Schiff **I U4,** 61
book [bʊk] Buch **I U1,** 14
address book [ə'dres ˌbʊk] Adressbuch **I U6,** 90
exercise book ['eksəsaɪz ˌbʊk] Heft **I U1,** 16
boring ['bɔːrɪŋ] langweilig **I U1,** 20
bottle ['bɒtl] Flasche **I U7,** 104
bottom ['bɒtəm] unteres Ende, Boden **I U3,** 46
on the bottom [ɒn ðə 'bɒtəm] unten **I U3,** 46
bowl [bəʊl] Schüssel **I U7,** 110; ⟨**I U5,** 79⟩
box [bɒks] Box, Kasten, Kästchen, Schachtel **I U3,** 43
a box of ... [ə 'bɒks‿əv] eine Schachtel ..., ein Karton ... **I U5,** 78
boy [bɔɪ] Junge **I U1,** 14
boy band ['bɔɪ ˌbænd] Boygroup **I U3,** 40
to **break** [breɪk] (zer)brechen, kaputtgehen **I U5,** 78
break-dance ['breɪkdɑːns] Breakdance ⟨**I U3,** 50⟩
breakfast ['brekfəst] Frühstück **I U3,** 48
to have breakfast [hæv 'brekfəst] frühstücken **I U6,** 93
bridge [brɪdʒ] Brücke **I PUC,** 54
to **bring** [brɪŋ] (mit)bringen **I U3,** 48
British ['brɪtɪʃ] britisch **I U3,** 40
brochure ['brəʊʃə] Broschüre **I U4,** 56
brother ['brʌðə] Bruder **I PUA,** 25
brown [braʊn] braun **I PUA,** 24
to **build** [bɪld] bauen **I U6,** 90
bus pl. **buses** [bʌs; bʌsɪz] Bus **I ZI,** 9
bus stop ['bʌs ˌstɒp] Bushaltestelle **I PUC,** 54
busy (with) ['bɪzi ˌwɪð] beschäftigt (mit) **I U2,** 34
but [bʌt] aber **I U1,** 12
to **buy** [baɪ] kaufen **I U5,** 72
by (Underground) [baɪ] mit (der U-Bahn), per **I U4,** 58
bye [baɪ] tschüss **I U1,** 19

C

café ['kæfeɪ] Café **I U3,** 48
jazz café ['dʒæz ˌkæfeɪ] Jazzcafé **I U3,** 48
cafeteria [kæfə'tɪərɪə] Cafeteria **I U1,** 20
cake [keɪk] Kuchen, Torte **I U5,** 74
(phone) **call** ['fəʊn ˌkɔːl] (Telefon)Anruf **I U3,** 42
to **call** [kɔːl] rufen, schreien **I U3,** 48; nennen **I U4,** 57
calm [kɑːm] ruhig, friedlich **I U7,** 104
camera ['kæmrə] Fotoapparat, Kamera **I U7,** 108
can [kæn; kən] können, dürfen **I U1,** 19
can't *(=cannot)* [kɑːnt; 'kænɒt] nicht können **I U2,** 32
How can I do my homework? ['haʊ kən‿aɪ ˌduː maɪ 'həʊmwɜːk] Wie soll ich meine Hausaufgaben machen? **I U2,** 32
candle ['kændl] Kerze **I U5,** 78
captain ['kæptɪn] Kapitän **I U4,** 66
car [kɑː] Auto **I U2,** 31
card [kɑːd] Karte, Spielkarte **I PUA,** 24; Chip, Speicherkarte *(für Digitalkameras)* **I U7,** 108
caretaker ['keəteɪkə] Hausmeister, Hausmeisterin **I U1,** 12
castle ['kɑːsl] Burg, Schloss **I PUC,** 54
sand castle ['sænd ˌkɑːsl] Sandburg **I U6,** 90
cat [kæt] Katze **I U2,** 26
cat food ['kæt ˌfuːd] Katzenfutter **I U3,** 44
to **catch** [kætʃ] nehmen *(Bus, Zug)*; (ein)fangen **I U4,** 58
CD [ˌsiː'diː] CD **I U2,** 32
centre ['sentə] Zentrum, Center **I PUC,** 54
information centre [ˌɪnfə'meɪʃn 'sentə] Touristeninformation **I PUC,** 54
chair [tʃeə] Stuhl **I U1,** 18
to **chase** [tʃeɪs] verfolgen **I U3,** 44
cheap [tʃiːp] billig, preiswert **I U6,** 94
check-in ['tʃekɪn] Einchecken **I U1,** 10
check-out ['tʃekaʊt] Auschecken **I U1,** 23
cheese [tʃiːz] Käse **I U4,** 62
chemistry set ['kemɪstri set] Chemiekasten **I U2,** 26
chicken ['tʃɪkɪn] Huhn; Hähnchen, Hühnchen **I U7,** 102
chicken flavour ['tʃɪkɪn ˌfleɪvə] Geschmacksrichtung "Hühnchen" **I U3,** 44
child pl. **children** ['tʃaɪld; 'tʃɪldrn] Kind **I U2,** 26
only child [ˌəʊnli 'tʃaɪld] Einzelkind **I U2,** 26
chocolate ['tʃɒklət] Schokolade **I U1,** 18
plain chocolate [ˌpleɪn 'tʃɒklət] (Halb)Bitterschokolade ⟨**I U5,** 79⟩
to **choose** [tʃuːz] (aus)wählen **I U7,** 106
chorus ['kɔːrəs] Refrain ⟨**I ZI,** 9⟩
church [tʃɜːtʃ] Kirche **I PUC,** 54
cinema ['sɪnəmə] Kino **I U3,** 40
city ['sɪti] Großstadt **I U7,** 102
to **clap** [klæp] klatschen **I U1,** 17
class [klɑːs] (Schul-)Klasse **I U4,** 59
class trip [ˌklɑːs 'trɪp] Klassenfahrt, Klassenausflug **I U7,** 104

classroom ['klɑ:srʊm] Klassenzimmer **I U1,** 14
classroom phrases *(pl.)* ['klɑ:srʊm ˌfreɪzɪz] Redewendungen für den Unterricht **I U1,** 19
clear [klɪə] klar, verständlich **I U7,** 111
to **click on** ['klɪk‿ɒn] anklicken **I U6,** 90
to **climb** [klaɪm] (hinauf)steigen, hinaufklettern, erklimmen **I U6,** 88
clock [klɒk] Uhr **I ZI,** 9
alarm clock [ə'lɑ:m ˌklɒk] Wecker **I U5,** 80
o'clock [ə'klɒk] Uhr *(Zeitangabe bei vollen Stunden)* **I U3,** 40
to **close** [kləʊz] schließen, zumachen **I PUA,** 24
clothes *(pl.)* [kləʊðz] Kleidung, Kleider **I U5,** 72
club [klʌb] Klub, Verein **I U3,** 40
computer club [kəm'pju:tə ˌklʌb] Computerklub **I U3,** 40
cooking club ['kʊkɪŋ ˌklʌb] Kochklub **I U3,** 40
coast [kəʊst] Küste **I U6,** 88
cold [kəʊld] kalt **I U6,** 88
to **collect** [kə'lekt] sammeln, einsammeln **I PUB,** 38
colour ['kʌlə] Farbe **I PUA,** 24
What colour are ...? [wɒt 'kʌlə‿ɑ:] Welche Farbe haben ... ? **I PUA,** 25
to **come** [kʌm] kommen **I U2,** 34
Come on! [kʌm‿'ɒn] Komm schon!/ Komm jetzt! **I U3,** 40
to come in [kʌm 'ɪn] hereinkommen **I U3,** 44
to come over [kʌm 'əʊvə] herüberkommen, vorbeischauen **I U2,** 34
communication skills [kəˌmju:nɪ'keɪʃn ˌskɪlz] Sprechfertigkeiten, Kommunikationsfertigkeiten **I U4,** 59
competition [ˌkɒmpə'tɪʃn] Wettbewerb **I U7,** 108
to **complete** [kəm'pli:t] vervollständigen **I U1,** 21
computer [kəm'pju:tə] Computer **I PUA,** 25
computer club [kəm'pju:tə ˌklʌb] Computerklub **I U3,** 40
computer shop [kəm'pju:tə ˌʃɒp] Computergeschäft **I U2,** 26
cook [kʊk] Koch, Köchin **I U5,** 78
cooking club ['kʊkɪŋ ˌklʌb] Kochklub **I U3,** 40
cool [ku:l] cool, super **I U1,** 13
to **copy** ['kɒpi] abschreiben, abmalen **I U1,** 16
cornflakes ['kɔ:nfleɪks] Cornflakes ⟨**I U5,** 79⟩
to **correct** [kə'rekt] korrigieren, berichtigen **I U4,** 64
correct [kə'rekt] richtig **I PUA,** 24
could [kʊd] könnte/-n ⟨**I U7,** 116⟩
to **count** [kaʊnt] zählen **I U5,** 78
of **course** [əv 'kɔ:s] natürlich, selbstverständlich **I U4,** 59
cousin ['kʌzn] Cousin, Cousine **I U2,** 28
covered ['kʌvəd] bedeckt ⟨**I U5,** 79⟩
cow [kaʊ] Kuh **I U7,** 102
to **crash** [kræʃ] aufprallen, zusammenstoßen **I U6,** 96
crisp [krɪsp] Kartoffelchip **I U1,** 18
chocolate **crispies** *(pl.)* ['tʃɒklət ˌkrɪspɪz] Schokoplätzchen **I U5,** 79
rice crispies *(pl.)* ['raɪs ˌkrɪspɪz] Reis-Knusperflocken ⟨**I U5,** 79⟩
to **cross** [krɒs] überqueren, über ... gehen **I PUC,** 55
crow's nest ['krəʊz ˌnest] Ausguck, Krähennest **I U4,** 66
crystal ['krɪstl] Kristall **I U2,** 35
CU (= See you) ['si: ju:] bis bald *(Abkürzung in SMS oder E-Mail)* **I U5,** 75
a **cup of** [ə 'kʌp‿əv] eine Tasse ... **I U5,** 78
cupboard ['kʌbəd] Schrank **I U1,** 18
customer ['kʌstəmə] Kunde, Kundin **I U5,** 73
cyberpet ['saɪbəpet] virtuelles Haustier **I U7,** 106

D

dad [dæd] Papa, Vati **I PUA,** 25
daily ['deɪli] täglich **I U3,** 42
to **dance** [dɑ:ns] tanzen **I U5,** 76; ⟨**I U3,** 50⟩
dancing lessons *(pl.)* ['dɑ:nsɪŋ ˌlesnz] Tanzunterricht, Tanzstunden **I U3,** 42
dark [dɑ:k] dunkel **I U7,** 110
date [deɪt] Datum **I U5,** 74
day [deɪ] Tag **I PUB,** 39
days of the week *(pl.)* [ˌdeɪz‿ɒv ðə 'wi:k] Wochentage *(pl.)* **I PUB,** 39
dead [ded] tot **I U7,** 111
dear [dɪə] Schatz **I U4,** 62
December [dɪ'sembə] Dezember **I U5,** 75
department store [dɪ'pɑ:tmənt ˌstɔ:] Kaufhaus **I U5,** 76
to **describe** [dɪ'skraɪb] beschreiben **I PUA,** 25
desk [desk] Schreibtisch **I U1,** 18
dialogue ['daɪəlɒg] Dialog **I U1,** 21; ⟨**I U1,** 19⟩
nine of **diamonds** [naɪn‿əv 'daɪəməndz] Karoneun *(beim Kartenspiel)* **I U3,** 46
diary ['daɪəri] Tagebuch **I U1,** 15
dictionary ['dɪkʃnri] Wörterbuch **I U5,** 84
to **die** [daɪ] sterben **I U6,** 97
different ['dɪfrnt] anders, unterschiedlich **I U1,** 23
dirty ['dɜ:ti] dreckig, schmutzig **I U2,** 30
Discman ['dɪskmæn] Discman **I U2,** 30
divorced from [dɪ'vɔ:st frəm] geschieden von **I U2,** 28
DJ ['di: ˌdʒeɪ] DJ, Discjockey **I U5,** 81
to **do** [du:; də; du] machen, tun **I U1,** 17
Don't you listen to the radio? [dəʊnt jə ˌlɪsn tə ðə 'reɪdiəʊ] Hörst du kein Radio? **I U5,** 81
dog [dɒg] Hund **I U2,** 27
doghouse ['dɒghaʊs] Hundehütte **I U6,** 92
dog-tired [dɒg'taɪəd] hundemüde **I U3,** 49
door [dɔ:] Tür **I U1,** 18
down [daʊn] herunter, hinunter, nach unten, hinab **I PUC,** 55
downstairs [daʊn'steəz] unten, im Untergeschoss **I U2,** 27
to **draw** [drɔ:] zeichnen **I PUA,** 25
dream [dri:m] Traum **I PUA,** 25
drink [drɪŋk] Getränk **I U3,** 49
to **drink** [drɪŋk] trinken **I U7,** 111
to **drive** [draɪv] fahren **I U4,** 58
driver ['draɪvə] Fahrer, Fahrerin **I U4,** 58
drums *(pl.)* [drʌmz] Schlagzeug **I U2,** 26
duty ['dju:ti] Pflicht **I U7,** 104

E

ear [ɪə] Ohr **I U7,** 106
early ['ɜ:li] früh **I U3,** 42
east [i:st] Osten **I U4,** 57
east of ['i:st‿əv] östlich von **I U6,** 88
easy ['i:zi] leicht, einfach **I U1,** 20
easy-peasy [ˌi:zi'pi:zi] babyleicht **I U4,** 62
to **eat** [i:t] essen **I U3,** 42
eatery ['i:tri] Kantine, Restaurant **I U1,** 20
egg [eg] Ei **I U5,** 78
Eh? [eɪ] Was? Nicht wahr? **I U5,** 80
eight [eɪt] acht **I U1,** 11
eighteen [ˌeɪ'ti:n] achtzehn **I U1,** 16
eighty ['eɪti] achtzig **I U1,** 16
eleven [ɪ'levn] elf **I U1,** 10
e-mail ['i:meɪl] E-Mail **I U2,** 33
empty ['emti] leer **I U7,** 111
to **end** [end] enden **I U4,** 62
English ['ɪŋglɪʃ] Englisch **I U1,** 11; englisch, aus England **I U2,** 29
in English [ɪn‿'ɪŋglɪʃ] auf Englisch **I U1,** 19

to enjoy [ɪn'dʒɔɪ] genießen **I U6,** 100
enough [ɪ'nʌf] genug ⟨**I U6,** 91⟩
er [ɜ:] äh **I U1,** 12
etc. (= et cetera) [ɪt'setrə] usw. (= und so weiter) **I U5,** 84
European [ˌjʊərə'pi:ən] europäisch, aus Europa; Europäer/-in **I U2,** 29
even ['i:vn] sogar, selbst **I U5,** 80
not even [nɒt 'i:vn] (noch) nicht einmal **I U6,** 95
evening ['i:vnɪŋ] Abend **I U3,** 42
in the evening [ɪn ði‿'i:vnɪŋ] abends **I U3,** 42
one evening [wʌn‿'i:vnɪŋ] eines Abends **I U7,** 110
every ['evri] jede/-r/-s **I U3,** 42
every ten minutes [ˌevri ten 'mɪnɪts] alle zehn Minuten **I U4,** 70
everyone ['evriwʌn] jeder **I U5,** 80
everything ['evriθɪŋ] alles **I U4,** 59
everywhere ['evriweə] überall **I U2,** 34
He takes us everywhere. [hi ˌteɪks‿əs‿'evriweə] Er bringt uns überallhin. **I U4,** 71
example [ɪg'zɑ:mpl] Beispiel **I U1,** 13
excited [ɪk'saɪtɪd] aufgeregt, begeistert **I U5,** 80
Excuse me. [ɪk'skju:s mi] Entschuldigung./Entschuldigen Sie. **I PUC,** 55
exercise ['eksəsaɪz] Übung **I U1,** 16
exercise book ['eksəsaɪz ˌbʊk] Heft **I U1,** 16
expensive [ɪk'spensɪv] teuer **I U5,** 73
to explain [ɪk'spleɪn] erklären **I U7,** 110
extra large (XL) ['ekstrə ˌlɑ:dʒ] besonders groß **I U5,** 72
eye [aɪ] Auge **I U3,** 46
He can't believe his eyes. [hi kɑ:nt bɪˌli:v hɪz 'aɪz] Er traut seinen Augen nicht. **I U3,** 46

F

face [feɪs] Gesicht **I U3,** 48
fair [feə] gerecht, fair **I U4,** 62
to fall [fɔ:l] (hin)fallen **I U3,** 42
to fall asleep [fɔ:l‿ə'sli:p] einschlafen **I U3,** 42
to fall over [fɔ:l 'əʊvə] umfallen, hinfallen **I U3,** 49
family ['fæmli] Familie **I PUA,** 25
family fun ['fæmli ˌfʌn] Spaß für die ganze Familie **I U6,** 90
family tree ['fæmli ˌtri:] Familienstammbaum **I U2,** 28
famous ['feɪməs] berühmt **I U4,** 57
farm [fɑ:m] Bauernhof **I U7,** 102
farmhand ['fɑ:mhænd] Landarbeiter, Landarbeiterin **I U7,** 102
fast [fɑ:st] schnell **I U4,** 64
father ['fɑ:ðə] Vater **I PUA,** 25
favourite ['feɪvrɪt] Lieblings- **I U1,** 12
February ['februri] Februar **I U5,** 75
to feed [fi:d] füttern **I U3,** 44
he is fed up (with) [hi: ɪz fed 'ʌp wɪð] er ist sauer, er hat die Nase voll (von) **I U2,** 34
ferris wheel ['ferɪs ˌwi:l] Riesenrad **I U6,** 100
festival ['festɪvl] Fest, Festival **I U6,** 88
kite festival ['kaɪt ˌfestɪvl] Drachenfest **I U6,** 88
a few [ə 'fju:] ein paar, einige; wenige **I U5,** 78
field [fi:ld] Wiese, Weide, Acker **I U7,** 102
fifteen [fɪf'ti:n] fünfzehn **I U1,** 16
fifty ['fɪfti] fünfzig **I U1,** 16
to fight [faɪt] kämpfen; sich streiten **I U4,** 67
to fight over [faɪt‿'əʊvə] sich streiten um **I U7,** 104
to fill in [fɪl‿'ɪn] ausfüllen **I U1,** 16
film [fɪlm] Film **I U3,** 40
finally ['faɪnli] schließlich, endlich, zum Schluss **I U3,** 44
to find [faɪnd] finden **I U1,** 22
finding the way [ˌfaɪndɪŋ ðə 'weɪ] den Weg finden **I U4,** 59
finding words [ˌfaɪndɪŋ 'wɜ:dz] Wörter finden **I U5,** 84
fine [faɪn] in Ordnung, gut **I U3,** 40
I'm fine. [ˌaɪm 'faɪn] Mir geht es gut. **I U3,** 42; ⟨**I U1,** 13⟩
finger ['fɪŋgə] Finger ⟨**I U4,** 67⟩
to finish ['fɪnɪʃ] (be)enden, fertig stellen **I U2,** 34
first [fɜ:st] zuerst, als Erstes **I U3,** 42; erste/-r/-s **I U4,** 60
fish pl. **fish** [fɪʃ] Fisch **I U6,** 100
five [faɪv] fünf **I U1,** 11
flat [flæt] Wohnung **I U2,** 26
flavour ['fleɪvə] Geschmack, Geschmacksrichtung, Aroma, Sorte **I U3,** 44
chicken flavour ['tʃɪkɪn ˌfleɪvə] Geschmacksrichtung „Hühnchen" **I U3,** 44
flour [flaʊə] Mehl **I U5,** 78
flower [flaʊə] Blume **I U4,** 62
to fly [flaɪ] fliegen **I U6,** 88
to fly a kite [flaɪ ə 'kaɪt] einen Drachen steigen lassen **I U6,** 88
folder ['fəʊldə] Ordner, Mappe **I U1,** 11
food [fu:d] Essen, Nahrung, Nahrungsmittel **I U3,** 44
cat food ['kæt ˌfu:d] Katzenfutter **I U3,** 44
foot pl. **feet** [fʊt; fi:t] Fuß **I U4,** 57
football ['fʊtbɔ:l] Fußball **I U1,** 12
for [fɔ:; fə] für **I ZI,** 8
for (many) hours [fə ˌmeni 'aʊəz] stundenlang **I U7,** 107
for (many) years [fə ˌmeni 'jɪəz] jahrelang **I U7,** 107
to forget [fə'get] vergessen **I U3,** 46
form [fɔ:m] Form **I U1,** 14
forty ['fɔ:ti] vierzig **I U1,** 16
four [fɔ:] vier **I U1,** 11
four of them ['fɔ:r‿əv ðəm] vier davon (Personen, Tiere, ...) **I U7,** 104
fourteen [fɔ:'ti:n] vierzehn **I U1,** 16
fox [fɒks] Fuchs **I U7,** 102
free time ['fri: ˌtaɪm] Freizeit **I U3,** 40
fresh [freʃ] frisch **I U6,** 100
Friday ['fraɪdeɪ] Freitag **I PUB,** 39
fried [fraɪd] gebraten ⟨**I U6,** 100⟩
friend [frend] Freund **I U1,** 12
from [frɒm; frəm] aus, von **I U1,** 10; von ... entfernt **I U6,** 88
from ... to ['frəm tə] von ... bis **I U3,** 40
Where are you from? [ˌweər‿ə jə 'frɒm] Woher kommst du? **I U1,** 10
in front of [ɪn 'frʌnt‿əv] vor **I U1,** 18
... is fun [ɪz 'fʌn] ... macht Spaß, ... ist witzig **I U2,** 35
Lisa is great fun. ['li:sə ɪz 'greɪt ˌfʌn] Lisa ist echt witzig. **I U3,** 42
to have fun [hæv 'fʌn] Spaß haben, sich amüsieren **I U5,** 78
funny ['fʌni] lustig, witzig **I PUA,** 25
fur [fɜ:] Fell ⟨**I U7,** 116⟩
furniture ['fɜ:nɪtʃə] Möbel **I PUA,** 25

G

game [geɪm] Spiel **I U1,** 13
garage ['gærɑ:ʒ] Garage; Werkstatt; Tankstelle **I U7,** 110
garden ['gɑ:dn] Garten **I U2,** 26
German ['dʒɜ:mən] Deutsch; deutsch, aus Deutschland **I U1,** 12
German teacher ['dʒɜ:mən ˌti:tʃə] Deutschlehrer, Deutschlehrerin **I U1,** 12
to get [get] holen, bringen; bekommen **I U4,** 58
to get into [get‿'ɪntə] (ein)steigen **I U6,** 97
to get lost [get 'lɒst] sich verirren **I U3,** 48
to get near [get 'nɪə] sich nähern ⟨**I U6,** 91⟩
to get to ['get tə] kommen zu, kommen nach, erreichen **I PUC,** 55
to get up [get 'ʌp] aufstehen **I U3,** 42
You've got me there! [jʊv ˌgɒt mi 'ðeə] Da habt ihr mich kalt erwischt! **I U4,** 60

girl [gɜ:l] Mädchen **I U1,** 14
to **give** [gɪv] geben; schenken **I U4,** 59
to give tours [gɪv 'tʊəz] Stadtrundfahrten leiten **I U4,** 60
to **go** [gəʊ] gehen, fahren **I U1,** 19; führen **I U4,** 56
go on, please [gəʊ‿'ɒn pli:z] Mach/Macht bitte weiter. **I U1,** 13
Let's go! [lets 'gəʊ] Lass(t) uns anfangen!/Lass(t) uns gehen! **I PUB,** 39; ⟨**I ZI,** 9⟩
to go back [gəʊ 'bæk] zurückgehen **I U3,** 44
to go down [gəʊ 'daʊn] hinuntergehen; entlanggehen **I PUC,** 55; nach unten gehen **I U5,** 79
to go for a picnic [gəʊ fər‿ə 'pɪknɪk] ein Picknick machen ⟨**I U5,** 75⟩
to go home [gəʊ 'həʊm] nach Hause gehen **I U3,** 42
to go on holiday [gəʊ ɒn 'hɒlədeɪ] in Urlaub gehen, in Urlaub fahren **I U6,** 100
to go shopping [gəʊ 'ʃɒpɪŋ] einkaufen gehen **I U5,** 73
to go surfing [gəʊ 'sɜ:fɪŋ] surfen gehen **I U6,** 88
to go to bed [gəʊ tə 'bed] ins Bett gehen **I U3,** 49
to go up [gəʊ 'ʌp] nach oben gehen **I U5,** 79
to go with [gəʊ 'wɪð] passen zu, gehören zu **I U4,** 56
goal [gəʊl] Tor **I U1,** 12
good [gʊd] gut **I U1,** 22
Emma is good with ... [ˌemə ɪz 'gʊd wɪð] **Emma kann mit ... gut umgehen** **I U2,** 33
Good morning. [gʊd 'mɔ:nɪŋ] Guten Morgen. **I U1,** 14; ⟨**I U1,** 13⟩
she is good at [ʃi‿ɪz 'gʊd‿ət] sie ist gut in/bei ... **I U1,** 20
goodbye [gʊd'baɪ] auf Wiedersehen **I U1,** 19
she has **got** [ʃi həz 'gɒt] sie hat ... **I U2,** 30
to have (got) [hæv 'gɒt] besitzen, haben **I U2,** 30
gram [græm] Gramm ⟨**I U5,** 79⟩
grammar ['græmə] Grammatik **I U1,** 15
grandad ['grændæd] Opa **I PUA,** 25
grandfather ['grænˌfɑ:ðə] Großvater **I PUA,** 25
grandma ['grænmɑ:] Oma **I PUA,** 25
grandmother ['grænˌmʌðə] Großmutter **I PUA,** 25
grass [grɑ:s] Gras **I U7,** 104
great [greɪt] toll, großartig **I U2,** 33; groß, riesig **I U6,** 96
Greek [gri:k] griechisch, aus Griechenland; Griechisch **I U2,** 29
green [gri:n] grün **I PUA,** 24
grey [greɪ] grau **I PUA,** 24
grid [grɪd] Raster, Tabelle **I U1,** 16
group [gru:p] Gruppe **I U2,** 36; ⟨**I U1,** 21⟩
grown [grəʊn] ausgewachsen; erwachsen ⟨**I U7,** 116⟩
to **guess** [ges] (er)raten; vermuten **I U4,** 63
guitar [gɪ'tɑ:] Gitarre **I PUB,** 38

H

half [hɑ:f] halb **I U3,** 41
half-sister ['hɑ:fˌsɪstə] Halbschwester **I U2,** 26
hamster ['hæmstə] Hamster ⟨**I U7,** 116⟩
hand [hænd] Hand **I U7,** 105
Hands on [hændz‿'ɒn] Pack's an! **I U1,** 11
to **happen** ['hæpn] passieren, geschehen **I U3,** 47
happy ['hæpi] glücklich, fröhlich **I PUA,** 25
Happy birthday! [ˌhæpi 'bɜ:θdeɪ] Alles Gute zum Geburtstag! **I U5,** 80
harbour ['hɑ:bə] Hafen **I U6,** 90
hard [hɑ:d] hart ⟨**I U5,** 79⟩
she **has got** [ʃi həz 'gɒt] sie hat ... **I U2,** 30
to have (got) [hæv 'gɒt] besitzen, haben **I U2,** 30
to have a party [hæv ə 'pɑ:ti] eine Party feiern **I U2,** 33
to have breakfast [hæv 'brekfəst] frühstücken **I U6,** 93
to have fun [hæv 'fʌn] Spaß haben, sich amüsieren **I U5,** 78
he [hi:] er **I U1,** 12
heading ['hedɪŋ] Überschrift, Titel **I U5,** 81
to **hear** [hɪə] hören **I U6,** 96
heart [hɑ:t] Herz **I PUA,** 25
eight of hearts [ˌeɪt‿əv 'hɑ:ts] Herzacht *(beim Kartenspiel)* **I U3,** 46
to learn by heart [ˌlɜ:n baɪ 'hɑ:t] auswendig lernen **I PUA,** 25
Hello. [hel'əʊ] Hallo. **I U1,** 10
to say hello [seɪ hel'əʊ] jemanden begrüßen **I U1,** 11
to say hello to [seɪ hel'əʊ tə] grüßen, Grüße ausrichten **I U2,** 33
help [help] Hilfe **I U3,** 44
to **help** [help] helfen **I U2,** 32
her [hɜ:] ihr/-e **I U1,** 15
here [hɪə] hier **I U1,** 12; hierher, hierhin **I U4,** 56
Here it is. [ˌhɪər‿ɪt‿'ɪz] Hier ist es. **I U2,** 30
Here you are. [ˌhɪə ju‿'ɑ:] Bitte schön. **I U5,** 73; ⟨**I U2,** 31⟩
in here [ɪn 'hi:ə] hier drin **I U6,** 94
It's Mum here. [ɪts 'mʌm ˌhɪə] Hier spricht Mama. **I U3,** 42
Hey! [heɪ] Hey! **I U1,** 12
Hi. [haɪ] Hi./Hallo. **I U1,** 10
his [hɪz] sein/-e **I PUA,** 25
hm [m] hm **I U1,** 21
hobby *pl.* **hobbies** ['hɒbi; 'hɒbiz] Hobby **I PUB,** 38
to **hold** [həʊld] halten, festhalten **I U3,** 46
to hold up [həʊld 'ʌp] hochhalten **I PUA,** 24
hole [həʊl] Loch **I U3,** 44
holiday(s) ['hɒlədeɪ; 'hɒlədeɪz] Ferien, Urlaub **I U6,** 88
beach holiday ['bi:tʃ ˌhɒlədeɪ] Strandurlaub **I U6,** 88
holiday home ['hɒlədeɪ ˌhəʊm] *(hier:)* Tierpension **I U7,** 106
planning your holidays [ˌplænɪŋ jə 'hɒlədeɪz] den Urlaub planen **I U6,** 90
to go on holiday [gəʊ ɒn 'hɒlədeɪ] in Urlaub gehen, in Urlaub fahren **I U6,** 100
holiday-maker ['hɒlədeɪˌmeɪkə] Urlauber, Urlauberin **I U6,** 100
home [həʊm] Zuhause **I U1,** 10
at home [æt 'həʊm] zu Hause **I U2,** 26
holiday home ['hɒlədeɪ ˌhəʊm] *(hier:)* Tierpension **I U7,** 106
home page ['həʊm ˌpeɪdʒ] Homepage **I U6,** 90
home sweet home ['həʊm ˌswi:t 'həʊm] trautes Heim *(Sprichwort)* **I PUA,** 24
on the way home [ˌɒn ðe weɪ 'həʊm] auf dem Weg nach Hause **I U6,** 94
to go home [gəʊ 'həʊm] nach Hause gehen **I U3,** 42
homework ['həʊmwɜ:k] Hausaufgabe, Hausaufgaben **I U1,** 19
How can I do my homework? ['haʊ kən‿aɪ ˌdu: maɪ 'həʊmwɜ:k] Wie soll ich meine Hausaufgaben machen? **I U2,** 32
What's for homework, please? [wɒts fə 'həʊmwɜ:k ˌpli:z] Was haben wir als Hausaufgabe auf? **I U1,** 19
Hooray! [hʊ'reɪ] Hurra! **I U6,** 92; ⟨**I ZI,** 9⟩
horse [hɔ:s] Pferd **I U7,** 102
hot [hɒt] heiß ⟨**I U5,** 79⟩
hour [aʊə] Stunde **I U4,** 57
for (many) hours [fə ˌmeni 'aʊəz] stundenlang **I U7,** 107
24-hour [twentiˌfɔ:‿'aʊə] 24-Stunden **I ZI,** 9
house [haʊs] Haus **I PUA,** 25
at my house [ət 'maɪ haʊs] bei mir zu Hause **I U3,** 41

how [haʊ] wie **I U1,** 10
How about ... [haʊ ə'baʊt] Wie wäre es mit ... **I U3,** 40
How are you? [ˌhaʊ‿ɑː 'jə] Wie geht es dir/Ihnen? **I U3,** 42; ⟨**I U1,** 13⟩
How can I do my homework? ['haʊ kən‿aɪ ˌduː maɪ 'həʊmwɜːk] Wie soll ich meine Hausaufgaben machen? **I U2,** 32
How many ... ? [haʊ 'meni] Wie viele ... ? **I U4,** 60
How much ... ? [haʊ 'mʌtʃ] Wie viel ... ? **I U5,** 78
How much is ... ? ['haʊ mʌtʃ‿ɪz] Wie viel kostet ... ? **I U5,** 72
How old are you? [haʊ‿'əʊld‿ɑː 'juː] Wie alt bist du? **I U1,** 10
How to ... ['haʊ tə] Wie man ... **I U1,** 11
a/one **hundred** [ə 'hʌndrəd; wʌn 'hʌndrəd] einhundert **I U1,** 16
hurry ['hʌri] Eile, Hast **I U2,** 30
She is in a hurry. [ˌʃi‿ɪz ɪn ə 'hʌri] Sie hat es eilig. **I U2,** 30
to **hurry up** [ˌhʌri 'ʌp] sich beeilen **I U4,** 67

I

I [aɪ] ich **I U1,** 10
I'm (= I am) [aɪm; ˌaɪ 'æm] ich bin **I U1,** 10
ice-cream [ˌaɪs'kriːm] Eiscreme, Eis **I U6,** 90
idea [aɪ'dɪə] Idee **I U2,** 32
if [ɪf] wenn, falls; ob **I U7,** 111
important [ɪm'pɔːtnt] wichtig **I U3,** 40
in [ɪn] in **I U1,** 10; im **I U1,** 18
in English [ɪn‿'ɪŋglɪʃ] auf Englisch **I U1,** 19
in front of [ɪn 'frʌnt‿əv] vor **I U1,** 18
in here [ɪn 'hiːə] hier drin **I U6,** 94
in the evening [ɪn ðiˌ'iːvnɪŋ] abends **I U3,** 42
in the street [ɪn ðə 'striːt] auf der Straße **I U7,** 116
in the town of Penzance [ɪn ðə 'taʊn‿əv pen'zæns] in der Stadt Penzance **I U6,** 88
information *(no pl.)* [ˌɪnfə'meɪʃn] Information, Informationen **I PUC,** 54
information centre [ˌɪnfə'meɪʃn 'sentə] Touristeninformation **I PUC,** 54
inside [ˌɪn'saɪd] in ⟨**I U7,** 116⟩
interested in ['ɪntrəstɪd] interessiert an **I U2,** 26
interesting ['ɪntrəstɪŋ] interessant **I U4,** 56
Internet ['ɪntənet] Internet **I U6,** 90
to surf on the Internet [ˌsɜːf‿ɒn ðiˌ'ɪntənet] im Internet surfen **I U6,** 90
into ['ɪntə] in (hinein) **I U3,** 44
invitation [ˌɪnvɪ'teɪʃn] Einladung **I U5,** 74
to **invite** [ɪn'vaɪt] einladen **I U5,** 74
to invite ... out [ɪnˌvaɪt 'aʊt] ... (zu etwas) einladen **I U5,** 74
is [ɪz] ist **I U1,** 10
island ['aɪlənd] Insel **I U4,** 66
it [ɪt] es **I U1,** 12
It's Mum here. [ɪts 'mʌm ˌhɪə] Hier spricht Mama. **I U3,** 42
It's two pounds. [ɪts ˌtuː 'paʊndz] Es kostet zwei Pfund. **I U5,** 72
Italian [ɪ'tæliən] italienisch, aus Italien; Italienisch **I U2,** 29
its [ɪts] sein **I U2,** 26

J

January ['dʒænjuri] Januar **I U5,** 75
jeans *(pl.)* [dʒiːnz] Jeans **I U5,** 76
job [dʒɒb] Arbeit, Aufgabe, Tätigkeit **I U7,** 104
joke [dʒəʊk] Witz **I U1,** 20
jolly ['dʒɒli] lustig, vergnügt ⟨**I U4,** 67⟩
July [dʒʊ'laɪ] Juli **I U5,** 75
jumbled ['dʒʌmbld] durcheinander geraten, vermischt **I U4,** 59
to **jump** [dʒʌmp] springen **I U5,** 80
June [dʒuːn] Juni **I U5,** 75
just [dʒʌst] nur **I U2,** 30; einfach **I U3,** 46; gerade (eben), soeben **I U5,** 76
just now [ˌdʒʌst 'naʊ] gerade, im Augenblick **I U7,** 116

K

karaoke machine [ˌkæri'əʊki mə'ʃiːn] Karaokegerät **I U5,** 80
to **keep** [kiːp] behalten, aufbewahren **I U6,** 94
to **kick** [kɪk] schießen; treten **I U3,** 47
kid [kɪd] Kind, Jugendlicher, Jugendliche **I U4,** 60
kitchen ['kɪtʃɪn] Küche **I PUA,** 24
kite [kaɪt] Drachen **I U6,** 88
kite festival ['kaɪt ˌfestɪvl] Drachenfest **I U6,** 88
to fly a kite [flaɪ ə 'kaɪt] einen Drachen steigen lassen **I U6,** 88
to **know** [nəʊ] kennen; wissen **I U1,** 11
I don't know! [ˌaɪ dəʊnt 'nəʊ] Ich weiß (es) nicht! **I U4,** 60
I have known [aɪ həv 'nəʊn] ich habe gekannt, ich kannte ⟨**I U7,** 116⟩
I know a fox when I see one! [aɪ ˌnəʊ ə 'fɒks wen‿aɪ 'siː wʌn] Ich erkenne einen Fuchs sofort! **I U7,** 110

L

land [lænd] Land **I PUB,** 38
language ['læŋgwɪdʒ] Sprache **I U1,** 12
laptop ['læptɒp] Laptop **I U2,** 34
large (L) [lɑːdʒ] groß **I U5,** 72
extra large (XL) ['ekstrə ˌlɑːdʒ] besonders groß **I U5,** 72
last [lɑːst] letzte/-r/-s **I U4,** 62
late [leɪt] (zu) spät **I U1,** 14
He's late. [hiːz 'leɪt] Er kommt zu spät./Er ist spät dran. **I U1,** 14
Sorry I'm late. [ˌsɒri‿aɪm 'leɪt] Tut mir Leid, dass ich zu spät komme. **I U1,** 19
to be late for school [bi ˌleɪt fə 'skuːl] zu spät zur Schule kommen **I U5,** 80
later ['leɪtə] später **I U2,** 30
to **laugh** [lɑːf] lachen **I U5,** 78
to **learn** [lɜːn] lernen **I PUA,** 25
to learn by heart [ˌlɜːn baɪ 'hɑːt] auswendig lernen **I PUA,** 25
we're learning English [wɪə ˌlɜːnɪŋ‿'ɪŋglɪʃ] wir lernen Englisch ⟨**I ZI,** 9⟩
left [left] linke/-r/-s; links **I PUC,** 55
on the left [ɒn ðə 'left] auf der linken Seite, links **I PUC,** 55; ⟨**I U2,** 28⟩
on your left/right [ɒn jə 'left, 'raɪt] links/rechts, auf der linken/rechten Seite **I PUC,** 55
leg [leg] Bein **I U7,** 110; ⟨**I U4,** 67⟩
lesson ['lesn] Unterrichtsstunde **I U1,** 17
dancing lessons *(pl.)* ['dɑːnsɪŋ ˌlesnz] Tanzunterricht, Tanzstunden **I U3,** 42
to **let** [let] lassen **I ZI,** 9
let's (= let us) [lets; let‿'ʌs] lass(t) uns **I ZI,** 9
let's get started [lets get 'stɑːtɪd] lass(t) uns beginnen, lass(t) uns anfangen ⟨**I ZI,** 9⟩
Let's go! [lets 'gəʊ] Lass(t) uns anfangen!/Lass(t) uns gehen! **I PUB,** 39; ⟨**I ZI,** 9⟩
let's listen [lets 'lɪsn] lass(t) uns zuhören **I ZI,** 9
letter ['letə] Buchstabe **I U1,** 20; ⟨**I U1,** 17⟩
to **lick** [lɪk] (ab)lecken **I U4,** 67
life pl. **lives** [laɪf; laɪvz] Leben **I U4,** 57
lighthouse ['laɪthaʊs] Leuchtturm **I U6,** 88
to **like** [laɪk] mögen **I U3,** 45
I don't like them. [aɪ dəʊnt 'laɪk ˌðəm] Sie gefallen mir nicht. **I U6,** 94
like [laɪk] wie **I PUA,** 25

like this [laɪk ˈðɪs] so, auf diese Weise **I PUA, 25**
what it looks like [ˌwɒt‿ɪt ˈlʊks laɪk] wie es aussieht **I U7, 107**
line [laɪn] Linie; Zeile **I U4, 57**
to **link** [lɪŋk] verbinden **I U3, 47**
linking sounds [ˌlɪŋkɪŋ ˈsaʊndz] das Verbinden von Lauten **I U3, 47**
list [lɪst] Liste **I U1, 16**
to **listen** [ˈlɪsn] zuhören **I ZI, 9**
let's listen [lets ˈlɪsn] lass(t) uns zuhören **I ZI, 9**
to listen for [ˈlɪsn fə] heraushören **I U1, 16**
to listen to [ˈlɪsn tə] jemandem zuhören **I U2, 27**
Listening [ˈlɪsnɪŋ] *(hier:)* Hörverstehensübung **I U1, 11**
little [ˈlɪtl] klein **I U5, 74**; wenig **I U5, 78**
a little [ə ˈlɪtl] ein wenig, etwas **I U5, 78**
to **live** [lɪv] wohnen, leben **I U5, 81**; ⟨**I U4, 65**⟩
living room [ˈlɪvɪŋ ruːm] Wohnzimmer **I PUA, 24**
long [lɒŋ] lang **I U1, 14**
a pier a mile long [ə ˈpɪə ə ˌmaɪl ˈlɒŋ] ein Pier, der eine Meile lang ist **I U6, 88**
to **look** [lʊk] schauen, sehen, gucken **I U1, 20**; nachschauen, suchen **I U2, 30**; aussehen **I U3, 44**
to look after [lʊk‿ˈɑːftə] sich kümmern um; aufpassen auf **I U7, 104**
to look at [ˈlʊk‿æt] anschauen, ansehen **I U1, 15**
to look for [ˈlʊk fə] suchen (nach) **I U5, 76**
to look up [lʊk‿ˈʌp] nachschlagen, nachschauen **I U6, 100**
what it looks like [ˌwɒt‿ɪt ˈlʊks laɪk] wie es aussieht **I U7, 107**
to get **lost** [get ˈlɒst] sich verirren **I U3, 48**
a **lot of** [ə ˈlɒt‿əv] viel/-e, eine Menge **I U2, 30**
lots of [ˈlɒts‿əv] viel/-e, jede Menge **I U5, 78**
loud [laʊd] laut **I U5, 80**
to **love** [lʌv] lieben **I U3, 45**
You're **lucky.** [jʊə ˈlʌki] Du hast Glück./Ihr habt Glück. **I U1, 14**
lunch [lʌnʃ] Mittagessen **I U2, 29**; ⟨**I U2, 28**⟩
lunchtime [ˈlʌnʃtaɪm] Mittagszeit, Mittagspause **I U1, 20**

M

machine [məˈʃiːn] Maschine, Apparat, Gerät; Automat **I U5, 80**
karaoke machine [ˌkæriˈəʊki məˈʃiːn] Karaokegerät **I U5, 80**
magazine [ˌmægəˈziːn] Zeitschrift **I U2, 30**
to **make** [meɪk] machen, bilden **I U1, 15**
Make up your mind! [ˌmeɪk‿ˈʌp jə ˈmaɪnd] Entscheide dich! **I U4, 62**
man pl. **men** [mæn; men] Mann **I U5, 74**
manager [ˈmænɪdʒə] Geschäftsführer, Geschäftsführerin **I U2, 26**
many [ˈmeni] viele **I U5, 78**
How many ... ? [haʊ ˈmeni] Wie viele ... ? **I U4, 60**
map [mæp] Stadtplan, Landkarte **I PUC, 54**
treasure map [ˈtreʒə ˌmæp] Schatzkarte **I U4, 66**
March [mɑːtʃ] März **I U5, 75**
the third of March [ðə ˌθɜːd‿əv ˈmɑːtʃ] der dritte März **I U5, 74**
market [ˈmɑːkɪt] Markt **I U4, 62**
married to [ˈmærid tə] verheiratet mit **I U2, 28**
to **match** [mætʃ] zuordnen **I U2, 27**
mate [meɪt] (Schiffs)Offizier; Freund, Freundin **I U4, 66**
may [meɪ] (vielleicht) können; dürfen **I U7, 110**
May [meɪ] Mai **I U5, 75**
maybe [ˈmeɪbi] vielleicht **I U2, 30**
me [miː] mich; mir **I U3, 48**
Me? [miː; mi] Ich? **I U4, 62**
meal [miːl] Mahlzeit, Essen **I U6, 90**
to **mean** [miːn] bedeuten; meinen **I U4, 64**
meaning [ˈmiːnɪŋ] Bedeutung **I U7, 116**
medium (M) [ˈmiːdiəm] mittel(groß) **I U5, 72**
to **meet** [miːt] (sich) treffen **I U3, 40**
meeting people [ˈmiːtɪŋ ˌpiːpl] Leute kennen lernen, Leute treffen **I U1, 12**
to **melt** [melt] schmelzen ⟨**I U5, 79**⟩
to **mend** [mend] heilen; reparieren **I U7, 110**
mess [mes] Unordnung, Durcheinander **I U2, 30**
What a mess! [wɒt‿ə ˈmes] Was für eine Unordnung! **I U2, 30**
mile [maɪl] Meile **I U6, 88**
milk [mɪlk] Milch **I U7, 104**
to **milk** [mɪlk] melken **I U7, 104**
Make up your **mind!** [ˌmeɪk‿ˈʌp jə ˈmaɪnd] Entscheide dich! **I U4, 62**
minute [ˈmɪnɪt] Minute **I U3, 41**; ⟨**I U2, 28**⟩
missing [ˈmɪsɪŋ] fehlend, verschwunden **I U1, 23**
What is missing? [ˌwɒt‿ɪz ˈmɪsɪŋ] Was fehlt? **I U1, 23**
to **mix** [mɪks] verrühren ⟨**I U5, 79**⟩
mixed [mɪkst] gemischt **I U3, 50**
mixed bag [ˌmɪkst ˈbæg] bunte Mischung **I U3, 50**
mmm [m] mmm, lecker **I U1, 16**
mobile [ˈməʊbaɪl] Handy, Mobiltelefon **I U1, 11**
moment [ˈməʊmənt] Moment, Augenblick **I U7, 108**
Monday [ˈmʌndeɪ] Montag **I PUB, 39**
money [ˈmʌni] Geld **I U5, 73**
monkey [ˈmʌŋki] Affe **I U7, 102**
month [mʌnθ] Monat **I U5, 75**
more [mɔː] mehr; weitere **I U1, 11**
morning [ˈmɔːnɪŋ] Morgen, Vormittag **I U1, 14**
Good morning. [gʊd ˈmɔːnɪŋ] Guten Morgen. **I U1, 14**; ⟨**I U1, 13**⟩
this morning [ðɪs ˈmɔːnɪŋ] heute Morgen **I U6, 93**
mother [ˈmʌðə] Mutter **I PUA, 25**
mountain [ˈmaʊntɪn] Berg **I U6, 88**
mouse pl. **mice** [maʊs; maɪs] Maus **I U1, 10**
mouth jogging [ˈmaʊθ ˌdʒɒgɪŋ] „Sprachjoggen" ⟨**I U1, 22**⟩
Mr [ˈmɪstə] Herr *(Anrede)* **I U1, 12**
Mrs [ˈmɪsɪz] Frau *(Anrede)* **I U1, 12**
much [mʌtʃ] viel **I U4, 57**
How much ... ? [haʊ ˈmʌtʃ] Wie viel ... ? **I U5, 78**
How much is ... ? [ˈhaʊ mʌtʃ‿ɪz] Wie viel kostet ... ? **I U5, 72**
to **muck out** [mʌk‿ˈaʊt] ausmisten **I U7, 104**
mug [mʌg] Becher **I U6, 94**
mum [mʌm] Mama **I U1, 14**
museum [mjuːˈziːəm] Museum **I PUC, 54**
music [ˈmjuːzɪk] Musik **I U2, 32**
must [mʌst] müssen **I U6, 90**
mustn't [ˈmʌsnt] nicht dürfen **I U7, 104**
my [maɪ] mein/-e **I U1, 10**
My name is .... . [maɪ ˈneɪm‿ɪz] Ich heiße ... **I U1, 10**

N

name [neɪm] Name **I U1, 10**
My name is .... . [maɪ ˈneɪm‿ɪz] Ich heiße ... **I U1, 10**
What's your name? [wɒts jɔː ˈneɪm] Wie heißt du? **I U1, 10**
nasty [ˈnɑːsti] böse, gemein ⟨**I U1, 21**⟩

nationality [ˌnæʃn'æləti] Nationalität **I U2,** 28
near [nɪə] nahe, in der Nähe von **I PUC,** 54
to **need** [ni:d] brauchen **I U5,** 78
neighbour ['neɪbə] Nachbar, Nachbarin **I U3,** 44
nervous ['nɜ:vəs] nervös, aufgeregt **I U7,** 104
never ['nevə] nie, niemals **I U3,** 42
new [nju:] neu **I U1,** 10
newsagent ['nju:zˌeɪdʒnt] Zeitschriftengeschäft **I U5,** 72
next [nekst] nächste/-r/-s **I U7,** 116
next to ['nekst tə] neben **I U3,** 44; ⟨**I U2,** 28⟩
nice [naɪs] nett, sympathisch **I U1,** 14; schön, gut **I U3,** 42
the nicest [ðə 'naɪsɪst] die schönsten, die nettesten ⟨**I U7,** 116⟩
night [naɪt] Nacht **I U7,** 110
nine [naɪn] neun **I U1,** 11
nineteen [ˌnaɪn'ti:n] neunzehn **I U1,** 16
ninety ['naɪnti] neunzig **I U1,** 16
no [nəʊ] kein/-e **I U1,** 20
no [nəʊ] nein **I U1,** 14
north [nɔ:θ] Norden **I U4,** 57
North Sea [ˌnɔ:θ 'si:] Nordsee **I U4,** 57
not [nɒt] nicht **I U1,** 14
not even [nɒt 'i:vn] (noch) nicht einmal **I U6,** 95
note [nəʊt] Notiz, Nachricht **I U3,** 44
to take notes [teɪk 'nəʊts] sich Notizen machen **I U5,** 81
noun [naʊn] Nomen, Hauptwort **I U6,** 100
November [nə'vembə] November **I U5,** 75
now [naʊ] jetzt, nun, gerade **I U1,** 14
right now [raɪt 'naʊ] jetzt, sofort, gerade **I U5,** 74
number ['nʌmbə] Nummer, Hausnummer; Zahl **I U1,** 11

O

o'clock [ə'klɒk] Uhr (*Zeitangabe bei vollen Stunden*) **I U3,** 40
object ['ɒbdʒɪkt] Objekt, Satzergänzung **I U7,** 107
object pronoun ['ɒbdʒɪkt ˌprəʊnaʊn] Objektpronomen ⟨**I U4,** 59⟩
ocean ['əʊʃn] Ozean **I U6,** 89
October [ɒk'təʊbə] Oktober **I U5,** 75
of [ɒv; əv] von **I PUC,** 54
four of them ['fɔ:r‿əv ðəm] vier davon (Personen, Tiere, …) **I U7,** 104
in the town of Penzance [ɪn ðə 'taʊn‿əv pen'zæns] in der Stadt Penzance **I U6,** 88
of course [əv 'kɔ:s] natürlich, selbstverständlich **I U4,** 59
often ['ɒfn] oft, häufig **I U3,** 42
oh [əʊ] null (*bei Telefonnummern*) **I U1,** 11
Oh! [əʊ] Oh! **I U1,** 12
OK [əʊ'keɪ] okay **I U1,** 12
old [əʊld] alt **I U1,** 10
How old are you? [haʊ‿'əʊld‿ɑ: 'ju:] Wie alt bist du? **I U1,** 10
on [ɒn] auf; an **I U1,** 14
on a train [ɒn‿ə 'treɪn] im Zug **I U6,** 97
on the beach [ɒn ðə 'bi:tʃ] am Strand **I U6,** 92
on the bottom [ɒn ðə 'bɒtəm] unten **I U3,** 46
on the left [ɒn ðə 'left] auf der linken Seite, links **I PUC,** 55; ⟨**I U2,** 28⟩
on the right [ɒn ðə 'raɪt] auf der rechten Seite, rechts **I PUC,** 55; ⟨**I U2,** 28⟩
on the top [ɒn ðə 'tɒp] oben **I U3,** 46
on top of [ɒn 'tɒp‿əv] auf … hinauf, oben (auf) **I U3,** 46
on Tuesdays [ɒn 'tju:zdeɪz] dienstags **I U3,** 40
on TV [ɒn ˌti:'vi:] im Fernsehen **I U3,** 42
on your right/left [ɒn jə 'raɪt, 'left] rechts/links, auf der rechten/linken Seite **I PUC,** 55
at **once** [ət 'wʌns] auf einmal; sofort **I U6,** 96
one [wʌn] eins **I U1,** 10
one evening [wʌn‿'i:vnɪŋ] eines Abends **I U7,** 110
one Saturday afternoon [wʌn 'sætədeɪ ˌɑ:ftə'nu:n] an einem Samstag Nachmittag **I U2,** 34
online [ˌɒn'laɪn] online **I U7,** 106
only child [ˌəʊnli 'tʃaɪld] Einzelkind **I U2,** 26
only ['əʊnli] nur, bloß **I U2,** 30
Oops! [u:ps] Hoppla! **I U6,** 101
to **open** ['əʊpn] öffnen, aufmachen **I U2,** 33
open ['əʊpn] geöffnet, offen; aufgeschlagen **I PUA,** 24
opposite ['ɒpəzɪt] gegenüber **I PUC,** 54
or [ɔ:] oder **I U1,** 11
orange ['ɒrɪndʒ] orange **I PUA,** 24
orchestra ['ɔ:kɪstrə] Orchester **I U3,** 40
order ['ɔ:də] Reihenfolge **I U1,** 13
other ['ʌðə] andere/-r/-s, weitere/-r/-s **I U1,** 22
the others [ðiˌ'ʌðəz] die anderen **I U5,** 77
our [aʊə; ɑ:] unser/-e **I U2,** 26
out [aʊt] heraus, hinaus, nach draußen **I U6,** 96
outside [ˌaʊt'saɪd] außen, draußen, im Freien; außerhalb **I U2,** 30
over there [ˌəʊvə 'ðeə] (nach) dort drüben **I U6,** 91
over ['əʊvə] über **I U2,** 26
to **own** [əʊn] besitzen ⟨**I U7,** 116⟩
own [əʊn] eigene/-r/-s **I U2,** 30
her own room [hər‿ˌəʊn 'ru:m] ihr eigenes Zimmer **I U2,** 30
owner ['əʊnə] Besitzer, Besitzerin **I U7,** 106

P

to **pack** [pæk] (ein)packen **I U6,** 90
page [peɪdʒ] Seite **I U1,** 14
home page ['həʊm ˌpeɪdʒ] Homepage **I U6,** 90
Nasreen is a **pain.** [nʌsˌri:n‿ɪz ə 'peɪn] Nasreen geht mir auf die Nerven. **I U2,** 34
pair [peə] Paar **I U6,** 94
paper case ['peɪpə ˌkeɪs] Papierbackförmchen ⟨**I U5,** 79⟩
parents *pl.* ['peərənts] Eltern **I U2,** 26
park [pɑ:k] Park **I U3,** 40
to **park** [pɑ:k] parken **I U4,** 60
parrot ['pærət] Papagei ⟨**I U4,** 67⟩
part [pɑ:t] Teil **I U4,** 56
partner ['pɑ:tnə] Partner, Partnerin **I U1,** 11
party ['pɑ:ti] Party, Feier **I U1,** 18
birthday party ['bɜ:θdeɪ ˌpɑ:ti] Geburtstagsfeier **I U5,** 72
to have a party [hæv ə 'pɑ:ti] eine Party feiern **I U2,** 33
past [pɑ:st] nach (*bei Uhrzeitangaben*) **I U3,** 41
pen [pen] Füller **I U1,** 16
pencil ['pensl] Bleistift **I U1,** 16
pencil-case ['pensl keɪs] Federmäppchen **I U1,** 16
penny pl. **pence** [peni; pens] Penny, Pence (*brit. Währungseinheit*) **I U5,** 73
people *(pl.)* ['pi:pl] Leute *(pl.)*, Menschen *(pl.)* **I U1,** 14
per [pɜ:; pə] pro **I PUA,** 24
person pl. **people** ['pɜ:sn; pi:pl] Person, Mensch **I U6,** 100
pet [pet] Haustier **I U3,** 48
phone [fəʊn] Telefon **I U1,** 11
phone call ['fəʊn ˌkɔ:l] (Telefon)Anruf **I U3,** 42

phone number ['fəʊn ˌnʌmbə] Telefonnummer **I U1,** 11
to **phone** [fəʊn] anrufen **I U1,** 18
photo ['fəʊtəʊ] Foto **I U2,** 27
phrase [freɪz] Satz, Redewendung **I U1,** 11
classroom phrases *(pl.)* ['klɑ:srʊm ˌfreɪzɪz] Redewendungen für den Unterricht **I U1,** 19
pick-up ['pɪkʌp] Pick-up, Kleintransporter **I U1,** 10
to **pick up** [pɪk‿'ʌp] abholen, mitnehmen **I U1,** 10
picnic ['pɪknɪk] Picknick **I U3,** 49
to go for a picnic [gəʊ fər‿ə 'pɪknɪk] ein Picknick machen ⟨**I U5,** 75⟩
picture ['pɪktʃə] Bild **I U1,** 15
piece [pi:s] Stück ⟨**I U5,** 79⟩
pier [pɪə] Pier, Hafendamm **I U6,** 88
pig [pɪg] Schwein **I U7,** 102
pink [pɪŋk] rosa, pink **I PUA,** 24
pirate ['paɪrət] Pirat, Seeräuber **I U4,** 66
to **pitter-patter** ['pɪtəˌpætə] prasseln, klopfen, trappeln **I U6,** 96
pizza ['pi:tsə] Pizza **I U5,** 74
pizza place ['pi:tsə ˌpleɪs] Pizzeria **I U5,** 74
place [pleɪs] Ort **I PUC,** 54
to **plan** [plæn] planen **I U6,** 90
planning your holidays [ˌplænɪŋ jə 'hɒlədeɪz] den Urlaub planen **I U6,** 90
plank [plæŋk] Brett, Planke **I U4,** 67
to walk the plank [ˌwɔ:k ðə 'plæŋk] über eine Schiffsplanke ins Wasser getrieben werden *(alte Strafe für Seeleute)* **I U4,** 67
role **play** ['rəʊl pleɪ] Rollenspiel **I PUB,** 39; ⟨**I U1,** 19⟩
to **play** [pleɪ] spielen **I U1,** 16; (ab)spielen *(CD, Radio etc.)* **I U2,** 32
playground ['pleɪgraʊnd] Schulhof; Spielplatz **I U1,** 20
please [pli:z] bitte **I U1,** 13
plural ['plʊərl] Plural, Mehrzahl **I U1,** 16
pm [ˌpi:'em] nachmittags *(Uhrzeit)* **I U3,** 40
pocket ['pɒkɪt] Hosentasche ⟨**I U7,** 116⟩
poem ['pəʊɪm] Gedicht **I U3,** 50
to **point** [pɔɪnt] zeigen **I ZI,** 9
police [pə'li:s] Polizei **I PUC,** 54
police station [pə'li:s ˌsteɪʃn] Polizeirevier, Polizeiwache **I PUC,** 54
Polish ['pəʊlɪʃ] polnisch, aus Polen; Polnisch **I U2,** 29
polite [pə'laɪt] höflich **I U1,** 21
Pooh! [pu:] Igitt! **I U7,** 104
pop star ['pɒp stɑ:] Popstar **I U5,** 80
postcard ['pəʊskɑ:d] Postkarte **I U6,** 90
poster ['pəʊstə] Poster **I U1,** 18
pound [paʊnd] Pfund *(Währung)* **I U5,** 72
It's two pounds. [ɪts ˌtu: 'paʊndz] Es kostet zwei Pfund. **I U5,** 72
present ['preznt] Gegenwart; Präsens **I U3,** 51; Geschenk **I U5,** 72
present progressive [ˌpreznt prə'gresɪv] Verlaufsform des Präsens/ der Gegenwart **I U6,** 92
simple present [ˌsɪmpl 'preznt] Gegenwart, Präsens **I U3,** 51
primary school ['praɪmri ˌsku:l] Grundschule **I U1,** 11
prize [praɪz] Preis, Gewinn **I U4,** 62
problem ['prɒbləm] Problem **I U1,** 20
project ['prɒdʒekt] Projekt **I U2,** 34
pronoun ['prəʊnaʊn] Pronomen, Fürwort **I U4,** 59
object pronoun ['ɒbdʒɪkt ˌprəʊnaʊn] Objektpronomen ⟨**I U4,** 59⟩
public ['pʌblɪk] öffentlich **I U4,** 61
pupil ['pju:pl] Schüler, Schülerin **I U1,** 10
purple ['pɜ:pl] violett, lila **I PUA,** 24
purr [pɜ:] *(Schnurren einer Katze)* **I U3,** 44
to **put** [pʊt] stellen, setzen, legen **I U1,** 21
to put in [pʊt 'ɪn] einsetzen **I U1,** 14
puzzle ['pʌzl] Rätsel, Puzzle ⟨**I U1,** 17⟩
word puzzle ['wɜ:d ˌpʌzl] Worträtsel ⟨**I U1,** 17⟩

Q

quarter ['kwɔ:tə] Viertel **I U3,** 41
question ['kwestʃən] Frage **I U1,** 15
question word ['kwestʃən ˌwɜ:d] Fragewort **I U4,** 64
quiet [kwaɪət] leise, ruhig, still **I U2,** 32
quiz [kwɪz] Quiz, Ratespiel **I U1,** 13

R

radio ['reɪdiəʊ] Radio **I U5,** 81
radio station ['reɪdiəʊ ˌsteɪʃn] Radiosender **I U5,** 81
rain [reɪn] Regen **I U6,** 90
to **rain** [reɪn] regnen **I U6,** 96
raisin ['reɪzn] Rosine ⟨**I U5,** 79⟩
rap [ræp] Rap **I U1,** 17
to **read** [ri:d] lesen **I PUB,** 38
reading a story ['ri:dɪŋ ə 'stɔ:ri] eine Geschichte lesen **I U5,** 80
to read to [ri:d 'tə] jemandem vorlesen **I U6,** 96
ready ['redi] fertig, bereit **I U5,** 80; fertig ⟨**I U5,** 79⟩
really ['rɪəli] wirklich ⟨**I U7,** 108⟩
recipe ['resɪpi] Rezept **I U5,** 78
red [red] rot **I PUA,** 24
relative ['relətɪv] Verwandter, Verwandte ⟨**I U2,** 30⟩
to **remember** [rɪ'membə] sich erinnern (an); denken an **I U3,** 46
to **repeat** [rɪ'pi:t] wiederholen **I U4,** 59
restaurant ['restrɑ:ŋ] Restaurant, Gaststätte **I U6,** 90
to **retell** [ri:'tel] nacherzählen; nochmals erzählen **I U6,** 97
revision [rɪ'vɪʒn] Wiederholung **I U2,** 33
rhyme [raɪm] Reim **I PUA,** 25
rich [rɪtʃ] reich **I U5,** 74
to **ride** [raɪd] reiten, fahren **I PUB,** 38
right [raɪt] richtig **I U1,** 13; rechte/-r/-s; rechts **I PUC,** 55
on the right [ɒn ðə 'raɪt] auf der rechten Seite, rechts **I PUC,** 55; ⟨**I U2,** 28⟩
on your right/left [ɒn jə 'raɪt, 'left] rechts/links, auf der rechten/linken Seite **I PUC,** 55
to be right [bɪ 'raɪt] Recht haben **I U7,** 110
to turn right [ˌtɜ:n 'raɪt] (nach) rechts abbiegen **I PUC,** 55
right now [raɪt 'naʊ] jetzt, sofort, gerade **I U5,** 74
to **ring** [rɪŋ] klingeln, läuten **I U1,** 11
river ['rɪvə] Fluss **I PUC,** 54
road [rəʊd] Straße **I U2,** 26
to **roast** [rəʊst] braten, rösten ⟨**I U6,** 91⟩
rock [rɒk] Fels, Riff, Stein **I U6,** 96
rocky ['rɒki] felsig, steinig **I U6,** 100
role play ['rəʊl pleɪ] Rollenspiel **I PUB,** 39; ⟨**I U1,** 19⟩
the **roof** is **down** [ðə 'ru:f‿ɪz ˌdaʊn] *(hier:)* das Faltdach (am Auto) ist heruntergeklappt ⟨**I U6,** 91⟩
room [ru:m] Zimmer, Raum **I U1,** 14
living room ['lɪvɪŋ ru:m] Wohnzimmer **I PUA,** 24
from all **round** the world [frəm‿'ɔ:l ˌraʊnd ðə 'wɜ:ld] aus aller Welt **I U4,** 57
round the garden [raʊnd ðə 'gɑ:dn] durch den ganzen Garten **I U3,** 44
She runs all round him. [ʃi ˌrʌnz ɔ:l 'raʊnd hɪm] Sie rennt um ihn herum. **I U4,** 67
routine [ru:'ti:n] Routine **I U3,** 42
to **row** [rəʊ] rudern **I U6,** 96
rubber ['rʌbə] Radiergummi **I U1,** 16
rubber ball [ˌrʌbə 'bɔ:l] Gummiball **I U2,** 33
to **ruin** ['ru:ɪn] zerstören, ruinieren **I U6,** 92
rule [ru:l] Regel **I U2,** 32
ruler ['ru:lə] Lineal **I U1,** 16
to **run** [rʌn] laufen, rennen **I U3,** 44

She runs all round him. [ʃi ˌrʌnz ɔːl ˈraʊnd hɪm] Sie rennt um ihn herum. I U4, 67
to run after [rʌn‿ˈɑːftə] hinterherrennen I U7, 110
to run away [rʌn‿əˈweɪ] weglaufen I U3, 44
Russian [ˈrʌʃn] russisch, aus Russland; Russisch I U2, 29

S

sad [sæd] traurig I U7, 110
safe [seɪf] sicher, ungefährlich I U6, 92
to sail [seɪl] segeln I U4, 66
the same [ðə ˈseɪm] der-/die-/dasselbe, der/die/das Gleiche I U2, 33
sand [sænd] Sand I U6, 90
sand castle [ˈsænd ˌkɑːsl] Sandburg I U6, 90
sandwich [ˈsænwɪdʒ] Sandwich I U1, 16
sandy [ˈsændi] sandig I U6, 100
Saturday [ˈsætədeɪ] Samstag I U2, 34
to say [seɪ] sagen I U1, 11
saying what you've got [ˈseɪɪŋ ˌwɒt jʊv ˈgɒt] sagen, was jemand hat I U2, 30
to say hello [seɪ helˈəʊ] jemanden begrüßen I U1, 11
to say hello to [seɪ helˈəʊ tə] grüßen, Grüße ausrichten I U2, 33
scared [skeəd] verängstigt I U6, 96
to be scared for [bi ˈskeəd fə] Angst haben um I U6, 96
scarf pl. scarves [skɑːf; skɑːvz] Schal, Tuch I U6, 100
scary [ˈskeəri] beängstigend, unheimlich I U1, 12
school [skuːl] Schule I U1, 10
primary school [ˈpraɪmri ˌskuːl] Grundschule I U1, 11
school day [ˈskuːl deɪ] Schultag I U3, 42
schools officer [ˈskuːlz ˌɒfɪsə] *(hier:)* Beauftragter/Beauftragte für Schulklassen I U7, 102
school things *(pl.)* [ˈskuːl ˌθɪŋz] Schulsachen *(pl.)* I U1, 16
to be late for school [bi ˌleɪt fə ˈskuːl] zu spät zur Schule kommen I U5, 80
schoolbag [ˈskuːlbæg] Schultasche I U1, 16
sea [siː] Meer, die See I U4, 57
North Sea [ˌnɔːθ ˈsiː] Nordsee I U4, 57
seashore [ˈsiːʃɔː] Strand, Meeresküste ⟨I U6, 100⟩
seaside [ˈsiːsaɪd] (Meeres)Küste I U6, 89
seaside town [ˌsiːsaɪd ˈtaʊn] Küstenstadt I U6, 89
season [ˈsiːzn] Jahreszeit; Saison I U6, 90
second [ˈseknd] Sekunde I U2, 30
to see [siː] sehen I U3, 40
See you there. [siː jə ˈðeə] Wir sehen uns dort. I U3, 40
to sell [sel] verkaufen I U4, 62
sentence [ˈsentəns] Satz I U1, 15
September [sepˈtembə] September I U5, 75
seven [ˈsevn] sieben I U1, 10
seventeen [ˌsevnˈtiːn] siebzehn I U1, 16
seventy [ˈsevnti] siebzig I U1, 16
s-genitive [esˈdʒenɪtɪv] s-Genitiv I U2, 37
she [ʃiː] sie I U1, 12
shed [ʃed] Schuppen, Gartenhäuschen I U2, 26; Stall I U7, 104
sheep pl. sheep [ʃiːp] Schaf I U7, 102
shelf pl. shelves [ʃelf; ʃelvz] Regal, Regalbrett I U6, 94
shell [ʃel] Muschel ⟨I U6, 100⟩
ship [ʃɪp] Schiff I U4, 57
shock [ʃɒk] Schock, Schreck I U7, 110
shoe [ʃuː] Schuh I U1, 12
shop [ʃɒp] Geschäft, Laden I U2, 26
computer shop [kəmˈpjuːtə ˌʃɒp] Computergeschäft I U2, 26
sports shop [ˈspɔːts ˌʃɒp] Sportgeschäft I U5, 72
shopping [ˈʃɒpɪŋ] Einkaufen I U5, 73
to go shopping [gəʊ ˈʃɒpɪŋ] einkaufen gehen I U5, 73
short [ʃɔːt] kurz I U1, 14
should [ʃʊd] sollte/-est/-en/-et I U7, 106
to shout [ʃaʊt] rufen, schreien I U1, 17
to show [ʃəʊ] zeigen I U3, 46
to shuffle [ˈʃʌfl] mischen I U3, 46
sights *(pl.)* [saɪts] Sehenswürdigkeiten I U4, 56
signal [ˈsɪgnl] Zeichen, Signal I U6, 93
silly [ˈsɪli] Dummkopf I U4, 62
simple present [ˌsɪmpl ˈpreznt] Gegenwart, Präsens I U3, 51
silly [ˈsɪli] albern, dumm I U2, 30
to sing [sɪŋ] singen I U5, 77; ⟨I ZI, 9⟩
third person singular [θɜːd ˈpɜːsn ˈsɪŋgjələ] dritte Person Singular (Einzahl) I U3, 44
to sink [sɪŋk] untergehen, sinken I U6, 96
sister [ˈsɪstə] Schwester I PUA, 25
to sit [sɪt] sitzen I U1, 19
to sit down [sɪt ˈdaʊn] sich hinsetzen I U1, 19
six [sɪks] sechs I U1, 11
sixteen [ˌsɪkˈstiːn] sechzehn I U1, 16
sixty [ˈsɪksti] sechzig I U1, 16
size [saɪz] Größe I U5, 72
skateboard [ˈskeɪtbɔːd] Skateboard I U4, 56
skill [skɪl] Fertigkeit I U1, 22
communication skills [kəˌmjuːnɪˈkeɪʃn ˌskɪlz] Sprechfertigkeiten, Kommunikationsfertigkeiten I U4, 59
to sleep [sliːp] schlafen I U3, 49
slow [sləʊ] langsam I U2, 34
small [smɔːl] klein I U2, 26
smell [smel] Geruch, Duft, Gestank I U2, 34
to smile [smaɪl] lächeln I U7, 110
smoke [sməʊk] Rauch I U2, 34
so [səʊ] so I U1, 15
so [səʊ] also, folglich, deshalb I U1, 12
sofa [ˈsəʊfə] Sofa, Couch I PUA, 25
soft [sɒft] weich ⟨I U7, 116⟩
some [sʌm] einige, ein paar; etwas I U6, 94
sometimes [ˈsʌmtaɪmz] manchmal I U3, 42
song [sɒŋ] Lied, Song I PUB, 39; ⟨I ZI, 9⟩
soon [suːn] bald I U2, 34
I'm sorry. [aɪm ˈsɒri] Es tut mir Leid. I U1, 14
Sorry I'm late. [ˌsɒri‿aɪm ˈleɪt] Tut mir Leid, dass ich zu spät komme. I U1, 19
to sort [sɔːt] sortieren I U2, 35
to sort out [sɔːt ˈaʊt] klären, regeln I U2, 30
sound [saʊnd] Geräusch I ZI, 9; Laut I U1, 16
south [saʊθ] Süden I U6, 89
souvenir [ˌsuːvnˈɪə] Andenken, Souvenir I U6, 94
spaghetti [spəˈgeti] Spaghetti I U2, 29
Spanish [ˈspænɪʃ] spanisch, aus Spanien; Spanisch I U2, 29
to speak (to) [spiːk tə] sprechen (mit) I U4, 58
special [ˈspeʃl] besondere/-r/-s I U4, 58
to spell [spel] buchstabieren I U1, 17
to spend [spend] verbringen *(Urlaub, Zeit etc.)* I U6, 100
spoonful [ˈspuːnfʊl] Löffel *(Mengenangabe)* ⟨I U5, 79⟩
sport [spɔːt] Sport, Sportart I U1, 12
sports shop [ˈspɔːts ˌʃɒp] Sportgeschäft I U5, 72
spring [sprɪŋ] Frühling I U6, 90
Sssh! [ʃ] Psst! I U1, 20
to stand [stænd] stehen I U7, 110
star [stɑː] Star I U1, 17
pop star [ˈpɒp stɑː] Popstar I U5, 80
to start [stɑːt] anfangen, beginnen I U1, 11
let's get started [lets get ˈstɑːtɪd] lass(t) uns beginnen, lass(t) uns anfangen ⟨I ZI, 9⟩

station ['steɪʃn] Station, Bahnhof **I U4,** 56
radio station ['reɪdiəʊ ˌsteɪʃn] Radiosender **I U5,** 81
step-father ['stepˌfɑːðə] Stiefvater **I U2,** 26
still [stɪl] noch, immer noch **I U5,** 76
to **stink** [stɪŋk] stinken **I U7,** 104
to **stop** [stɒp] aufhören, beenden **I U2,** 34
department **store** [dɪ'pɑːtmənt ˌstɔː] Kaufhaus **I U5,** 76
storm [stɔːm] Sturm, Unwetter, Gewitter **I U6,** 96
stormy ['stɔːmi] stürmisch **I U6,** 96
story ['stɔːri] Geschichte, Erzählung **I U3,** 48; ⟨**I U2,** 35⟩
straight [streɪt] gerade(aus); direkt **I PUC,** 55
straight on [streɪt‿'ɒn] geradeaus **I PUC,** 55
street [striːt] Straße **I U3,** 44
in the street [ɪn ðə 'striːt] auf der Straße **I U7,** 116
strong [strɒŋ] stark, kräftig **I U6,** 96
subject ['sʌbdʒɪkt] Subjekt, Satzgegenstand **I U7,** 107
suddenly ['sʌdnli] plötzlich, auf einmal **I U5,** 80
sugar ['ʃʊgə] Zucker **I U5,** 78
summer ['sʌmə] Sommer **I U6,** 88
sun [sʌn] Sonne **I U6,** 100; ⟨**I U6,** 91⟩
Sunday ['sʌndeɪ] Sonntag **I PUB,** 39
sunglasses *(pl.)* ['sʌnˌglɑːsɪz] Sonnenbrille **I U6,** 90
sure [ʃɔː; ʃʊə] sicher **I U1,** 14
to **surf** [sɜːf] (wind)surfen **I U6,** 88
to go surfing [gəʊ 'sɜːfɪŋ] surfen gehen **I U6,** 88
to surf on the Internet [ˌsɜːf‿ɒn ði‿'ɪntənet] im Internet surfen **I U6,** 90
surprise [sə'praɪz] Überraschung **I U5,** 80
to **survive** [sə'vaɪv] überleben **I U6,** 97
sweatshirt ['swetʃɜːt] Sweatshirt **I U5,** 73
sweet [swiːt] süß **I PUA,** 24
sweets *(pl.)* [swiːts] Süßigkeiten **I U6,** 95
sweet shop ['swiːt ˌʃɒp] Süßwarenladen **I PUC,** 54
to **swim** [swɪm] schwimmen **I PUB,** 38
swimming pool ['swɪmɪŋ ˌpuːl] Schwimmbad, Schwimmbecken **I U4,** 65; ⟨**I U4,** 61⟩
to go swimming [gəʊ 'swɪmɪŋ] schwimmen gehen **I PUB,** 38
swimsuit ['swɪmsuːt] Badeanzug **I U6,** 90

T

table ['teɪbl] Tisch **I U1,** 18
tablespoon ['teɪblspuːn] Esslöffel ⟨**I U5,** 79⟩
to **take** [teɪk] (weg)nehmen **I U2,** 32; (mit)nehmen; bringen **I U3,** 48
He takes us everywhere. [hi ˌteɪks‿əs‿'evriweə] Er bringt uns überallhin. **I U4,** 71
to take a photo [ˌteɪk‿ə 'fəʊtəʊ] ein Foto machen **I U7,** 108
to take notes [teɪk 'nəʊts] sich Notizen machen **I U5,** 81
to take off [teɪk‿'ɒf] abnehmen, ausziehen, herunternehmen **I U6,** 94
to take out [teɪk‿'aʊt] ausführen **I U3,** 49
to take turns [teɪk 'tɜːnz] sich abwechseln **I U2,** 32
to **talk** [tɔːk] sprechen, reden **I PUA,** 25
to talk about [tɔːk ə'baʊt] sprechen über **I U2,** 35
to talk to [tɔːk tə] sprechen mit, reden mit **I PUA,** 25
tasty ['teɪsti] lecker **I U3,** 44
taxi ['tæksi] Taxi **I U4,** 58
tea [tiː] Tee **I U4,** 66
to **teach** [tiːtʃ] unterrichten, lehren, beibringen **I U3,** 48
teacher ['tiːtʃə] Lehrer, Lehrerin **I U1,** 12
German teacher ['dʒɜːmən ˌtiːtʃə] Deutschlehrer, Deutschlehrerin **I U1,** 12
team [tiːm] Team, Gruppe **I U4,** 56
to **tell** [tel] erzählen, sagen **I U2,** 29
to tell the time [ˌtel ðə 'taɪm] die Uhr lesen **I U3,** 41
ten [ten] zehn **I U1,** 11
terrible ['terəbl] schrecklich, schlimm, furchtbar **I U1,** 20
territory ['terɪtri] Gebiet, Revier, Territorium **I U7,** 110
test [test] Test, Prüfung **I U4,** 62
text [tekst] Text **I U1,** 20
to **text** [tekst] eine SMS schicken **I U5,** 74
than [ðæn; ðən] als *(bei Vergleichen)* ⟨**I U7,** 116⟩
thank you ['θæŋk ju] danke **I U1,** 12
thanks [θæŋks] danke **I U2,** 34
thanks a lot [ˌθæŋks‿ə 'lɒt] vielen Dank **I U6,** 92
thanks to ['θæŋks tə] dank (dir/Ihnen), wegen **I U7,** 111
that [ðæt; ðət] dass **I U4,** 66
that [ðæt] das; jenes **I U1,** 12
that day [ðæt 'deɪ] an jenem Tag **I U6,** 97
that [ðæt; ðət] die *(Relativpronomen)* **I U1,** 17

the [ðə; ði] der, die *(auch pl.)*, das **I U1,** 11
their [ðeə] ihr, ihre *(Plural)* **I U2,** 29
them [ðem; ðəm] sie *(Plural)* **I U3,** 49
then [ðen] dann, danach **I PUA,** 24
there [ðeə] da, dort **I U1,** 18; dorthin, dahin **I U3,** 40
over there [ˌəʊvə 'ðeə] (nach) dort drüben **I U6,** 91
There she is. ['ðeə ʃi‿ɪz] Da ist sie ja. **I U3,** 44
You've got me there! [jʊv ˌgɒt mi 'ðeə] Da habt ihr mich kalt erwischt! **I U4,** 60
these [ðiːz] diese (hier) **I U3,** 46
they [ðeɪ] sie **I U1,** 14
thief pl. **thieves** [θiːf; θiːvz] Dieb **I U5,** 76
thing [θɪŋ] Ding, Sache **I U1,** 16
… is his thing [ɪz hɪz 'θɪŋ] … macht er gerne/ … kann er gut ⟨**I U3,** 50⟩
school things *(pl.)* ['skuːl ˌθɪŋz] Schulsachen *(pl.)* **I U1,** 16
to **think** [θɪŋk] (nach)denken; finden, glauben **I U4,** 61
to think about [θɪŋk‿ə'baʊt] halten von, denken über **I U6,** 97
to think of ['θɪŋk‿əv] halten von, denken über **I U6,** 90; (sich) ausdenken, sich etwas einfallen lassen **I U7,** 108; ⟨**I U7,** 107⟩
third [θɜːd] dritte/-r/-s **I U5,** 74
the third of March [ðə ˌθɜːd‿əv 'mɑːtʃ] der dritte März **I U5,** 74
thirteen [θɜː'tiːn] dreizehn **I U1,** 16
thirty ['θɜːti] dreißig **I U1,** 16
this [ðɪs] diese/-r/-s **I U1,** 10
like this [laɪk 'ðɪs] so, auf diese Weise **I PUA,** 25
this is … ['ðɪs‿ɪz] hier ist … *(am Telefon)* **I U3,** 43
this morning [ðɪs 'mɔːnɪŋ] heute Morgen **I U6,** 93
those [ðəʊz] diese dort, jene **I U3,** 46
a/one **thousand** [ə 'θaʊznd; wʌn 'θaʊznd] eintausend **I U6,** 89
three [θriː] drei **I U1,** 11
to **throw** [θrəʊ] werfen **I U3,** 48
Thursday ['θɜːzdeɪ] Donnerstag **I PUB,** 39
tiger ['taɪgə] Tiger **I U2,** 26
time [taɪm] Zeit **I ZI,** 8
at the same time [ət ðə ˌseɪm 'taɪm] zur selben Zeit, gleichzeitig **I U7,** 102
from time to time [frəm ˌtaɪm tə 'taɪm] von Zeit zu Zeit **I U7,** 106
It's time to go home. [ɪts ˌtaɪm tə gəʊ 'həʊm] Es ist Zeit, nach Hause zu gehen. **I U3,** 44
to tell the time [ˌtel ðə 'taɪm] die Uhr lesen **I U3,** 41

What time is it, please? [wɒt 'taɪm‿ɪz‿ɪt ˌpli:z] Wie spät ist es, bitte? **I U3,** 41
tin [tɪn] Dose, Büchse **I U3,** 44
tiny ['taɪni] klein, winzig **I U1,** 10
tip [tɪp] Tipp, Ratschlag **I U1,** 13
tired ['taɪəd] müde **I U3,** 49
dog-tired [dɒg'taɪəd] hundemüde **I U3,** 49
title ['taɪtl] Titel **I U5,** 80
to [tu:; tʊ; tə] nach, zu, in **I ZI,** 9; an **I U2,** 33; vor *(bei Uhrzeitangaben)* **I U3,** 41
today [tə'deɪ] heute **I U2,** 29
together [tə'geðə] zusammen; gemeinsam **I U3,** 44
toilet ['tɔɪlət] Toilette **I U1,** 19
Can I go to the toilet, please? [kən‿aɪ ˌgəʊ tə ðə 'tɔɪlət pli:z] Kann ich bitte zur Toilette gehen? **I U1,** 19
tongue twister ['tʌŋ ˌtwɪstə] Zungenbrecher 〈**I U6,** 100〉
too [tu:] auch **I U1,** 10; zu **I U4,** 57
too much [tu: 'mʌtʃ] zu viel **I U4,** 57
tooth pl. **teeth** [tu:θ; ti:θ] Zahn **I U6,** 92
top [tɒp] oberes Ende, Spitze **I U3,** 46
on the top [ɒn ðə 'tɒp] oben **I U3,** 46
on top of [ɒn 'tɒp‿əv] auf … hinauf, oben (auf) **I U3,** 46
top 10 [ˌtɒp 'ten] Top 10, die besten Zehn **I U7,** 106
tour [tʊə] Reise, Tour, Rundgang **I PUC,** 55
to give tours [gɪv 'tʊəz] Stadtrundfahrten leiten **I U4,** 60
tourist ['tʊərɪst] Tourist, Touristin **I U4,** 56
town [taʊn] Stadt **I U3,** 41
in the town of Penzance [ɪn ðə 'taʊn‿əv pen'zæns] in der Stadt Penzance **I U6,** 88
seaside town [ˌsi:saɪd 'taʊn] Küstenstadt **I U6,** 89
toy [tɔɪ] Spielzeug 〈**I U6,** 100〉
train [treɪn] Zug **I U4,** 56
on a train [ɒn‿ə 'treɪn] im Zug **I U6,** 97
transport *(no pl.)* ['trænspɔ:t] Verkehrsmittel, Beförderung **I U4,** 58
treasure ['treʒə] Schatz **I U4,** 66
treasure map ['treʒə ˌmæp] Schatzkarte **I U4,** 66
tree [tri:] Baum **I U1,** 20
trick [trɪk] Trick, Kunststück **I U3,** 46
card trick ['kɑ:d ˌtrɪk] Kartenkunststück **I U3,** 46
trip [trɪp] Reise, Fahrt, Ausflug **I U6,** 90
class trip [ˌklɑ:s 'trɪp] Klassenfahrt, Klassenausflug **I U7,** 104
trouble ['trʌbl] Ärger, Schwierigkeiten **I U2,** 30
to **try on** [traɪ‿'ɒn] anprobieren **I U5,** 73
T-shirt ['ti:ʃɜ:t] T-Shirt **I U2,** 30
Tuesday ['tju:zdeɪ] Dienstag **I PUB,** 39
tunnel ['tʌnl] Tunnel **I U4,** 56
Turkish ['tɜ:kɪʃ] türkisch, aus der Türkei; Türkisch **I U2,** 29
to take **turns** [teɪk 'tɜ:nz] sich abwechseln **I U2,** 32
Your turn. ['jɔ: tɜ:n] Du bist dran. **I U1,** 13
to **turn** [tɜ:n] einbiegen, abbiegen **I PUC,** 55
to turn right [ˌtɜ:n 'raɪt] (nach) rechts abbiegen **I PUC,** 55
tutor ['tju:tə] Klassenlehrer, Klassenlehrerin **I U1,** 12
tutor group ['tju:tə gru:p] Klasse *(in einer englischen Schule)* **I U1,** 12
TV [ˌti:'vi:] Fernseher **I PUA,** 25
on TV [ɒn ˌti:'vi:] im Fernsehen **I U3,** 42
twelve [twelv] zwölf **I U1,** 10
twenty ['twenti] zwanzig **I U1,** 16
twenty-one [ˌtwenti'wʌn] einundzwanzig **I U1,** 16
two [tu:] zwei **I U1,** 11

U

ugh [ʊh] i, igitt **I U4,** 58
uh [ə] äh **I U1,** 20
uncle ['ʌŋkl] Onkel **I U2,** 28
under ['ʌndə] unter **I U1,** 18
Underground ['ʌndəgraʊnd] U-Bahn **I U4,** 56
to **underline** [ˌʌndə'laɪn] unterstreichen **I U2,** 36
unit ['ju:nɪt] Lektion, Kapitel, Einheit **I U1,** 10
until [ʌn'tɪl] bis 〈**I U5,** 79〉
What's **up?** [wɒts‿'ʌp] Was ist los? **I U1,** 14
upstairs [ʌp'steəz] oben, im Obergeschoss **I U2,** 27
us [ʌs; əs] uns **I U3,** 42
to **use** [ju:z] benutzen, verwenden, gebrauchen **I U1,** 19
using the present progressive ['ju:zɪŋ ðə ˌpreznt prə'gresɪv] das *present progressive* benutzen **I U5,** 76
useful ['ju:sfl] nützlich, hilfreich **I U1,** 11
usually ['ju:ʒli] gewöhnlich, normalerweise **I U3,** 42

V

verb [vɜ:b] Verb, Zeitwort **I U6,** 100
very ['veri] sehr **I U1,** 15
vet [vet] Tierarzt, Tierärztin **I U7,** 110
video ['vɪdiəʊ] Video **I PUB,** 38
village ['vɪlɪdʒ] Dorf **I U6,** 88
to **visit** ['vɪzɪt] besuchen **I U3,** 42
visitor ['vɪzɪtə] Besucher, Besucherin **I U4,** 57
vocabulary [və'kæbjəlri] Vokabular, Wortschatz **I U1,** 22
volleyball ['vɒlibɔ:l] Volleyball **I U6,** 88

W

to **wait** [weɪt] warten **I U3,** 44
to wait for ['weɪt fə] warten auf **I U6,** 94
to **wake up** [weɪk‿'ʌp] aufwecken; aufwachen **I U3,** 48
to **walk** [wɔ:k] gehen *(zu Fuß)* **I U3,** 42
to walk the dog [wɔ:k ðə 'dɒg] den Hund ausführen **I U3,** 42
to walk the plank [ˌwɔ:k ðə 'plæŋk] über eine Schiffsplanke ins Wasser getrieben werden *(alte Strafe für Seeleute)* **I U4,** 67
wall [wɔ:l] Wand, Mauer **I U1,** 18
to **want** [wɒnt] wollen, mögen **I U4,** 66
I want to … [aɪ 'wɒnt tə] ich möchte …/ich will … **I U5,** 74
to want to know [ˌwɒnt tə 'nəʊ] wissen wollen **I U5,** 78
wardrobe ['wɔ:drəʊb] Kleiderschrank **I U2,** 30
warm [wɔ:m] warm **I U6,** 88
to **wash** [wɒʃ] waschen **I U3,** 48
to **watch** [wɒtʃ] ansehen; beobachten **I PUB,** 38; aufpassen auf, achten auf 〈**I U5,** 77〉
to watch out [wɒtʃ 'aʊt] aufpassen **I U1,** 20
water ['wɔ:tə] Wasser **I U3,** 40
wave [weɪv] Welle, Woge **I U6,** 88
way [weɪ] Weg **I PUC,** 55
finding the way [ˌfaɪndɪŋ ðə 'weɪ] den Weg finden **I U4,** 59
on his way [ˌɒn hɪz 'weɪ] auf dem Weg, unterwegs **I PUC,** 55
we're on our way [wɪər‿ɒn‿aʊə 'weɪ] wir sind auf dem Weg 〈**I ZI,** 9〉
we [wi:; wi] wir **I U1,** 14
Wednesday ['wenzdeɪ] Mittwoch **I PUB,** 39
week [wi:k] Woche **I PUB,** 39
days of the week *(pl.)* [ˌdeɪz‿ɒv ðə 'wi:k] Wochentage *(pl.)* **I PUB,** 39

weekend [ˌwi:k'end] Wochenende **I U3,** 40
  at the weekend [æt ðə ˌwi:k'end] am Wochenende **I U3,** 40
You're **welcome.** [jɔ: 'welkəm] Bitte schön./Nichts zu danken./Gern geschehen. **I U1,** 19
well [wel] tja, nun **I U2,** 30
welly pl. **wellies** ['weli; weliz] Gummistiefel **I U6,** 90
west [west] Westen **I U4,** 57
what [wɒt] was **I U1,** 10
  What about ... ? [wɒt‿ə'baʊt] Was ist mit ... ? **I U3,** 42
  What colour are ...? [wɒt 'kʌlə‿ɑ:] Welche Farbe haben ... ? **I PUA,** 25
  what it looks like [ˌwɒt‿ɪt 'lʊks laɪk] wie es aussieht **I U7,** 107
  what's (= what is) [wɒts; ˌwɒt 'ɪz] was ist **I U1,** 10
  What's for homework, please? [wɒts fə 'həʊmwɜ:k ˌpli:z] Was haben wir als Hausaufgabe auf, bitte? **I U1,** 19
  What's that song? [wɒts ðæt 'sɒŋ] Was ist das für ein Lied? **I U5,** 80
  What's up? [wɒts‿'ʌp] Was ist los? **I U1,** 14
  What's your name? [wɒts jɔ: 'neɪm] Wie heißt du? **I U1,** 10
  What time is it, please? [wɒt 'taɪm‿ɪz‿ɪt ˌpli:z] Wie spät ist es, bitte? **I U3,** 41
wheel [wi:l] Steuerrad, Steuer, Rad **I U4,** 66
when [wen] wenn, als **I U2,** 32; wann **I U3,** 40
where [weə] wo, wohin, woher **I U1,** 10
  Where are you from? [ˌweər‿ə jə 'frɒm] Woher kommst du? **I U1,** 10
which [wɪtʃ] welche/-r/-s **I U3,** 46
white [waɪt] weiß **I PUA,** 24
who [hu:] wer **I U1,** 14
whole [həʊl] ganz **I U6,** 100
why [waɪ] warum **I U2,** 27
  Why don't you invite ...? [waɪ dəʊnt jə ɪn'vaɪt] Warum lädst du nicht ... ein? **I U5,** 74
wild [waɪld] wild **I U7,** 102
will [wɪl] Wille **I U6,** 96
to **win** [wɪn] gewinnen **I U4,** 62
wind [wɪnd] Wind **I U6,** 96
window ['wɪndəʊ] Fenster **I U1,** 18
windy ['wɪndi] windig **I U6,** 88
winner ['wɪnə] Gewinner, Gewinnerin **I U4,** 64
winter ['wɪntə] Winter **I U6,** 88
with [wɪð] mit **I U1,** 14
  I'm with ... [aɪm 'wɪð] Ich bin bei ... **I U2,** 33

woman pl. **women** ['wʊmən; 'wɪmɪn] Frau **I U6,** 100
wonder ['wʌndə] Wunder **I U4,** 57
wooden ['wʊdən] hölzern, aus Holz ⟨**I U4,** 67⟩
Woof! [wʊf] Wau! **I U2,** 27
Woosh! [wʊʃ] Zisch! **I U6,** 96
word [wɜ:d] Wort **I U1,** 11
  question word ['kwestʃən ˌwɜ:d] Fragewort **I U4,** 64
  signal word ['sɪgnl ˌwɜ:d] Signalwort **I U6,** 93
  word bank ['wɜ:d ˌbæŋk] Wortsammlung **I U1,** 11
  word order ['wɜ:d‿ɔ:də] Wortstellung, Satzstellung **I U7,** 107
  word web ['wɜ:d web] Wortnetz **I U1,** 22
wordwise ['wɜ:dwaɪz] „wortschlau", „wortgewandt" **I U1,** 22
to **work** [wɜ:k] funktionieren **I U3,** 46; arbeiten **I U4,** 56
world [wɜ:ld] Welt **I U4,** 57
  in the world [ɪn ðə 'wɜ:ld] auf der Welt **I U5,** 78
worried ['wʌrɪd] beunruhigt, besorgt **I U7,** 110
to **worry** ['wʌri] sich Sorgen machen **I U6,** 96
  Don't worry. [dəʊnt 'wʌri] Mach dir keine Sorgen. **I U6,** 96
I'd like to ... *(= I would like to)* [aɪd 'laɪk tə] ich möchte .../ich würde gerne ... **I U5,** 74
Wow! [waʊ] Wow!/Toll! **I U1,** 18
to **write** [raɪt] schreiben **I U1,** 11
  to write down [raɪt 'daʊn] aufschreiben **I U4,** 60
wrong [rɒŋ] falsch **I U1,** 13
  you're wrong [jɔ: 'rɒŋ] du hast Unrecht, du irrst dich **I U1,** 21

Y

year [jɪə] Jahr; Jahrgangsstufe, Klasse, Schuljahr **I U1,** 10
  for (many) years [fə ˌmeni 'jɪəz] jahrelang **I U7,** 107
yellow ['jeləʊ] gelb **I PUA,** 24
yes [jes] ja **I U1,** 14
  Yes, we are. [jes wi‿'ɑ:] Ja, das sind wir. **I U1,** 14
you [ju:] du **I U1,** 10
young [jʌŋ] jung **I U4,** 56
your [jɔ:] dein, deine **I U1,** 10; euer, eure; Ihr(e) **I U2,** 29
yourself [jɔ:'self] dich selbst **I U1,** 11
yuk [jʌk] i, igitt **I U2,** 34

Z

zero ['zɪərəʊ, əʊ] null **I U1,** 11
zoo [zu:] Zoo **I U7,** 102
zoom-in [zu:m'ɪn] Heranzoomen, Heranfahren **I ZI,** 8
Zzz ... [z] Schnarch! **I U4,** 66

Boys' names

Ben [ben] **I U2,** 27
David ['deɪvɪd] **I U2,** 28
James [dʒeɪmz] **I U2,** 28
Jonathan ['dʒɒnəθn] **I U6,** 88
Martin ['mɑ:tɪn] **I U6,** 88
Nelson ['nelsn] **I U1,** 13
Phil [fɪl] **I U2,** 28
Richard ['rɪtʃəd] **I U2,** 27
Rob [rɒb] **I U2,** 26
Sam [sæm] **I U1,** 14
Samuel ['sæmjʊəl] **I U2,** 28
Scott [skɒt] **I U6,** 88
Ted [ted] **I U2,** 26
Terry ['teri] **I U1,** 10
Tim [tɪm] **I U2,** 28
Tom [tɒm] **I U1,** 10

Girls' names

Amanda [ə'mændə] **I U4,** 59
Debbie ['debi] **I U6,** 88
Denise [də'ni:z] **I U7,** 104
Elena ['elənə] **I U2,** 28
Elsie ['elsi] **I U6,** 88
Emma ['emə] **I U1,** 12
Farah ['fɑ:rə] **I U2,** 26
Fiona [fi'əʊnə] **I U2,** 37
Grace [greɪs] **I U2,** 26
Jade [dʒeɪd] **I U2,** 27
Kim [kɪm] **I U1,** 23
Lisa ['li:sə] **I U1,** 10
Marci ['mɑ:si] ⟨**I U7,** 116⟩
Nasreen [nəs'ri:n] **I U2,** 26
Nicola ['nɪklə] **I U2,** 33
Rachel ['reɪtʃl] **I U2,** 28
Sarah ['seərə] **I U2,** 28
Sue [su:] **I U2,** 27
Susan ['su:zn] **I U2,** 28
Tess [tes] **I PUB,** 39
Tracy ['treɪsi] **I U2,** 28
Yoko ['jəʊkəʊ] **I U4,** 66

Surnames

Barker ['bɑ:kə] **I U4,** 64
Brook [brʊk] **I U1,** 12
Brown [braʊn] **I U5,** 80
Carter ['kɑ:tə] **I U1,** 12

Darling ['dɑ:lɪŋ] **I U6**, 96
Green [gri:n] **I U2**, 37
Jackson ['dʒæksn] **I U1**, 10
Nelson ['nelsn] **I U4**, 64
Newman ['nju:mən] **I U1**, 12
Peterson ['pi:təsn] **I U4**, 59
Pilch [pɪltʃ] **I U2**, 28
Ridlon ['rɪdlən] ⟨**I U7**, 116⟩
Smith [smɪθ] **I U2**, 28
Spencer ['spensə] **I U1**, 14
Stavros ['stævrəs] **I U2**, 28
Taylor ['teɪlə] **I U1**, 10
Tiny ['taɪni] **I U1**, 11
Wendover ['wendəʊvə] **I U4**, 64

Place names

Bamburgh ['bæmbrə] **I U6**, 88
Berlin [bɜ:'lɪn] **I U1**, 11
Blackheath Park [ˌblækhi:θ 'pɑ:k] **I U3**, 40
Brighton ['braɪtn] **I U6**, 88
Bristol ['brɪstl] **I U1**, 12
Canary Wharf [kə'neəri ˌwɔ:f] **I U4**, 56
Cardiff ['kɑ:dɪf] **I U1**, 14
Charlton ['tʃɑ:ltn] **I U4**, 57
Church Street ['tʃɜ:tʃ ˌstri:t] **I U4**, 57
Golden Mile [ˌgəʊldn 'maɪl] **I U6**, 88
Greenwich ['grenɪdʒ] **I ZI**, 8
Greenwich Park [ˌgrenɪdʒ 'pɑ:k] **I ZI**, 9
Harlech ['hɑ:lek] **I U6**, 88
High Road ['haɪ ˌrəʊd] **I U4**, 58
Hither Farm Road ['hɪðə fɑ:m ˌrəʊd] **I U2**, 26
Holburne Road ['hɒlbɜ:n ˌrəʊd] **I U2**, 26
Istanbul [ˌɪstæn'bʊl] **I U1**, 13
Kidbrooke Park Road [ˌkɪdbrʊk 'pɑ:k ˌrəʊd] **I U4**, 58
Leicester ['lestə] **I U2**, 31
London ['lʌndən] **I U1**, 10
Madrid [mə'drɪd] **I U1**, 13
Nairobi [naɪ'rəʊbi] **I U1**, 13
Observatory Station [əbˌzɜ:vətri 'steɪʃn] **I U4**, 57
Paris ['pærɪs] **I U1**, 13
Penzance [pen'zæns] **I U6**, 88
Pond Road ['pɒnd ˌrəʊd] **I U2**, 27
Shanghai [ʃæŋ'haɪ] **I U4**, 66
Southend-on-Sea [ˌsaʊθ'end ɒn 'si:] **I U6**, 88
Stockwell Street ['stɒkwel ˌstri:t] **I U4**, 59
Tokyo ['təʊkiəʊ] **I U1**, 13
Wendover Road ['wendəʊvə ˌrəʊd] **I U2**, 28

Geographical names

Big Harcar Rock [bɪg ˌhɑ:kə 'rɒk] **I U6**, 96
Britain ['brɪtn] Großbritannien **I U6**, 88
Cornwall ['kɔ:nwɔ:l] **I U6**, 88
England ['ɪŋglənd] **I U1**, 12
Farne Islands [fɑ:n 'aɪləndz] **I U6**, 88
Germany ['dʒɜ:məni] Deutschland **I U2**, 29
Greece [gri:s] Griechenland **I U2**, 29
Isle of Dogs [ˌaɪl əv 'dɒgz] **I U4**, 56
Italy ['ɪtli] Italien **I U2**, 29
Mount Snowdon [ˌmaʊnt 'snəʊdn] **I U6**, 88
Poland ['pəʊlənd] Polen **I U2**, 29
River Thames [ˌrɪvə 'temz] **I U4**, 56
Russia ['rʌʃə] Russland **I U2**, 29
Sennen Beach [ˌsenən 'bi:tʃ] **I U6**, 88
Spain [speɪn] Spanien **I U2**, 29
St Michael's Mount [snˌmaɪklz 'maʊnt] **I U6**, 90
Turkey ['tɜ:ki] Türkei **I U2**, 29
Wales [weɪlz] **I U6**, 88

Other names

Angelo's ['ændʒələʊz] **I U5**, 74
Barker ['bɑ:kə] **I U2**, 27
Bonza ['bɒnzə] **I U7**, 106
buzz [bʌz] *(hier:) Name eines Spiels* **I U1**, 16
Chocolate Islands ['tʃɒklət ˌaɪləndz] **I U4**, 66
Cool Cat [ˌku:l 'kæt] **I U5**, 81
Cutty Sark [ˌkʌti 'sɑ:k] **I U4**, 56
Docklands Light Railway [ˌdɒklændz laɪt 'reɪlweɪ] **I U4**, 56
Greenwich Foot Tunnel [ˌgrenɪdʒ 'fʊt tʌnl] **I U4**, 56
Greenwich Market [ˌgrenɪdʒ 'mɑ:kɪt] **I ZI**, 8
Grumpy Greg [ˌgrʌmpi 'greg] ⟨**I U4**, 67⟩
Hobbyland ['hɒbilænd] **I PUB**, 38
Millennium Dome [mɪ'leniəm ˌdəʊm] **I ZI**, 8
Mousehole Harbour [ˌmaʊzl 'hɑ:bə] **I U6**, 90
Mudchute Farm [ˌmʌdʃu:t 'fɑ:m] **I U7**, 102
Peg [peg] ⟨**I U4**, 67⟩
Royal Observatory [ˌrɔɪəl əb'zɜ:vətri] **I U4**, 57
Rusty ['rʌsti] **I U7**, 110
Thames Barrier [ˌtemz 'bæriə] **I ZI**, 8
Thomas Tallis [ˌtɒməs 'tælɪs] **I U1**, 10
Thomas Tallis School [ˌtɒməs 'tælɪs ˌsku:l] **I U1**, 10
Tiger ['taɪgə] **I U2**, 26
Tokyo Tigers [ˌtəʊkiəʊ 'taɪgəz] **I U4**, 67
4U [fə 'ju] **I U3**, 40
Water Park ['wɔ:tə ˌpɑ:k] **I U3**, 40

Famous names

Mickey Mouse ['mɪki maʊs] **I U1**, 17

Bildquellen:
U1/U4: Ernst Klett Verlag/Fletcher; S. 8: Corbis/London Aerial Photo Library; S. 9: (1) ullstein bild/Minehan; (2) Collections Picture Gallery/Haggerty; (3) Corbis/Everton; (4) National Maritime Museum; (5) Corbis/Horner; (6) Schmidt; S. 10: Ernst Klett Verlag/Hacker; S. 11: (1) Ernst Klett Verlag/Fletcher; (2-3) Ernst Klett Verlag/Hacker; S. 13: (1) Ernst Klett Verlag/Hacker; (2-4, 7) Bananastock RF/Watlington; (5-6) Corbis; S. 14: Ernst Klett Verlag/Fletcher; S. 17: (1-2) Ernst Klett Verlag/Fletcher; S. 19: Ernst Klett Verlag/Fletcher; S. 21: (1-2) Ernst Klett Verlag/Fletcher; S. 24: MEV; S. 26: (1) Klett-Archiv/McBride; (2-3) Ernst Klett Verlag/Fletcher; S. 27: (1) Corbis/Edifice; (2) Alamy Images RM/Arcaid/Knight; (3) Alamy Images RM/Harding; (4) Ernst Klett Verlag/Fletcher; (5) Klett-Archiv/Smith; (6) Klett-Archiv/McBride; S. 28: (1,9) Corbis; (2,4,7) Ernst Klett Verlag/Fletcher; (3,5-6,8,10) Bananastock RF/Watlington; S. 30: (1) Ernst Klett Verlag/Fletcher; S. 31: mecom/Bilderbox/Wod; S. 38: MEV; S. 40: (1-4) Ernst Klett Verlag/Fletcher; S. 41: (1) Fotosearch RF; (2) Mauritius/Mittenwald; (3) Avenue Images GmbH/image 100; (4) Picture-Alliance/A0759; S. 46: Ernst Klett Verlag/Fletcher; S. 54: MEV; S. 56: (1) Ernst Klett Verlag/Schmidt; (2) National Maritime Museum; (3) Topham Picturepoint/UPPA Ltd; S. 57: (1) Getty Images RF/Photodisc; (2) Bananastock RF/Watlington; (3) Mauritius/O'Brien; (4) Getty Images/taxi/Kings; (5) Corbis/Shelley; (6) Alamy Images RM/FCL Photogr. RF; (7) Corbis/Hawkins; S. 59: (1) Ernst Klett Verlag/Fletcher; (2) Inmagine/Brand X Pictures RF; S. 61: (1) Transport for London; (2) Corbis/Kähler; (3) Schmidt; (4) Avenue Images GmbH/thinkstock; S. 63: Ernst Klett Verlag/Fletcher; S. 65: (1) Getty Images/taxi/Benelux Press; (2) Ernst Klett Verlag/Fletcher; S. 70: Corbis/Garratt; S. 71: Palmer; S. 72: (1-5) Ernst Klett Verlag/Hacker; S. 73: Klett-Archiv; S. 74: Ernst Klett Verlag/Hacker; S. 77: (1) Ernst Klett Verlag/Hacker; (2) Ernst Klett Verlag/Fletcher; S. 79: The Anthony Blake Photo Library Ltd/Skipper; S. 80-81: Ernst Klett Verlag/Fletcher; S. 85: Alamy Images RM/Creatas RF; S. 86: Ernst Klett Verlag/Fletcher; S. 88: (1, 3-5) Avenue Images GmbH/Rubberball RF; (2) Getty Image S. 89: (1) Alamy Images RM/Moore; (2) Alamy Images RF/RF; (3) Corbis/Cormack; (4) Alamy Images RM/Atmosphere; (5) Getty Images/Porro/Contributor; (6) Alamy Images RM/Kase; S. 90: (1) Getty Images/stone/Barraud; (2) Alamy Images RM/Sullivan; S. 93: Ernst Klett Verlag/Fletcher; S. 95: (1) PhotoDisc; (2-3) Ernst Klett Verlag/Fletcher; (4-5) Ernst Klett Verlag/Hacker; S. 100: Corbis/Thompson; S. 101: www.britainonview.com; S. 102: (1-7) Ernst Klett Verlag/Hacker; S. 103: (1-4) Ernst Klett Verlag/Hacker; S. 106: Ernst Klett Verlag/Fletcher; S. 108: Ernst Klett Verlag/Hacker; S. 120: Picture-Alliance/Hirschberger; S. 126: Corbis/Nicholson; S. 128: Alamy Images RM/Worldwide Pict. Lib./Belcher; S. 130: (1-2, 4) Corel Corporation; (3) Corbis/Conrad; S. 131: (1,4) Corel Corporation; (2) Fotosearch RF/Digital Vision; (3) MEV; (5) Angermayer; S. 132: NewsCast/Harrods; (2) Picture-Alliance/dpa/Conran; S. 133: Avenue Images GmbH/Bananastock RF; S. 171: (1) Getty Images/DigitalVision; (2) Niehoff
Textquelle:
S. 116: © by Marci Ridlon

⟨In the classroom⟩

You can say

Before the lesson

Good morning, Mr / Mrs … — Guten Morgen, Herr / Frau …
Hello, Mr / Mrs … — Hallo, Herr / Frau …
Sorry I'm late. — Tut mir Leid, dass ich zu spät komme.

Asking for help

Can you help me, please? — Kannst du / Können Sie mir bitte helfen?
How do you do this exercise? — Wie macht man diese Übung?
Is this right? I'm not sure. — Ist das richtig? Ich bin mir nicht sicher.
Sorry, I don't know. Ask … — Tut mir Leid, das weiß ich nicht. Frag …!
Why don't you ask the teacher? — Frag doch den Lehrer / die Lehrerin!
Sorry. Can you say that again, please? — Wie bitte? Können Sie das bitte wiederholen?
What page are we on? — Auf welcher Seite sind wir?
Can we open the window, please? — Können wir bitte das Fenster aufmachen?
Can I go to the toilet, please? — Kann ich bitte zur Toilette gehen?
What's for homework? — Was haben wir als Hausaufgabe auf?

Asking for information

What's that in English / German? — Was heißt das auf Englisch / Deutsch?
What does that mean? — Was bedeutet das?
How do you spell … , please? — Wie schreibt man … , bitte?
What time is it, please? — Wie spät ist es, bitte?
Where's the …? / Where are the …? — Wo ist der / die / das …? / Wo sind die …?

Working in class

Thank you. / Thanks. — Danke.
You're welcome. — Bitte. / Bitte schön!
Now it's your turn. — Jetzt bist du an der Reihe.
Let's make / draw a … — Lasst uns ein / eine / einen … machen / zeichnen.
Let's act the story / dialogue. — Lasst uns die Geschichte / den Dialog spielen.

Your teacher can say

Open your books at page … — Öffnet eure Bücher auf Seite …
Do exercise … on page … for homework. — Macht Übung … auf Seite … als Hausaufgabe.
Where's your book, Sam? — Sam, wo ist dein Buch?
Sit down, please. — Setz dich. / Setzt euch bitte.
Say that again, please. — Wiederhole / Wiederholt es bitte.
We're on page 19. — Wir sind auf Seite 19.
It's on the board. — Es steht an der Tafel.
That's very good! — Das ist sehr gut!
That's all for today. — Das wäre es für heute.

Lösungen Check-out

Unit 1 page 23

Exercise 1

1. This is Lisa. She**'s eleven**. 2. Look, it's Terry and Sam. They**'re in my tutor group, too**. 3. My name is Emma. I**'m from Bristol**. 4. Here's Mr Newman. He**'s the caretaker**. 5. Hi, we**'re new here.**

Exercise 2

Emma: *(Ring! Ring!)* Oh, hi, Kim!
Kim: Hello, Emma. **Is** your new school OK?
Emma: Yes, **it is.**
Kim: And your tutor and teachers? **Are** they nice, too?
Emma: Yes, **they are.** Mrs Carter is very nice.
Kim: **Is** she your English teacher?
Emma: No, **she isn't.** She's my tutor and my German teacher.
Kim: Hey, cool! You**'re** lucky.
Emma: Yes, **I am.** Bye, Kim!
Kim: Bye, Emma.

Exercise 3

In A there is a pencil-case on the table. In B there are three pencils on the table.
In A there is a schoolbag on the chair. In B there is a schoolbag under the chair.
In A there are two books in the cupboard. In B there are four books in the cupboard.
In A there is a football behind the door. In B Tom is behind the door.
In A there are two posters on the wall. In B there is one poster on the wall.

Exercise 4

Hier sollst du selbst über deine neue Schule schreiben.
Musterlösung: My new school is the Kepler-Gymnasium. It is a big Gymnasium in Stuttgart. Mrs Schneider is my tutor and my German teacher. Mr Maier is my English teacher. He is very nice.

Exercise 5

1. **Who** is from Greenwich?
2. **Who** is Mr Newman?
3. **What** (oder: **who**) is Thomas Tallis?
4. **Where** is Emma from?
5. **Who** is eleven?
6. **Where** (oder: **what**) is Greenwich?

Unit 2 page 37

Exercise 1

a) 1. Ben's sisters are Lisa and Jade.
2. Their mum's bag is new.
3. Barker's ball is in the garden.

b) 1. The Taylors' garden is small.
2. The girls' brother is sixteen.
3. Their parents' car is old.

Exercise 2

Hier sollst du selbst über deine Familie schreiben.
Musterlösung: My parents are Silke Schneider and Hans Schneider. I have got a sister, too. Her name is Anja. She is 15. Luzie is our cat. Our flat is in Schwetzingen.

Exercise 3

Lisa: Let's look at **your** pictures from Bristol, Emma. Who's the girl here?
Emma: She's a friend from **my** old school. **Her** name is Fiona Green. The Greens have got a funny house. **Their** house has got a living room upstairs – and **its** walls are pink and yellow! And Fiona's dad is funny, too. He's always got funny pictures on **his** T-shirts!
Lisa: Ha, ha! Is that a dog with Fiona – or a mouse?! We've got a dog, but **our** dog is big.
Emma: Yes, **your** dog is very big – but Fiona's dog is nice, too.

Exercise 4

1. Emma: My sisters and I **have** got a small room. We**'ve** got a computer in our room. **Have** you got a computer in your room, Terry?
Terry: No, I **haven't** got a computer. But I**'ve** got Dad's old laptop.

2. Emma: The Jacksons **have** got a shed. **Have** you got a shed, too, Lisa?
Lisa: No, we **haven't**. But we**'ve** got a garden.
Emma: **Has** Sam got a garden?
Lisa: No, he **hasn't**.

Exercise 5

1. Can you **help**, please?
2. Don't **play football in the classroom.**
3. **Can you open the door, please?**
4. **Don't use your mobile in the classroom.**

Unit 3 page 51

Exercise 1

A: Hey – let's **go to the cinema.**
B: **Good idea!**

A: There's a **great film about a girl and a boy.**
B: **A girl and a boy?! That's boring.**

A: Oh, please – **let's see the film!**
B: **Oh – OK. When can we go?**

A: How about Friday **at six at the Bristol Cinema?**
B: **Fine. See you on Friday. Bye.**

Exercise 2

It's eight fifty-seven. (*Oder:* It's three minutes to nine.) – It's ten past four. – It's ten sixteen. – It's three thirty-three. – It's four minutes past two. – It's quarter past five. – It's one thirty. – It's twelve forty-five. (*Oder:* It's quarter to one.)

Exercise 3

Emma: Greenwich 84007433.
Lisa: Hi, Emma. It's Lisa. How are you?
Emma: Hi, Lisa. I'm fine. And you?
Lisa: Fine. Listen, Emma. I've got a problem.
Emma: Oh – What's the problem?
Lisa: I can't take Barker to the park this weekend. Can you help?
Emma: Yes, Lisa. No problem. I like Barker.
Lisa: Thanks a lot. See you. Bye.
Emma: Bye, Lisa. See you.

Exercise 4

Hier sollst du über deine Freizeit schreiben.
Musterlösung: I have got a good friend.
Her name is Annika. At the weekend we have fun.
We meet on Saturday morning and
we ride our bikes. In the evening we watch TV or play computer games.

Exercise 5

1. On Saturdays Jade gets up at six thirty.
2. Then she makes her breakfast at quarter to seven.
3. After that she wakes up her parents at quarter past seven.
4. At ten thirty she plays with Barker.
5. In the afternoon at three o'clock she feeds Barker.

Unit 4 page 71

Exercise 1

Hier sollst du darüber schreiben, wie du von zu Hause zur Schule kommst.
Musterlösung: First I walk to the bus stop. Then I catch the bus number 22 to school. I am at school in twenty minutes.

Exercise 2

1. I'm not sure, but Mr Jackson knows the way. Ask **him**. 2. Hey – we're lucky. My dad can pick **us** up for a special tour! 3. Mr Jackson drives the friends all round town. He takes **them** everywhere.
4. The Cutty Sark is great. I like **it** because it's so beautiful. 5. Emma always writes down everything about Greenwich. Ask **her**. 6. I can't find the Dome. – It's easy-peasy! Please give **me** the map

Exercise 3

Beispiele:
Do **you come to school by bus / … ? – Yes, I do. / No, I don't.**
Do **your friends go to the town centre by bike / … ? – Yes, they do. / No, they don't.**
Does **your teacher go to the park by Underground / … ? – Yes, she does. / No, she doesn't.**

Exercise 4

Where **do a lot of Greenwich kids go with their skateboards? – They go to Greenwich Park.**
When **does Mr Jackson pick the friends up for the tour? – He picks them up at four o'clock.**
Why **does Mr Jackson know a lot about Greenwich? – He knows a lot about Greenwich because he drives a taxi in Greenwich.**
Why **doesn't Captain Terry win the fight? – Captain Terry doesn't win the fight because Lisa-Yoko is fast and she plays for the Tokyo Tigers.**

Unit 5 page 85

Exercise 1

Beispiele:
1. Customer: How much is this sweatshirt, please?
2. Customer: And what size is it?
3. Customer: Have you got other sizes?
4. Customer: Can I try them on, please?
5. Customer: Do you sell T-shirts here?

Exercise 2

1. Would you like a little birthday cake?
2. I'd like to do karaoke.
3. Would you like to come to my party?
4. I'd like my cat food!

Exercise 3

1. "Yes, OK. **I'm not using it right now.**"
2. "Again?! **What's he buying today?**"
3. "No, she isn't. Look, **she's coming now.**"
4. "No. **They aren't talking today.**"
5. "Oh no! **Are we doing the wrong homework?**"

Exercise 4

*Hier sollst du über deine Zeichnung einer Party schreiben. Benütze in jedem Satz das **Present progressive!***

Musterlösung: In my party picture everyone is having fun. Two girls and two boys are dancing. A girl is singing with a karoke machine. Three people are listening to her and they are laughing. One boy is opening a present – it is *my* present!

Exercise 5

Mrs Taylor: What do we need from the shops, Lisa? How **much** flour have we still got?
Lisa: Let's see. There's only **a little** flour here. And there isn't **much** sugar.
Mrs Taylor: And can you please look and see how **many** eggs we've got? I want to make a cake, so I need **a few** eggs for that. Three or four.
Lisa: No, we don't need eggs. There are six in the box. But there's only **a little** cheese. It's for a mouse, but not **much** for a big family!
Mrs Taylor: OK. So we need flour, sugar, cheese. Oh, and **a few** tins of dog food, too. I know there aren't **many** tins in the cupboard. – Do you want to come to the shops with me, Lisa? I can use **a little** help with the shopping.

Unit 6 page 101

Exercise 1

Hier sollst du über eine Reise schreiben, die du mit deiner Familie machen möchtest.
Musterlösung: I would like to go to Britain because I am learning English. I would like to go swimming in Penzance and see Cornwall. I would like to take my swimsuit with me. I want to take my sweatshirt and my wellies with me, too. Sometimes it rains there in the summer. I don't like the rain but I want to see St Michael's Mount and the little beach in Mousehole Harbour.

Exercise 2

1. My Discman is still in the room. Jade, can you **bring** me my Discman, please? 2. Can you **take** our bag to the car, Ben? 3. Lisa, can you please **bring** me my wellies? 4. Please **take** the map to the car. Mum would like to look at it. 5. No, Barker, we can't **take** your new dog friend with us!

Exercise 3

Dear Terry, We **are** in Penzance this year. I **am sitting** on the beach now. I can **see** St Michael's Mount from here. Some people **are surfing** today. Mum and Dad **go** in the water every day, but today it **is** too cold for me! Jade and I often **build** sand castles on the beach and **walk** Barker in town. Some kites **are flying** over the beach now. Oops! One kite **is falling** into the sea. CU soon. Lisa

Exercise 4

Mrs Taylor: OK. Let's see what we've got. We've got **some** water. Now let's get **some** picnic food.
Lisa: Have they got **any** sandwiches here?
Mrs Taylor: Yes, they have. And they've got **some** little cakes, too.
Lisa: Yes, nice. Have they got **any** apples?
Mrs Taylor: OK, let's get **some** apples and **some** chocolate, too!
Lisa: And what about Barker? Is there **any** dog food here?
Mrs Taylor: Yes, there is. They've got **some** tins of his favourite dog food over there.
Barker: Woof!

Unit 7 page 117

Exercise 1

Hier schreibst du über dein Lieblingstier.
Musterlösung: My favourite animals are cats. I have got a cat and her name is Fluffy. I love her and she loves me because I am very good to her. She is a sweet cat and she likes milk. I feed her in the morning and in the evening. She wants her milk only from me, and she is a great friend.

Exercise 2

1. Are you busy? I can take the dog to the park today. You **needn't** do it. 2. Hey, you **mustn't** throw water at the neighbours' cat. That isn't nice! 3. We've got chickens in our garden. So we **needn't** go to the shops for eggs. 4. My horse has got a problem with her leg. I **must** phone the vet. 5. We **mustn't** forget to take a camera with us when we go to the zoo on Sunday. 6. The sheep eat the grass in the field, so we **needn't** feed them in summer.

Exercise 3

Hier schreibst du über deine Aktivitäten zu Hause und in der Umgebung.
Musterlösung: 1. I do my homework in my room in the afternoon. 2. I meet my friends at the weekend and we have fun in the park. 3. I listen to music in the evening. 4. I have breakfast at six thirty but at the weekend at ten o'clock!

Exercise 4

1. The trees are nice for the people here **and / but** they are nice for birds, too. 2. The birds start to sing early in the morning **so / and** they wake up my brother and me. 3. I like my 'alarm clock' **but** my brother doesn't like it. 4. I love birds **because / and** I think their songs are beautiful. 5. I always get up with the birds **so** I'm never late for school!

Exercise 5

Toms Ferienrap kannst du lesen, sprechen und auswendig lernen.

Dictionary (German–English)

A

abbiegen to turn **I PUC**, 55
(nach) rechts abbiegen to turn right **I PUC**, 55
Abend evening **I U3**, 42
eines Abends one evening **I U7**, 110
abends in the evening **I U3**, 42
Abenteuer adventure **I U6**, 96
aber but **I U1**, 12
abholen to pick up **I U1**, 10
ablecken to lick **I U4**, 67
abmalen to copy **I U1**, 16
abschreiben to copy **I U1**, 16
abspielen to play **I U2**, 32
sich **abwechseln** to take turns **I U2**, 32
acht eight **I U1**, 11
achtzehn eighteen **I U1**, 16
achtzig eighty **I U1**, 16
Acker field **I U7**, 102
Adjektiv adjective **I U1**, 22
Adressbuch address book **I U6**, 90
Adresse address **I U6**, 90
Affe monkey **I U7**, 102
Aktivität activity **I U7**, 102
albern silly **I U2**, 30
alle zehn Minuten every ten minutes **I U4**, 70
aus aller Welt from all round the world **I U4**, 57
allein alone **I U6**, 92
allergisch auf allergic to **I U7**, 104
alle/-s all **I U4**, 58
alles everything **I U4**, 59
Alphabet alphabet **I U1**, 17
alphabetisch alphabetical **I U5**, 84
als when **I U2**, 32
also so **I U1**, 12
alt old **I U1**, 10
am Strand on the beach **I U6**, 92
sich **amüsieren** to have fun **I U5**, 78
an at **I U1**, 10; to **I U2**, 33; on **I U1**, 14
anbellen to bark at **I U3**, 49
Andenken souvenir **I U6**, 94
andere/-r/-s other **I U1**, 22
die anderen the others **I U5**, 77
ein/-e andere/-r/-s another **I U6**, 94
anders different **I U1**, 23
anfangen to start **I U1**, 11
Angst haben um to be scared for **I U6**, 96
anklicken to click on **I U6**, 90
anprobieren to try on **I U5**, 73
(Telefon)**Anruf** phone call **I U3**, 42
anrufen to phone **I U1**, 18
anschauen to look at **I U1**, 15
ansehen to watch **I PUB**, 38; to look at **I U1**, 15
Antwort answer **I U1**, 15
(be)**antworten** to answer **I PUA**, 24
Apfel apple **I U1**, 16
Apparat machine **I U5**, 80
April April **I U5**, 75
Arbeit job **I U7**, 104
arbeiten to work **I U4**, 56
Ärger trouble **I U2**, 30
Aroma flavour **I U3**, 44
auch too **I U1**, 10
auf at **I U1**, 10; on **I U1**, 14
auf der linken Seite on the left **I PUC**, 55
auf Englisch in English **I U1**, 19
auf ... hinauf on top of **I U3**, 46
aufbewahren to keep **I U6**, 94
Aufgabe job **I U7**, 104
aufgeregt nervous **I U7**, 104; excited **I U5**, 80
aufhören to stop **I U2**, 34
aufmachen to open **I U2**, 33
aufpassen to watch out **I U1**, 20
aufpassen auf to look after **I U7**, 104
aufprallen to crash **I U6**, 96
aufschreiben to write down **I U4**, 60
aufstehen to get up **I U3**, 42
aufwachen to wake up **I U3**, 48
aufwecken to wake up **I U3**, 48
Auge eye **I U3**, 46
Augenblick moment **I U7**, 108
im Augenblick just now **I U7**, 116
August August **I U5**, 75
aus from **I U1**, 10
Auschecken check-out **I U1**, 23
(sich) **ausdenken** to think of **I U7**, 108
Ausflug trip **I U6**, 90
ausführen to take out **I U3**, 49
den Hund ausführen to walk the dog **I U3**, 42
ausfüllen to fill in **I U1**, 16
Ausguck crow's nest **I U4**, 66
ausmisten to muck out **I U7**, 104
Grüße **ausrichten** to say hello to **I U2**, 33
aussehen to look **I U3**, 44
außen outside **I U2**, 30
außerhalb outside **I U2**, 30
auswählen to choose **I U7**, 106
ausziehen to take off **I U6**, 94
Auto car **I U2**, 31

B

babyleicht easy-peasy **I U4**, 62
Bad(ezimmer) bathroom **I PUA**, 24
Badeanzug swimsuit **I U6**, 90
Bahnhof station **I U4**, 56
bald soon **I U2**, 34
Ball ball **I U1**, 20
Band band **I U3**, 40
Basketball basketball **I PUB**, 38
bauen to build **I U6**, 90
Bauernhof farm **I U7**, 102
Baum tree **I U1**, 20
beängstigend scary **I U1**, 12
Becher mug **I U6**, 94
bedeuten to mean **I U4**, 64
Bedeutung meaning **I U7**, 116
sich **beeilen** to hurry up **I U4**, 67
beenden to stop **I U2**, 34
Beförderung transport *(no pl.)* **I U4**, 58
begeistert excited **I U5**, 80
beginnen to start **I U1**, 11
jemanden **begrüßen** to say hello **I U1**, 11
behalten to keep **I U6**, 94
bei at **I U1**, 10
beibringen to teach **I U3**, 48
Bein leg **I U7**, 110
Beispiel example **I U1**, 13
bekommen to get **I U4**, 58
bellen to bark **I U3**, 48
benutzen to use **I U1**, 19
beobachten to watch **I PUB**, 38
bereit ready **I U5**, 80
bereits already **I U7**, 103
Berg mountain **I U6**, 88
berichtigen to correct **I U4**, 64
berühmt famous **I U4**, 57
beschäftigt (mit) busy (with) **I U2**, 34
beschreiben to describe **I PUA**, 25
besitzen to have got **I U2**, 30
Besitzer, Besitzerin owner **I U7**, 106
besondere/-r/-s special **I U4**, 58
besorgt worried **I U7**, 110
beste/-r/-s best **I U4**, 62
besuchen to visit **I U3**, 42
Besucher, Besucherin visitor **I U4**, 57
Bett bed **I PUA**, 25
beunruhigt worried **I U7**, 110
bevor before **I U2**, 34
Bild picture **I U1**, 15
bilden to make **I U1**, 15
billig cheap **I U6**, 94
bis before **I U5**, 78
bitte please **I U1**, 13
Bitte schön. You're welcome. **I U1**, 19; Here you are. **I U5**, 73
blau blue **I PUA**, 24
Bleistift pencil **I U1**, 16
bloß only **I U2**, 30
Blume flower **I U4**, 62
Boden bottom **I U3**, 46
Boot boat **I U4**, 61
böse bad **I U7**, 106
Box box **I U3**, 43
Boygroup boy band **I U3**, 40
brauchen to need **I U5**, 78
braun brown **I PUA**, 24
brechen to break **I U5**, 78
Brett plank **I U4**, 67; board **I U1**, 18
bringen to take **I U3**, 48; to get **I U4**, 58
(mit)bringen to bring **I U3**, 48
britisch British **I U3**, 40
Broschüre brochure **I U4**, 56
Brücke bridge **I PUC**, 54

Bruder brother I **PUA**, 25
Buch book I **U1**, 14
Büchse tin I **U3**, 44
Buchstabe letter I **U1**, 20
buchstabieren to spell I **U1**, 17
Burg castle I **PUC**, 54
Bus bus pl. buses I **ZI**, 9
Bushaltestelle bus stop I **PUC**, 54

C

Café café I **U3**, 48
Cafeteria cafeteria I **U1**, 20
CD CD I **U2**, 32
Center centre I **PUC**, 54
Chemiekasten chemistry set I **U2**, 26
Chip card I **U7**, 108
Computer computer I **PUA**, 25
Computergeschäft computer shop I **U2**, 26
Computerklub computer club I **U3**, 40
cool cool I **U1**, 13
Couch sofa I **PUA**, 25
Cousin cousin I **U2**, 28
Cousine cousin I **U2**, 28

D

da there I **U1**, 18
da because I **U2**, 29
dahin there I **U3**, 40
danach after that I **U3**, 44; then I **PUA**, 24
dank thanks to I **U7**, 111
vielen **Dank** thanks a lot I **U6**, 92
danke thank you I **U1**, 12; thanks I **U2**, 34
Nichts zu **danken**. You're welcome. I **U1**, 19
dann then I **PUA**, 24
das that I **U1**, 12
das the I **U1**, 11
dass that I **U4**, 66
Datum date I **U5**, 74
dein(e) your I **U1**, 10
(nach)**denken** to think I **U4**, 61
  denken über to think of I **U6**, 90; to think about I **U6**, 97
der the I **U1**, 11
der-/die-/dasselbe the same I **U2**, 33
deshalb so I **U1**, 12
deutsch German I **U1**, 12
Deutsch German I **U1**, 12
aus **Deutschland** German I **U1**, 12
Deutschlehrer, Deutschlehrerin German teacher I **U1**, 12
Dezember December I **U5**, 75
Dialog dialogue I **U1**, 21
dich selbst yourself I **U1**, 11
die *(Relativpronomen)* that I **U1**, 17
die the I **U1**, 11
Dieb thief pl. thieves I **U5**, 76
Dienstag Tuesday I **PUB**, 39
dienstags on Tuesdays I **U3**, 40
diese (hier) these I **U3**, 46
  diese (dort) those I **U3**, 46
diese/-r/-s this I **U1**, 10
Ding thing I **U1**, 16
direkt straight I **PUC**, 55
Discjockey DJ I **U5**, 81
Discman Discman I **U2**, 30
DJ DJ I **U5**, 81
Donnerstag Thursday I **PUB**, 39
Dorf village I **U6**, 88
dort there I **U1**, 18
  (nach) dort drüben over there I **U6**, 91
  dort ist there's (= there is) I **U1**, 18
dorthin there I **U3**, 40
Dose tin I **U3**, 44
Drachen kite I **U6**, 88
  einen Drachen steigen lassen to fly a kite I **U6**, 88
Drachenfest kite festival I **U6**, 88
draußen outside I **U2**, 30
  nach draußen out I **U6**, 96
dreckig dirty I **U2**, 30
drei three I **U1**, 11
dreißig thirty I **U1**, 16
dreizehn thirteen I **U1**, 16
dritte/-r/-s third I **U5**, 74
du you I **U1**, 10
Duft smell I **U2**, 34
dumm silly I **U2**, 30
Dummkopf silly I **U4**, 62
dunkel dark I **U7**, 110
durcheinander geraten jumbled I **U4**, 59
Durcheinander mess I **U2**, 30
dürfen may I **U7**, 110; can I **U1**, 19
  nicht dürfen mustn't I **U7**, 104

E

Ei egg I **U5**, 78
eigene/-r/-s own I **U2**, 30
Eigenschaftswort adjective I **U1**, 22
Eile hurry I **U2**, 30
ein/-e a, an I **U1**, 10
  ein/-e andere/-r/-s another I **U6**, 94
  noch ein/-e another I **U6**, 94
einbiegen to turn I **PUC**, 55
Einchecken check-in I **U1**, 10
einfach just I **U3**, 46
einfach easy I **U1**, 20
sich etwas **einfallen lassen** to think of I **U7**, 108
Einheit unit I **U1**, 10
einhundert a/one hundred I **U1**, 16
einige a few I **U5**, 78; some I **U6**, 94
einkaufen gehen to go shopping I **U5**, 73
Einkaufen shopping I **U5**, 73
einladen to invite I **U5**, 74
  ... (zu etwas) einladen to invite ... out I **U5**, 74
Einladung invitation I **U5**, 74
(noch) nicht **einmal** not even I **U6**, 95
  auf einmal suddenly I **U5**, 80; at once I **U6**, 96
eins one I **U1**, 10
einsammeln to collect I **PUB**, 38
einschlafen to fall asleep I **U3**, 42
einsetzen to put in I **U1**, 14
einsteigen to get into I **U6**, 97
Einzelkind only child I **U2**, 26
Eiscreme ice-cream I **U6**, 90
elf eleven I **U1**, 10
Eltern parents *(pl.)* I **U2**, 26
E-Mail e-mail I **U2**, 33
(be)**enden** to finish I **U2**, 34
enden to end I **U4**, 62
endlich finally I **U3**, 44
aus **England** English I **U2**, 29
englisch English I **U2**, 29
Englisch English I **U1**, 11
entlanggehen to go down I **PUC**, 55
Entschuldigung. Excuse me. I **PUC**, 55
er he I **U1**, 12
sich **erinnern (an)** to remember I **U3**, 46
erklären to explain I **U7**, 110
erklimmen to climb I **U6**, 88
erreichen to get to I **PUC**, 55
als **Erstes** first I **U3**, 42
  erste/-r/-s first I **U4**, 60
erzählen to tell I **U2**, 29
Erzählung story I **U3**, 48
es it I **U1**, 12
essen to eat I **U3**, 42
Essen meal I **U6**, 90; food I **U3**, 44
etwas a little I **U5**, 78; some I **U6**, 94
euer, eure your I **U2**, 29
aus **Europa** European I **U2**, 29
europäisch European I **U2**, 29

F

fahren to drive I **U4**, 58; to go I **U1**, 19; to ride I **PUB**, 38
  in Urlaub fahren to go on holiday I **U6**, 100
Fahrer, Fahrerin driver I **U4**, 58
Fahrrad bike I **PUB**, 38
Fahrt trip I **U6**, 90
fair fair I **U4**, 62
(hin)**fallen** to fall I **U3**, 42
falls if I **U7**, 111
falsch wrong I **U1**, 13
Familie family I **PUA**, 25
Familienstammbaum family tree I **U2**, 28
(ein)**fangen** to catch I **U4**, 58
Farbe colour I **PUA**, 24
Februar February I **U5**, 75
Federmäppchen pencil-case I **U1**, 16
fehlend missing I **U1**, 23
Feier party I **U1**, 18
eine Party **feiern** to have a party I **U2**, 33
Fels rock I **U6**, 96
felsig rocky I **U6**, 100
Fenster window I **U1**, 18
Ferien holiday(s) I **U6**, 88
Fernseher TV I **PUA**, 25
  im Fernsehen on TV I **U3**, 42
fertig ready I **U5**, 80

fertig stellen to finish | U2, 34
Fertigkeit skill | U1, 22
Fest festival | U6, 88
festhalten to hold | U3, 46
Festival festival | U6, 88
Film film | U3, 40
finden to think | U4, 61
finden to find | U1, 22
Fisch fish pl. fish | U6, 100
Flasche bottle | U7, 104
fliegen to fly | U6, 88
Fluss river | PUC, 54
folglich so | U1, 12
Form form | U1, 14
Foto photo | U2, 27
ein Foto machen to take a photo | U7, 108
Fotoapparat camera | U7, 108
Frage question | U1, 15
fragen to ask | PUA, 24
nach ... fragen to ask for ... | U4, 59
Fragewort question word | U4, 64
Frau *(Anrede)* Mrs | U1, 12
Frau woman pl. women | U6, 100
im Freien outside | U2, 30
Freitag Friday | PUB, 39
Freizeit free time | U3, 40
Freund, Freundin friend | U1, 12; mate | U4, 66
friedlich calm | U7, 104
frisch fresh | U6, 100
fröhlich happy | PUA, 25
früh early | U3, 42
Frühling spring | U6, 90
Frühstück breakfast | U3, 48
frühstücken to have breakfast | U6, 93
Fuchs fox | U7, 102
führen to go | U4, 56
Füller pen | U1, 16
fünf five | U1, 11
fünfzehn fifteen | U1, 16
fünfzig fifty | U1, 16
funktionieren to work | U3, 46
für for | ZI, 8
furchtbar terrible | U1, 20
Fürwort pronoun | U4, 59
Fuß foot pl. feet | U4, 57
Fußball football | U1, 12
füttern to feed | U3, 44

G

ganz all | U4, 58; whole | U6, 100
Garage garage | U7, 110
Garten garden | U2, 26
Gartenhäuschen shed | U2, 26
Gaststätte restaurant | U6, 90
geben to give | U4, 59
es gibt there are | U1, 18; there's (= there is) | U1, 18
Gebiet territory | U7, 110
gebrauchen to use | U1, 19
Geburtstag birthday | U5, 72
Alles Gute zum Geburtstag! Happy birthday! | U5, 80
Geburtstagsfeier birthday party | U5, 72
gegen against | U6, 96
gegenüber opposite | PUC, 54
Gegenwart present | U3, 51
gehen to go | U1, 19
gehen *(zu Fuß)* to walk | U3, 42
in Urlaub gehen to go on holiday | U6, 100
ins Bett gehen to go to bed | U3, 49
nach oben gehen to go up | U5, 79
nach unten gehen to go down | U5, 79
surfen gehen to go surfing | U6, 88
über ... gehen to cross | PUC, 55
gehören zu to go with | U4, 56
gelb yellow | PUA, 24
Geld money | U5, 73
gemeinsam together | U3, 44
gemischt mixed | U3, 50
genießen to enjoy | U6, 100
geöffnet open | PUA, 24
gerade just now | U7, 116; right now | U5, 74; now | U1, 19
geradeaus straight on | PUC, 55
Gerät machine | U5, 80
Geräusch sound | ZI, 9
gerecht fair | U4, 62
Gern geschehen. You're welcome. | U1, 19
Geruch smell | U2, 34
Geschäft shop | U2, 26
Geschäftsführer, Geschäftsführerin manager | U2, 26
geschehen to happen | U3, 47
Geschenk present | U5, 72
Geschichte story | U3, 48
geschieden von divorced from | U2, 28
Geschmack flavour | U3, 44
Geschmacksrichtung flavour | U3, 44
Gesicht face | U3, 48
Gestank smell | U2, 34
Getränk drink | U3, 49
Gewinn prize | U4, 62
gewinnen to win | U4, 62
Gewinner winner | U4, 64
Gewitter storm | U6, 96
gewöhnlich usually | U3, 42
Gitarre guitar | PUB, 38
glauben to think | U4, 61; to believe | U3, 46
der/die/das Gleiche the same | U2, 33
gleichzeitig at the same time | U7, 102
glücklich happy | PUA, 25
Grammatik grammar | U1, 15
Gras grass | U7, 104
grau grey | PUA, 24
aus Griechenland Greek | U2, 29
griechisch Greek | U2, 29
Griechisch Greek | U2, 29
groß large (L) | U5, 72; big | U1, 12; great | U6, 96
besonders groß extra large (XL) | U5, 72
großartig great | U2, 33
Größe size | U5, 72
Großmutter grandmother | PUA, 25
Großstadt city | U7, 102
Großvater grandfather | PUA, 25
grün green | PUA, 24
Grundschule primary school | U1, 11
Gruppe group | U2, 36; team | U4, 56
Grüße ausrichten to say hello to | U2, 33
grüßen to say hello to | U2, 33
gucken to look | U1, 20
Gummiball rubber ball | U2, 33
Gummistiefel welly pl. wellies | U6, 90
gut fine | U3, 40; good | U1, 22; nice | U3, 42
sie ist gut in/bei ... she is good at | U1, 20

H

haben to have got | U2, 30
Hafen harbour | U6, 90
Hafendamm pier | U6, 88
Hähnchen chicken | U7, 102
halb half | U3, 41
Halbschwester half-sister | U2, 26
Hallo. Hi. | U1, 10; Hello. | U1, 10
halten to hold | U3, 46
halten von to think of | U6, 90; to think about | U6, 97
Hand hand | U7, 105
Handy mobile | U1, 11
Hast hurry | U2, 30
häufig often | U3, 42
Hauptwort noun | U6, 100
Haus house | PUA, 25
Hausaufgabe, Hausaufgaben homework | U1, 19
auf dem Weg nach Hause on the way home | U6, 94
bei mir zu Hause at my house | U3, 41
nach Hause gehen to go home | U3, 42
zu Hause at home | U2, 26
Hausmeister, Hausmeisterin caretaker | U1, 12
Hausnummer number | U1, 11
Haustier pet | U3, 48
virtuelles Haustier cyberpet | U7, 106
Heft exercise book | U1, 16
heilen to mend | U7, 110
helfen to help | U2, 32
Heranzoomen zoom-in | ZI, 8
heraus out | U6, 96
heraushören to listen for | U1, 16
Herbst autumn | U6, 90
hereinkommen to come in | U3, 44
Herr *(Anrede)* Mr | U1, 12
herüberkommen to come over | U2, 34
herunter down | PUC, 55
herunternehmen to take off | U6, 94
Herz heart | PUA, 25
heute today | U2, 29
Hi. Hi. | U1, 10
hier here | U1, 12

hier drin in here I U6, 94
hierher here I U4, 56
hierhin here I U4, 56
Hilfe help I U3, 44
hilfreich useful I U1, 11
hinab down I PUC, 55
hinaufklettern to climb I U6, 88
hinaufsteigen to climb I U6, 88
hinaus out I U6, 96
hinfallen to fall over I U3, 49
sich hinsetzen to sit down I U1, 19
hinter behind I U1, 18
hinterherrennen to run after I U7, 110
hinunter down I PUC, 55
hinuntergehen to go down I PUC, 55
Hobby hobby pl. hobbies I PUB, 38
hochhalten to hold up I PUA, 24
höflich polite I U1, 21
holen to get I U4, 58
Homepage home page I U6, 90
hören to hear I U6, 96
Huhn chicken I U7, 102
Hühnchen chicken I U7, 102
Hund dog I U2, 27
Hundehütte doghouse I U6, 92
hundemüde dog-tired I U3, 49
Hurra! Hooray! I U6, 92

I

ich I I U1, 10
Idee idea I U2, 32
igitt yuk I U2, 34
ihr/-e her I U1, 15; their I U2, 29
Ihr/-e your I U2, 29
im in I U1, 18
immer always I U1, 14
immer noch still I U5, 76
in at I U1, 10; in I U1, 10; to I ZI, 9
in (hinein) into I U3, 44
in Ordnung fine I U3, 40
Information, Informationen information I PUC, 54
Insel island I U4, 66
interessant interesting I U4, 56
interessiert an interested in I U2, 26
Internet Internet I U6, 90
im Internet surfen to surf on the Internet I U6, 90
irgendein/-e/-er any I U6, 94
irgendwelche any I U6, 94
aus Italien Italian I U2, 29
italienisch Italian I U2, 29
Italienisch Italian I U2, 29

J

ja yes I U1, 14
Jahr year I U1, 10
jahrelang for (many) years I U7, 107
Jahreszeit season I U6, 90
Jahrgangsstufe year I U1, 10
Januar January I U5, 75
Jazzcafé jazz café I U3, 48
Jeans jeans *(pl.)* I U5, 76
jeder everyone I U5, 80
jede/-r/-s every I U3, 42
jene those I U3, 46
jenes that I U1, 12
an jenem Tag that day I U6, 97
jetzt right now I U5, 74; now I U1, 19
Jugendlicher, Jugendliche kid I U4, 60
Juli July I U5, 75
jung young I U4, 56
Junge boy I U1, 14
Juni June I U5, 75

K

kalt cold I U6, 88
Kamera camera I U7, 108
kämpfen to fight I U4, 67
Kantine eatery I U1, 20
Kapitän captain I U4, 66
Kapitel unit I U1, 10
kaputtgehen to break I U5, 78
Karaokegerät karaoke machine I U5, 80
Karte card I PUA, 24
Kartenkunststück card trick I U3, 46
Kartoffelchip crisp I U1, 18
ein Karton ... a box of ... I U5, 78
Käse cheese I U4, 62
Kästchen box I U3, 43
Kasten box I U3, 43
Katze cat I U2, 26
Katzenfutter cat food I U3, 44
kaufen to buy I U5, 72
Kaufhaus department store I U5, 76
kein/-e no I U1, 20
kennen to know I U1, 11
Kerze candle I U5, 78
Kind kid I U4, 60; child pl. children I U2, 26
Kino cinema I U3, 40
Kirche church I PUC, 54
klar clear I U7, 111
klären to sort out I U2, 30
(Schul)Klasse class I U4, 59
Klasse *(in einer englischen Schule)* tutor group I U1, 12; year I U1, 10
Klassenausflug class trip I U7, 104
Klassenfahrt class trip I U7, 104
Klassenlehrer, Klassenlehrerin tutor I U1, 12
Klassenzimmer classroom I U1, 14
klatschen to clap I U1, 17
Kleider clothes *(pl.)* I U5, 72
Kleiderschrank wardrobe I U2, 30
Kleidung clothes *(pl.)* I U5, 72
klein tiny I U1, 10; small I U2, 26; little I U5, 74
Kleintransporter pick-up I U1, 10
klingeln to ring I U1, 11
klopfen to pitter-patter I U6, 96
Klub club I U3, 40
Knall bang I U4, 66
knallen to bang I U3, 46
Koch, Köchin cook I U5, 78
Kochklub cooking club I U3, 40
kommen to come I U2, 34
Komm jetzt! Come on! I U3, 40
Komm schon! Come on! I U3, 40
kommen nach to get to I PUC, 55
kommen zu to get to I PUC, 55
Kommunikationsfertigkeiten communication skills I U4, 59
können can I U1, 19
(vielleicht) können may I U7, 110
korrigieren to correct I U4, 64
Wie viel kostet ... ? How much is ... ? I U5, 72
kräftig strong I U6, 96
Krähennest crow's nest I U4, 66
Kristall crystal I U2, 35
Küche kitchen I PUA, 24
Kuchen cake I U5, 74
Kuh cow I U7, 102
sich kümmern um to look after I U7, 104
Kunde, Kundin customer I U5, 73
Kunststück trick I U3, 46
kurz short I U1, 14
(Meeres)küste seaside I U6, 89
Küste coast I U6, 88
Küstenstadt seaside town I U6, 89

L

lächeln to smile I U7, 110
lachen to laugh I U5, 78
Laden shop I U2, 26
Land land I PUB, 38
Landarbeiter, Landarbeiterin farmhand I U7, 102
Landkarte map I PUC, 54
lang long I U1, 14
langsam slow I U2, 34
langweilig boring I U1, 20
Laptop laptop I U2, 34
lassen to let I ZI, 9
laufen to run I U3, 44
laut loud I U5, 80
Laut sound I U1, 16
läuten to ring I U1, 11
leben to live I U5, 81
Leben life pl. lives I U4, 57
lecken to lick I U4, 67
lecker tasty I U3, 44
leer empty I U7, 111
legen to put I U1, 21
lehren to teach I U3, 48
Lehrer, Lehrerin teacher I U1, 12
leicht easy I U1, 20
leise quiet I U2, 32
Stadtrundfahrten leiten to give tours I U4, 60
Lektion unit I U1, 10
lernen to learn I PUA, 25
auswendig lernen to learn by heart I PUA, 25
lesen to read I PUB, 38
letzte/-r/-s last I U4, 62
Leuchtturm lighthouse I U6, 88
Leute people *(pl.)* I U1, 14
lieben to love I U3, 45
Lieblings- favourite I U1, 12

Lied song I PUB, 39
lila purple I PUA, 24
Lineal ruler I U1, 16
Linie line I U4, 57
linke/-r/-s left I PUC, 55
links left I PUC, 55; on the left I PUC, 55
auf der linken Seite on the left I PUC, 55
Liste list I U1, 16
Loch hole I U3, 44
Luft air I U6, 100
lustig funny I PUA, 25

M

machen to do I U1, 17; to make I U1, 15
ein Foto machen to take a photo I U7, 108
sich Notizen machen to take notes I U5, 81
Mädchen girl I U1, 14
Mahlzeit meal I U6, 90
Mai May I U5, 75
Mama mum I U1, 14
manchmal sometimes I U3, 42
Mann man pl. men I U5, 74
Mappe folder I U1, 11
Markt market I U4, 62
März March I U5, 75
Maschine machine I U5, 80
Mauer wall I U1, 18
Maus mouse pl. mice I U1, 10
Meer sea I U4, 57
Mehl flour I U5, 78
mehr more I U1, 11
Mehrzahl plural I U1, 16
Meile mile I U6, 88
mein/-e my I U1, 10
meinen to mean I U4, 64
melken to milk I U7, 104
eine Menge a lot of I U2, 30
jede Menge lots of I U5, 78
Mensch person pl. people I U6, 100
mich me I U3, 48
Milch milk I U7, 104
Minute minute I U3, 41
mir me I U3, 48
mischen to shuffle I U3, 46
bunte Mischung mixed bag I U3, 50
mit with I U1, 14
mit (der U-Bahn) by (Underground) I U4, 58
mitnehmen to pick up I U1, 10
Mittagessen lunch I U2, 29
Mittagspause lunchtime I U1, 20
Mittagszeit lunchtime I U1, 20
mittel(groß) medium (M) I U5, 72
Mittwoch Wednesday I PUB, 39
Möbel furniture I PUA, 25
Mobiltelefon mobile I U1, 11
mögen to want I U4, 66; to like I U3, 45
ich möchte ... I'd like to ... *(= I would like to)* I U5, 74
Moment moment I U7, 108
Monat month I U5, 75
Montag Monday I PUB, 39
Morgen morning I U1, 14
Guten Morgen. Good morning. I U1, 14
heute Morgen this morning I U6, 93
müde tired I U3, 49
Museum museum I PUC, 54
Musik music I U2, 32
Musikgruppe band I U3, 40
müssen must I U6, 90
Mutter mother I PUA, 25

N

nach *(bei Uhrzeitangaben)* past I U3, 41
nach to I ZI, 9; after I U3, 42
Nachbar, Nachbarin neighbour I U3, 44
nachdem after I U3, 42
nacherzählen to retell I U6, 97
Nachmittag afternoon I U2, 34
nachmittags *(Uhrzeit)* pm I U3, 40
Nachricht note I U3, 44
nachschauen to look I U2, 30; to look up I U6, 100
nachschlagen to look up I U6, 100
nächste/-r/-s next I U7, 116
Nacht night I U7, 110
nahe near I PUC, 54
in der Nähe von near I PUC, 54
Nahrung food I U3, 44
Nahrungsmittel food I U3, 44
Name name I U1, 10
Nationalität nationality I U2, 28
natürlich of course I U4, 59
neben next to I U3, 44
nehmen *(Bus, Zug)* to catch I U4, 58
(mit)nehmen to take I U3, 48
(weg)nehmen to take I U2, 32
nein no I U1, 14
nennen to call I U4, 57
nervös nervous I U7, 104
nett nice I U1, 14
neu new I U1, 10
neun nine I U1, 11
neunzehn nineteen I U1, 16
neunzig ninety I U1, 16
nicht not I U1, 14
nie never I U3, 42
niemals never I U3, 42
noch still I U5, 76
noch ein/-e another I U6, 94
noch einmal again I U3, 42
nochmal again I U3, 42
nochmals erzählen to retell I U6, 97
Nomen noun I U6, 100
Norden north I U4, 57
Nordsee North Sea I U4, 57
normalerweise usually I U3, 42
Notiz note I U3, 44
sich Notizen machen to take notes I U5, 81
November November I U5, 75
null *(bei Telefonnummern)* oh I U1, 11
null zero I U1, 11
Nummer number I U1, 11
nun well I U2, 30
nun now I U1, 19
nur only I U2, 30; just I U2, 30
nützlich useful I U1, 11

O

ob if I U7, 111
oben upstairs I U2, 27; on the top I U3, 46
oben (auf) on top of I U3, 46
oberes Ende top I U3, 46
im Obergeschoss upstairs I U2, 27
oder or I U1, 11
offen open I PUA, 24
öffentlich public I U4, 61
öffnen to open I U2, 33
oft often I U3, 42
Ohr ear I U7, 106
okay OK I U1, 12
Oktober October I U5, 75
Oma grandma I PUA, 25
Onkel uncle I U2, 28
online online I U7, 106
Opa grandad I PUA, 25
orange orange I PUA, 24
Orchester orchestra I U3, 40
Ordner folder I U1, 11
Ort place I PUC, 54
Osten east I U4, 57
östlich von east of I U6, 88
Ozean ocean I U6, 89

P

ein paar a few I U5, 78; some I U6, 94
Paar pair I U6, 94
(ein)packen to pack I U6, 90
Papa dad I PUA, 25
Park park I U3, 40
parken to park I U4, 60
Partner, Partnerin partner I U1, 11
Party party I U1, 18
eine Party feiern to have a party I U2, 33
passen zu to go with I U4, 56
passieren to happen I U3, 47
Penny, Pence *(brit. Währungseinheit)* penny pl. pence I U5, 73
per by (Underground) I U4, 58
Person person pl. people I U6, 100
Pferd horse I U7, 102
Pflicht duty I U7, 104
Pfund *(Währung)* pound I U5, 72
Picknick picnic I U3, 49
Pick-up pick-up I U1, 10
Pier pier I U6, 88
pink pink I PUA, 24
Pirat pirate I U4, 66
Pizza pizza I U5, 74
Pizzeria pizza place I U5, 74
planen to plan I U6, 90
Planke plank I U4, 67
plötzlich suddenly I U5, 80
Plural plural I U1, 16

aus **Polen** Polish | **U2**, 29
Polizei police | **PUC**, 54
Polizeirevier police station | **PUC**, 54
Polizeiwache police station | **PUC**, 54
polnisch Polish | **U2**, 29
Polnisch Polish | **U2**, 29
Popstar pop star | **U5**, 80
Poster poster | **U1**, 18
Postkarte postcard | **U6**, 90
Präsens present | **U3**, 51
prasseln to pitter-patter | **U6**, 96
Preis prize | **U4**, 62
preiswert cheap | **U6**, 94
pro per | **PUA**, 24
Problem problem | **U1**, 20
Projekt project | **U2**, 34
Pronomen pronoun | **U4**, 59
Prüfung test | **U4**, 62

Q

Quiz quiz | **U1**, 13

R

Rad wheel | **U4**, 66
Radiergummi rubber | **U1**, 16
Radio radio | **U5**, 81
Radiosender radio station | **U5**, 81
Rap rap | **U1**, 17
Raster grid | **U1**, 16
(er)**raten** to guess | **U4**, 63
Ratespiel quiz | **U1**, 13
Ratschlag tip | **U1**, 13
Rauch smoke | **U2**, 34
Raum room | **U1**, 14
Recht haben to be right | **U7**, 110
rechte/-r/-s right | **PUC**, 55
rechts right | **PUC**, 55; on the right | **PUC**, 55
  auf der rechten Seite on the right | **PUC**, 55
reden to talk | **PUA**, 25
  reden mit to talk to | **PUA**, 25
Redewendung phrase | **U1**, 11
Regal shelf pl. shelves | **U6**, 94
Regalbrett shelf pl. shelves | **U6**, 94
Regel rule | **U2**, 32
regeln to sort out | **U2**, 30
Regen rain | **U6**, 90
regnen to rain | **U6**, 96
reich rich | **U5**, 74
Reihenfolge order | **U1**, 13
Reim rhyme | **PUA**, 25
Reise tour | **PUC**, 55; trip | **U6**, 90
reiten to ride | **PUB**, 38
rennen to run | **U3**, 44
reparieren to mend | **U7**, 110
Restaurant restaurant | **U6**, 90; eatery | **U1**, 20
Revier territory | **U7**, 110
Rezept recipe | **U5**, 78
richtig right | **U1**, 13; correct | **PUA**, 24
Riesenrad ferris wheel | **U6**, 100
riesig great | **U6**, 96
Riff rock | **U6**, 96
Rollenspiel role play | **PUB**, 39
rosa pink | **PUA**, 24
rot red | **PUA**, 24
Routine routine | **U3**, 42
rudern to row | **U6**, 96
rufen to shout | **U1**, 17; to call | **U3**, 48
ruhig calm | **U7**, 104; quiet | **U2**, 32
ruinieren to ruin | **U6**, 92
Rundgang tour | **PUC**, 55
russisch Russian | **U2**, 29
Russisch Russian | **U2**, 29
aus **Russland** Russian | **U2**, 29

S

Sache thing | **U1**, 16
sagen to say | **U1**, 11; to tell | **U2**, 29
Saison season | **U6**, 90
sammeln to collect | **PUB**, 38
Samstag Saturday | **U2**, 34
Sand sand | **U6**, 90
Sandburg sand castle | **U6**, 90
sandig sandy | **U6**, 100
Sandwich sandwich | **U1**, 16
Satz phrase | **U1**, 11; sentence | **U1**, 15
Satzstellung word order | **U7**, 107
Schachtel box | **U3**, 43
  eine Schachtel ... a box of ... | **U5**, 78
Schaf sheep pl. sheep | **U7**, 102
Schal scarf pl. scarves | **U6**, 100
Schatz treasure | **U4**, 66; dear | **U4**, 62
Schatzkarte treasure map | **U4**, 66
schauen to look | **U1**, 20
schenken to give | **U4**, 59
schießen to kick | **U3**, 47
Schiff boat | **U4**, 61; ship | **U4**, 57
schlafen to sleep | **U3**, 49
schlafend asleep | **U3**, 42
Schlafzimmer bedroom | **PUA**, 24
Schlag bang | **U4**, 66
schlagen to bang | **U3**, 46
Schlagzeug drums *(pl.)* | **U2**, 26
schlecht bad | **U7**, 106
schließen to close | **PUA**, 24
schließlich finally | **U3**, 44
schlimm terrible | **U1**, 20
Schloss castle | **PUC**, 54
schmutzig dirty | **U2**, 30
schnell fast | **U4**, 64
Schock shock | **U7**, 110
Schokolade chocolate | **U1**, 18
Schokoplätzchen chocolate crispies *(pl.)* | **U5**, 79
schon already | **U7**, 103
schön nice | **U3**, 42; beautiful | **U2**, 35
Schrank cupboard | **U1**, 18
Schreck shock | **U7**, 110
schrecklich terrible | **U1**, 20
schreiben to write | **U1**, 11
Schreibtisch desk | **U1**, 18
schreien to shout | **U1**, 17; to call | **U3**, 48
Schuh shoe | **U1**, 12
Schule school | **U1**, 10
  zu spät zur Schule kommen to be late for school | **U5**, 80
Schüler, Schülerin pupil | **U1**, 10
Schulhof playground | **U1**, 20
Schuljahr year | **U1**, 10
(Schul)Klasse class | **U4**, 59
Schulsachen *(pl.)* school things *(pl.)* | **U1**, 16
Schultag school day | **U3**, 42
Schultasche schoolbag | **U1**, 16
Schuppen shed | **U2**, 26
Schüssel bowl | **U7**, 110
schwarz black | **PUA**, 24
Schwein pig | **U7**, 102
Schwester sister | **PUA**, 25
Schwierigkeiten trouble | **U2**, 30
Schwimmbad swimming pool | **U4**, 65
Schwimmbecken swimming pool | **U4**, 65
schwimmen to swim | **PUB**, 38
  schwimmen gehen to go swimming | **PUB**, 38
sechs six | **U1**, 11
sechzehn sixteen | **U1**, 16
sechzig sixty | **U1**, 16
See sea | **U4**, 57
Seeräuber pirate | **U4**, 66
segeln to sail | **U4**, 66
sehen to see | **U3**, 40; to look | **U1**, 20
Sehenswürdigkeiten sights *(pl.)* | **U4**, 56
sehr very | **U1**, 15
sein its | **U2**, 26
sein to be | **U1**, 15
sein/-e his | **PUA**, 25
Seite page | **U1**, 14
Sekunde second | **U2**, 30
selbst even | **U5**, 80
dich **selbst** yourself | **U1**, 11
selbstverständlich of course | **U4**, 59
September September | **U5**, 75
setzen to put | **U1**, 21
s-Genitiv s-genitive | **U2**, 37
sicher sure | **U1**, 14; safe | **U6**, 92
sie them | **U3**, 49; she | **U1**, 12; they | **U1**, 14
sieben seven | **U1**, 10
siebzehn seventeen | **U1**, 16
siebzig seventy | **U1**, 16
Signal signal | **U6**, 93
Signalwort signal word | **U6**, 93
singen to sing | **U5**, 77
sinken to sink | **U6**, 96
sitzen to sit | **U1**, 19
Skateboard skateboard | **U4**, 56
eine **SMS schicken** to text | **U5**, 74
so like this | **PUA**, 25; so | **U1**, 15
soeben just | **U5**, 76
Sofa sofa | **PUA**, 25
sofort at once | **U6**, 96; right now | **U5**, 74
sogar even | **U5**, 80
sollte/-est/-en/-et should | **U7**, 106
Sommer summer | **U6**, 88
Sonne sun | **U6**, 100

Sonnenbrille sunglasses *(pl.)* I **U6**, 90
Sonntag Sunday I **PUB**, 39
sich Sorgen machen to worry I **U6**, 96
Sorte flavour I **U3**, 44
sortieren to sort I **U2**, 35
Souvenir souvenir I **U6**, 94
Spaghetti spaghetti I **U2**, 29
aus Spanien Spanish I **U2**, 29
spanisch Spanish I **U2**, 29
Spanisch Spanish I **U2**, 29
Spaß haben to have fun I **U5**, 78
(zu) spät late I **U1**, 14
später later I **U2**, 30
(Schinken)Speck bacon I **U7**, 104
Speicherkarte *(für Digitalkameras)* card I **U7**, 108
Spiel game I **U1**, 13
Spielautomaten arcade games *(pl.)* I **U6**, 88
spielen to play I **U1**, 16; to act I **U4**, 67
(ab)spielen to play I **U2**, 32
Spielkarte card I **PUA**, 24
Spielplatz playground I **U1**, 20
Spitze top I **U3**, 46
Sport sport I **U1**, 12
Sportart sport I **U1**, 12
Sportgeschäft sports shop I **U5**, 72
Sprache language I **U1**, 12
sprechen to speak (to) I **U4**, 58; to talk I **PUA**, 25
sprechen mit to talk to I **PUA**, 25
sprechen über to talk about I **U2**, 35
Sprechfertigkeiten communication skills I **U4**, 59
springen to jump I **U5**, 80
Stadt town I **U3**, 41
Großstadt city I **U7**, 102
Stadtplan map I **PUC**, 54
Stadtrundfahrten leiten to give tours I **U4**, 60
Stall shed I **U7**, 104
Star star I **U1**, 17
stark strong I **U6**, 96
Station station I **U4**, 56
stehen to stand I **U7**, 110
steigen to climb I **U6**, 88
einen Drachen steigen lassen to fly a kite I **U6**, 88
Stein rock I **U6**, 96
steinig rocky I **U6**, 100
stellen to put I **U1**, 21
sterben to die I **U6**, 97
Steuer wheel I **U4**, 66
Steuerrad wheel I **U4**, 66
Stiefvater step-father I **U2**, 26
still quiet I **U2**, 32
stinken to stink I **U7**, 104
Strand beach I **U6**, 88
Strandurlaub beach holiday I **U6**, 88
Straße street I **U3**, 44; road I **U2**, 26
auf der Straße in the street I **U7**, 116
sich streiten to fight I **U4**, 67
sich streiten um to fight over I **U7**, 104
Stuhl chair I **U1**, 18
Stunde hour I **U4**, 57
stundenlang for (many) hours I **U7**, 107
Sturm storm I **U6**, 96
stürmisch stormy I **U6**, 96
suchen to look I **U2**, 30
suchen (nach) to look for I **U5**, 76
Süden south I **U6**, 89
super cool I **U1**, 13
surfen to surf I **U6**, 88
im Internet surfen to surf on the Internet I **U6**, 90
süß sweet I **PUA**, 24
Süßigkeiten sweets *(pl.)* I **U6**, 95
Süßwarenladen sweet shop I **PUC**, 54
Sweatshirt sweatshirt I **U5**, 73
sympathisch nice I **U1**, 14

T

Tabelle grid I **U1**, 16
Tafel board I **U1**, 18
Tag day I **PUB**, 39
Tagebuch diary I **U1**, 15
täglich daily I **U3**, 42
Tankstelle garage I **U7**, 110
Tante aunt I **U2**, 28
tanzen to dance I **U5**, 76
Tanzstunden dancing lessons *(pl.)* I **U3**, 42
Tanzunterricht dancing lessons *(pl.)* I **U3**, 42
Tasche bag I **U1**, 14
eine Tasse ... a cup of I **U5**, 78
Tätigkeit job I **U7**, 104
Taxi taxi I **U4**, 58
Team team I **U4**, 56
Tee tea I **U4**, 66
Teil part I **U4**, 56
Telefon phone I **U1**, 11
Telefonnummer phone number I **U1**, 11
Territorium territory I **U7**, 110
Test test I **U4**, 62
teuer expensive I **U5**, 73
Text text I **U1**, 20
Tier animal I **U7**, 102
Tierarzt, Tierärztin vet I **U7**, 110
Tiger tiger I **U2**, 26
Tipp tip I **U1**, 13
Tisch table I **U1**, 18
Titel title I **U5**, 80; heading I **U5**, 81
tja well I **U2**, 30
Toilette toilet I **U1**, 19
toll great I **U2**, 33
Tor goal I **U1**, 12
Torte cake I **U5**, 74
tot dead I **U7**, 111
Tour tour I **PUC**, 55
Tourist, Touristin tourist I **U4**, 56
Touristeninformation information centre I **PUC**, 54
trappeln to pitter-patter I **U6**, 96
Traum dream I **PUA**, 25
traurig sad I **U7**, 110
treffen to meet I **U3**, 40
sich treffen to meet I **U3**, 40
treten to kick I **U3**, 47
Trick trick I **U3**, 46
trinken to drink I **U7**, 111
tschüss bye I **U1**, 19
T-Shirt T-shirt I **U2**, 30
Tuch scarf pl. scarves I **U6**, 100
tun to do I **U1**, 17
Tunnel tunnel I **U4**, 56
Tür door I **U1**, 18
aus der Türkei Turkish I **U2**, 29
türkisch Turkish I **U2**, 29
Türkisch Turkish I **U2**, 29
eine Tüte ... a bag of ... I **U5**, 78

U

U-Bahn Underground I **U4**, 56
über over I **U2**, 26; about I **U1**, 11
überall everywhere I **U2**, 34
überleben to survive I **U6**, 97
überqueren to cross I **PUC**, 55
Überraschung surprise I **U5**, 80
Überschrift heading I **U5**, 81
Übung exercise I **U1**, 16
Uhr *(Zeitangabe bei vollen Stunden)* o'clock I **U3**, 40
Uhr clock I **ZI**, 9
die Uhr lesen to tell the time I **U3**, 41
umfallen to fall over I **U3**, 49
und and I **U1**, 10
ungefährlich safe I **U6**, 92
unheimlich scary I **U1**, 12
Unordnung mess I **U2**, 30
uns us I **U3**, 42
unser/-e our I **U2**, 26
unten downstairs I **U2**, 27
unten on the bottom I **U3**, 46
nach unten down I **PUC**, 55
unter under I **U1**, 18
unteres Ende bottom I **U3**, 46
untergehen to sink I **U6**, 96
im Untergeschoss downstairs I **U2**, 27
unterrichten to teach I **U3**, 48
Unterrichtsstunde lesson I **U1**, 17
unterschiedlich different I **U1**, 23
unterstreichen to underline I **U2**, 36
unterwegs on his way I **PUC**, 55
Unwetter storm I **U6**, 96
Urlaub holiday(s) I **U6**, 88
Urlauber, Urlauberin holiday-maker I **U6**, 100
usw. (= und so weiter) etc. (= et cetera) I **U5**, 84

V

Vater father I **PUA**, 25
Vati dad I **PUA**, 25
verängstigt scared I **U6**, 96
Verb verb I **U6**, 100
verbinden to link I **U3**, 47
verbringen *(Urlaub, Zeit etc.)* to spend I **U6**, 100
Verein club I **U3**, 40
verfolgen to chase I **U3**, 44

THE BRITISH ISLES